TEACHING CHILDREN 3–11

TEACHING CHILDREN 3–11

A STUDENT'S GUIDE

THIRD EDITION

Edited By

ANNE D. COCKBURN & GRAHAM HANDSCOMB

Los Angeles | London | New Delhi
Singapore | Washington DC

Reprinted 2013

SAGE Publications Ltd
1 Oliver's Yard
55 City Road
London EC1Y 1SP

SAGE Publications Inc.
2455 Teller Road
Thousand Oaks, California 91320

SAGE Publications India Pvt Ltd
B1/11 Mohan Cooperative Industrial Area
Mathura Road
New Delhi 110 044

SAGE Publications Asia-Pacific Pte Ltd
3 Church Street
#10-04 Samsung Hub
Singapore 049483

Library of Congress Control Number: 2011925168

British Library Cataloguing in Publication data

A catalogue record for this book is available from the British Library

ISBN 978-0-85702-486-2
ISBN 978-0-85702-487-9 (pbk)

Typeset by C&M Digitals (P) Ltd, Chennai, India
Printed in Great Britain by Ashford Colour Press Ltd, Gosport, Hampshire

CONTENTS

LIST OF FIGURES AND TABLES

Tables

LIST OF ABBREVIATIONS

AfL   Assessment for Learning
APP   Assessing Pupils' Progress
ARG   Assessment Reform Group
AT   Attainment Target
BBC   British Broadcasting Corporation
CACE   Central Advisory Council for Education
CAF   Common Assessment Framework
CEDP   Career Entry and Development Profile
CPD   Continuing Professional Development
CUREE   Centre for the Use of Research and Evidence in Education
CV   Curriculum Vitae
D&T   Design and Technology
DCSF   Department for Children, Schools and Families (2007–10)
DES   Department of Education and Science (1964–92)
DfE   Department for Education (2010–)
DfEE   Department for Education and Employment (1999–2001)
DfES   Department for Education and Skills (2001–7)
EAL   English as an Additional Language
EPPE   Effective Pre-school and Primary Education
EYFS   Early Years Foundation Stage
FLARE   Forum for Learning and Research Enquiry

GTP	Graduate Teacher Programme
HMI	Her Majesty's Inspectorate
HMSO	Her Majesty's Stationery Office
ICT	Information and Communications Technology
IT	Information Technology
IWB	Interactive Whiteboard
LA	Local Authority
LDD	Learning Difficulties and Disabilities
LSA	Learning Support Assistant
NACCE	National Advisory Committee on Creative and Cultural Education
NALDIC	National Association for Language Development in the Curriculum
NCC	National Curriculum Council
NFER	National Foundation for Educational Research
NQT	Newly Qualified Teacher
OFSTED	Office for Standards in Education (later Ofsted)
PE	Physical Education
PGCE	Post Graduate Certificate of Education
PPA	Planning, Preparation and Assessment
PSHE	Personal, Social and Health Education
QCA	Qualifications and Curriculum Authority
QCDA	Qualifications and Curriculum Development Agency
SCITT	School Centred Initial Teacher Training
SEAL	Social and Emotional Aspects of Learning
SEN	Special Educational Needs
SENCo	Special Educational Needs Coordinator
SLT	Senior Leadership Team
TA	Teaching Assistant
TDA	Training and Development Agency for Schools
TGAT	Task Group on Assessment and Testing
TTA	Teacher Training Agency
UEA	University of East Anglia
UNESCO	United Nations Educational, Scientific and Cultural Organisation
VAK	Visual, Auditory and Kinaesthetic
VLE	Virtual Learning Environment
WALT	'What we are learning today' or 'We are learning to …'
WILF	'What I am looking for'

NOTES ON THE EDITORS AND CONTRIBUTORS

Editors

Anne Cockburn is a Professor in Early Years' Education at the University of East Anglia (UEA). She has been a teacher and researcher for many years and her publications include *Recruiting and Retaining Teachers* (with Terry Haydn and published by RoutledgeFalmer, 2004) and *Mathematical Misconceptions* (edited with Graham Littler and published by Sage, 2008).

Graham Handscomb has a wide range of senior management experience in local authorities and schools. He was Senior Manager, Strategic Development in Essex County Council and is now an independent consultant. Graham was initially both primary and secondary trained and has taught for 18 years. He is external examiner for all education Masters programmes at the University of Wales and is a Fellow and Associate of many universities throughout the UK. Graham has led national and international professional development initiatives and has pioneered the concept of the *Research Engaged School*.

Contributors

Stephen Chynoweth is currently Principal of the GEMS Hamsphire School, Kensington. Previously he was Principal of an International School in Dubai and led an outstanding primary school in Essex. Stephen is passionate about whole-child centred learning, the well-being and confidence of children and the provision of skills, knowledge, attitudes and emotional security for them all.

Eleanor Cockerton has many years' experience teaching in a variety of schools across the 3–11 age range. She joined the Primary PGCE team at UEA in 2007 as a maths tutor and is also responsible for the early years component of the course.

Elizabeth Cornish is an experienced mainstream senior leader and SENCo; she has been influential in shaping pivotal pilot projects such as multi-agency working and the TDA School Improvement Framework. Liz currently works in the Essex Strategic Development Team.

Sue Cox is a former primary teacher and senior lecturer at UEA where she is a member of the Primary PGCE team teaching professional studies and art and design. She also coordinates Masters level courses. Her research interests include children's drawing and primary curriculum and pedagogy, with a particular interest in teaching art and design, children's participation and decision-making and children's voice.

Fiona Dorey is a Primary Lead Curriculum Adviser for Essex County Council. Her main areas of expertise are supporting schools with the development of a curriculum to match local needs, developing and embedding assessment for learning and whole-school improvement. She has also worked as a Primary Strategy Consultant and previously was a teacher and subject leader in primary and junior schools in North Essex.

Melanie Foster's association within the field of education is both diverse and long-standing. She has 26 years' teaching experience across mainstream and special schools, with 12 years' experience as a senior SEN Advisory Officer working in partnership with schools to promote excellence in learning and teaching for *all* children.

Helena Gillespie is lecturer in education at UEA Norwich. She teaches undergraduates and postgraduates who would like to be teachers and her research interests include virtual learning and the effect of media on children.

Jo Lang has worked widely in education and the voluntary sector, where she has specialised in communications and problem-solving, as a trainer, coach, consultant and employee. As a confirmed cockeyed optimist, she believes there is no problem that can't be resolved through good communication and bad humour.

Lorraine Laudrum has spent most of her career as a senior leader in Essex primary schools. She was committed to the classroom and thus became a 'serial deputy', enjoying both the world of teaching and the contribution to leadership this role afforded. More recently she joined Essex LA to work as part of the strategic development team, facilitating schools' educational visions for the Primary Capital Programme. She is currently seconded to acting headship in a large primary school.

Ralph Manning is a lecturer in primary education at the UEA, with subject responsibilities in mathematics and physical education. Ralph taught in primary schools in

Bedfordshire and Norfolk following an earlier career in IT, and continues to teach occasionally in partnership schools. His other interests are in developing children's thinking skills, assessment and planning, and using ICT effectively to support these.

Ann Oliver taught in primary schools for several years before becoming a lecturer in primary science education at the UEA. She has worked in teacher education for 18 years which included being a director of the Primary PGCE. Her book, *Creative Teaching: Science in the Early Years and Primary Classroom* (David Fulton, 2006), provides suggestions on how to develop the primary science curriculum in interesting and cross-curricular ways.

Michele Otway is a lecturer teaching English at the UEA. She also contributes to components of the early years' curriculum course. Prior to joining the university, she taught in a range of Norfolk first schools for a number of years.

Alan Pagden worked for many years as a teacher and manager in primary schools in England and abroad before joining the primary team at UEA. His recently completed PhD thesis looks at how children represent/construct their geographies through drawing. He is currently lecturing in primary humanities at Canterbury Christ Church University.

Paul Parslow-Williams taught in primary schools for eight years prior to joining the PGCE team at UEA in 2006. He has a wide range of interests including science, ICT and children with special educational needs. He has been known to contribute to books on mathematics such as *Mathematical Misconceptions* (edited by Anne Cockburn and Graham Littler in 2008 and published by Sage).

Michael Pond is a retired headteacher who is currently working as an associate tutor in the School of Education at UEA. He has 47 years' experience of working with children in a range of schools and residential settings in the primary years as well as brief spells in higher education.

Jenifer Smith is a lecturer in education and course director for the Primary PGCE in the School of Education and Lifelong Learning at UEA. She runs Writing Teachers groups and has too many interests in children and learning to list here!

Abigail Williams draws upon her 12 years' experience of working as a senior strategic leader and operational manager of ICT learning and development programmes within the public and private sector. As a teacher, lecturer and consultant, she has pioneered new working practices and implemented complex ICT projects within primary, secondary and special schools. Abigail was Lead ICT Strategic Development Officer for the Future Schools Programme and is now Head of Schools' Learning and Development with Essex County Council.

PREFACE TO THE THIRD EDITION

We are delighted to present the third edition of *Teaching Children 3–11*. It has been written during exciting times of change. The Coalition Government in England has been reshaping a good deal of the education policy landscape and plans for National Curriculum requirements and teacher education are still evolving. We are confident that this new edition anticipates the developments emerging from this changing scene. We also see this as an excellent opportunity to focus on key principles of teaching and learning which we believe are enduring and transcend changes in particular attitudes to education which can tend to be more transitory. Such principles include, for instance, the vital importance of the teacher–learner relationship, keeping a focus on classroom practice and creating a positive learning ethos. As we hope you will be working in schools for many years to come these will provide you with a secure foundation on which to build your own educational philosophy, enabling you to navigate your professional life confidently and effectively.

While we have retained many of the strengths of the first and second editions *Teaching Children 3–11* has been substantially revised and, as explained in Chapter 1, we are delighted to welcome several new contributors from the University of East Anglia, Essex local authority and schools. You will discover not only revised and updated content but also some entirely new chapters. We are also pleased to introduce a new feature – *Critical Issues* – designed to really challenge you. These may be of particular interest to those working at Masters' level. To help in your navigation of this new edition we have also grouped the chapters under the themes of: 'The Learning Teacher', 'Skills in Teaching and Learning'; 'Managing the Curriculum'; and 'The Child and the community' 'Developing the Teacher You Want to Be'.

Many people have worked towards the publication of this edition and we are most grateful for their help and advice. In particular we would like to thank James Clark and Monira Begum at Sage and our colleagues who – with varying degrees of speed – all managed to produce the goods in time for the deadline!

Anne Cockburn
Graham Handscomb

Section 1

THE LEARNING TEACHER

In this first section we introduce our overarching theme of the learning teacher.

The opening chapter sets out how we regard you the reader as a fellow traveller on the learning and development journey explored in this book. To be an effective teacher means becoming an equally effective learner, not just as you prepare for your first post but also throughout a career of professional development. We explain how this outlook has guided the style adopted of addressing you directly as a fellow professional in the second person. Other chapters explore the importance of collaboration with your colleagues within and beyond the school, and how you consider learning and teaching from a range of perspectives. We give guidance on how to develop as an enquiring teacher, always aiming to reflect and improve upon your classroom practice. Above all we emphasise the pivotal nature of the relationship you will forge with children and how to foster pupil voice as a key feature of the collaborative, learning culture of your school.

CHAPTER 1

SETTING OUT

Graham Handscomb and Anne Cockburn

Chapter overview

Teaching is a great paradox. On the one hand it can be one of the most rewarding and even life-enhancing experiences. On the other, teaching can be extremely demanding and challenging. In 'Setting out' Graham Handscomb and Anne Cockburn explain how reading this book will provide an overview of what a career in teaching might have to offer you. They stress, however, that it is essential to obtain practical primary classroom experience before embarking on any form of teacher training.

Introduction

Teaching can be unremittingly dull, repetitive and stressful. We know: we have been there. It can also be one of the most stimulating, enjoyable and rewarding jobs in the world. We know: we have been there too. This book is about how to make the difference.

It does not claim to have all the answers but it will certainly present enough material and thought-provoking ideas for you to see the tremendous possibilities which lie ahead. You may think that this is slightly over the top but, as you may already have discovered, very few people feel neutral about teachers and teaching! In this chapter we will very briefly describe the intended readership, authors, origins and uses of this book. We will then outline some of the most important issues you would be wise to consider before embarking on a course, let alone a career, in teaching.

So who are you?

We, the authors, envisage you, the reader, as:

- someone who might be contemplating primary teaching as a career
- someone who is about to embark on a 3–11 training course or one of the variations
- someone who has been accepted on a training programme (for example, 3–8, 7–11) and is about to embark on it
- a trainee already part-way through a teacher education qualification
- a tutor receiving books with a view to recommending them – or not as the case may be – to any of the above audience.

We also see you as someone who, although generally enthusiastic about the idea of teaching, sometimes becomes anxious and demoralised by the struggle. There is no doubt about it – learning to teach is hard work. It is not easy being an experienced learner one minute and a relatively inexperienced teacher the next. You are, however, undoubtedly intelligent and our intention is to demonstrate how, by making the most of your experiences, skills and intellectual capacity, you can gain the most from your training and chosen career. Even so, you will, inevitably, sometimes feel like packing the whole lot in. Obviously, if this feeling becomes all-consuming you should look for a career elsewhere: teaching – just like dentistry, social work and plumbing – is not for everyone and there is no reason to suppose that it should be. If, however, you just occasionally feel dispirited, overworked and under-appreciated, hang in there: it will be worth it!

So who are we?

This is not a profound philosophical question but rather a practical one about the nature of the contributors to this book. We feel it would be helpful for you to know something of the 'voices' that will be speaking to you through its pages.

When writing the first edition we were the nine members of the Primary PGCE Team at the University of East Anglia (UEA). Between us we had about 120 years' experience as school teachers and over 100 years in teacher education which, coupled with very high grades in HMI inspections, suggest that we had at least an idea of what we were talking about! The second edition saw the start of our fruitful collaboration with colleagues from Essex local authority. In particular, Graham Handscomb, Senior Manager in Essex School Improvement and Early Years Services, joined Anne Cockburn to become joint editor. Graham has a national reputation for his work on continuous professional development and brings a great deal of experience from how local authorities support training and development, including the wide-ranging initial teacher training group of programmes which have been judged as outstanding by Ofsted. These have incorporated the Graduate Training and School Centred Initial Teacher Training (SCITT) schemes. For this third edition we have an even greater collaborative mix between the UEA team and Essex colleagues. We are delighted to welcome new contributors Fiona Dorey, Melanie Foster, Jo Lang, Lorraine Laudrum, Elizabeth Cornish and Abigail Williams who have been involved in primary innovation and the new *Schools of the Future* development in Essex. Stephen Chynoweth, who contributed to the second edition, has moved from his headship in Essex to a headship in Dubai but we are pleased that he is still contributing to this issue, drawing on his varied experience. A number of the UEA contributors have retired since the second edition but their places have been very ably taken over by Ralph Manning, Eleanor Cockerton, Paul Parslow-Williams, Michele Otway, Helena Gillespie and Michael Pond who, between them, have stacked up over 100 years of recent and relevant classroom experience. So, in all, we represent a range of skills and understanding, combining considerable insight and expertise in teacher education, as well as continuing engagement with the classroom practicalities of teaching and learning. We might not always agree. It would be odd – and, indeed, rather disturbing – if we did. It is always healthy to have a good debate! Nevertheless, we all share the same underlying philosophy that reflection is a crucial aspect of professional development. Throughout the book therefore – and particularly at the end of every chapter – we will invite you to reflect on various issues in order to extend your own learning. We believe this to be an important feature of the book. The business of teaching is learning. Obviously, this particularly means promoting the learning of the children we teach. However, if we are to be effective teachers, and remain so throughout our careers, we also need to be accomplished learners who continue to reflect upon practice. So this book is designed to encourage you to connect with a range of issues and guidance within the body of each chapter, and then to actively reflect upon what this might mean for you in the context of your own particular outlook and experience.

Why did we write the book?

A simple serious answer would be because Marianne Lagrange of Sage Publications asked Anne to compile the first edition and Sage invited us to produce a second and then a third one! Flattered though we were, even that alone would have been insufficient to get our pencils and word processors going. Rather we wrote this book because – at the risk of sounding corny – we want to share our belief that education should be an enjoyable, challenging and valuable experience for teachers and learners alike. What also unites us is a conviction that you are the future of the teaching profession and our strong desire to make some contribution that you will find helpful at this early stage in your career. Given the media, some of your experiences and some of today's teaching materials, you might be forgiven for thinking that teaching is all about finding something to teach, teaching it and then testing your pupils to ensure that they have mastered the topic to a sufficiently high standard. Teaching can be about that but education cannot. Education is about engaging the mind and helping learners realise their full potential. It is also about a sense of worthwhileness, where those involved – teachers, pupils and others – share a belief in the fundamental value of the enterprise:

> Education is for individuality. We all think, feel and learn in distinctive ways. Good education works with the unique grain of our personal capacities to help each of us become a better version of ourselves – and with luck and determination, to make a living at it too. (Robinson, 2005, p. 6)

The best educators are those who inspire their pupils and enable them to continue learning long after they have left the confines of the classroom.

It would be ridiculous – not to say arrogant – to claim that this book covered everything you needed to know to become a successful primary school teacher. We recognise, however, that you are likely to be short of reading time. We have therefore endeavoured to focus on the issues we consider to be particularly important in the hope that we will complement your course and prompt you into continuing your own professional development. Should you find yourself becoming particularly intrigued by specific topics, we have listed and commented on books for further reading at the end of each chapter.

Changing times – lasting principles

Since the last edition of this book there have been many changes. Among these have been a number of attempts to review and redefine the primary curriculum, changing views about how schools should be established and organised, and a change of government. All these things, of course, affect the context in which we all work in school and there is often heated exchange about, for instance, the styles of teaching and how best to increase standards in our schools. A good example is the renewed debate about teachers focusing on helping pupils to acquire learning skills. Some are passionately clear about the importance of this: 'I can hardly think of anything more worthwhile than learning to learn. It's like money in the bank at compound interest' (Perkins, 2009, quoted in Watkins, 2010, p. 7). By contrast a new Schools Minister, Nick Gibb (2010, p. 4), challenges that children should be taught how to learn, saying instead: 'I believe very strongly that education is about the transfer of knowledge from one generation to another.'

Well, in the course of your teaching career, you will live through many changes in the educational landscape and shifts in thinking about educational practice. Part of your professionalism will include the need to be aware of this and indeed to actively engage in such dialogue and thinking yourself. The contributors of this book also have their clear views on education and, although these may vary among the different contributors, when you read this book we think you will find that there are certain principles that they all share, and which we believe transcend changes in particular public attitudes to education, which tend to come and go. Such principles include the vital importance of the teacher–learner relationship, keeping the focus on classroom practice and creating a positive learning ethos. As Watkins (2010, p. 6) reflects: 'Classrooms are the influential site in creating achievement at school. They have their impact not through particular practices but through the learning climate they create. When classrooms create a thoughtful and learner-centred climate, achievement is high.' One of the key messages we hope to convey in this book is that as a fellow professional you, the reader, should develop and clarify your own principles that underpin your approach to teaching.

How might you use this book?

This book does not need to be read in any particular order. Indeed, you may find that there are some chapters you wish to refer to immediately, others you will want to consult later and still others you would prefer to just dip into. We hope you find the chapter titles give a clear indication of their content but will briefly comment here on some of the key features that you will discover.

Each chapter begins with a small boxed 'banner' statement designed to give you a flavour of what follows. We hope you find that the content of each chapter is written in helpful accessible language, divided into useful sections indicated by subheadings. To help you engage and reflect on the content of this book we provide towards the end of each chapter a summary box and a general *Issues for Reflection* box. In this edition we also introduce within the body of each chapter *Critical Issues* inserts. These aim to prompt your engagement and thinking at a higher level by delving deeper into the subject of the chapter, exploring the issues more critically, and examining different and perhaps controversial perspectives. We hope you find this helpful.

You will find each of the chapters distinctive, reflecting the variety of contributors. However, what they all have in common is their approach to you, the reader. All the authors address the reader as a fellow professional, albeit a less experienced one. In a sense they adopt the stance of sitting alongside the reader, taking them through the issues and the learning journey of the book. Often this will mean addressing you in the first person, exploring and debating issues rather than just conveying information. This reflects the fundamental outlook of this book which is to see the teacher as a learner who is constantly honing and improving his/her craft and in this context to regard the reader as a professional enquirer and questioner.

This philosophy is very much reflected in the way we have reorganised the chapters in this third edition under five sections. The first, *The Learning Teacher*, sets the tone of the book, with its emphasis on you being a fellow professional with whom the authors are engaging. Section 2, *Skills in Teaching and Learning,* takes the reader straight to the business of developing the skills needed within the classroom. In Section 3, *Managing the Curriculum,* we look at the range of issues related to managing a curriculum that is dynamic and constantly changing to meet the needs of the child and of society. Section 4, *The Child and the Community,* looks at the important relationship between the school and the community and how we can ensure this contributes to the child's development. Finally the last section, *Developing the Teacher You Want to Be,* is focused on helping you to take stock of how you are developing as a teacher and to consider the kind of professional you want to be, as well as giving practical guidance on job applications and interviews.

In terms of the scope of the book, in Chapter 15 '*Continuity and progression from 3–11*' Alan Pagden discusses the similarities and differences between the phases currently used to describe children between 3 and 11 years of age – the Foundation Stage (3–5), Key Stage 1 (5–7) and Key Stage 2 (7–11). Unless otherwise stated, the principles considered in the book refer to all three of these phases. The chapter emphasises that whatever you teach, it is important for teachers to be aware of each phase and to help ensure children's educational journey is a joined-up and meaningful experience.

Preparing for your training

To make the most of this book and, more importantly your training, you would be wise to do some preparation.

School experience

Very occasionally we interview people with little school experience. Sometimes we accept them for teacher education programmes. Often all is well, but not always. Despite our detailed interviewing, two difficulties can arise. The first is when someone realises that they have opted for the wrong age group. Unfortunately this usually strikes them when they are several weeks into their training, when it may be difficult to change from a primary to a secondary course, for example.

The second problem is that a few people embark on their training with an insufficient appreciation of the demands and challenges of the teaching profession. We do our best to warn everyone at interview but, unless you have had first-hand experience of working closely with a teacher, you may not realise what you are undertaking.

In brief it is *essential* that you gain experience working in a school with a range of children from different age groups *before* submitting your application form. If you can, try for half a day a week in a school for a term. Even better is to gain experience in two or three schools, but this is not always possible if you are working or in full-time study. The chapters on the three related processes of observation (Chapter 5), learning and classroom skills (Chapter 6) and reflection (Chapter 9) will be particularly useful in helping you make full use of this opportunity. There are a number of ways to arrange work experience in a local school. You can simply telephone them and ask to make an appointment to discuss the possibility with the head teacher. You can make contact through your local careers centre. You can speak to someone in your local authority or you can ask advice from the Training and Development Agency (TDA) or the Department for Education (DfE). Schools will generally be positive about such requests, though occasionally – perhaps because of timing or particular school pressures – you may receive a negative response.

Pre-course reading

Some of you will be completing your degree when you read this. Others may not have done any studying for more years than you might care to remember. In both cases some pre-course – and, indeed, pre-interview – reading is strongly recommended. Not only will this prepare you for what is to come but it may also give you the opportunity to do some reading at a relatively leisurely pace: you'll soon discover that you'll have little time for it once you have started your teacher education course.

What you read is largely down to you, although it is likely that your intended teacher education provider will give you some suggestions. If you know you are weak in specific subjects, it is a good idea to do some work on them. At the end of this chapter are listed some books our students have found helpful in this respect. It is important to remember that you will be given up-to-date subject knowledge on your course but, with often only about 38 weeks, it is valuable to have a head start.

It is also useful to read general books about schools and schooling and some suggestions are given at the end of this chapter. Reading such books can help develop your insight into your chosen profession. The more you know about it the better prepared you'll be for your interview and, with luck, your training. If you have not done any studying for a while or, if you are lacking in confidence in your ability to work effectively, you would be wise to read a book on study skills. There are likely to be several examples in any good bookshop. Choose one that appeals to you and see if it does the trick. If, however, you find yourself struggling several weeks into the course, speak to your tutor who may be able to help directly or who might advise you to contact a study skills centre at, for example, your institution. Declaring such a difficulty is not a problem. Training institutions will be aware that many people entering the profession may not have had recent experience of study. Rather than feeling at all awkward about such a need, you may find that this helps you empathise with difficulties that children have with their learning and study.

Being organised

There is no doubt whatsoever that teacher training is highly demanding both intellectually and organisationally. If you secure a place on a course – given that you already have a degree, are well prepared and have succeeded on interview – you are likely to take the intellectual challenge in your stride. You may not, however, be so well prepared to meet the organisational challenges your teacher preparation presents. We suspect you will never have been so busy. For example, you will be expected in school no later than 8.30 a.m. – some schools say 8.00 a.m. – and questions will be asked if you leave before 4.30 p.m. There may well be staff meetings to attend and after-school clubs, reflections on your teaching and observations, the next day's marking and preparation. As will be discussed below, it *is* important that you have a life beyond teaching but, before embarking on a course, you must ensure that you are as well organised as you can possibly be. This might mean reducing your shopping from every two to three days to once a week, arranging for dependants to be cared for in your absence, ensuring that your car is in good working order, and so on.

Finally, before accepting an offer for a training place, talk it over with your family and friends. Ultimately it has to be your decision, but it is important that you have their confidence and support. You will find, for example, that your training will be a time of great personal discovery: this can be extremely exciting and liberating but it can also be a little daunting at times.

Your colleagues

Everything is in place and you are about to start your training. Who will your colleagues be? What will they be like?

In all probability there will be more females than males. This is particularly true if you have opted for early years or lower primary training. There will be a wide age range and we think you may well be surprised by the number of more mature people. Every year at the University of East Anglia, for example, we take students in their early twenties, some in their late forties and early fifties, and many in between. The average age is generally around 30 so you can be sure that many of your colleagues will have worked and had a range of life experiences prior to embarking on the course.

Attendance

Becoming a teacher is a full-time commitment. Before enlisting on a course or embarking on any training therefore it is *vital* that you recognise that you will be extremely busy and that you appreciate that – except in cases of illness or serious domestic need – missing sessions simply is not an option. Indeed, the Department for Education insists that everyone attends all timetabled sessions otherwise they will not issue you with a certificate.

Theory and practice

Sometimes when people come to interview for training they tend to think that this involves a programme of tips for teachers. Fortunately, teacher education is not like that. We are all individuals, we work in different situations with different people and we do not know what the curriculum of the future holds.

Accordingly, although we may suggest some handy hints and useful approaches from time to time, we strive to provide a dynamic mix of theory and practice. There are some in the profession – experienced as well as beginning teachers – who have a rather negative view of 'theory'. They tend to see it as an intellectual indulgence, at the expense of concentrating on the important matter of classroom practice. Theory has certainly got a bad name! However, this is rather a simplistic view as there is a crucial relationship between theory and practice: 'No action, unless it is the action of an irrational being, is devoid of theory, for theory involves beliefs, ideas, assumptions, values, and everything we do is influenced by theory' (Fish, 1995a, p. 57). Also, this is not just a 'one-way street' relationship – that is, that you learn some theory and then apply it in practice. The relationship is much more fundamental than that. It is about how you use theory to make sense of your practice and, indeed, as Fish powerfully explains, how as an individual you develop your own theory from your practice. 'At best in teacher education programmes, there exists a constant interplay between the taught course and the school experience through which students are encouraged to draw out personal theories from practice' (Fish, 1995b, p. 55).

You will find Chapter 2 by Graham Handscomb, 'Working together and enquiring within', and Chapter 9 by Jenifer Smith, 'Reflective practice', explore the need for teachers to reflect upon and critique their work. In Chapter 3, 'Approaches to learning and teaching', Sue Cox demonstrates that the kind of teacher you become will depend on the personal qualities and values that you bring to your teaching. So, developing as an effective teacher entails emerging as a reflective practitioner where you ask searching questions of your teaching, and by striving to increase understanding of your practice are able to feed this into further improvement. In this way we produce flexible teachers fit for the demands of the twenty-first century curriculum and the adults of the future: in other words, people with a real understanding of teaching and learning, classrooms and schools, pupils and colleagues, and themselves as educators.

CRITICAL ISSUES

Jerome Bruner (1960) proposed that:

> We begin with the hypothesis that any subject can be taught effectively in some intellectually honest form to any child at any stage of development. (p. 33)

Can you think of arguments for and against this hypothesis? How would you set about gathering evidence to support these arguments? Having reflected on this through this activity, try to say what your view/position is and why.

Maintaining perspective

As we mentioned earlier, teaching is not an easy option. It is important, however, that you do not let it consume your life. If you do, you will cease to be a first-rate practitioner. It is undoubtedly true that you must be prepared to work hard, but you must also be prepared to play hard. Too many teachers suffer from stress having succumbed to the pressures of the job. Added to which, your hobbies can provide an interesting and important dimension to your teaching: your musical or sporting talents, for example, will almost certainly enhance your own and your pupils' experience in the classroom. While you may find teaching satisfyingly challenging and enjoyable, make sure that there are other dimensions to your life which are equally fulfilling.

Concluding remarks

Some might feel that we have painted a slightly negative picture of teaching in this chapter. This has not been our intention: far from it. We both find teaching – whether it be at school, college or university level – to be an immensely satisfying career. It is also important that you see the stresses as well as the triumphs, the challenges as well as the rewards. It is not, however, the job for everyone and you would be doing both yourself and numerous children a disservice if you entered the profession unknowingly.

In brief, primary teaching is hard work but, ultimately for many, worthwhile and personally satisfying. We hope that this book will help you as you move towards your goal.

Summary

Successful primary teaching is:

- a highly satisfying career
- hard work and demanding
- not for everyone.

It is, however, ultimately a vocation in which you can make a real difference for children and their lives.

The authors of this book are:

- successful teachers and teacher educators
- people who enjoy teaching
- educators who consider reflective practice to be of fundamental importance.

Make sure that you are well prepared for your training by:

- gaining experience in schools
- doing some pre-course reading
- addressing the need to develop organised behaviours
- remembering that commitment to training and 'follow-through' is important
- recognising the value of theory and practice, and their interrelationship
- ensuring you care for yourself and have a life beyond teaching.

Issues for reflection

- What do you think a career in teaching has to offer you?
- What do you consider to be the main aims of primary education? Why?
- Think about the most inspiring teachers in your life. What made them such successful educators?

Further reading

Pollard, A. (2010) *Professionalism and Pedagogy: A Contemporary Opportunity*. A commentary by the Teaching and Learning Research programme and the General Teaching Council. This is a 30 paged publication which gives teachers and others a comprehensive guide to how teaching and learning can be at the heart of your professionalism.

Watkins C (2010) *Learning, Performance and Improvement*. Research Matters. The Research Publication of the International Network for School Improvement. Summer 2010, Issue 34. This is a short 12 page paper which looks at the tension between promoting learning and increasing performance of pupils. You should find this a stimulating read which will help you reflect on the principles that are to be at the heart of your teaching.

And here are some books that our students have found particularly helpful:

Crystal, D. (2007) *How Language Works*. London: Penguin.

Eyres, I. (2007) *English for Primary and Early Years: Developing Subject Knowledge*. 2nd edition. London: Paul Chapman Publishing.

Harlen, W. (2006) *Teaching, Learning and Assessing Science 5–12*. London: Sage.

Haylock, D. (2010) *Mathematics Explained for Primary Teachers*. 4th edition. London: Sage.

Oliver, A. (2007) *Creative Teaching: Science in the Early Years and Primary Classroom*. London: David Fulton.

Wood, D. (1997) *How Children Think and Learn: the social contexts of cognitive development*. Oxford: Blackwell.

Bruce, T. (2006) *Early Childhood: A Guide for Students*. London: Sage.

Fisher, J. (2007) *Starting from the Child*. Buckingham: Open University Press.

Moyles, J. (2007) *Beginning Teaching: Beginning Learning in Primary Education*. Buckingham: Open University Press.

CHAPTER 2

WORKING TOGETHER AND ENQUIRING WITHIN

Graham Handscomb

Chapter overview

Gone are the days when teachers were left to sink or swim behind the closed doors of their classrooms. Graham Handscomb explains that it is cool to collaborate and how communities of practice within and beyond the school can provide extended opportunities to develop your teaching and enrich pupils' learning. Schools are about learning and working together to promote a culture of joint learning between all members of the community and the sharing of practice. Graham shows how enquiring and researching into your own practice is a key part of this new shared professionalism, and how genuine partnership, particularly with one key group – the children – is at the heart of successful teaching.

No one had told her that teaching was difficult, and beginning as a teacher most difficult of all. (Stevenson, 1989, p. 116)

There are few professions like teaching, where one individual is called upon to give in such a personal way to, possibly, 30 other individuals on a day-to-day basis. This personal dimension of teaching is probably what you will find most rewarding and why you went into teaching in the first place. At the same time you will also find the specific, individual demands made on you as one of the most challenging features of the job. Teaching can be daunting and stressful, and there are occasions when you may feel rather isolated and alone in your endeavours. But it does not need to be like this, and indeed you will find that in order to grow into an effective teacher you will need to work collaboratively with others.

You are not alone

The quote at the beginning of this chapter comes from Anne Stevenson's (1989) biography of the poet Sylvia Plath. At one time Plath was a teacher and prior to this quote we are given extended extracts from her diary at the time. In this she describes her feelings, which reflect the pendulum swing of emotions experienced by many beginning teachers, alternating between soaring confidence when things appear to be going well, to abject despair when lesson planning seems to fall apart and her students are unresponsive. Plath's response to the low times is to feel inadequate and inferior compared to her more experienced colleagues. So she decides to keep the 'demon' of her doubts to herself:

> I shall show a calm front & fight it in the precincts of my own self, but never give it the social dignity of a public appearance, me running from it, & giving in to it. (Stevenson, 1989 p. 115)

She makes the fundamental mistake that is still common among teachers starting out on their career – of feeling that difficulties encountered are an individual failing and must be struggled with on one's own. Consequently, as Stevenson notes, 'none of her colleagues, young or old, had the least inkling of her personal distress' (Stevenson, 1989, p. 116).

In today's schools and classrooms collaboration and teamwork are vital. On your teaching placements you will find that a great deal of emphasis is placed on teachers working together. This may involve joint planning (short, medium and long term – see Chapter 15) and development of schemes of work, but you may also have the opportunity to be involved in team teaching. In most schools there may be arrangements for trainee teachers to be allocated a personal mentor who will be available to give one-to-one support and critique. Indeed most regard this as basic good practice. There may also be coaching opportunities, where you can work with experienced colleagues on specific teaching skills through observing each other's lessons, giving reciprocal feedback and thus honing and improving your teaching technique. In some cases this can effectively be done as a trio of teachers, where teacher A observes teacher B, teacher B observes teacher C and teacher C observes teacher A (see also Chapter 5). Schools that have established such mentoring or coaching arrangements find that it is not just beginning teachers who benefit. What happens is that a true sense of partnership and collaborative working is developed where the mentor and coach find they reflect on their own practice and learn as much as those they are assisting (Cordingley et al., 2005). Excellent guides to mentoring and coaching and the benefits they provide can be found by reading the 'How To' guide produced by Chris Chapman and Francis Gallannaugh (2008) or the CUREE (2010) website. If you have the good fortune to teach within a school that fosters such a culture of mentoring and coaching, be sure to grasp the opportunity with both hands.

Collaboration and teaching in the primary classroom

So working as a team is to be seen not as a desirable extra on top of the main business of you coping on your own and 'cutting it' in your classroom. It has now become a fundamental part of teaching. You will find the schools you work in are highly complex places where people have to deal continually with an array of changes, ranging from new developments in curriculum to revised approaches to behaviour management. Moving forward on all these things requires that school staff work effectively together. Indeed, it is not an overstatement to say that it would be difficult to survive and flourish in a school today without learning to work as part of a team.

Your common purpose is the learning and development of the children you teach. This is not a solitary exercise and can only be achieved effectively through the joint approach of a whole range of people within and beyond the school. The effective management of your classroom, and making sure you address the needs of all the individuals within it, will depend on how you work with a number of others – including teachers, teaching assistants and parents (see Chapter 16). These collaborations tend to work best when they are part of a genuine partnership in which there are no distinctions of status between yourself as the teacher and the parent or teaching assistant who works alongside you in the classroom. Rather, you fulfil different roles operating within a complementary team. Being part of such an atmosphere can be one of the most rewarding aspects of your teaching experience. So be prepared to share, to open up your classroom to others, and to support and be supported. MacBeath and Stoll describe what this collaborative culture looks like when it dynamically takes off in a school – aim to be part of this:

> Collaboration and partnership are a way of life. People work together. People are not left to sink or swim. People are available to help each other. Team teaching, mentoring, peer coaching, joint planning and mutual observation and feedback are a normal part of the everyday life of the school. (2001, p. 154)

Professional learning communities

When such collaboration takes off within a school there is a real sense of a gathering of colleagues committing to each other to bring about professional learning and growth among staff and children. This exciting development has been a focus of major research on what has become known as 'professional learning communities' (see Stoll et al., 2006; Stoll and Seashore Louis, 2007). In schools where such a community flourishes 'the staff collectively takes responsibility to learn new content, strategies, or approaches to increase its effectiveness in teaching' (Hord, 2009, p. 40) and 'work together towards a common understanding of concepts and practices' (Stoll and Seashore Louis, 2007, p. 3). Sometimes this can be manifested as a group of staff forming an 'action learning set' focused on exploring one particular aspect of teaching and learning (see O'Brien, 2010, p. 29).

How will you recognise whether such an ethos is present within the school where you teach? Well one guide is that:

> … you know that one exists when you can see a group of teachers (and others) sharing and critically interrogating their practice in an ongoing, reflective, collaborative, inclusive, learning orientated, growth promoting way. (Stoll and Seashore Louis, 2007, p. 1)

There is a sense of the gains of such a group being more than a sum of the parts so that 'what is held in common supplements, but does not supplant, what teachers learn individually and bring to their classroom' (Stoll and Seashore Louis, 2007, p. 3). If you are not fortunate to join a school where such a culture is already established, then as a new member of staff with a fresh outlook why not look to work with like-minded colleagues to help develop such a community yourself? In doing this it might be helpful to bear in mind the following five headings which summarise the key features of professional learning communities (Stoll et al., 2006, p. 34):

- Shared values and vision that focus on improving learning and teaching
- Collective responsibility for the learning of all pupils
- Reflective professional enquiry to deepen practice
- Collaboration and teamwork
- Group and collective learning, as well as individual learning.

Collaboration beyond the school

In your teaching practice placements you will gain experience of working in a number of schools. If you are trained as part of a School Centred Initial Teacher Training (SCITT) partnership, your training will be organised and delivered by a group of schools working together. So, for example, in Essex there are a number of SCITTs where head teachers and teachers from a range of primary schools get together to plan how trainee teachers will have experience of teaching in at least two schools. Trainees' academic training, together with the development of curriculum and assessment knowledge and expertise, also takes place within this collaborative on-the-job setting. Following the government statement that it 'will reform teacher training to shift trainee teachers out of college and into the classroom' (Gove, 2010, p. 10) it is likely that the recommendations of the report *More Good Teachers* by the Policy Exchange think tank which has influenced government thinking will be implemented. This includes the proposals that school-based and employment routes to teacher training be made more attractive and expanded to become the default option – so in the future it may well be that many readers of this book will be trained via these routes (Freedman et al., 2008).

This is just one example of how schools are increasingly working together in ways that would have been unheard of even a few years ago. Nowadays it is very likely that in whichever school you work you will also have a range of opportunities to link with colleagues in other schools. In the past this was less common. During the mid-1990s the government emphasised that schools were autonomous and self-managing, and the responsibility for school performance and improvement rested primarily with schools themselves. This meant that schools tended to be locked in competition to attract pupils. Nevertheless there were many people working in schools during this time, myself among them, who felt that this overemphasis on competition rather than cooperation between schools was not the way forward. I remember somewhat idealistically portraying this as:

> … taking a stand against the view that a coherent education system can be built from the innumerable, self-interested decisions of individual parents and schools. It means holding proudly aloft the banner declaring that schools need to collaborate and share good practice to achieve the best for all our children. (Handscomb, 1995, p. 12)

Well, much changed in the intervening years and it became 'cool to collaborate' (Handscomb, 2002, p. 3). The reason for this was not just a cosy view that it is nice for schools and their teachers to work together, but a growing realisation that further improvement and the raising of standards rely on such collaboration. So, for instance, Clarke argued that as schools continue to improve, 'they will eventually come to a point when they need to communicate and examine what other schools are doing' (2000, p. 16). Above all, the momentum towards greater joint working between clusters of schools was given new impetus by the government itself lending political weight to this development. Since the political changes introduced in 2010 there has been a greatly renewed emphasis on school 'freedoms' and autonomy which some fear may act as a restraint to such collaborative working between schools. However, the government sought to give clear reassurance on this as shown in one of the first statements by the then new Secretary of State:

> I know some have expressed concern that this offer of greater autonomy for schools will work against the collaborative model of school improvement that has grown up over the past 15 or so years … I would not be going down this road if I thought it would in any way set back the process of school improvement … or if it would in any way fracture the culture of collaboration which has driven school improvement over the last decade. (Gove, 2010, p. 3)

So in your training and ongoing career, collaboration with colleagues in the wider profession and in other agencies will continue to be a very important part of development as a teacher.

Collaborative professional development and growth

Initial teacher training is an intensive period of professional training and development. During your placements in schools you will quickly discover that this emphasis on the importance of professional development is a continuing feature of what it means to be a teacher. There will be a range of continuing professional development (CPD) experiences provided by the school. Much of this will take place within the school itself while other activities will take place outside the school, facilitated in some cases by the local authority or, increasingly, by a local cluster or network of schools. While you are on placement you are a member of the school, and it is obviously important that, if given the opportunity, you participate in these activities and, of course, make the most of the benefits that they provide. This experience will also help you appreciate that your initial teacher training is but the first part of a continuing process of professional learning throughout your teaching career.

It is useful to consider the nature of this ongoing development and its important connection with collaboration. There is now a growing and authoritative consensus that the most effective professional learning is focused on teachers' classroom practice and is collaborative – learning from other teachers' good practice (Handscomb, 2009).

So learning together is advocated because it tends to focus development on classroom practice. As Harris (2002) puts it, '… improvements in teaching are most likely to occur where there are opportunities to work together and to learn from each other' (p. 102). There are particular benefits to be gained for beginning teachers from schools working together on professional development. I discovered this through a year-long research project undertaken by Essex local authority and some major national agencies. It involved 21 schools working in eight clusters and over 120 teachers at the beginning of their career (Essex County Council, 2003). The investigation clearly showed that clusters of schools were able to develop joint approaches to the identification of beginning teachers' needs, and were able to draw on a wider range of CPD opportunity and training expertise from across the variety of schools in each cluster. The teachers also greatly valued the facility to visit other schools and exchange experiences. These positive learning outcomes were clearly reflected in the comments of the teachers involved (see Figure 2.1).

Reflecting on your own practice is a key factor in developing as a learner and teacher (see Chapter 9). To be able to do this with other colleagues in a collaborative setting

- I have found the activities I have undertaken very useful and I have a much better idea of how to develop professionally.
- The area that was extremely beneficial to me was the opportunity to visit another school. This developed me as a teacher and I took many ideas back to school, some of which I could implement immediately, others that I will include in my next action plan.
- Networking for Foundation Stage coordinators was valuable.
- Talking to other beginning teachers about professional issues has made me realise that many of us have the same concerns and issues. This project has given me some time to reflect on professional knowledge and understanding. It has afforded me with opportunities to develop and consolidate transferable skills such as those connected to classroom management.

Figure 2.1   Some beginning teachers' comments on the value of collaborative professional development

Source: Essex County Council (2003, pp. 11 and 13).

across a number of schools can be particularly powerful, and it will be important to make the most of such an opportunity when it arises.

The other important thing to bear in mind about your continuing professional development is that it should have an impact on the work that you do in the classroom and with children. Rather than think of what kind of course or CPD activities I need to undertake, it is better to consider what development experiences I need to bring about a positive difference in my teaching and to improve the behaviours, attitude and achievement of the children I teach (Earley and Porritt, 2010a, 2010b). Based on this approach there are now some very helpful guides on how to make the most of professional development opportunities in schools to ensure they make a real difference to improving your performance in the classroom (Bubb and Earley, 2010).

School networks and communities of practice

To a certain extent schools have always loosely liaised with each other, even in times of intense competition between them. Recently there has been a considerably increased drive for schools to work in more structured networks that make a significant contribution to learning and teaching.

Hargreaves (2003) sees networks as one of the most significant educational developments in modern times. He portrays them as potential hotbeds of innovation in which good practice can be identified and spread more quickly than it has done between teachers and between schools in the past. Networking between primary schools has certainly arrived, and it is highly likely that the schools where you have your placements will be active members of one of these networks. Although many schools and networks will wish to involve trainee teachers in their activities, it is also fair to warn you that there may be some cases where this practice is less developed. However, if these networks are effective then they will increasingly be an aspect of school life that you will experience and that will influence the way in which you plan and teach.

One of the greatest benefits of networking between schools is that it provides teachers, including those at the beginning of their career, with opportunities to work in a wider community where practice can be shared and compared. You will find that this is an exciting time to be entering the teaching profession. Too often in the past teachers operated behind the 'closed doors' of their classrooms and schools, and this meant that often valuable experience was not shared and the profession failed to learn and grow.

Nowadays this has changed and communities of practice have developed within and between schools. One of the most valuable features of these communities is that they can foster a climate of dialogue, reflection and exchange between teachers. This is so important because research has indicated that the communication and transference of practice from one teacher to another is difficult to achieve. This is because good teaching is often intuitive, uses tacit experience and knowledge, and is focused on the particular and immediate context of the individual teacher (McIntyre, 2001). Hargreaves has given considerable thought to this problem of how to 'bottle' and share teacher practitioner knowledge:

> If one teacher tells another about a practice that he (she) finds effective, the second teacher has merely acquired information, not personal knowledge. Transfer occurs only when the knowledge of the first becomes information for the second, who then works on that information in such a way that it becomes part of his or her context of meaning and purpose and pre-existing knowledge and then is applied in action ... Transfer is the conversion of information about one person's practice into another's know-how. (1998, p. 46)

One of the problems in this area is the casual ease with which people sometimes talk of sharing best practice to be used as models for others to emulate, when actually what is being disseminated is untried, untested interesting practice. 'The sharing of good practice and the dissemination of best practice is widely advocated. Unfortunately our knowledge of how to do this is frighteningly slight' (Hargreaves, 2003, p. 44). David Woods makes the following helpful distinctions:

> In the literature on school improvement the terms 'best', 'good' and 'innovative' practice are used in a variety of ways. Good practice is generally used to mean practice which is professionally judged to be effective, but may require further evidence and validation; best practice is used to mean practice which is proven over time, backed by supporting evidence; innovative practice may highlight new and interesting ways of doing things, with early indications of success. (2000, p. 2)

This is perhaps most helpfully illustrated as a continuum (see Figure 2.2) ranging from innovative practice, to good practice, to best practice. So, for example, if you develop a set of practices in your classroom that works well with your group of learners, this might be characterised as being at the left-hand side of the continuum. As this is shared with other school colleagues, who adapt and apply it in their different settings, it gets tested against a range of teacher perspectives and might then be termed 'good practice'.

Interesting and innovative practice	Good practice	Best practice
Encouraging creativity, innovation and a sense of dynamism. Generating a culture of dialogue and exchange. 'Letting a thousand flowers bloom.'	Effective practice. Ideas shared with others, adapted to new contexts and tried out. Learning communities which promote sharing and trialling and critique of practice.	Best practice validated by supporting evidence and proven over time. Structured systems: benchmarking, monitoring and evaluation, quality assurance, formal dissemination.

Figure 2.2   A continuum of practice

Source: Handscomb, (2002/3, p. 20)

Eventually it might be developed into school-wide approaches, shared in other school settings, benchmarked and validated by supporting evidence and proven over time – and thus merit the accolade 'best practice'. Clearly calibration and judgements made about such distinctions should be part and parcel of the professional discussion, debate and collaborative agreement among teachers, schools and other parties like higher education institutions and local authorities.

As part of your training, and as you begin in your first teaching post, you may have the opportunity to be part of, for instance, a newly qualified teachers' cluster within which colleagues can share their experiences and recognise different strengths and areas for development. Figure 2.3 gives a flavour of the benefits that one group found.

Lorna
Sharing ideas about how to approach problems has been helpful. It is great to hear about ideas that have worked and that you can adopt.

Claire
We encouraged each other to reflect upon lessons during all meetings but the two sessions on good/bad lessons that we had taught and creativity are the most memorable.

Gill
By becoming reflective practitioners we were constantly reflecting on (our own) practice and that of others at the meetings.

Martin
It was really good when Gill and Lorna led the meeting on subject knowledge and the sharing of resources and lesson plans has helped us all.

(Adapted from McAteer et al., 2010)

If you have the chance to be part of such a dynamic professional community then count it as good fortune and be ready to contribute!

Figure 2.3   Sharing experiences within a newly qualified teachers' cluster

CRITICAL ISSUES

Effective collaboration?

This chapter argues that collaboration within and between schools can result in significant gains to teachers' well-being and professionalism. However, there is always the danger that this could surface as a kind of cosy collegiality, an easy staffroom banter or school cluster social get-together. These can be pleasant enough social events, worthwhile in themselves, but they may lack the challenge and opportunity for growth that you would wish to gain from a community of practice.

What ingredients would you see as being essential to a community of teachers from a cluster of schools meeting regularly to develop their thinking and practice? Try to specify in particular what features will help to keep the experience of the group sharp, challenging and replenishing.

Enquiry and research

We have seen that there are likely to be opportunities to work collaboratively with a range of colleagues within your school and with others in the wider educational community. We have also reflected on how powerful these opportunities can be, but also that energies devoted to such collaborative activities can be wasted if they lack rigour and focus. This concern about 'soft' unproductive collaboration is resolved in Alma Harris' view if a strategic link is made with teacher enquiry and research:

> For teacher development ... to occur commitment to certain kinds of collaboration is centrally important. However, collaboration without reflection and enquiry is little more than working collegially. For collaboration to influence personal growth and development it has to be premised upon mutual enquiry and sharing. (2002, p. 103)

I will argue in the next few pages the merits of research practice in schools and of you developing as a teacher enquirer. This may appear to you to be a rather strange proposal. The image of educational research for many teachers is something done by others in academic institutions – complex, difficult to access and of limited relevance. You only need to look at the range of publications by the authors of this book, however, to see that educational research can be highly relevant and practical. Unfortunately this is not always the case but this is changing. Increasingly, classroom practitioners have discovered the merits of investigating an aspect of their work that directly contributes to improved practice and benefits the children they teach. I have worked with teachers at

Teachers who have engaged in researching their own classrooms and schools have found that it:

- encourages them to question, explore and develop their practice
- is a highly satisfying and energising professional activity
- has become an integral part of their continuing professional development
- has enhanced the quality of teaching and learning.

Figure 2.4   Why engage in research?

various stages of their career – during initial training, as newly qualified or as experienced teachers – where they have actively undertaken enquiry into their practice and all have found this experience manageable, relevant and often transforming. Figure 2.4 summarises the key benefits for teachers researching their classrooms.

Many teachers would not readily engage with the notion of being a 'teacher-researcher'. A more helpful term, which describes the skills that are part of good teaching, is the teacher as enquirer. This alludes to teachers who are keen to reflect upon and critique their practices. They make good use of research and evidence to stimulate new ways of thinking and to try out new ideas, and then systematically to evaluate the impact of any subsequent change they have brought about (see also Chapter 9).

Teachers have long been involved in examining their practice in this way to make further improvements. But when does such activity 'count' as research? What is the relationship between large-scale research conducted by, for instance, a university department and a piece of evidence-informed practice carried out by a teacher within the classroom? And how is such evidence-informed practice any different from what good teachers do anyway in refining and honing their craft in day-to-day lesson preparation and evaluation?

One view is that evidence-informed practice typically involves individual teachers reflecting on their own classroom practice and sharing this with colleagues; in contrast, 'research' is seen as involving a larger-scale more systematic enquiry. Another view is that these two characterisations are not different in kind, but rather two ends of a continuum of practice in which 'evidence-informed practice' merges into 'research'. However, many have found this a difficult debate and would be uncomfortable about making too sharp a distinction between evidence-informed practice and research. There are tensions between the world of academic research and teachers pursuing research as part of their professional learning and practice, but many have become convinced of the great potential of practitioner research to transform both the classroom and the teacher (Handscomb, 2004).

In fact it may be useful for you as a teacher approaching this area to adopt the definition of research as simply being 'systematic enquiry made public' (Stenhouse, 1981, p. 34). In other words, it is not different in kind to good classroom practice and reflection, but requires that you do this systematically and share both how you went about it and the outcomes (Essex County Council, 2002). I think this idea of incorporating rigorous enquiry into your everyday practice is best explained by John Mason (2002) who sees it as a disciplined approach to 'noticing':

> The Discipline of Noticing is nothing more than an attempt to be systematic and methodical without being mechanical. It is a collection of practices which together can enhance sensitivity to notice opportunities to act freshly in the future. (p. 59)

It is a powerful argument that as teachers we are continually encouraging our pupils to engage in enquiry, systematically and with a concern for evidence. So why do we not apply these same principles of learning and development to ourselves as teachers? To get under way, just start by asking the everyday but critical questions that are live issues for you. Why do children behave the way they do? Why do some children find it difficult to stay on task? Why is my teaching sometimes effective and at other times not? How can I foster a more stimulating and productive classroom environment? Once having arrived at a focus for an area of your practice that interests you, embarking upon the investigation is not as forbidding as it may seem.

There tends to be a rather off-putting mystique about the steps involved in the research process but in fact it mainly involves those listed in Figure 2.5. These are basic, but rigorous, stages and, perhaps with the help of a mentor within the school or possibly a colleague from the local authority or a partner university, are well within the scope of classroom teachers wanting to enquire into their practice.

Certainly there is now a view held by many that:

> All teachers should have an entitlement to research thinking in order to develop their role as critical users of research. All schools and colleges should have an entitlement and perhaps a responsibility, to participate in a relevant research partnership for appropriate periods. (Dyson, 2001, p. 7)

Such voices are arguing that teacher enquiry and school-based research are not just desirable extras once the core business of teaching and raising standards is done, but

---

- What do you want to find out? (The research problem and research questions)
- What is already known on this issue? (A basic web-search)
- What information do you need?
- What information is already available in the school or elsewhere?
- How will you obtain the information?
- How will you check that the information gathered is sound and the methods for gathering it effective?
- How will you make sense of, and use, the information?
- How do you draw secure conclusions?
- Make judgements about recommendations for changed practice.

Figure 2.5   Steps in the enquiry process

that such activity is becoming essential to school performance and success. There is evidence that it also affects the quality of pupils' learning and how they come to become confident independent learners: 'The key condition for promoting learner autonomy is classroom-focussed inquiry by teachers' (Watkins, 2010, p. 11; see also Swaffield and MacBeath, 2006).

In some schools and local authorities in which you will work there may be a growing commitment to supporting teachers enquiring into their own practice. For instance, Essex has established a Forum for Learning and Research Enquiry (FLARE) which is made up of teachers and headteachers dedicated to promoting teacher and school-based research. Building on what is known about teachers as researchers FLARE explored the features that might typically be found in a school that was 'research engaged'. FLARE's thinking is that in such a school, research and enquiry are integral to its approach to teaching and learning. It is built into the school culture, fostering research in collaborative groups and partnerships within and beyond the school. Above all, what distinguishes a research-engaged school is that such activity is at the very heart of the school, pervading its outlook, informing its systems and stimulating learning at every level (Handscomb and MacBeath, 2003).

Of course, this is the ideal and the schools that you experience may not exhibit all these characteristics and to this degree. However, it is possible that in many schools there will be opportunities for you to investigate an aspect of your practice, and be given the support needed to do this. The great thing is that you are now no longer on your own as there are a number of helpful and accessible guides to help you become an enquirer into your own practice. This includes a short comprehensive Research Tool-kit and book on Action Research from the National Foundation for Educational Research (NFER) (Lawson, 2008, 2009), and articles on the benefits of being a practitioner researcher (Handscomb and MacBeath, 2009), how to plan your research project (Rickinson, 2009) and how to ask the right questions (Sharp, 2009).

Collaboration with pupils

It may seem self-evident and somewhat superfluous to advocate collaboration with pupils! Surely this is something you will do automatically. Gone are the days when teaching was seen in terms of simply filling empty vessels, but there remains concern that we insufficiently take account of the 'voice' of pupils. Yet it is essential that, as teachers, we work in a truly collaborative way with children in order for effective teaching and successful learning to take place.

The emphasis on the collaboration, consultation and participation of pupils has gained momentum in recent times as the result of a number of important developments. Possibly one of the most important is the work done by Jean Rudduck and her colleagues on how giving pupils a voice and listening to what they say can make a significant difference to how they perform and achieve. So, for instance, from the early

1990s the Chief Inspector's Annual Reports showed that there was a sustained 'dip' in the progress of children at Year 3. The initial reaction was to blame the teaching but, by conducting extensive research into the pupils' view, the situation was shown to be far more complex and related to a whole range of issues such as different expectations, different ways of working and features of the curriculum and school organisation (Doddington and Flutter with Berne and Demetriou, 2001). By listening to what children had to say, and attempting to gain an appreciation of their perspective, new light was shed on problems of this kind. The power of Rudduck's work is that it clearly shows how important it is for you and I as teachers to really engage with pupils, and the benefits of genuinely making them partners in the teaching and learning enterprise. On your teaching placement, and in your teaching career beyond, you can do no worse than to have the following exhortations always in mind:

We should

- take seriously what pupils can tell us about their experiences of being a learner in school – about what gets in the way of their learning and what helps them to learn
- find ways of involving pupils more closely in decisions that affect their lives in school, whether at the level of the classroom or the institution.

(Rudduck and Flutter, 2004, p. 2)

CRITICAL ISSUES

Pupil Power?

Teachers' union criticises demeaning treatment by children selection panels

This headline reflects a number of press reports that appeared in April 2010. Teachers were complaining to their unions that when children have been used in the selection process for appointing staff this led in a number of cases to humiliating experiences. One candidate complained of not been recommended for appointment because he looked liked 'Humpty Dumpty'. Another said that, as an internal candidate, he had been marked down because he had previously given the child interviewer a detention.

How would you respond to these criticisms, drawing on what you have read in this chapter about the importance of collaborating with children and pupil voice?

What sort of preparation and training should be available for schools, children and candidates to avoid the problems encountered in such press reports?

Other work about the value of teachers overtly consulting pupils about their teaching has been equally illuminating. Dave Pedder (2005) reflects that although some teachers may find this a rather vulnerable thing to do, children usually are very constructive.

When consulted, rather than wanting the teacher to stop doing some things, they often select some aspects of the teacher's repertoire and ask for more of this! So, if you build in consultation with children as part of your teaching, this can be liberating rather than threatening:

> You know – that's what made me enthusiastic, because I suddenly saw all that untapped creativity really. You can use pupils' ideas in a very valid, interesting way and it can make the pupil excited, the teacher excited and you know obviously the lessons will take off from there. If you can actually collaborate with pupils it's equally – I didn't realise it – it's equally exciting, isn't it? (Pedder and McIntyre, 2004, p. 30)

The potential for consulting pupils and actively using pupil voice is therefore great. The important thing is that you genuinely let the pupil's voice count, and Michael Fielding (2004) warns against making this a passive token exercise. It is only by embracing real collaboration with pupils that dividends will be gained in the quality of teaching and learning in your classroom.

This issue of how we work collaboratively with pupils is a crucial one that relates both to your whole outlook as a teacher and to your practice. It grows out of the understanding of the school as a learning organisation in which all its members are fellow learners, and the implications of this for the teacher–pupil learning relationship:

> It raises potentially fundamental issues about the learning enterprise being a collaborative venture and poses challenging questions about the dynamic of control and empowerment of young people in our schools. (Handscomb, 2009, p. 5)

This is particularly brought into sharp relief by the exciting development of pupils as researchers of their schools. In recent years the value of young people developing enquiry skills has been recognised, not just as valuable for investigation as part of the curriculum but also in making a contribution to researching the school: 'Involving young people not just in School Council activity but also as co-evaluators can pay great dividends in the process of school self-evaluation' (Frost et al., 2009, p. 4). The important issue here is that this does not just become a token exercise but one which may very well fundamentally question current school arrangements. As Cook-Sather points out, it is dishonest to authorise student voice where the context does not allow an implied challenge (Cook-Sather, 2007). It can bring a marvellous new dimension to your relationship and work with children to develop their enquiry skills in this way and there are resources like *Active Enquiring Minds* (Frost et al., 2009) which can support you in this.

So achieving your intended outcomes for children will necessarily involve you in a range of collaborations with others, including people from other professional areas like health and social care. Thus collaboration with a host of colleagues within and beyond the school, and particularly with children themselves, has come to centre stage and will be a fundamental feature of your role as a teacher.

Summary

- Beginning as a teacher can feel a daunting and isolating experience, but it is important to remember that you are not alone.
- Teachers, together with other colleagues, rely on one another and often bring the best out of each other when working together.
- Teamwork is now a fundamental feature of teaching in the modern primary school.
- There is a strong push for all primary schools to be active participants in school networks.
- Collaboration and networking between schools has considerable potential to promote innovation and help share successful practice more widely.
- Some of the most effective professional development experiences are when teachers undertake them together.
- It is valuable to share interesting practice, and to identify and disseminate proven best practice.
- Enquiring into your practice can be a very rewarding experience, and can help transform your teaching and improve pupil learning.
- Teacher research, through systematic enquiry which is shared with colleagues, is within the reach of all, including beginning teachers.
- Partnership and consultation with pupils can pay great dividends in your teaching.
- Paying attention to the 'voice' and perceptions of pupils is an important ingredient in promoting successful learning. Think of how you might go about developing the enquiry skills of your pupils so that they can be actively involved in reflecting on their learning and their school.

Issues for reflection

- Make arrangements with a fellow trainee to talk about the difficulties you each encounter on your placements. When listening, try not to make evaluative comments or pass judgement but concentrate on letting each other tell the details of what happened and share how it felt. Talking about your experience in this way may help to put incidents in perspective and avoid blowing them up into major crises.

(Continued)

(Continued)

- During your placement explore whether it would be possible to plan a number of lessons with an experienced school colleague, to observe each other teaching this programme of lessons and to have time together to reflect on the observations.
- Think of a time when you have been involved in a collaborative activity with another person or a team. What were the advantages in doing this? What difficulties and strains were encountered? How were these dealt with?
- Think of a network to which you belong (this can be a 'local' one involving meetings and activities, or a virtual online network). How would you describe the main features of this network to someone who knew little about it? What aspects of the network are key factors in keeping it going?
- 'To get under way, just start by asking the everyday but critical questions that are live issues for you' (this chapter, p. 26). Consider what classroom practice issues might be of interest to you as potential areas for investigation and enquiry.
- Consider in what ways children perceive school differently to adults. What do you think would be the main significant features of school and classroom experience from the child's perspective?

Further reading

Frost, R., Handscomb, G. and Prince, R. (2009) *Active Enquiring Minds: Supporting Young Researchers*. Essex: Forum for Learning and Research Enquiry (FLARE), Essex County Council. This is a comprehensive folder of material for supporting pupil researchers. It contains a resource pack for the young researchers, guidance material for adults supporting young researchers, work booklets for pupils and the facility for pupils to apply for a Certificate of Enquiry and Research.

Handscomb, G. and MacBeath, J. (2003) *The Research Engaged School*. Essex: Forum for Learning and Research Enquiry (FLARE), Essex County Council. This 15-page booklet describes the main features of a school that is research-engaged and includes a basic health-check audit to help teachers and schools to check out their own practice.

Lawson, A. (ed.) (2009) *Action Research: Making a Difference in Education*. Slough: NFER. This is a concise book of 70 pages written in accessible language with illustrative examples in which the authors present research that has made a difference.

Mason, J. (2002) *The Discipline of Noticing*. London: RoutledgeFalmer. A very readable manual to help you develop practical approaches to incorporating 'noticing' and enquiry into your everyday practice and professional development.

Rudduck, J. and Flutter, J. (2004) *How to Improve Your School: Giving Pupils a Voice*. London: Continuum. This book gives a compelling account of schooling from the pupils' perspective. It brings together all the major work done on 'pupil voice' and conveys the important messages: not to underestimate pupils and to ensure you work in partnership with them.

http://www.curee-paccts.com/mentoring-and-coaching (2010). CUREE were commissioned to produce the national guidance on mentoring and coaching and are leaders in this field. CUREE has produced a comprehensive range of materials on mentoring and coaching for school practitioners.

CHAPTER 3

APPROACHES TO LEARNING AND TEACHING

Sue Cox

Chapter overview

The sort of teacher you become will not be about how well you apply a prescribed set of techniques or approaches provided by others, but rather dependent on how you learn to think critically about your teaching. In this chapter Sue Cox delves deep. She demonstrates the need for you to develop a broader understanding of the education process and appreciate how the ways you teach are shaped by values in the wider society and culture. This should help you to see how your approaches to teaching might be challenged and improved. You are invited to consider learning and teaching from a range of different perspectives, the values and outlook that will help shape the teacher you want to be, and key elements to address in your teaching in order to help children to learn.

Introduction

From your experience as a pupil and student you will already know that there is no single answer to the question of what makes a good teacher. If you think about why you have admired particular teachers you will probably come up with a variety of reasons. What they taught you and how they taught you, as well as their personal qualities and characteristics, will, no doubt, come to mind. In this chapter, I intend to focus on the question of 'how' teachers teach and how this is bound up with values – those of wider society as well as those to which they are personally committed. I will show how, as a member of the teaching profession, it is important to think about this relationship between approaches to teaching and values and to develop a critical perspective. To help clarify this I will explain some of the influences on primary practice, in a historical sense. The chapter as a whole explores the way in which you might develop your own approach to teaching in order to become a good teacher.

Becoming a 'good' teacher

To some extent, the way in which a teacher teaches is inextricably bound up with what sort of person they are and the kind of thing they are teaching. For instance, my 'best' teacher from my own primary school days was the caring and imaginative Miss T, who was my class teacher when I was 7. One thing I remember is that she taught us about all the interesting plant life in the vicinity of the school, by taking us out into the environment to investigate and observe it. It was because she was a caring kind of person, who had imagination, that she made sure what she taught us was always interesting in itself. But it wasn't only the subject matter which was engaging: it was also the way in which we learned about it, from first-hand experience and through working together with our friends. As well as setting things up in this way, Miss T excited us by helping us to notice things. She encouraged us to be curious and to ask questions, and was always ready to listen to us.

What a contrast this was with the teacher I had had the year before, who provided us with endless little printed workbooks which we worked through, with hardly an opportunity to talk to the teacher. Likewise, I remember the teacher I had the following year as one who talked at us from the front of the class and did not want to hear what her pupils had to say. As well as wanting to emulate the 'good' teachers you have known, you may also have a feeling that you could make a better job of it than some of the less memorable ones! Your own reflections will inevitably reveal that you value certain approaches to teaching more than others.

Making judgements

There is an understandable temptation, when you begin a teacher education course, to believe that you will be provided with a simple 'how to do it' kit that you can put into practice in the classroom. If teaching were as straightforward as this then it would lose much of what makes it infinitely interesting, challenging and worthwhile. Teaching is a complex business in which there are almost endless questions to be asked about what to do and how to do it. It is the fact that there are no simple, incontestable answers to these that makes your 'training' much more than merely acquiring a predetermined set of skills.

There is no straightforward solution because how one will act depends on what one ought to do. This takes us into the area of values, which, of course, are always open to debate. In other words, the questions of what and how will inevitably be linked to the larger issue of 'why': why do this rather than that? It is probable that, from your own point of view, some personal, deeply held beliefs or ideas connected to this question about 'aims' or 'ends' will have been part of your motivation for embarking on a career in education.

There are many issues that might be addressed here. There are those about what is worthwhile or important educationally. What should children be learning and what are educationally worthwhile ways of doing this? Then again, these kinds of questions are grounded in the larger moral issues of how we should treat other people – in the case of primary teaching, how we should treat children. The decisions that are required, then, are fundamentally ethical ones: it is this that makes teaching professional work. You are not training to be a technician: considering the questions of how to go about the business of teaching, and deciding to do things one way rather than another, entails making judgements. Furthermore, it is not enough, as a professional, simply to assert that your way is the right way. If your way of doing things is to be professionally valid rather than just a matter of personal whim, then it must be justifiable.

Reflecting on practice

However, the need to address these kinds of issues should not prevent you from getting started on some teaching. After all, we wouldn't be able to live if our every action required us to think out beforehand what we should do and why. Since we all learn how to go about our lives among the people in the communities – or the social situations – in which we find ourselves from the moment we are born, we are quite able to act appropriately in the course of our daily existence, without this level of reflection. Likewise, when starting out on your training, you will already have enough 'inside knowledge' of teaching to be able to take on the role of a teacher in a classroom. However, whatever we do, in whatever situation, reflects the values – even if we are not aware of them – that we implicitly hold as members of a social or cultural group that does things in particular ways, for particular reasons, in particular contexts. To bring those values into sharper focus we need to question what we do and why. This applies to what we do in the classroom in the same way as it applies to any other of our actions.

So this suggests looking at things the other way round. Rather than working out what you ought to do and how to achieve those aims before you start teaching, you can begin to make sense of what you actually do and then develop and improve it. You will be able to participate as a teacher in a classroom when you first go into school, whether you are a student teacher on a Graduate Training Programme, a member of an undergraduate or postgraduate course, or a trainee on a SCITT programme, because you already know about the kinds of things that teachers do, both from your own experience as a learner in educational settings and, perhaps, from having had some kind of work experience in school before embarking on your teacher education programme. You will already have some role models to follow from your previous experience, or you could simply follow the examples of the teachers you are working with. You can also develop your teaching skills by practising what you already know how to do from your own experience. This is a valid and appropriate starting point. However, more will be needed if you are to develop your professional abilities.

Following a role model or honing your existing skills, in themselves, will not develop your understanding or your ability to make judgements. It may be appropriate for a technician to follow procedures with no concern for the reasons behind them, but being a professional demands more than merely doing what you have seen others do, doing what you have been told to do, or doing what you have done before. You need to make sense of what you are doing and to evaluate it.

The sort of questions you might ask yourself to help you to do this include:

- What am I doing? (Describing actions)
- What does it mean? (Interpreting actions)
- What values are implicit? (Analysing actions; identifying assumptions)
- What other interpretations are there? (Questioning interpretations; challenging assumptions)
- What other courses of action might there be? (Questioning actions)
- What alternative value positions might thus be brought into play? (Questioning values)

Learning from experience, then, requires reflecting on what you are doing and becoming aware of things that you do almost unconsciously when you are using your existing 'know-how'. It requires that you look critically and analytically at what might otherwise become a matter of habit or routine (see also Chapter 9).

As well as thinking about what you yourself do, you will look at what the children and the class teacher are doing. Do their actions tell you how they understand what is going on? Are there any differences between your own perspectives and those of the class teacher? Do the teacher's decisions differ from those you would make? If there are differences, does this tell you anything about the different kinds of values coming into play? Can you learn about your own practice from reflecting in this way on the practice of others?

Conceptions of teaching and learning

As you consider your approach to teaching, and begin to assess the underlying values, it may be useful to ask yourself an underlying question. Which, of the many and varied ways in which you might act in the classroom, would you count as teaching and why. This might help you to work out whether your actions are educationally valid.

To illustrate what I am saying, it can be helpful to reflect on 'learning' from the point of view of being a learner. This will help to throw light on the idea of teaching, for, if there is one general point that can be made about teaching, it is that it is conceptually connected with learning. We can hardly think of ourselves as teaching unless we at least intend that learning will come about as a consequence of what we are doing. It can be taken as read that schools exist to help children to learn.

'What is your idea of learning?' When I have asked prospective teachers this question a common response is that learning is acquiring new knowledge – getting to know something that they didn't know before. The role of the teacher in this process is seen as in some way 'transmitting' that knowledge to the learner – 'passing on' knowledge, or 'telling' the learner what they need to know. However, I have then asked these same people to reflect on experiences they have had which have changed them in some important way. It is impossible to do justice here to the range of stories which they have told, but there is space to list some of the ways in which they have gone on to characterise the experience, and these may resonate with experiences of your own.

Some people have suggested that the personal changes occurred as a result of solving a problem, questioning their established ideas or being brought to see something from another point of view. Some had acquired a new skill. Others recognised that they had been responding to a new challenge, had persevered in the face of difficulty or had collaborated with other people. Yet others had changed as a result of having experienced something first hand or through having time to think and experiment, or had seen new value in what they were doing. For others, the experience had been an emotional one, or one where they had been able to empathise with another person, or had needed to handle failure or insecurity. When I asked whether they would count these as learning experiences, they have always affirmed that they would. What is interesting to note is that none of these learning experiences involved 'the acquisition of new knowledge' in the way anticipated. It was rarely the case that a teacher had directly 'transmitted' what the learner had learned. All the learning had occurred in a context that was personally meaningful to the learner.

Learning in classrooms

If we go back to your classroom, where you can observe children and teachers, you may well find them doing things which challenge your initial ideas about teaching and learning. To look at an example, you might go into a classroom where the children are examining a collection of toys from the Victorian era. They are working in a group, sharing their ideas on what these artefacts tell them about the lives of children at that time. As far as you can see, the teacher's role is that of joining in the conversation to make observations that encourage the children to notice more features about the toys.

She responds to comments that the children make and she asks questions which encourage them to make deductions. At no time does she appear to tell them directly how children lived in Victorian times. She keeps them focused on the clues that are presented by the artefacts. For instance, she asks them questions about similarities and differences between these toys and their own toys, and they very quickly realise that none of the Victorian toys are made of plastic and none of them are electronic. She prompts them to put forward their own ideas about what this suggests.

Again, imagine going into a reception classroom to find that the children are playing in an area that has been converted into a shoe shop, with pairs of shoes in boxes, seats for the customers and a till with coins in it. The teacher is joining in the children's play as a customer in the shop. The children are also in role as customers and shop assistants, and the teacher responds to what they say to him. He initiates conversations about which pair of shoes he wants to try and talks about the size he needs and the price he wants to pay. Then again, there might be some children in the outdoor play area of the nursery. The teacher had been throwing and catching balls with them, but now they are all on their own, using balls of different sizes and weight, which the teacher has provided.

In all these situations, it might seem that the teachers are not doing their jobs as they do not seem to be 'teaching' in that apparently obvious sense of directly transmitting knowledge. But, given that they are competent and professional teachers who know what they are doing, perhaps there is a wider definition to be given to teaching that would include these actions. Starting by asking what the children are learning and what part the teachers are playing in that, it does appear that there is more to teaching than simply sitting the children down and giving them information.

In the first example here, the teacher is challenging the children to think about the toys as evidence of how people lived in the Victorian era. She could simply tell them – but she wants them to think about how we know about the past, to look at the kind of evidence that is available and to make inferences. These are the kinds of things that historians do to arrive at the facts. Clearly, this teacher thinks it is important for children to understand this process, as well as knowing the facts. And again, she doesn't only tell them about what historians do, she lets them experience this for themselves, to join in and gain first-hand insight into what the process involves. The teacher values children's participation and independence. She clearly believes that this is an effective way for children to learn, partly because her definition of learning is the kind of expanded one that I discussed above.

In the second example, the teacher, likewise, wants the children to understand what goes on in a shop and how we buy things. The children are not being formally taught that shoes come in different sizes and that coins have value and can be exchanged for other things – rather they are learning this in a context which is meaningful: it has the features of a real life situation where these are the common practices. The teacher lets the children take the lead in their play and participates in it on their terms.

In the third example, the teacher has let the children continue practising throwing and catching the balls on their own, knowing that they need time to master this. She has made it quite challenging by providing a range of different balls. Her actions, in both instances, suggest that she respects and values children's play and, furthermore, sees it as a vehicle for learning and, in this case, for developing their physical abilities.

There are parallels to be drawn with the examples of learning processes I discussed earlier provided by prospective teachers. The children, here, are facing challenges, solving problems, seeing things differently, finding new ways of thinking about things, experiencing things first hand and having an opportunity to work things out and try things for themselves, using these processes to make sense of what goes on around them.

So, while the 'transmission' view of teaching may seem obvious enough, it may well be the kind of commonly held conception that belies the complexity of teaching and learning.

What I hope is becoming clear from all the above examples is that if learning can involve a range of processes that extend beyond 'being on the receiving end' of knowledge that is 'transmitted' to the learner, this has implications for the way we might see teaching. As well as providing information through imparting, instructing, telling and explaining, which are sometimes described as 'didactic' approaches to teaching, there are other ways of helping children to learn. In the above examples of teaching, some children are making deductions from primary sources of evidence, some are learning through playing, while others are learning through practising a new skill. The teacher's role is partly one of providing the right kinds of situations and resources to allow this to happen. Children cannot learn to make inferences unless they are given some sources of evidence, nor can they master the skill of ball-throwing without the balls and the space in which to throw them being made available. Children cannot, of course, learn through playing unless they are given the opportunity to play. Crucially, however, the teacher's role entails interacting with the children in productive ways within these situations, having conversations with the children, responding to them and asking them questions. The teacher can create collaborative contexts, where both children and teachers join in so that teachers play and work along with the children, They can 'model' how to do things they want their pupils to learn, especially when what they want them to learn is a process or practice (such as 'making deductions from evidence' and 'giving change') or a skill (such as throwing a ball).

In contrast, the examples of trainee teachers' learning given earlier show how we can learn from our life experiences – and these are always a very important aspect of everyone's education – which tend to happen randomly. Teachers, however, take responsibility for making sure that children are also provided with specific and valued learning experiences. Moreover, teachers can also ensure that children get the most out of the learning experiences which both life and school may offer, by making sure that they learn how to learn. They can ensure that the children encounter and learn from the many and varied processes or practices involved in learning for oneself, some of which were identified in the examples of trainee teachers' learning – for example collaborating, cooperating, communicating, responding, questioning, investigating, experimenting, enquiring, exploring, creating, inferring and solving problems. Clearly, they all require the involvement of the learner in many more ways than as a passive recipient of the teacher's word! Again, they demand the involvement of the teacher, interacting with the children in ways that help them understand what these processes involve. While teachers may model these processes, as did the teachers who worked alongside the children interpreting evidence from the past, they might make sure that this is sometimes in response to activities the children have initiated themselves, as in the example of playing shoe shops. They might also provide opportunities for children to learn in these ways with their peers or, where it is appropriate, on their own. Such teachers clearly value children's self direction and independence.

Values and primary practice

At this point I want to explore further this relationship between approaches to teaching and the issue of values. The examples, given above, help to bring different perspectives to thinking about learning and teaching. If these more broadly based interpretations are given to learning and teaching, then you will be able to consider the value of a wider range of approaches than you might otherwise have done.

One way of understanding teaching approaches is to be aware of the way in which, historically, primary teaching methods have evolved. Changing values in the wider world of education shape what happens in schools and influence the way we see learning and teaching in the classroom. It is useful to see how different ways of approaching learning and teaching are aligned to distinctive ways of looking at children and thinking about education, and how these have influenced developments in primary practice. To make sense of your teaching in today's classrooms and to evaluate it in the ways I have suggested, it is helpful to be aware of the range of approaches and how these have come about, and to recognise and possibly challenge some of the assumptions that underlie what happens in classrooms.

Historical developments – changes in educational thinking and policy

During the late 1980s and 1990s there was a period of far-reaching change in primary education. An important turning point at this time was the Education Act 1988, which was arguably the most significant Education Act of recent times. It brought about radical changes in educational policy and practice that have shaped where we are today. Although it did not legislate on teaching methods, as such, it did bring in a new era in education, which was characterised by centralised control. Wide-ranging initiatives were introduced at the level of central government which had major implications for approaches to learning and teaching in classrooms. It was this Act that brought in the National Curriculum.

To go further back in time, the 1988 Act was the result of an educational debate which ran through the 1970s. This had grown out of a mistrust and critique of 'child-centred' education – an approach that prevailed at that time in people's imaginations and in the rhetoric about primary education, if not always in reality. Child-centred or 'progressive' education became prominent following the publication of the Plowden Report in 1967 (CACE, 1967), but it originated much earlier. A significant move towards the progressive position, for instance, was the Hadow Report of 1931. This declared that 'the curriculum is to be thought of in terms of activity and experience rather than of knowledge to be acquired and facts to be stored' (Board of Education, 1931, p. 93). The values and theories inherent in this way of thinking contrasted markedly with those that underpinned traditional forms of education that were often associated with the late nineteenth century and the early days of compulsory education. The didactic teaching methods of that earlier era were caricatured by Dickens in his novel, *Hard Times*, in which the teacher, Gradgrind, insisted on the rote learning of facts which his charges clearly did not understand. There is not space here to discuss whether this was an accurate representation but it remains a popular view of Victorian elementary education.

By the 1960s, ways of approaching learning and teaching that conformed to traditional ideas of both children and education were being widely challenged. For instance, the common practice of streaming in primary schools (putting children into different classes according to their ability) had begun to disappear, as it had become apparent that children were being segregated more on the basis of their social class than on their ability. The Plowden Report (CACE, 1967) embodied different values. Children were no longer to be treated as belonging to a category, but were to be seen as having individual needs. The report made extensive, if not necessarily well argued, recommendations about 'good practice' in primary education that placed the child 'at the heart' of the educational process, and promoted an informal, individualised approach to learning.

Knowledge, rather than being seen as a predetermined body of information to be passed on from teacher to child, was seen as the achievement of the individual learner through 'learning by discovery'. This is problematic. Even at the time, this was acknowledged to be a flawed view of knowledge and of learning. It is clear that there are limits to what a child can 'discover' for themselves. Take, as examples, ideas in mathematics, science, art and music. Knowledge and understanding in these areas have been constructed over time by the collaborative efforts of those who have engaged in the complex practices of mathematics, science and music. Learning in those areas means joining in with the activities of mathematicians, scientists, artists and musicians – seeing how they do things and how they make sense of the world, rather than acting entirely on one's own. It is the same for any other area of human endeavour. Nevertheless, the typical view of a 'Plowden' classroom was an informal setting where children worked on individualised tasks, possibly self-chosen, with the teacher tending to stand back, always allowing children to take the lead, rather than formally teaching them or interacting with the whole class as a group.

The popular conception of this 'progressive' approach was that children were not to be 'told things'. This emphasis on children finding out for themselves led to a perception of schools as undisciplined places where children were allowed to do as they liked, and it was not long before growing concern about falling educational standards came to a head and there was a backlash against 'child-centred progressivism'. The Labour leader James Callaghan in the late 1970s initiated what was sometimes referred to as the 'Great Debate' on education to address these concerns, and the Conservatives took up the cause to 'raise standards' during their period of office throughout the 1980s and 1990s. The call was for a return to more 'traditional' methods – which for the government of the day implied more formal, 'teacher- directed' approaches.

Famously, John Major announced at the Conservative Party conference in 1991 that 'the progressives have had their say and they have had their day'. A return to not only the methods but also the values of the past was seen as the way forward.

Research on approaches to learning and teaching

'Progressive' values became a convenient scapegoat as the cause of low standards (though whether and in which ways standards were low was a matter of dispute). However, it is questionable whether 'Plowden' approaches had ever been as widely adopted as politicians and others supposed. The prevalence of child-centred teaching may have been a matter of myth more than fact (Richards, 1999). For instance, the observations from the 'Oracle Project' (Galton et al., 1980) showed that rather than being encouraged to find things out for themselves, 'the opposite was taking place. Children were being told what to do more frequently than under any other form of organisation' (Galton, 1995, p. 18). Galton suggested that this resulted from the increased time which teachers using individualised forms of organisation must spend on providing children with instructions about what to do next and on giving information which children needed to complete their tasks.

According to Galton, what tended to be lacking under this form of organisation were the kinds of interaction that the teacher might have with the child which would develop their ability to reason and to think for themselves – for instance, such interactions as asking challenging questions and giving the kind of feedback that would stimulate thought and enquiry (what are referred to as 'higher-order' interactions). Galton's study, as well as those carried out by other researchers (for example, Mortimore et al., 1988), concluded that each individual child generally received very little of the teacher's attention, even when the teacher was constantly interacting with the children. The studies showed that interactions were very short and did not really engage the child's thinking. Tizard and Hughes (1984), who carried out research with younger children, likewise found that interactions involving 'intellectual challenge' were, alarmingly, less evident in the classroom than they were in the children's homes before they started going to school. In addition, an important evaluation project of primary education in Leeds carried out by Alexander raised many similar issues. In a book that followed up his report of the project, Alexander (1992) commented: 'Teacher–pupil talk was often dominated by the teacher's questions, frequently of a rhetorical, closed or token kind. Questions inviting or encouraging the child to think were much rarer' (p. 51).

Engaging and challenging children is the key

It needs to be noted that the evidence of these classroom-based studies does not in itself undermine any aims or values. What the research did show was what was actually going on in classrooms. It provided evidence about the particular kinds of teaching that were occurring, revealing that teachers tended not to be challenging children's thinking, as well as they might, to promote learning. In reality, while teachers may have adopted individualised approaches, this was not necessarily creating the kind of child-centredness that might have enhanced children's learning. Some of the practice that was going on did not appear, in actuality, to reflect the values of those teachers whose enthusiasm for child–centred approaches was based on concern for each individual child's educational interests. Although individualisation might potentially offer the scope for engaging with children in intellectually challenging ways, this did not seem to be happening. Perhaps this was a question of the practical difficulties of managing the activities of a large number of individual children and finding the time to engage with them on an appropriate level. On the other hand, perhaps it was related to the misconceived notion that children would learn best if left to their own discoveries – the mistaken belief that children could somehow extract knowledge from their experience in the absence of constructive interaction with others.

In either case, those who were making generalised criticisms of child-centred practice were arguably making two incorrect assumptions: first, that teachers were actually engaging in such practice and, second, that the outcomes of it showed that child-centred approaches were wrong in principle. The first of these assumptions was, at least to some extent, shown to be false by the research. The second rests on the false premise that if children were not learning then this must be a consequence of child-centred values. Whatever the research evidence shows, however, it cannot, in itself, invalidate principles such as respect for children as persons, the promotion of self-direction and independence and the overriding principle of fairness which would ensure that every individual would be given the opportunity to learn.

In other words, the values or aims that might underlie a child-centred approach to learning and teaching, and may indeed be the kind of altruistic and caring concerns that would motivate many people to pursue a career in teaching, cannot be shown to be at fault by these empirical research findings in themselves. Such studies may provide information that is useful in other ways, but the questions as to whether, for example, it is worthwhile to ensure that children are respected as individuals, that their empowerment through education is important and that they should have a voice in their education and in society are matters to be settled through debate.

There is reason to believe, then, that the politicians' response back in the late 1980s to the apparent decline in educational standards of bringing back traditional values was a reaction that could not lay claim to being justified by the evidence of research. To explain 'falling standards' by polarising approaches along stereotypical lines and to advocate a wholesale return to a more traditional set of values seems unhelpful and inappropriate.

To illustrate this further, one of the government's priorities in the 1990s became a return to more 'whole-class' teaching – which is often associated with traditional teacher-centred approaches. In contrast with the scenario where the teacher moves around the classroom supporting individuals' learning in response to their needs, the teacher addresses the whole group, usually from the front of the class.

Unhelpful swings

The problem here, as Galton argued, is that the swing from one approach to the other was, in reality, a shift between different forms of organisation rather than a move towards better teaching. Galton observed that neither of these forms of organisation in themselves necessarily addressed the quality of interaction between teacher and child that was the central factor in children's learning. Galton (1995) had pointed out that the Oracle studies showed that 'it was not in itself class teaching or individualised instruction that made the difference, but the opportunity that the use of a particular method provided for a teacher to engage in certain types of exchanges with children' (p. 17). On the one hand, while an individualised form of organisation might have been typical of a child-centred classroom, this was not necessarily – as Galton showed – going to produce the level of intellectual engagement and challenge that might be desirable. But, similarly, the move to whole-class teaching approaches was also found to be wanting. It was thought, when whole-class teaching was reintroduced, that it could be 'interactive' in ways that would engage children's thinking and reasoning, Again, however, the research on classroom practice suggests that this was not necessarily achieved, as both Galton's (2007) and Alexander's (2010) reviews of the research have shown.

Appropriate interaction

Galton suggests that this underlying confusion has been perpetuated for years (Galton, 2007) – both during the era of so-called child-centred teaching and during the more formal forms of organisation that emerged during the 1990s. During that decade, the organisation of primary classrooms was transformed by policymakers with a view to improving children's achievements. Timetables, which had been associated with secondary rather than primary schools, were introduced so that subject-focused teaching could take place. Whole-class teaching became the norm. The election of the New Labour government in 1997 continued these kinds of changes with the introduction of the National Literacy and Numeracy Strategies. In the first years of this century, 'Literacy' and 'Numeracy' lessons took up two hours each day and were organised into small-group activities and whole-class introductions and plenaries, as centrally prescribed by government bodies. But such moves did not in themselves improve the quality of participation and interaction within the classroom that makes the difference to learning. What goes on between teacher and child is much more important. The ways of working described earlier in this chapter, where children were working sometimes independently, sometimes with their peers, were effective ways of bringing about learning because the teacher was interacting appropriately with the children and providing the right levels of engagement and challenge.

The kind of interaction that would promote the kind of higher-order thinking that researchers found to be often lacking in classrooms is referred to by Mercer (Mercer and

Littleton, 2007; Mercer and Hodgkinson, 2008) as 'exploratory talk'. This is the kind of talk which, Mercer argues, both teacher and child use to explore and question ideas together and through which reasoning is made more visible. In exploratory talk, 'partners engage critically but constructively with each other's ideas. Statements and suggestions are offered for joint consideration. These may be challenged and counter-challenged, but challenges are justified and alternative hypotheses are offered. Partners all actively participate, and opinions are sought and considered before decisions are jointly made' (Mercer and Littleton, 2007, p. 59). Mercer argues for the need for 'dialogic teaching', an approach to learning and teaching that has developed from his own research and the work of other researchers such as Wells (1999) and has been presented in particular by Alexander (2008).

Learning as collaboration

Dialogic teaching has in recent years become more widely understood. In dialogic class-rooms 'talk is used effectively as a tool for joint enquiry' (Mercer and Dawes, 2008, p. 69). The teacher is less the source of knowledge and more the guide who respects children's ideas, values their active participation and encourages them to reflect upon and extend their ideas. Rather than being the authority figure who transmits what they know to those who don't know, their relationship with the children is more collabora-tive. Learning is seen as a shared process. It reflects a different view of knowledge. Knowledge is neither 'discovered' by children, nor is it 'delivered' to them by their teachers through predetermined programmes. Rather, it is constructed jointly. As Alexander argues, 'dialogic teaching reflects a view that knowledge and understanding come from testing evidence, analysing ideas and exploring values, rather than unques-tioningly accepting someone else's certainties' (Alexander, 2008, p. 32).

CRITICAL ISSUES

Wells and Ball (2008) write:

> Given the long-term dominance of information transmission in the history of schooling (Cole, 1996), it is not surprising that, despite repeated calls for a more dialogic form of interaction, transmission remains the default option in most classrooms. (p. 169).

Consider how you might begin to change this dominant classroom culture. What principles for action might you adopt in your own classroom in relation, for instance, to how children participate in classroom activities; how children's and teacher's contributions are valued; how 'knowledge' is viewed; how learning is understood; how and why dialogue should be fostered. You will find that chapters in Mercer and Hodgkinson (2008) will help you to do this.

The influence of central government and ways forward

Following the era of progressivism, when standards were perceived to be falling, the Conservative government of the time moved steadily towards centralised control of education (see Lawton, 1994). Until then, teachers had considerable professional autonomy and could make their own decisions about the curriculum and about organisation and methods, but as different governments have come into power, they have continually introduced and imposed new initiatives on schools and teachers. Central control of the curriculum was established in 1988. Even though teachers have always retained the statutory right to decide how they teach, government influence has been powerful in this area too. The system of Ofsted inspections has meant that teachers have been obliged to comply with government recommendations as to how they should go about their work as well as with the statutory orders on what they should teach.

The rise of the targets and performance culture

It became the norm for lessons to be planned to achieve specific, predetermined objectives. The overriding emphasis was on 'outcomes' as the drive to raise achievement in the statutory tests to meet government targets and to gain high positions in the 'league tables' and good Ofsted reports became the priority. The requirement to raise children's achievement led to more 'targeted' teaching, with official encouragement for teachers to classify children, once more, according to their ability. Teachers began to divide their classes into low, average and high achievers, and they were encouraged to do so by Ofsted inspectors.

The last thirty years have seen the establishment of this target-driven education system and a 'performance culture', with teachers increasingly held accountable for their pupils' levels of achievement and children once again categorised and labelled. Yet, as Galton (2007), and Alexander (2010) and other researchers have shown, the policy-makers' recommendations may have led to changes in how teachers organise their teaching but have not led to significant development in the ways that teachers engage with children to extend their learning. Furthermore, research projects have been highly critical of ability grouping of children. Hart et al. (2004), for example, reporting on the research project 'Learning Without Limits', argue that this kind of classification by ability limits the children's opportunities to learn, by narrowing the learning experiences offered to different groups of children and imposing limited expectations.

CRITICAL ISSUES

The 'performance culture' may have led teachers to think about children only in terms of their potential to achieve particular 'levels' and to focus their teaching on the achievement of limited targets. Think about the implications of this – what values are implicit in this approach? Outline the possible alternatives – both in terms of values and practices.

You should find the material in Hart et al. (2004) very thought-provoking. Gleeson and Husbands (2001) provide an analysis of the focus on performance and the development of the 'performance culture' that you may find interesting.

At pivotal moments of change, such as the 1988 Act and the introduction of the Literacy and Numeracy Strategies in 1999, politicians and policymakers failed to address the need to clarify educational values. The Primary Strategy, introduced in 2003, made a point of emphasising enjoyment as well as excellence, but was similarly found to have an inadequate grounding in educational aims and principles (see Alexander, 2004). Instead, there has been much talk about 'effective' teaching – of giving priority to 'what works'. But this raises the crucial question: 'Effective in terms of what?' This question has been eclipsed by the focus on achieving measurable results. In focusing on raising levels of performance there has been a danger of losing sight of the broader issues. The performance culture, in schools and wider society, has not helped teachers think more clearly about what they are trying to achieve for children and their learning. It focuses their minds on end results rather than on the processes of learning and encourages them to adopt a 'top-down' approach in their classroom. It encourages them to 'deliver' their lessons – pre-packaged, with no opportunity for children to reshape their contents. If we make assumptions about what we are working towards, focusing only on the means of achieving the pre-specified end result and neglecting to examine what aims and values underpin these assumptions, then teaching is merely a technical activity rather than a professional one.

Engage and develop children's thinking

Opportunities for teachers themselves to innovate and develop their teaching have, perhaps, been opening up during this century. Since the introduction of the Primary Strategy it is true that teachers have felt encouraged to be more creative in how they teach the curriculum, not just with reference to the creative subjects such as art and design, drama and music, but in relation to the whole curriculum. Teachers are once again finding 'cross-curricular' ways of structuring the curriculum as an alternative to teaching different subjects in timetabled slots (see Chapter 14). The opportunities to make meaningful links across different areas of the curriculum and to focus on learning how to learn can potentially enable teachers to focus on the child's perspective rather than on outcomes and performance for their own sake. But, unless this potential is recognised and realised, these new ways of organising the curriculum, in themselves, may again make little difference to children's learning. Teachers need to be clear that the aim is to engage and develop children's thinking, and the new approaches need to promote such processes as collaborative enquiry and meaningful dialogue, otherwise they may remain at the level of organisational changes.

There are also signs, as the twenty-first century progresses, that values within the wider policy context have changed. The publication of Every Child Matters was an important milestone (DfES, 2004b), arising out of an enquiry into a particularly tragic case of child abuse. It resulted in the Children Act 2004 which provided legislation to integrate the different services available to children across care, health and education, with the aim of protecting children from risk and supporting every child so that they can develop to their full potential. The focus has been on developing the services available to children around their needs and there is a requirement to listen to children's views. The emphasis on relationships with children and their families was sustained in the Children's Plan (DCSF, 2007) and the theme of 'personalisation' permeated all the previous government's more recent proposals and became one of the key principles of reform in the Five Year Strategy (DfES, 2004c): 'Greater personalisation and choice – with the wishes and needs of children, parents and learners centre-stage' (p. 7). The Secretary of State asserted that 'the learner is a partner in learning, not a passive recipient' (p. 5).

An important opportunity was missed, however, in 2010 for the Labour government to respond to the comprehensive Cambridge Primary Review (Alexander, 2010) which laid out the strongest possible case for more extensive reform to the system. At the time of writing it remains to be seen what changes the Coalition government will introduce, but it is unlikely that targets and testing will be relinquished.

A question of values

Teachers can struggle with the fact that any developments they make in their practice remain within a framework of national testing and league tables. You, too, may find that the need to produce the required results and reach the prescribed targets comes into conflict with your concerns for the individual child, your respect for their rights and their perspectives and motivations, as well as your concerns for their learning. These kinds of values tend to resonate with those of the earlier child-centred era. While some of the recommended practices of child-centred education may not have materialised in classrooms or may seem to have been misguided now that understanding of how children learn and theories of knowledge have moved on, some of the values that informed them may yet be relevant. As you develop sound pedagogical approaches for the twenty-first century and learn how to engage in dialogic teaching, such values might provide a rationale for your approaches to learning and teaching that you may not be able to find within the discourse of targets and testing.

Developing critical perspectives

To return to my earlier point, it is only through analysis of practice in relation to those larger questions of value (what ought we to do) that we can gain some sense of direction in our teaching – its larger educational aims and moral purpose. This kind of critical evaluation can help you, at all stages of your career, to improve your teaching. The discussion of changes in educational thinking, policy and practice that I have presented in this chapter should help provide a context for understanding your practice and for making your decisions about the best way to teach. Insight from a historical perspective – understanding more about how schools came to be the way they are, what has changed, what hasn't changed and why – and giving consideration to the place of values in educational practices can provide the means to think critically about what you do so that you can improve it. As someone not only learning to teach, but also becoming professional, it is most important to develop these critical perspectives on your approaches to teaching.

Summary

What I hope has emerged from this chapter is that approaches to learning and teaching are bound up with values. I have presented some illustrations of ways of looking at learning that go beyond a simplistic 'transmission' model. By providing a historical context, I have shown how influences beyond the classroom can shape teachers' values and practice and how important it is to retain a clear sense of aims and principles. What needs to be recognised is the complexity of the teaching and learning process. To maintain their professionalism teachers must take full account of the 'why' and the 'what for' as well as the 'how' of their practice.

Having described and interpreted your own teaching approaches, explored the values inherent in them and considered whether these are what you would aspire to as a 'good' teacher, you may need to modify your practice. If you find yourself professionally committed to engaging children's minds to develop their ability to think and reason, and if you are to respect them as thinking individuals and as people with equal rights to empowerment through education, to participate, to be heard and to create their own learning journey, what kinds of decisions for action would you make?

Issues for reflection

Once you have started on some teaching and you begin to analyse your practice and that of those around you, you may find that the way you or others do things does not conform to the narrower definitions of teaching and learning, but is, instead, valid in terms of broader and more complex understandings. In asking yourself what underlying values these practices reveal, you will need to avoid those assumptions that can so easily be made. In particular it is important to avoid mistaking changes in ways of organising teaching for changes in classroom communication and interaction and changes in teachers' values. The range of variables you will need to critically address to gain this sort of insight is very wide, and cannot be fully discussed within this single chapter. However, the following list may be helpful as an indication:

(Continued)

(Continued)

- The kinds of relationships which teachers have with children.
- The kinds of interaction between children and teachers. (What forms of interaction are used and for what purposes?)
- The ways in which children are encouraged to think for themselves, to take risks, to be creative, to learn how to learn, to participate and negotiate, to take responsibility for and control of their own learning.
- The kinds of groups children work in. (For what purposes children are grouped – for example: administrative convenience or educationally rich collaborative work. Which criteria are used for grouping children and for what purpose – for example: ability, friendship, task, interest, gender.)
- The structure of activities in the classroom. (For example: how and when the children work alone, with each other in groups or with the teacher; the pattern of the day; the pattern of a particular session; the kind of time constraints.)
- The way the learning environment is set up. (For example: how the classroom furniture and equipment is arranged so that particular forms of interaction and activity can take place; what resources and learning materials there are and how they are made available for children to learn from them.)
- The structure and content of the curriculum. (For example: whether there are set times for different subjects; whether the children are put into 'sets' for specific subjects, taught by specialist teachers in different curriculum areas or always taught by their class teacher; whether 'cross-curricular' connections are made in the content of what the children learn; whether any of the content of the curriculum is linked to children's own interests or centred around questions which they have asked themselves; whether different children do different activities at the same time or do the same thing at the same time.)
- The ways in which teachers assess children's learning and the purposes behind it. (For example: is it just to find out whether targets have been reached or is it used to help teachers extend children's learning and engage with them in more meaningful and productive ways?)

Further reading

Alexander, R. (2008) *Towards Dialogic Teaching: Re-thinking Classroom Talk*. 4th edition. York: Dialogos. This is an important book in which Alexander explains what is meant by Dialogic Teaching. It should provide food for thought in developing your ideas about your own practice and primary pedagogy for the future.

Fisher, J. (2007) *Starting from the Child*. 3rd edition. Milton Keynes: Open University Press. This book provides both theoretical insights into and practical advice on approaches to learning and teaching that start from the child.

Section 2

SKILLS IN TEACHING AND LEARNING

This second section is aimed at helping you develop a wide variety of skills in teaching and learning which we anticipate will be fundamental to your work. They include how to use talk and dialogue with children, how to develop your observation skills and also a range of other classroom-based skills connected to managing classroom interactions and the pacing of lessons. We explore with you crucial issues related to inclusion and ensuring we do the best for each child. There are chapters on how to maintain high expectations in terms of pupil motivation and behaviour and on how to develop the vital skills of reflective teaching. We show how successful lessons are built upon the twin pillars of assessment and planning and we aim to develop your confidence in using new technologies to serve the needs of the learners you teach.

CHAPTER 4

TALKING IN CLASS

Jenifer Smith and Michele Otway

Chapter overview

Talking is vital. It is central to personal growth, making relationships, expressing feelings and enabling children to become fully functioning members of the community. Jenifer Smith and Michele Otway show how talk with children is one of the most crucial resources for teaching and learning that you have. They give a detailed guide to making the most of this important tool in all its rich forms, including discussion, dialogue, storytelling and drama.

Eyes on me; ears listening; hands in laps.

Children know very well that it is the teacher who does the talking in class. And yet the value of talk in our development as individuals, thinkers and social beings is well documented. As a teacher one must think about and act on the ways that talk can and does feature in one's plans and teaching. We need to consider our own use of talk and how we model and facilitate talk in the classroom, how we can shape our utterances so that children can develop their thinking and understanding through talk. We need to think about how talk appears in our planning so that children become increasingly confident and versatile speakers and listeners. The hope is that this chapter will begin to help you to extend your thinking about how you plan for talking within your classroom.

List the talk that you have been involved in over the last two or three hours – longer if you have been in a talk-free context during that time. Note your audiences and the purposes for talk, the subject matter/content and whether your talk was formal or informal. How much time did you spend talking – and listening? For you, how are those different? How many stories do you hear – and tell? Where was the talk involved in making sense of the world – and in what ways?

From home to school

By the time they arrive in school, most children are accomplished talkers. Immersed in a language-using community, they will have participated in rich everyday conversations with many different people and have used talk to communicate their needs and to make sense of the world around them. In everyday situations at home, talk between parent and child is characterised by immediate interest and need and is in essence a shared dialogue. Here is an example, from the work of Gordon Wells (1987) of an impromptu conversation between Penny and her mother. Penny is watching her mother do the washing:

Penny: It ain't hot-look. The froth ain't.

Mother (referring to the water in the machine):   It is hot.

Penny: The froth ain't.
Mother: No, not the froth.
Penny: It's not froth, it's suds.
Mother: It's suds, it is.
Penny (sings): Roundy roundy roundy roundy. Still it goes. (She puts her hand in the machine.) Ma, it ain't hurting me – look.
Mother: No it's not going, that's why.

In this unremarkable, everyday conversation, Penny is being actively immersed into the language of her community by her mother through, what Maggie Maclure (1992) terms 'the four Ss': *shaping* – treating children's utterances as meaningful and responding to them with more conventional language and phrasing; *sharing* – emotions, ideas, experiences and opinions through conversation; *supporting* – providing children with enough response and input to sustain conversation without doing the talking for them; *stretching* – in a range of ordinary ways, adults extend children's conversations by commenting, asking genuine questions or asking children to give their opinions. Such conversations take place over time and, through them, both child and adult cumulate shared understandings of the world.

For many children entering a reception class, one of the most difficult accomplishments is to make sense of classroom talk. Being asked to reply to your name in the register, seeking permission to go to the toilet and having to respond to the question, 'Are you hot or packed?' are all about understanding some of the seemingly bizarre demands of the primary classroom. But more importantly, there can be a stark discontinuity between the conversations between parents and children at home and the same children with professionals at school. Let's look again at Penny, but this time talking with a teaching assistant:

Assistant:	Would you like to run your finger round (a section of toilet paper roll)? What can you tell me about the round?
Penny (feeling it):	Giddy.
Assistant:	Your finger goes giddy. Put your finger all round it. Has it got any sharp corners like a square? Put your finger round. No, it hasn't got corners like a square. It just goes all the way round, doesn't it? David, will you watch please? Scissors have got nothing to do with a round. It does go all the way round, doesn't it? (pointing to sections from an egg container). What are those?
Penny:	Egg box.
Assistant:	Egg box. They're round, aren't they? (demonstrating) They're round that way and they're round that way …

(Wells, 1987, p. 37)

What is different? There is a lack of life in the exchange not apparent in the dialogue between Penny and her mother. There is also a marked asymmetry. For while there is an equality of talk between mother and child, in the case of the teaching assistant, it is she who initiates the subject of the conversation and decides on its duration giving little opportunity for Penny and the other children in the group to use the kind of exploratory talk that they were using successfully at home. There is none of the shaping, sharing, supporting and stretching aspects of talk that Penny's mother uses at home.

Very quickly, it appears, children grasp the subtle rules that govern talk in the classroom. In the study by Mary Willes (1983) of young children entering reception class, it became apparent that mastering the discourse patterns of the setting was an important requirement of fulfilling their role as pupils. Indeed, even on their first day, Willes memorably describes children's learning about the rules of listening to a story:

… they have already learned that the questions asked by the teacher require brief answers. They seem not yet to realise that answers that have to do with their own preoccupations, rather than the facts of the story, or the facts of the world of shared experience, just will not do. There is early opportunity to learn that it is the teacher, not the pupil, who makes the crucial decision about what is, and is not, relevant. (p. 77)

Increasingly, in the last two decades there has been a greater awareness of the cultural capital that children bring to school and the need to ensure that children have plenty of opportunities to talk with adults and their peers. Classrooms are generally characterised as places where talk, both teacher and child-led, is valued with a marked encouragement for children to explore ideas, speculate, analyse and criticise. However, there is still plenty of evidence to suggest that there remains a marked inequality in the extent to which different children participate in classroom discussions. In a recent project by Myhill (2006), early observations of classes suggested that it was the high achievers who were more likely to participate in whole-class discussion than low achievers and that girls were more likely to participate than boys. The off-task behaviour and shouting out that was characteristic of many boys and low achievers began in Year 2 and continued into Year 6. The other main finding that came from this initial observation was that there was very little talk initiated by children.

When observing a classroom, take the opportunity to focus on children's talk. Notice the kind of talk that children engage in and what prompts it. Take the opportunity to listen to children talking in pairs or small groups. Consider their purposes for talking and how that has an impact on what they talk about and how. Notice the times when child and adult conversations involve shaping, sharing, supporting and stretching. Note down what is said. How was that achieved?

The importance of talk

So why is children's talk in class important? First of all talk has an important role in personal growth. It allows us to make relationships with each other, to express our feelings, moods and attitudes – in short, to express our personality. Talk is also crucial in enabling us to be fully functional members of a community. The speech of our home and community may be reflected in our dialect, accent and expression, but through talking and listening to others, we also learn about the social purposes of talk: the need to take turns and the conventions of spoken etiquette and when it is appropriate to use our local dialect or to choose formal or informal language. Finally, talk is essential to the development of thought.

Perhaps the most common form of talk in the classroom is its use as a tool to communicate learning. Reporting on our learning and answering questions are familiar repertoires of talk used by teachers. Much of this talk between teacher and children, according to Alexander (2001), takes the form of three predominant types of teacher talk:

- Rote, which involves the drilling of facts, ideas and routines through constant repetition, e.g. a brisk oral and mental mathematical starter;
- Recitation, tends to involve strong cuing of answers and the use of closed questions designed to test or stimulate recall of what has been previously learnt;
- Instruction, telling the pupil what to do, imparting information and explaining facts, principles and procedures.

(p. 526)

Alexander (2006) observes that there remains a scarcity of talk which challenges children to think for themselves. Rather, the low-level cognitive demand of many classroom questions and the bland all-purpose feedback of praise is not uncommon. There is no shortage of research evidence to suggest that, in English classrooms, there is an emphasis on whole-class talk where the teacher takes the lion's share of time for talk and controls classroom talk in a way which guides children towards a 'right answer'. Tony Edwards (2003) describes the teacher's skill in asking closed and pseudo-open questions which are 'progressively closed down in ways which make it obvious that an answer is already there for pupils' (p. 39) and in shaping and redirecting questions and answers to help the lesson's progress. Children become well practised in listening out for the clues that will tell them what the teacher is looking for and, in some cases, where the clues are so prolific 'that even a wild guess will lead the teacher to answer for them' (p. 39).

Talk should be used for something more than simply transmitting information from teacher to learner. Language and thought are deeply interconnected. In the words of Edwards and Mercer (1987), talk 'is one of the materials from which a child constructs a way of thinking' (p. 20). It is this connection between thinking and speech that enables us to articulate our thinking for ourselves and others. The process of verbalising our thoughts gives substance to thought. Interacting with others enables individual minds to be combined in a collective form of thinking so that we do not just 'interact' with others, we can 'interthink' (Mercer, 2000).

The implications of viewing talk as a means for developing thought are profound. Our talk with children is the most important resource we possess for teaching and learning. The simple transmission forms of talk simply won't suffice; classroom talk needs to have a cognitive basis if it is to develop children's thinking. In terms of Alexander's repertoire of talk, teachers need also to be using dialogue that ultimately leads to deeper learning. Such talk happens over a number of exchanges and there should be a high degree of cognitive challenge rather than the more commonly observed short answers from a greater number of children.

Learning, of course, does not just take place between teachers and children but also through productive talk between children themselves. If children are able to learn to use exploratory forms of language to think together with others, then they will be able to develop ways of how to think as individuals. Sadly, the practical reality is that, without guidance, children tend to interact with their peers at a basic, often social, level and that collaborative talk does not necessarily derive from a seemingly collaborative task. It is little wonder that teachers show a marked reluctance to use group work as a major teaching strategy. Research shows good evidence to support their disillusionment as, even when children are on task in groups, interactions are more about simply exchanging information rather than discussing ideas (Bennett and Dunne, 1992; Galton and Williamson, 1992). Our responsibility is clear: to help children to use talk to think together.

CRITICAL ISSUES

James Britton's book (1992) *Language and Learning: The Importance of Speech in Children's Development* remains one of the most important and accessible considerations of the crucial connections between speech and learning. Talk in school, he argues, is a direct continuation of a young child's talk with his family and is essential to learning to read and write. Teachers must always remember the operational value of language use.

> Putting this at its simplest, what children use language for in school must be 'operations' and not 'dummy runs'. They must continue to use it to make sense of the world: they must *practise* language in the sense in which a doctor 'practises' medicine and a lawyer 'practises' law and *not* in the sense in which a juggler 'practises' a new trick before he performs it. This way of working does not make difficult things easy: what it does is make them worth the struggle. (p. 130)

Teachers need to ensure as far as they possibly can that what children do in school offers genuine challenge and so leads to the extension and deepening of experience. The provision of a rich environment which engages and challenges children and, thus, gives rise to the need for developmental talk is hugely challenging.

Consider the times when you have seen children really using language to make sense of the world. What has the teacher done, if anything, to facilitate that? Find out more about the ways in which you can make difficult things 'worth the struggle'.

The teacher's role

To develop children as speakers, an ethos needs to be established where children feel secure and free to talk without being judged. Teachers need to acknowledge and value the language that children bring to school and this includes not just the languages of children of different nationalities but the variety of accents and dialects of our own language. Through what teachers say or how they respond (both in spoken and unspoken ways), children develop a sense of how they are valued as speakers. This focus on building respectful relationships is crucially important in the early years as it provides the basis for 'genuinely mutual conversations between children and adults, and between children and children' (Whitehead, 2004, p. 106). Classrooms where sustained shared thinking/dialogue can take place are created by the way teachers converse with children. We need to listen very carefully to what children say and build on their contributions by commenting or reflecting or adding information as well as by asking questions. What the child says is at the heart of the conversation about learning and teachers need to convey that message through their own part in the conversation.

It is important to plan real reasons for talking. Where conversations arise out of shared activity there is the opportunity for children to be involved in meaningful dialogue which develops and extends thought. In the best early years' practice the potential of activities such as cooking, gardening and building offer opportunities for many different types of thoughtful talk between adults and children including sorting, ordering, speculating and planning.

One of the most important things that teachers can do to develop the quality of children's talk in the class is to make explicit the kinds of talk they want children to use. These include the eleven different kinds of learning talk identified by Robin Alexander (2001) in *Culture and Pedagogy*:

- narrate
- explain
- instruct
- ask different kinds of questions
- perceive, build upon answers
- analyse, solve problems
- specialise and imagine
- explore and evaluate ideas
- discuss
- argue or defend a position
- negotiate.

The challenge is to consider how best to set the conditions for these different kinds of talk to arise and develop. You might consider the language that you use, the questions you ask, the language modelled by adults in the class, the language you expect from children and the kinds of language you might expect from the tasks that you set. Some of these types of talk are more commonly used than others and so you may wish to think about how you directly teach these kinds of talk and how you reflect on and develop skills in all of them. Another consideration is the language demands not only of the task but of the subject itself. Science, for example, is a rich context for asking questions, analysing, hypothesising, exploring and evaluating ideas and for doing so in particular ways that are different from the ways in which you might engage with the same kinds of talk in art or in history. Consider the questions that children might ask having heard a story or poem, and those they might formulate in response to a collection of primary sources from domestic life in 1930s Britain or in anticipation of a mini-beast hunt in the school's grounds. The ways in which children talk depends very much on teachers' expectations of talk and how they plan for it. Children also learn about talk through the way teachers themselves talk, the way they respond to what children say and the kinds of task that teachers ask them to engage with. A mathematics class where children are used to articulating how they arrived at a solution to a problem is a much more vibrant learning environment than one where answers are accepted or rejected without explanation.

CRITICAL ISSUES

Look at the list of different types of talk. Identify the curriculum areas and the activities within them that demand these different kinds of talk. Consider the modes of thinking demanded by a subject and the way that they can be reflected and developed through particular kinds of talk.

Another important aspect of the teacher's role is to help children to use talk to think together in groups. Inspired by Douglas Barnes's (1976) classroom-based research on how productive group discussion can contribute not only to the development of children's language and reasoning skills but also their individual learning, Dawes et al. (2000) have devised practical, research-based guidelines designed to teach children explicitly how to use exploratory forms of talk. Such talk requires children not only to use language to explore ideas and possibilities, share information and give reasons for their viewpoint, but also to constructively, but respectfully, engage critically with each other's ideas to ensure that all possible insights inform final agreement. However, children need to be supported in establishing ground rules for talk and teachers need to actively model (sometimes with a willing TA or placement student) how to talk effectively in groups. The value of talking partners cannot be overestimated in introducing this kind of work. Indeed, the pair may be the essential context for the majority of child-to-child talk. Having an explicit set of rules for group talk enables children to self-regulate their talk while sometimes it can be useful to assign key roles to individuals in groups in order to focus more on cooperation between members of a group. Alongside rules, children should hear and experience what exploratory talk means and learn to use the affordances of dialogic talk.

Dialogic talk

Robin Alexander's work on dialogic talk arises from his experience of observing classrooms across the world. The practice in South Korea and Russia had a particular impact on his thinking which is set out clearly in his pamphlet *Towards Dialogic Teaching* (Alexander, 2006). In this call to rethink classroom talk Alexander makes the distinction between discussion – 'the exchange of ideas with a view to sharing information and solving problems' – and dialogue – 'achieving common understanding through structured cumulative questioning and discussion which guide and prompt, reduce choice, minimise risk and error, and expedite "handover" of concepts and principles.' This drive towards a 'handover' may not chime well with the cultural context of English schools which are more competitive and individualistic than Russian classes where there is an expectation that learning will be collective. You will have to think whether this is something that you would like to develop. You may want to think about what handing over knowledge might look like and how dialogic talk makes it possible for children to make new knowledge their own and to reach new understandings.

CRITICAL ISSUES

Dialogic teaching is:

collective: teachers and children address learning tasks together, as a group or as a class;

reciprocal: teachers and children listen to each other, share ideas and consider alternative viewpoints;

supportive: children articulate their ideas freely, without fear of embarrassment over 'wrong' answers, and they help each other to reach common understandings;

cumulative: teachers and children build on their own and each other's ideas and chain them into coherent lines of thinking and enquiry;

purposeful: teachers plan and steer classroom talk with specific educational goals.

(Alexander, 2006)

Dialogic teaching is recognised as an approach to teaching that supports children's critical thinking and their awareness of the global dimension of their lives and learning. It could be seen as a step towards the democratisation of the

(Continued)

(Continued)

classroom. Alexander suggests that dialogue minimises 'risk and error'. Is the reduction of risk such that creative mistakes are not made, or does the security of the dialogic classroom allow for children to take greater risks in their thinking? Maybe both these things are possible. What is your view? What would you encourage in your classroom? Read Alexander's pamphlet and consider how you might introduce dialogic teaching into your own practice.

Alexander applies dialogic teaching to whole-class, group and pair work, including that of the adult and child. In a class where a student teacher explored this way of working, the modelling of her whole-class discussion was evident in the way children worked together in groups. Dialogic teaching opens up the possibility of a more equal exchange between adult and teacher and demands that the teacher listen carefully to what children say. It requires longer turns from children and more sustained exchanges between one child and the teacher. If you worry about what other children are doing, these exchanges are usually much more interesting than most classroom question-and-answer sessions and children will learn that their turn to have this attention will come. These are conversations that are intellectually and emotionally engaging. Listening carefully to what children say and responding to what they reveal lies at the heart of productive teaching and learning though it is easier said than done. You may find that you have to be quite deliberate about what you say and how you respond at first. This is hard to do and mistakes are made in many conversations. A teacher is likely to learn about this alongside the children. However, when everyone feels genuinely part of the dialogue, and children have time to extend their thinking, teaching suddenly becomes much more exciting.

In classrooms where teachers developed dialogic talk many changes took place that resulted in greater involvement of all children and an improvement in the reading and writing of all children. More meta-cognitive talk was observed, teachers' questions became at once more focused and yet more genuinely open and children were speculating, thinking aloud and helping each other rather than competing to spot the right answer. Teachers were finding that their role was shifting from controlling discussion to facilitating and participating in discussion (Alexander, 2004).

Questioning is often the default mode for a teacher when faced with the whole class and we often see students painfully dragging information from children about a previous lesson with one leading question after another. If you want to recap, think about different ways in which to do it. Why not just give a brief reminder and children could add to that, or you could provide a concept map of the topic so far or a picture or object which will serve as both recap and starting point. How many times, faced with an obvious question, have you been reluctant to answer it? Why not provide the information and give children the opportunity to re-engage with it in a different way?

Nevertheless, questions are a crucial element of dialogic teaching and it is really helpful to identify them in your plans. You might display key questions during the lesson – these could be rather more interesting and enlivening than many learning objectives I have seen. It is worth thinking about questions and the work they can do. We could devote a separate chapter to the art of using questions and to inviting talk without using questions. Think about the way questions are framed and about other ways of initiating talk. 'I wonder …' is a very good opener, and simply stating what you think and being open to challengers is another.

Storytelling and drama

At the head of his list of talk types, Alexander places narration. Storytelling makes a particular contribution to children's learning and is something that is worth recognising. In *The Culture of Education,* Bruner (1996) explores the way in which narrative permeates all disciplines. While there is a value in introducing children to different kinds of discourse, narrative can provide a bedrock for the development of confidence in speech and the development of thought. A teacher who is a good storyteller has a great gift. Whether the story is a traditional tale, a personal memory or the story of the Armada, the life cycle of a frog or number bonds to ten, storytelling is both engaging and enabling. It is a skill that can be learned. Give children the opportunity to tell the stories of their experiences and their growing understanding and hone those skills through storytelling in English. If you can tell the story aloud, you will be surprised at how well children remember and retell it themselves. Their making the story their own develops their capacity to imagine, to find the telling turn of phrase and to develop the logic of action. These skills will inform their talk in other areas of the curriculum. Sometimes one is led to believe that storytelling, and drama, are of less value than other forms of talk because children take pleasure in them and are often successful. Perhaps we should think about the ways in which these pleasurable events, where children clearly do develop their skills, have an impact on children's capacity to use talk in a variety of contexts.

For younger children, especially, the fostering of storytelling develops both the social and cognitive aspects of talk. Talk is central to the imaginative engagement which arises in role play and drama. In Vivian Gussin Paley's early years settings storytelling and the exploration of first-hand experiences are given a premium. "'When my babies do their stories," Mrs Tully had told me, "they really see each other. That's what we need to go after in school, the seeing and the listening to each other"' (Paley, 2001, p. 23). Children's stories are valued and placed at the centre of whole-class talk in ways that help children to develop understandings of themselves, their place in the community and the wider world. The opportunities for scribing and then performing children's stories acknowledge inner and outer lives and the ways in which talk can mediate these. It also provides opportunities for kid-watching in ways that are so very well explored in *Listening to Children Think: Exploring Talk in the Early Years* (Hall and Martello, 1996) in which the collected essayists show not only how they reflect on what children say, but how they set up the classroom so that children may talk constructively and teachers have time to listen. Storytelling and drawing are part of a continuum that leads naturally to writing (Vygotsky, 1978). Their power to inform children's thinking and their development as readers and writers should not be underestimated. Stories, and story drama, provide the context for children to assume roles and to engage with problems and situations that they may not otherwise encounter. Drama, working in role, has a magic way of transforming children's way of being in the classroom and often makes way for otherwise reluctant individuals of all ages to talk in mature and surprisingly knowledgeable and perceptive ways.

Working in role is a way of taking on other ideas and voices. The teacher as an incompetent little pig, an eye witness from a plague village or a scientist with an interest in insects can engage and challenge children in ways that sometimes they are less able to do as their humdrum selves. Many tutors have observed otherwise fidgety classes galvanised into action by the quiet announcement from the teacher that they are going to be, for example, a Tudor merchant or Farmer Duck. Working in role allows the teacher to model, channel and extend language so that children are encouraged to reason, challenge, persuade, defend a position or negotiate in ways they may not in other contexts. When faced with the Big Bad Wolf, a Year 3 class asked questions which showed a sophistication laced with humour that they had not shown before, and the teacher, who had begun her role play using an ordinary voice and posture, became more wolf-like with every answer. You do not have to have fine acting skills to work in role but you can add to the repertoire of people who enter the classroom and prompt children to engage with problems from different points of view. Drama provides many opportunities for talk, some more structured than others, and we advise you to find out more about strategies such as conscience alley, meet and greet, thought-tracking or hot-seating, each of which will give rise to different kinds of thinking and talk. Use these techniques across the curriculum to inform more formal contexts for talk.

Planning for talk

When planning, consider the purpose of each section of the lesson and the kinds of talk that will best serve that purpose. If you have in mind the main purpose of whole-class introductions and explanations it will help you to consider the kinds of questions and responses you might plan for. Will it be mainly:

- exposition – explaining and presenting content
- discussion – conversations around a topic
- skill learning – teaching a skill to children
- investigative – experimenting?

Your answer to this question will help to determine the kind of discourse you will use – questions, perhaps, but other ways of beginning such as making a statement or beginning with 'I wonder ...' Teachers' questions are often more preoccupied with teaching than learning so you need to make a major shift. You will be accustomed to the common practice of using closed and pseudo open questions, both as a pupil and as a new teacher. When you identify questions in your plans include questions which promote thinking about concepts and personal response. Try not to use questions as a way of asking children to tell you what happened in the last lesson.

You may wish to begin with a story or an explanation. Both of these need some planning, though the explanation is something that needs more attention, especially when you begin teaching. You need to think carefully about the structure of the explanation, how gradually you introduce new ideas, how you build these on familiar ideas and how you will introduce any new vocabulary. You might want an aide-memoire of definitions, synonyms, hyponymy and characteristic features. You might think about creating a concept map and using objects, pictures or the children themselves. Be aware, also, of you own use of voice. Be clear and varied in tone. Your intonation itself can convey meaning and help children to follow your thread. You may wish to include a story in your explanation – they are not mutually exclusive. What you are wanting to do is to activate children's imaginations, their capacity to link what you have to say with what they already know and to arouse their interest and curiosity. You should be thinking about how children will make connections between the known and the about to be known. You may wish to begin by truly discovering what children already know. That in itself may be a revelation. If you follow up your explanation with an invitation for them to ask questions you are likely to know how much they have understood and what it is that interests them.

Listening carefully to children, hearing what they have to say and acting on it seems to us to be a crucial element of talking to learn. A challenge for teachers is the move from the self as the centre of the action to that of the child at its centre. This is less easy to plan and important to prepare for. Myhill (2006), among others, found that teachers tend to listen out for their own answers and not to engage with answers that do not lead towards their pre-planned outcome. If there is to be fruitful dialogic talk, then this may require a serious shift of focus on the part of the teacher. However, once you have started really listening, then the job of teaching becomes truly interesting. It is possible to reach that changed viewpoint through adopting strategies which will give children greater voice and keep you feeling relatively secure. Sometimes, when we start on a line of questioning carefully planned to take children down a certain route, some bright spark is there before you have a chance. That can be rather off-putting, so one strategy is to place the knowledgeable child in the hot seat and invite children to ask questions. At other times you may welcome a variety of ways to ensure you encourage longer turns. Try 'tell me more ...', 'keep going ...', 'can you explain how you came to that conclusion?', 'could you give an example?', 'can anyone build on what Ermintrude has said?', 'give some reasons ...' and so on.

Neil Mercer in *The Guided Construction of Knowledge* (1995) suggests a teacher's toolkit of responses which enable children to become effective and reflective speakers and listeners. He suggests that when teachers continually rephrase and respond to what children say, children emulate the teacher's higher-level model of talk. The toolkit involves a variety of techniques:

- Confirmations: 'Yes, that's right …'
- Repetitions: 'You've told us that "the ice-cap melted gradually"…'
- Reformulations: 'Over millions of years the ice-cap diminished …'
- Elaborations: 'Many scientists hypothesise that global warming is responsible for this …'
- 'We' statements: 'We've researched some evidence for this …'

Be careful not to simply repeat what children say. Think about how you can affirm or develop or challenge children's contributions. It has been our experience that much of our talk arises from unconscious behaviours and that in order to develop classroom talk we need to shift how we behave, using almost artificial actions. The use of planned questions and sentence starters for responses is one example. One of us found that, despite her best intentions, she was more likely to ask boys to answer than girls and so she simply decided to ask boys and girls alternately. Working in other people's classrooms, this reassured her that there was a gender balance and one consequence was that, in classrooms where either boys or girls were more reluctant to answer, she would eventually run out of children who were volunteering to answer. Once she had explained her dilemma, the minority group suddenly proved very keen to volunteer.

Reflecting on talk

Children can be of great help to any teacher wishing to think about developing their own teaching in relation to talk and there are a number of strategies you could introduce that will also encourage children to think about and be aware of their own talk. Simply asking children about anything raises its profile. You may like to ask some or all of the children in your class about talk. What do they know about how and where they learned to talk? Do they think they are good talkers and who would they pick out as good examples? What might their answer be to questions such as what talking do you do in school? Who do you talk to? What do you talk about and does your teacher like you to talk? These questions come from the Oracy Project (NCC, 1991) and we are sure you will think of others that would suit your context or a particular issue that you are interested in. Elizabeth Grugeon et al. (2005) suggest a variety of ways in which children can gather evidence and reflect upon their own talk. They can become talk detectives – working as a group to identify what kind of talk they might expect to hear in a specific lesson and then working individually or in pairs, observing groups at work and reporting back. This is seen more formally in the Speaking and Listening video materials produced for the QCA (1999) where children observe group talking, measuring performance against a set of agreed criteria. They can also keep their own talk diaries. Grugeon et al. (2005) provide a number of templates for these, or you can provide children with something less structured. If children tape their discussion, playing it back for them can give rise to further talk about what is and is not successful in the group and children can report back their findings. These strategies contribute to children's meta-cognitive awareness and to the teacher's understanding of the ways in which talk is more or less successful in the class as a whole and for individuals.

CRITICAL ISSUES

Consider the culture of talk that exists in schools where you are placed. Observe the way that adults use language and reflect on the messages that this conveys to children. Using the Oracy Project prompts or questions that you generate yourself, find out from children what they know and understand about talk. Identify and reflect upon what you consider to be the barriers to and the opportunities for rich thoughtful talk in classrooms.

Both the Oracy Project (1989) and Alexander's work on dialogic teaching (2006) emphasise the value of children's awareness of talk in terms of the development of skills. It is helpful to have a meta-language with which to talk about, in this instance, talk. Children should learn about talk itself: the nature of Standard English and other dialects, accent, register and phonological, lexical and syntactic systems; they should be able to articulate their understandings of when to speak and when not, what to talk about to whom and in what manner, and be able to match their talk to its purpose, learning what is effective and what not; and they should be able to evaluate their own speech and that of others and be able to take on and reflect upon different roles when talking in groups. This articulation of process and skill inevitably leads to greater accomplishment.

Debra Myhill's research (2006) explored how teachers use talk to scaffold whole-class teaching. The emphasis of the project was on reflection and, as part of that, participating teachers used the plenary in some lessons to ask children to share their views on what it was about the teacher's actions that helped or hindered their learning. Such an invitation is useful for both children and teachers and is likely to change everyone's talk behaviours. Be prepared to act on children's suggestions or to explain why you are not able to. Other opportunities for reflection included inviting a colleague to observe children's behaviours during whole-class dialogic teaching and to video a lesson about which you feel reasonably robust. Watch it in the privacy of your own home, Myhill advises, and identify one thing that you did that really engaged children and another that was less successful. It is fine to watch the film alone, but I suggest that you watch it with a friend, preferably someone who has filmed themselves also. That may prevent you from only spotting the worst things and wishing that you were taller, straighter, blonder and generally more photogenic than you are. Not the best idea with a takeaway and a bottle of wine on a Friday night.

The main thing that you have to think about is shifting the centre of gravity from you to the children without losing the challenge and difficulty of what you are providing. It is setting up the two-way traffic of talk between you and the class so that it is more evenly balanced and so that multiple voices are heard. You might want to begin by thinking about how the children are sitting and whether a different seating arrangement might change how talk happens. Your expectation should be that everyone will respond, so children may need more thinking time and time to talk in pairs, both to generate ideas and when everyone wants to speak at once. The idea is to make sure everyone gets to speak, although you must remember, also, a child's right to silence. Sometimes the time is not right for speech. Many children learn a great deal by listening. If you have managed to create the right atmosphere then children will value both speakers and listeners, the finely turned phrase and the moment when silence is just the right choice.

Talk encompasses the deeply serious and the joyfully playful. It is a part of who we are and can become. It is social, cultural and creative. Its place in the development of thought is crucial. Talk is part of the fabric of a classroom. How talk occurs will depend on the ethos of the school and the class and on the careful planning and philosophy of the classroom teacher. It is one of the most powerful tools that a teacher can use.

Summary

Talk is essential to learning and needs to be taught. Teachers need to take into account the richness of talk at home and to build on it rather than ignore it. Language and thought are interconnected. This is not sufficiently honoured in classrooms and this chapter suggests some of the ways in which teachers can and do promote the kinds of talk that generate thinking and learning, both in terms of teacher/child and child/child interactions. How teachers plan for talk across the curriculum can have a significant impact on children's social, cultural and cognitive development. Language through talk is both serious and celebratory.

Issues for reflection

- How can you make a link, as an educator, between the richness of talk at home and talk in the classroom? How can you create opportunities for authentic conversations in the early years classrooms that avoid the sterile lines of questioning seen in some of the classrooms depicted by Wells?

(Continued)

(Continued)

- Find out more about the work of Vivian Gussin Paley or, for older children, the work of Jack Zipes in relation to storytelling. Note down the stories that you hear in school. Who tells them? What are they about? How will you use story in the classroom?

- Think about your own history as a speaker and listener. Think about how your experience of home and family and then the widening world of school, higher education and work have changed your speech and language. What aspects of your speech have you held on to and what has changed? How do children experience you as a speaker and listener in their classrooms?

- Reflect on the ways you introduce new ideas, find out about what children know and your use of questions. Consider how, as an educator, you might use questions and other openings to enable children to be more fully involved in talk and in their own learning through talk. When might you use tentative, exploratory talk yourself?

- As we have seen, Vygotsky argued strongly that language structure directs the processes of thinking. Giving children opportunities to work together may help them to develop and recall solutions to problems that, alone, they could not achieve. What strategies as a teacher might you need to use to ensure that children use talk productively to think together?

Further reading

Alexander, R. (2006) *Towards Dialogic Teaching*. York: Dialogos. Very readable introduction to dialogic teaching.

Bearne, E. (ed.) (1998) *Use of Language Across the Primary Curriculum*. London: Routledge. An imaginative collection of writing about how language for thinking features in a variety of curriculum areas.

Cordon, R. (2000) *Literacy and Learning Through Talk: Strategies for the Primary Classroom*. Buckingham: Open University Press. This gives a good overview of the whole primary age range and combines theory and practice in a very accessible style.

Dawes, L. and Sams, C. (2004) *Talk Box: Speaking and Listening Activities for Learning at Key Stage 1*. London: David Fulton. Very practical ways of setting up and helping children to work successfully in groups.

Dawes, L., Mercer, N. and Wegerif, R. (2003) *Thinking Together: A Programme of Activities for Developing Speaking, Listening and Thinking Skills for Children Aged 8–11*. Birmingham: Imaginative Minds. Very practical ways of setting up and helping children to work successfully in groups.

Dickinson, R. and Neelands, J. (2006) *Improving Your Primary School Through Drama*. London: David Fulton. This is a very practical and thoughtful book about drama which answers many of the questions that inexperienced teachers ask about drama. It suggests many activities which generate children's thoughtful reflection.

Edwards, A.D. and Westgate, D.P.G. (1994) *Investigating Classroom Talk*. 2nd edition. London: Falmer. This is very helpful in suggesting ways of collecting samples of talk from the classroom.

Goodwin, P. (ed.) (2001) *The Articulate Classroom*. London: David Fulton. This edited book contains some excellent chapters which provide case studies of interesting practice.

Mercer, N. and Hodgkinson, S. (eds) (2008) *Exploring Talk in School*. London: Sage. Using the work of a range of researchers, this very good book considers ways of improving classroom talk.

CHAPTER 5

OBSERVATION

Stephen Chynoweth and Lorraine Laudrum

Chapter overview

What is one of the most crucial ingredients to becoming a better and more effective teacher? Observation, particularly when it has a clear purpose, structure and provides ample opportunity for professional reflection. Here Stephen Chynoweth and Lorraine Laudrum give down-to-earth guidance on how this lifelong skill can be learned, practised and refined.

Introduction

Stop for a minute and try to describe your usual journey home. How did you get on? Whether driving or walking, despite the fact that you may have made the journey many times, we suspect that you did not describe it at all well. We were very surprised to find that we were not able to describe our journey accurately and yet it's one we make daily. This activity demonstrates the difference between looking at something and noticing the information that you need, and observing what it is actually like. Even though looking at things is part of our everyday lives, detailed observation is not.

This exercise also suggests that when we look at things in order to gain specific information it is quite likely that we do not take in the context within which that information is situated: how often do we look but not really see? The main focus for this chapter is on trainee teachers as observers of classroom pedagogy and organisation and how this supports the honing of their skills through reflection on what they notice about the practice of others. But it also considers the vital contribution of observation to helping trainee teachers to understand the learning that is taking place in the classroom and to use their reflections to enable pupils to make progress. This dimension to observation is more fully explored in the suggested further reading.

Why observe?

The point about observation for you – as a trainee teacher – is that observation will help you learn a tremendous amount about teaching styles and techniques. It will also help you to gain considerable insight into how pupils learn. Most importantly, it will allow you to observe the impact a teacher has upon a pupil's learning and their well-being and the ways in which that impact can be measured. We must stress that effective teaching should always be focused upon the pupils' learning outcomes. We all know that there is 'more than one way to skin a cat' and so the purpose of observation is not necessarily to emulate a specific teacher but a way of observing the teaching styles of others to inform your own. Effective teaching should be judged in relation to how it facilitates learning and helps pupils to make gains in their attitudes, knowledge, understanding and skills. However, in observing detailed points about the way a classroom operates you must try not to lose sight of the context and the complex interactions which affect both teachers and pupils. Indeed, if you were to learn about the mechanics of a car, your learning would begin with how to change the oil or bleed the brakes rather than how to undertake a complete service!

Trainee teachers are often asked to make observations from the beginning of their teaching course. It is expected that, by looking closely enough at various forms of evidence, the trainee teacher will be able to focus on effective teaching and learning techniques. This osmosis approach provides a powerful first-hand experience of learning life within the primary classroom and, when broken down into 'bite-size' pieces and specific foci, provides a comprehensive catalogue of experiences and evidence on which to draw throughout your teaching career.

Observation is not just something trainee teachers do. Experienced teachers also use observation to help them to understand how the pupils in their class are learning new concepts and consolidating existing ones. Teachers also use observation to develop their own classroom management and teaching skills (see also Chapter 2). Teachers are used to working collaboratively, sharing ideas and strategies. Experienced teachers understand the importance of observing how other teachers teach and other pupils learn as well as allowing colleagues to observe them. Established teachers will often set up formal observation times when they can make assessments about the learning that has been taking place in their classroom. They will also make ad hoc observations or consult with their pupils on the impact of their teaching which will inform their assessments about both the learning taking place as well as the effectiveness of their teaching. This, in turn, allows teachers to alter their plans and activities to tailor them to the learning needs of their pupils.

Observation is a skill and, as with most skills, it requires practice, perseverance and regular reflection to become proficient in it. Classroom observation requires practice as there are so many things happening which require analysis both in terms of what is happening and in the observer's reaction to it. Each classroom or school setting will offer new experiences that will help an observer to build up a bank of knowledge and to develop a deeper understanding of what is occurring. When you are observing in the classroom remember that it has an end product – to make you a better and more effective teacher.

Teaching placements

Before commencing any placement, you would be well advised to carry out some pre-placement research on the context you are about to enter. The information you gather may take several forms: school policy documents, the school prospectus, conversations with teaching staff and/or the head teacher and, almost certainly, from reading the most recent inspection report. Most importantly, it would be beneficial to request time to observe the class within which you will be working.

Influencing practice

By observing the classroom setting in which you are placed you will begin to identify effective strategies which enhance the pupils' learning. The observations made can be both negative and positive – making judgements about why something appeared not to work can be as valuable a learning experience as noting positive things.

Preparation for observation

Before the observation period begins, try to find out in advance of your first visit as much information as you can about the school you will be visiting to help build a picture-information such as:

- the size of the school
- the socio-economic profile of the catchment area
- the name of the head teacher.

Much of this information, and more, will be available through recent inspection evidence, known as the Ofsted report. Try to read the school's most recent report available on the Internet (http://www.ofsted.gov.uk). Also, schools have become more self-evaluative and the Ofsted inspection process promotes schools to have a good understanding of how well they are providing for their pupils and the 'next-step' improvement priorities. All this information will be contained in the school's self-evaluation documentation which you could possibly discuss with your school's head teacher or a member of the senior leadership team (SLT).

CRITICAL ISSUES

Self-evaluation is key to improving schools, teachers and students and their learning. By reflecting upon performance against clear and measureable criteria, this provides an opportunity not only to critically evaluate how well someone performs but also the next steps to improve. Observation can be an invaluable tool to aid such self-evaluation.
Consider:

- How would you describe your strengths as a student teacher? How would you prioritise your immediate development needs?
- When you observe pupils and their learning, what opportunities does the class teacher provide in order for the pupils to recognise their own strengths as well as improvement priorities?

Once a class has been allocated to you ask for a class list, as learning the names of the pupils will help when making observations. It will also help when you take over responsibility for the class. A class list might also contain other information, such as the birthdays of the pupils, which will give you some idea as to whether the pupils' birthdays are fairly evenly spread out over the academic year or if there are many birthdays at one particular time. In Reception or Year 1 birthdays in the summer term usually mean that the pupils have not been in school for very long.

Gaining agreement

Once you have been introduced to the class teacher with whom you will be working, try to come to an agreement as to how the observation period will occur.

- How will you record your observations? Your college may have provided you with a pro forma.
- Does the teacher mind you making notes during the teaching sessions or will you be expected to jot down your observations during break times or after school?
- Will the teacher expect you to join in with lessons or taking notes?

Although at first this might appear quite daunting, working with the class teacher and sharing your observations will provide a positive foundation to the start of your teaching practice. The teacher might be able to pick up on areas of confusion and be able to explain why something was organised in the way it was, addressing misinterpretations which in turn might help you to understand better the organisation of that classroom.

If you are given the opportunity to sit apart from the class, not taking part in activities, try to ensure that you are as unobtrusive as possible, particularly while making any notes. This is not to suggest that you should be hidden, but try to be discreet when observing, preferably behind the learners. Should pupils approach you, then we feel you should be as honest as possible about what you are doing. We frequently find that pupils ask us what we are doing when we are observing trainee teachers on teaching practice. When asked the question 'Who are you and what are you doing?' we generally answer something like 'Ms/Mr X has told me about how well this class learns and I've come along to look at all the good learning that is happening.'

The profile of the class

While much of the attention paid in the initial stages of the observation can be towards the teacher the most important observations to be made involve how the pupils are learning. Issues include:

- How does the teacher engage all pupils?
- Which style of teaching appears to be most effective in a particular setting?
- Are different strategies adopted for different subjects?

You will also be gathering information about the pupils in the class to enable you to be able to plan your teaching with them effectively. For example:

- At what level are the pupils learning?
- Are there at least three clear levels of ability in the class?

This will help you to set appropriate tasks when your teaching practice starts. If the tasks set are too easy or too hard then this has a huge impact on how well the pupils learn. It can also start to affect the relationship you might have with a class if they perceive the tasks as being boring or unattainable.

To participate or not to participate?

As mentioned previously, it will not always be possible to have a choice as to whether you take part in a session or are allowed to sit apart from the class. There are advantages and disadvantages to both approaches. If you are a participant you have the opportunity:

- to speak with individual pupils and build up a relationship with them
- to work at close hand with the activities planned by the teacher
- to consider your own response, possibly reflecting on how you see your own teaching style, as well as adopting teaching methods used by the experienced class teacher.

However:

- you may be restricted in not being able to work alongside all the pupils
- it is easy to get caught up in the activity and to lose sight of the information which might be beneficial to you in the longer term.

You must also have thought carefully about any note-taking which you might wish to make while participating in an activity with pupils. The older the pupil the more inquisitive they are likely to be about what it is you are writing. Obviously the opposite situation is possible in non-participant observation; you may not build up a rapport with individuals or an adequate understanding of the type of activities planned by the teacher. Pupils may also deduce that you are a trainee teacher and this can present difficulties when you come to lead the class. We've all witnessed how pupils can adapt their behaviour to the environment, often presenting more behavioural difficulties with some adults than others, often depending upon the pupil's perception of authority figures within the community. Making it known too overtly to pupils that you are not yet a qualified teacher may give them the opportunity to 'push the boundaries' with you rather than simply accept your authority as their class teacher. However, non-participant observation will probably enable you to closely observe more general areas like classroom management strategies, use of resources to illustrate key teaching points and use of learning support assistants.

The ideal situation for a trainee teacher would therefore seem to be a balance between the two approaches: time to sit back and observe the general running of the classroom as well as opportunities to become involved in working on activities planned by the teacher with groups or individuals.

Making observations

Once you have agreed with the class teacher how the observation process will progress it will become evident that there is so much information to take on board it is difficult to know where to start. Returning to the analogy of car mechanics, it is much more effective to break down observations into 'bite-size' pieces, the same way in which you would learn how to change a car's oil, rather than attempting to do everything at once, such as a complete MoT! One approach is to try to focus your attention on particular aspects of the classroom rather than looking at and noting down everything that will be happening. Below we have listed some possible aspects of the classroom that you may want to focus upon first: perhaps discuss these with the class teacher before your first observation. This way other aspects can be planned into future observations so that each area of classroom teaching can be covered in smaller, manageable pieces. You may even want to break these aspects down into even smaller pieces, possibly as a chart or table, so that you can quickly make reference to your observations as you begin to plan lessons for the class at a later date.

1. Physical resources

Many aspects of this type of observation can occur without the pupils being in the room. Without providing an exhaustive list it is a good idea to note the following:

- How the room is laid out – are the tables in groups or pairs, for example? It is a good idea to draw a diagram of the classroom for you to look at later.
- Are the resources clearly accessible – are the pencils, rulers and so on stored in one place where the pupils are expected to go to get them or do the pupils have responsibility for looking after their own resources? Are dictionaries, information books and resources for supporting curriculum subjects such as mathematics and English easily accessible or are they stored away with the teacher responsible for handing them out?
- Are there pupil whiteboards/digit cards/resources that enable interactive learning with the class teacher? If so, where are these stored and what is the system for providing the pupils with them?
- Are there areas for the pupils to learn quietly and areas designated for more practical activities?
- Is there an interactive whiteboard in the classroom? What brand is it and what software is used? How does the teacher use it to enhance learning and teaching in their class?
- What are the displays like? Do the displays show examples of a range of abilities in the class? Do the displays simply celebrate pupil achievement or are they learning opportunities for the class, asking questions of pupils or raising questions from pupils? Do the displays concentrate on one subject area for each display, for example artwork, writing or mathematics? Or is a link made between the curriculum subjects which form the whole display, for example some poetry about flight, some design technology drawings and models of aeroplanes and a write-up of an experiment in connection with flight? This could be part of a whole-school policy or it might be the preferred way of working of the class teacher, but either way there should be a whole-school policy on it.

- Is there a 'talking wall' or well-being area in the classroom identifying pupils' concerns/comments with their school learning experiences?
- Is there an outside learning area? If so, how is it used?

Each classroom will be organised differently. This will depend on practical issues such as the space available but it will also reflect the preferred way that the class teacher likes to work.

Organisational issues, such as whether the pupils always sit in the same place or whether they learn in different places depending on the activity they are doing, are important to notice. It is not always possible to identify these issues without the pupils in the classroom, although the number of chairs to pupils in a class or name labels at each place may well give you a clue.

This is the time to put to one side your own experiences of how you remember learning when you were at school. It is the time to watch what happens in the forthcoming sessions, to try to understand why the teacher has organised things in the way they have and, most importantly, to consider how the learning environment is organised to best suit the learners in terms of effective learning.

2. Rules, routines, procedures

Like all organisations, schools are to some extent governed by a set of routines. Furthermore, pupils find security in routine; therefore it is important that your teaching practice continues them. Individual teachers will not be able to change some things that happen within a school day although many things will have been agreed by teachers as a whole-school policy. Policy and practice should be strongly linked. A good example of this is with behaviour management. Schools will often have agreed policies which all members of staff are expected to follow. It is important to have read the school's behaviour management policy before your teaching practice begins so that you feel confident in applying it; it would tend to undermine your teaching authority with a pupil if it appeared you 'did not know what to do'. It is also important to see the policy in operation in the classroom and in other areas of the school, for example in the playground and the school hall during PE and assembly. Other policies, which will have an immediate impact on the trainee teacher, include the marking of work, display and the school's Learning and Teaching policy.

3. Fixed points

There are many fixed points in a school day and it is worth observing how the teacher deals with these.

The start of the day

Schools vary in how the pupils start their day. Some schools allow the pupils to come into their classroom as they arrive or only after a set time. The teacher may have tasks or activities for the pupils to do independently until the official start time of the day. Some schools have all the pupils coming into school at the same time, usually after a bell or whistle has sounded and the pupils have been lined up and sent in class by class. Both of these approaches have organisational implications which you should observe as it will be important for you to fully understand and remember what happens when this becomes part of your responsibilities. Perhaps note down the different ways in which classes begin their day, commenting on possible advantages and disadvantages with both methods to help inform your own preference in the future.

Other fixed points

Try to observe the other fixed points of the day and how they are organised. Assembly times, playtimes, lunchtimes and the end of the day all bring their own organisational implications and it is important that you recognise the importance of continuing the practice of the class teacher. For example, being late for assembly upsets the routines of many other people, keeping the other classes waiting and possibly eating into valuable hall time at the end of the assembly time.

As well as clarifying the organisation of these fixed points throughout the school day, they also provide a rich source of understanding the ethos of the school. At playtimes, observe the interactions between pupils and staff as well as pupils with one another: how do speak to others? How do you know if pupils listen to others? How do pupils react to others? What body language do you observe during these interactions? How is conflict resolved by staff? By pupils? During assemblies observe how key points are conveyed to the pupils: are pupils hearing the assembly or listening to it? How do staff model the behaviour expected of pupils? How do you observe the 'feel' of the assembly? All of these fixed point activities during a school's working day will help you to align your teaching with the ethos and expectations of the school you will be working in.

4. Classroom management

Many areas of classroom management can be observed best when you are given the opportunity to sit back and observe without participating in a session. Observation times are an ideal way of learning from the class teacher how they achieve the working system that they do.

Style

It must be recognised that by the time you arrive in the classroom the teacher is likely to have been teaching the pupils for some time and to have established many routines. A teacher who appears relaxed and calm with a class, making jokes with individuals, has inevitably worked hard to gain a shared understanding with the class of an acceptable way of learning. It is inappropriate for a trainee to start their learning relationship with the class in the same way. The relationship that a successful teacher establishes with their class, over time, is based on clear expectations and boundaries which all members of the class adhere to.

Control and pace

Classroom management issues such as behaviour management, the timing of activities and the pace of pupils' learning are all important issues to consider when observing the teacher. These can be observed while participating in an activity, although a more accurate, holistic understanding of how these things work can be gained by watching the teacher as a non-participant. Observing the strategies that the teacher uses for behaviour management when they are effectively on their own in the classroom, for example, will help you to understand what will be expected of you when you take over responsibility for the class.

The physical and emotional learning environment

The most important aspect of classroom management is to ensure that all pupils feel safe, physically and emotionally. When observing an established teacher, identify how they provide security for their pupils so that the optimum conditions for learning are established for every pupil. How does the teacher encourage all pupils to participate in the lesson? How are answers encouraged from pupils? How are pupil errors addressed individually or in front of peers? By providing a secure learning environment, the teacher provides the ideal opportunity for the children to realise their own learning potential.

5. Teaching

When training to be a teacher, a common approach is to be thinking 'What will I do with the pupils?' Too much anxiety can be caused by thinking about how you will open the lesson, introduce the learning objectives, what questions you will ask and so on. While these are important facets of teaching, the teacher's mindset is, almost invariably, best focused on 'How will these pupils learn best?' So why not try imagining planning the perfect lesson backwards, considering what you want the pupils to have learnt/be able to do by the end of the lesson and then 'rewind back' through the lesson to consider what you will need to do to teach and facilitate that end aim? To put it another way, in order to make a cup of tea, we boil a kettle, put a tea bag in a mug, perhaps add sugar and milk before finally adding water and stirring to our preference. We don't necessarily go through the actions to see if we may make a cup of tea – the actions we undertake have a clear purpose towards the end aim of producing a delicious cup of tea.

Other areas to observe include teaching strategies such as, for example, the balance and choice of practical and written activities. When you are observing the class try to make a note of the type of activities organised by the class teacher. The teacher may have planned for their time to be spent working with one group. How then have the other groups been organised? Has the teacher been successful in planning activities that the remaining groups can maintain on their own with little input from the teacher? If it is a core subject, such as maths or English, is there a balance of activities across any given week? The independent activities planned may well be for reinforcement purposes, the teacher being confident that the pupils have previously been given a basis from which to learn. It is also worth noting how the teacher deals with hidden issues. For example, how does the teacher ensure equal access for boys and girls to all areas of the curriculum? This is a large area to observe and one that you may feel you do not have time to look at in depth, but it is certainly worth focusing upon over time.

CRITICAL ISSUES

I've realised it's not about teaching, it's about learning (An anonymous trainee teacher quoted by Black et al., 2003b, p. 95)

Ultimately, the only thing that matters in a classroom is how well the pupils are learning: learning about a curriculum, learning key skills, learning about positive attitudes and values, learning about themselves. Any quality assurance visit, whether it is an Ofsted inspection or your teaching course supervisor, should, ultimately, always focus on the impact of teaching for effective learning. Through observing lessons the temptation can be to focus solely on the teacher to the detriment of the pupils. However, ultimately, the effectiveness of a teacher will not be observed in that teacher but in the pupils that they are teaching. Consider:

- When speaking with other teachers, how do they know that pupils have learnt what they intended them to learn?
- How do they motivate the pupils to learn, inspire them and provide a context as well as a consequence for their learning?
- What different teaching strategies do teachers use? How do they use these different styles in order for all pupils to learn?
- When observing pupils learning, what does it look like?

6. Observing the use of ICT

The use of ICT, both as a teaching tool as well as a learning aid, should be implicit in a teacher's classroom practice. Pupils need to witness and understand the value of ICT in our daily lives and the ways in which it can enhance learning. You will observe a variety of ICT usage in classrooms including computers, interactive whiteboards, wireless/Bluetooth communication, multimedia equipment and an exhaustive range of software. The effective use of ICT in the primary classroom is explored in more depth later in this book (see Chapter 12); however, it is important to emphasise how you should look for its effective use during observations. Does the teacher use the whiteboard interactively with the pupils or is it merely a glorified screen show? Do the pupils explore, experiment and apply previous learning to the use of ICT or does the teacher lead through step-by-step instruction?

Does the use of ICT enhance the learning and the lesson or does it inhibit? As teachers, we must be mindful to avoid the use of ICT for the sake of it and ensure that it enhances the pupils' learning experience as well as facilitates the teacher's teaching.

7. Learning

It is imperative that pupils are partners in their own learning. Understanding the pupils' perceptions of how successful they are as learners as well as with their learning is key to informing how a teacher will ensure effective learning for all. When observing, how does the teacher gain the pupils' engagement? What instructions does the teacher give about what the pupils should do with their learning? Does the teacher share the learning objective with the class? In order for pupils to be able to reflect upon how well they are learning pupils need to know what the learning intentions of the lesson were in the first place. How does the teacher address misconceptions during the plenary session of the lesson? Do pupils reflect upon how successful they feel they've been with their learning? One useful tool to use here is the traffic light system. If a pupil has found their learning challenging, rewarding and successful then they are green, all systems go. If they have found their learning difficult and have had help along the way, then perhaps they are on amber, ready to go but require further assistance. If pupils have been 'stuck' and found their learning too difficult then they are at red, something is stopping them with their learning.

It is also beneficial to observe a pupil, or group of pupils, throughout a lesson or series of lessons. It is vital that a teacher meets all pupils' needs by differentiating activities and key teaching points: every pupil should be challenged appropriately. Track a particular pupil through a lesson, observing how they understand the learning objective, how they articulate their understanding and how they apply it. Does the pupil seem appropriately challenged or do they appear 'stuck', or do they speed through the activities with relative ease? Discussing with the teacher how they select key teaching points and activities for pupils of different abilities is a useful way to reflect upon the success of a lesson and outline the next steps in the pupils' learning.

Finally, when observing particular groups of pupils, consider how the teacher supports vulnerable groups, such as pupils with special educational needs or with English as an additional language, as well as the way the teacher ensures consistent challenge for gifted and talented pupils.

8. Movement around the classroom

Once the session is up and running, the teacher has delivered the key teaching points and the pupils are learning from the activities they have been assigned to, try to observe the movements of the teacher. Does the teacher sit in one place, working with one group of pupils? If so, there are several things to consider. Why do you think the teacher has selected that particular pupil or group of pupils to learn with? If the answer is not obvious to you it might be appropriate to ask at a later stage in the day or it may be outlined in the lesson plan. Teachers make choices like this for all sorts of reasons. For example, the teacher knows this group will need more support than the other groups to sustain this activity. Or the teacher wants to assess how the pupils are doing on this activity. Or there is one pupil in the group who is causing concern and the teacher wants to be able to support that child appropriately. We are sure there are many more reasons. It is also important to notice how the teacher has managed the rest of the class in order to concentrate time with this one group. Are the rest of the class free to come and ask questions of their teacher, or are they limited to going to the teacher one at a time? Is there a learning support assistant in the class assisting with the learning of the pupils? If so, how are they used? Is it the same throughout a week or different for different subjects and pupils? Have the pupils been given strategies for doing their activity independently?

A very common situation is where the teacher is expecting pupils to write independently so that he/she can support a guided reading group. Ultimately, if we really did not want to be disturbed while working with another group, we might say to the pupils that it did not matter if they made the occasional mistake, that we wanted them to 'have a go'. This is linked to building up a relationship with a class as they will not always have the confidence to 'have a go'. The pupils have to understand that you will not be cross if the attempt was not successful. Even so, if a teacher is working in a classroom on their own with no extra support it is almost inevitable, especially with younger pupils, that interruptions will occur.

It might be that, from time to time throughout such a session, the teacher makes a point of commenting on the behaviour of some of the pupils in the remaining groups, 'I can see Jo learning very hard, I will be interested to see what he has done at lunch time.' This is positive reinforcement of good learning habits and is good professional practice. Developing the teacher's mythical 'third eye' of peripheral awareness can be a real asset and a skill to refine as a trainee teacher.

There are occasions when teachers do not stay in one position throughout the session but decide to move freely around the room. It is also important to observe how this is done. Does the teacher move around stopping for a few minutes with each group, making sure the groups are on task and learning effectively? Or is their role identified in a more disciplinarian manner? It is important to observe how the pupils respond to these different approaches. Do you think that by moving around the class the teacher is able to support sufficiently those pupils who need it? Or are some pupils left unsupported because the teacher has been to them and has moved on to another group? Do you think that by the teacher staying with one group there are large numbers of pupils left unsupported? Does the teacher undertake mini-plenaries throughout the lesson? Are the pupils expected to line up before they leave the room, do they stand behind their chairs or do they leave the room as soon as their name has been called? Alternatively, does the teacher simply say that the children may now all leave the room? How does the teacher dismiss them?

All of these issues should then raise more questions for you which you could address with the class teacher at a more appropriate time.

9. Asking questions, giving answers, pupils raising questions

The power of the question is one of the most important factors in effective learning and teaching. The question stimulates curiosity, a desire to know, understand and learn. A healthy classroom should reflect a broad use of questioning: teacher questions, questions raised by the pupils, prompt questions in response to pupils' tasks, questions in displays. The use of questions should be planned on a daily basis. The mental and oral starters in the numeracy session and the whole-class introduction of the literacy session mean that teachers have had to address the most effective ways of asking questions to better assess the pupils' understanding of what is being taught and how the teacher uses questioning to informally assess achievement and inform next steps in planning the pupils' learning. Observing these parts of the sessions, as well as other times when questions are asked, will prove helpful to the trainee teacher.

When you are placed in the position of delivering your own numeracy session you will be able to bring to mind some of the questioning techniques you observed. You might try writing down the exact wording of the question asked and the answer that was given to it. If the correct answer was not given immediately but was perhaps given by the second pupil chosen, this might also be significant, so record both answers given. It can be useful to make a note of any groups of questions asked by the teacher, as there may be a progression or sequence which should be considered further. The same process is also useful for the explanations given by teachers to pupils' questions. For example, simply having large laminated cards with WHAT? WHY? HOW? WHAT IF? written on individual cards can help to prompt pupils to raise a variety of their own questions. It is also interesting to make a note of any situation where a teacher does not immediately know the answer to the question. How does the teacher respond? Does this response tell you anything about how you might respond in a similar situation?

It's all a matter of perspective

All these different methods will give you an insight into the ethos and style of the teacher. Every teaching style has advantages as well as disadvantages. Moreover, it should be recognised that each observer will have their own interpretations as to what is actually occurring in the classroom and that one example or incident should not necessarily be used as the only evidence for something. We cannot help but to reach conclusions based on our prior experiences of school and, sometimes, those conclusions may be too limited or naive. It is important that a trainee teacher gathers a variety of evidence and should try to look at things from different perspectives before making judgements about how effective their class teacher's methods might be.

Effective communication is key in the primary classroom; this includes those non-verbal methods of communication which are part of everybody's everyday life. What facial expressions does the teacher use with the class? The perceptive observer can begin to gain a better picture about the classroom environment and the relationship the teacher has with the pupils by trying to notice as many non-verbal messages as possible. For example, although formal and strict in the levels of discipline expected, does the teacher smile and nod approval a lot to encourage the pupils? When working with one group of pupils does the teacher take time to make eye contact with the pupils to demonstrate that they are aware of how well they are learning?

The other main methods of non-verbal communication employed include posture, gesture, facial expressions and different ways of moving around the room. All these things may be worth noting. It might well be inappropriate to expect you to imitate, for example, the class teacher's gestures, but observing the effect that the gestures have can help inform you as to how you would like to move and respond when working with children.

The same observations can also be made of the pupils in the class. Just because a child is sitting quietly, apparently with exercise book and activity to hand, does not necessarily mean that they are on task. Their body language or facial expressions may well signal to the teacher that the opposite situation is the case. Again, the way a teacher deals with such a pupil can be the result of the teacher's understanding of how that child will respond to them. Sometimes the best thing to do is to go and stand near the pupil in question and that will be enough to get the pupil back on task. It might require more direct questioning to discover what the problem is. For a trainee teacher, the danger of assuming that they have the same understanding as the teacher might lead to difficulties. The trainee teacher must realise that they will have to go through some process of establishing their own relationship with the pupils. Indeed, the crux of being an effective teacher is the attention and detail paid to relationships a teacher builds with their pupils and parents. Remember, you are not in the class to be a pupil's best friend or substitute parent; you are there to help them to learn as effectively as possible. Pupils need to know that you have their best interests at heart, that you care that they learn as well as you wanting them to feel happy, secure and stimulated in the learning environment around them. Ultimately, you want your pupils to grow in self-esteem and confidence, to possess a broad and balanced perspective on their school experiences so that they can develop the skills and understanding needed to equip them for their lives ahead. In a nutshell, you will want to lead their learning rather than simply manage your own teaching.

Earlier in the chapter we mentioned that one way to be productive in what you are observing is to focus closely on a specific aspect during different observation periods, for example to look at the behaviour management strategies employed by the teacher and to all intents and purposes ignore other aspects of the lesson such as timings, beginnings and endings, and so on. It is then possible to focus even more closely within the generic term of behaviour management strategies to look at the use of praise by the class teacher and the effectiveness of the praise and reward strategies that are employed. Wragg (1997) describes this as a 'critical event' approach; the trainee teacher should attempt to look for significant examples of a specific thing occurring and then should attempt to document this event. Wragg suggests that a description should be given of the situation leading up to this event, the actual event itself (including why it was significant) and what the outcome was. It may also be helpful to talk to the teacher and/or the pupils concerned to gain a better understanding of its significance. However, as Wragg comments: 'Talking to pupils either directly or indirectly about their teachers is not something that should be undertaken without permission, and even if agreement is secured, any interviews should be conducted in a sensitive manner' (p. 68). The term 'critical event' should not always imply something particularly important. Rather the events noted down should reflect something which is of interest to the observer. For a trainee teacher, the events should attempt to reflect something which will help them with their professional development in some way.

What do you do with your observations?

Observations you make in the classroom will help you become a more effective practitioner. The type of observations you make can be split broadly into two categories – observations about teaching and observations about learning, but you may wish to subcategorise beneath these two headings against the specific focus of each lesson observed.

Observations about teaching

You will use the observations that you make about the way a teacher operates in the classroom as a personal bank of information to help you inform and guide your practice. You may be expected to bring your observations back to your teaching course to discuss the implications and effectiveness of some of the things you have seen. However, the purpose of these observations as well as your discussions on your course is to help you to understand about effective teaching.

Observations about learning

The observations you make about the learning occurring in the class will help you to gain a better understanding of how pupils learn. You will also be able to use your observations to understand the role of the teacher in the learning which is taking place. For example, making judgements about how well the class has achieved an activity will help when you are responsible for planning the learning of that class on teaching practice. Additionally, you may be required to pass on the observations you have made to the class teacher who might wish to use your observations in the records of the class as well to help their planning of the curriculum.

Ethical issues

It is fundamental to your development as a professional teacher that observations are confidential. It would be advisable to avoid real names and simply refer to pupils as Pupil A, Pupil B, etc. It would also be appropriate to refer to the teacher as 'CT' in your notes (class teacher) so that, again, notes protect anonymity and focus on actions and outcomes rather than individuals. Also, when discussing individual situations during your teaching course, for example, retain the anonymity of all individuals being described. Remember, teachers may feel very nervous about being observed and defensive about their practice.

Additionally, it is important to respect their experience of the profession and to try to understand why a teacher may be using approaches with which you do not agree or that you perceive as ineffective. Being overly critical of the teacher or their practice is counterproductive. Do not discuss your observations in a negative way: focus on developing your understanding of the situation. You can then privately reflect on how you might have approached that teaching point and any advantages and disadvantages to your own approach.

Summary

Observation plays an important role in the routines and skills of the classroom practitioner. This is a lifelong skill which must be learned, practised and refined to build up a base of knowledge which will help to improve practice. At the beginning and end of your training you may well be given a chance to observe teachers and pupils in the classroom. This is only the beginning but these opportunities will provide a solid foundation that can be developed throughout your teaching career. Good teachers never stop observing and reflecting on how to translate their observations into better practice.

This chapter has dealt with how students can get the best out of the opportunities they are given to observe in schools. The key issues covered included:

- the purpose of observation
- how to prepare for observation
- types of observation
- what to observe
- how to interpret the observations
- what to do with the observations.

Issues for reflection

- Reflect on what it might be useful for you to observe on your next visit to school. Think about how you will discuss your ideas with the teacher and negotiate an appropriate focus. Consider how you might plan future observations in the light of what you see and hear.
- Observe teachers asking questions. What type of questions do they use? Do they encourage pupils to talk or give one-word answers? Are certain types of questions more suited to one situation rather than another? Why do you think this might be the case?
- Take the opportunity to focus on one pupil for a session. Look closely at what the pupil says and does. How do these relate to the teacher's plans, words and actions?
- Listen to the summaries that teachers give at the end of sessions and consider how they relate to the session plans and the content of what has taken place.

Further reading

Black, P., Harrison, C., Lee, C., Marshall, B. and Wiliam, D. (2003) *Assessment for Learning: Putting it into Practice*. Maidenhead: Open University Press. A clear guide to the effective use of assessment for learning in the primary classroom, enabling teachers to reflect upon their impact as a teacher.

Ginnis, P. (2002) *The Teacher's Toolkit*. Bancyfelin, Carmarthen: Crown House. A wonderful resource of inspiring teaching ideas coupled with a deep and precise understanding of pedagogy and how pupils learn best.

Wragg, E.C. (1997) *An Introduction to Classroom Observation*. London: Routledge. This is an excellent companion to accompany a structured approach to getting the most out of classroom observations.

CHAPTER 6

CLASSROOM SKILLS

Lorraine Laudrum and Stephen Chynoweth

Chapter overview

The primary classroom provides the foundations for a lifelong love of learning. This requires a strong focus on the development of skills, not only for pupils but also for the teacher. Skills-based learning needs to be embedded in the culture of the classroom and, for teachers, this begins with continuous refinement of our own classroom skills. Here Lorraine Laudrum and Stephen Chynoweth give down-to-earth guidance on how to develop classroom skills to promote lifelong learning.

Introduction

Every aspect of teaching is comprised of skills, some of which are organisational and some of which are personal and interpersonal. It is the honing of these skills that supports teachers' professional development at every level. Sharing the experience of skill refinement with other practitioners as well as with pupils makes the learning process explicit and models lifelong learning as an ongoing and iterative process. So when reading this chapter, consider how professional dialogue with other adults and classroom dialogue with pupils, can model the learning process and reflect the teacher not only as the deployer of skills but as a learner of skills.

We have selected a range of what we consider to be some of the most useful classroom skills for this chapter and isolated each for discussion but, in practice of course, we acknowledge they are interrelated and even interdependent.

Managing relationships

In our view, more important than any other element of the teacher role, is the ability to foster good relationships at every level. It may seem obvious but if children feel liked and valued, they are more likely to respond by learning well. Time spent getting to know the children's interests can be time well spent. Understanding what children enjoy outside of school, as well as in it, provides the class teacher with vital information that can be used to engage and excite children in their learning. For instance, delivering an aspect of maths through a sporting context will often motivate children to apply their new learning as it may have more relevance to their own lives (see Chapter 8). Getting to know individual pupils will enable them to feel valued by the class teacher, and this investment in each and every child will help to gain their trust and respect.

Talking explicitly to children about emotional literacy can be a very effective way of establishing the classroom ethos and setting up a framework for your own relationships with others in the school. This involves talking to the children about their emotions and how they affect and inform our interactions with our environment and others. Woolfolk et al. (2008, p. 138) pose an interesting question: 'Does intelligence inform emotions so we are clever about managing our feelings and impulses, or does emotion inform intelligence so we make good decisions and understand other people?' They suggest both may be true and the important thing to remember is that there is more to being successful in life than simply having good cognitive skills.

CRITICAL ISSUES

The SEAL curriculum (DfES, 2005) is a useful curriculum resource for underpinning all pupils' learning with the principles of social and emotional skills. Consider the importance of emotional literacy in the curriculum and reflect on the following:

- How might a focus on social and emotional skills with children support your skill development as a teacher?
- What are the risks of teaching without emotional intelligence and of producing pupils without emotional intelligence? What are the implications for your practice?

Channels of communication

Once relationships are productive, teachers can begin to practise their skill of creating and strengthening channels of communication in the classroom. There will be many channels for communication in a classroom where speaking and listening is promoted, valued and explicitly planned. These channels may include:

- children to teacher or other adult
- teacher or other adult to children
- peer to peer
- child to themselves in self-talk and self-assessment.

Children to teacher communication

This has two elements: encouraging the children to communicate and listening when they do. Children will usually feel comfortable engaging in classroom dialogue if it is always a win situation. Where children are used to voicing their thoughts without fear of 'making a mistake' or being 'wrong' the classroom dialogue becomes much richer and the children become more active in their learning. The child has nothing to lose in speaking if the content is always valued for its contribution to the learning. The teacher may, however, need to guide against comments from mischievous children who deliberately try to throw the dialogue off course. This can usually be handled by a confident and firm challenge to the comment which brings the lesson back on track.

Listening is a vital and often underestimated skill for teachers; this means listening to the children's ideas, hypotheses, concerns, questions and even social dialogue if invited. It is important to stress the difference between that of listening to children and merely hearing them. Consider your body language when you are listening to your children: maintaining eye contact, listening with a smile, facing the child or children. Where children are truly given a voice, the rewards can be significant. Consider the benefits of asking the children how they feel about their learning at any given point and, where the response is negative, how those views might be unpicked in order to provide useful feedback to move the lesson forward. In our experience, if children are encouraged to articulate the learning process, it can be invaluable for the teacher in honing the lesson for particular needs and identifying next steps for learning. Watkins (2010) points to film research which indicates that young children are often much more adept at meta-learning than professionals might expect and argues that, 'When we add an explicit focus on learning, children engage with the opportunity to talk about the processes and learn about them' (p. 3).

Teacher or other adult to children

Teachers can respond to children's ideas with further challenge, for example:

- Are you assuming that …?
- What is the thinking behind your idea?
- How can you investigate that hypothesis?
- How does your idea link to our learning about …?

And so in this way the children see the teacher's responses as having valued their contribution and the teacher's role as being that of lead learner rather than dispenser of knowledge and right answers. Where the teacher models non-judgemental listening, the children will follow and enrich discussions by building on the ideas of others or asking questions to deepen the thinking of their peers. It is also important for the teacher to model an approach to learning in which setbacks and mistakes are celebrated as a means to moving learning forward.

Peer to peer

Again this may be modelled by the way the teacher engages in dialogue with the children. It can be a good idea to have sentence starters for peer dialogue displayed in the room, for example:

- I agree/disagree with X when he says … because …
- I am not sure I understand X's point about …
- Do you mean …?
- I would like to add to X's point about …
- I liked X's sentence because …

Many experienced teachers will incorporate the use of 'talk partners' in their planning and teaching. Creating talk partners across a class could be based on a number of factors: ability, gender, particular interests in the subject-matter. Establishing talk partners is a wonderful vehicle for developing children's confidence in expressing their understanding as well as developing thinking skills and reflection on the everyday learning that is occurring within the classroom. As you undertake a teaching practice, it would be useful to discuss the use of talk partners with established teachers. It may be, for example, that their effective use is different from class to class as it is fashioned to the particular needs of the children.

Self-talk/self-assessment

This is explored more fully in the chapter on assessment (see Chapter 10) but where children are used to rich dialogue about learning they will be able to run this as an internal monologue to evaluate and improve their work. They will be critical thinkers, aware of how to challenge themselves and be open to new learning.

Parents

At this point it is worth considering how you will communicate with parents. Approaches to formal meetings and events are covered elsewhere in this book (Chapter 16) but it is worth considering how you communicate during those regular, informal meetings such as at the school gate or in the playground at the end of the day. Parents will want to know that their child is happy to be in your class and that you are an equal partner in the success of their child. Maintaining an approachable manner, smiling and being ready to listen at the appropriate times are simple ways in which you can gain parents' trust, respect and confidence in you as their child's teacher that will be encouraged within the home environment. During any interaction with parents, reflect not only on what you say but how you say it, your body language, your eye contact, your facial expressions. It is our experience that effectively engaging parents in the day-to-day learning of their child significantly increases the likelihood of a child's learning success and helps to contribute to a united approach to a child's school experience and well-being.

The elements of a lesson

Creating an engaging, challenging and effective lesson is a skilful process. Although experience helps, there are certain 'ingredients' for the shape of the lesson that can make all the difference. There is further information about the holistic picture of planning in Chapter 11.

The start of the lesson

Consider what needs to be gained from the start of a lesson:

- an understanding of the learning objective
- an understanding of the success criteria – where you want to be by the end of the lesson, what the children need to know, expectations
- an introduction to the area of learning
- engagement in learning and motivation for the next part of the lesson
- explore, explain, identify, model, instruct in order to move the children's learning on and prepare them for the next part of the lesson
- assess where the children are to inform you as to who may require further support and who could be pushed harder in the next part of the lesson.

In order to gain an understanding of the learning objectives and success criteria, it helps if the children play an active role in identifying them. Using the example of learning how to write a newspaper report, you may have been looking at examples the previous day and in today's lesson you're going to focus on the opening paragraph – its features and how to write one. If possible, encourage the children to identify the learning objective themselves. What do they want to be able to do by the end of the lesson? Once they know this, encourage the children to consider how they will know if they've done it successfully. Identify the success criteria together – what are the features of the examples that you've looked at? Clarke (2008) suggests it is most effective to have one set of success criteria for all abilities but to differentiate by activity and to give children certain priorities from within the success criteria. In this way, the children's potential is not artificially limited by expectations.

It is helpful if the start of the lesson demonstrates the success criteria in action. This may be done through a number of different methods, for example through the teacher modelling (in the previous newspaper example, actively writing an opening paragraph with the children's input and checking that it has all of the features identified). It may be through children exploring for themselves (perhaps writing a short paragraph in pairs on a mini-whiteboard) and checking against the success criteria, through identifying the success criteria in action (perhaps someone next to them has written a good example or they can highlight an example in a text), or by the children trying to instruct someone else (e.g. with children in role, teach the trainee reporter how to write an opening paragraph).

Consider how to engage the children at the start and motivate them to want to continue their learning in the next part of the lesson. Strategies might include the use of a particularly 'child-friendly' topic (e.g. a fictional newspaper report related to a book, television or film character), relating it to something that they might feel strongly about, using picture, film, suspense, employing a mixture of VAK approaches (visual, auditory and kinaesthetic – a term popularised through association with the work of Smith, 1996, on accelerated learning and Gardner, 1993, on multiple intelligences). It might also be motivating to give the children an audience or end-product to aim for (e.g. your newspaper report is going to be put on the school website), etc.

In order for the next part of the lesson to be successful, you also need to start by assessing where the children are in their learning. This can be effective if carried out after establishing the success criteria in order to check understanding against it before proceeding. On occasions, however, it may be more appropriate right at the start of the lesson to establish prior learning and understanding and thus inform the success criteria. This may be done through asking the children to give examples on mini-whiteboards, or asking the children directly to close their eyes and raise their hand if, for example, they feel confident getting there or would like a bit more input. This ensures that the remainder of the lesson is not wasted time for a child who either completes the work easily with little effort or a child who doesn't know where to begin but perhaps doesn't ask for help. Such information can be vital in ensuring that adult support is given to the appropriate children and that individuals are challenged appropriately. It does not always follow that a child who found the work on calculations simple yesterday will also find the work on shape easy today. While previous knowledge of children's ability is important, it is also vital (a) not to make assumptions and (b) to be ready to be flexible in the groupings of children.

During the lesson

Consider what needs to be gained from the main part of the lesson:

- new skill development or skill consolidation/practice – subject related or learning to learn skills
- moving knowledge and understanding forward
- time to engage with others in activity, dialogue or reflection
- sustaining motivation and children's engagement in their learning.

During the lesson it is important to maintain the appropriate atmosphere for the type of intended learning. If the lesson requires high energy and fast thinking, how is this achieved? High energy can be introduced by using very short snappy tasks and a sense of a race against time. To achieve this it is necessary to be explicit with the children about the amount of time they have for any given activity and to provide them with time checks as you remind them of your expectations. If, on the other hand the lesson requires quiet focused writing, a sense of calm can be introduced through the use of calm music or changes to lighting. During a day's learning it is important to balance these classroom moods and to consider which is more appropriate for certain times of the day or week.

Keeping the lesson moving at pace keeps the children engaged and motivated and supports good behaviour. Judging the pace takes practice; too fast and the learning can be superficial and too slow and the children will lose interest. Pace is about timing the elements of the lesson. While a teacher may set out with notional timescales for each part of the lesson or each activity, it is important to be flexible in response to the engagement of the children and their depth of understanding.

It takes confidence to divert from a plan but learning will not be effective if the children are bored because they have been given too much time to complete a task or if the lesson is hurried on when the children do not fully understand a concept. It is always worth carrying out regular checks on how far the children have got with a given activity and to consider what to do if some complete a task before others. Instead of giving more of the same it is more effective to plan extension activities or open-ended, child-led investigations.

It can be really effective to use a 'mini-plenary' during the lesson in which the teacher can ask how the children feel about their learning, check understanding, address misconceptions and share good examples. Better to pause for a few minutes to do this and then adjust the rest of the lesson than to carry on regardless.

Also during the lesson, it may be appropriate to completely rethink the direction of the learning. This can happen where the lesson is pitched at an inappropriate level or where prior learning has been assumed rather than evidenced. Children are usually very responsive in these situations if their learning has been explicitly discussed, and there is nothing wrong with saying 'We seem to be having some difficulties with this activity. Let's think about what we need to do in order to get things back on track.' It can seem daunting to have to revise a thoroughly planned series of lessons but better this than to attempt to build on weak foundations. Remember, a lesson plan sets out the learning and teaching intentions of a lesson but, ultimately, the response of the children will always inform the most effective and rewarding lessons.

In order to keep a close eye on the progress of all children during the lesson, it is helpful to devote some time to classroom climate walks. This is not to say it is not possible for the teacher to work with a group in a focused way but that this can be balanced with some time where the attention is on the whole class. Consider providing adults helping within the classroom with 'milepost' criteria so that, during classroom climate walks, they can inform you of the children's progress against their learning. Being flexible is the key to keeping lessons moving and to ensuring the learning is meaningful.

The end of the lesson

Consider what needs to be gained from the end of the lesson, for example:

- consolidation of learning/reinforcement of main points
- giving the children an audience for their learning
- checking understanding
- determining next steps
- homework
- a celebration of the learning achieved and providing children with a feeling of success with their learning.

Consolidation of learning and reinforcement of main points should consist of revisiting the success criteria and, where possible, giving the children opportunity to assess their own learning against this. This may be carried out in pairs, with the children highlighting and sharing examples of the success criteria in each other's work or through having some time to quietly look back and consider their own work. This could be done as a class with the children volunteering or you picking up on good examples of the success criteria in action.

Sometimes it is important to give the children an audience for their learning at the end of the lesson. This may involve feeding back and sharing with a partner, a group or the class. Apart from requiring the child to articulate their learning, this also encourages others to actively listen, identifying the success criteria in action and giving positive feedback. Such activity ensures that this is also a valuable activity for the rest of the class. Opportunities to speak and to share with a larger audience can also prove important in developing a child's self-esteem and confidence as well as their specific learning in a lesson.

The end of a lesson can be an important opportunity to check understanding and inform next steps. This may be through targeted questioning against the success criteria, a short activity which will demonstrate understanding (e.g. 'Which of the following sentences don't belong in a newspaper report?' 'Can you turn the sentence into one which would sound appropriate in a newspaper report?'). It is also sometimes appropriate to take a few minutes to allow children to mark their work against a set of answers. This gives them and you immediate feedback which allows any difficulties to be quickly addressed. Swift and direct feedback can also be given by asking the children how they feel about their learning, for example whether they feel 'red, amber or green' in their learning today through an eyes-closed, hands-up activity or a mark in their books. Taking a quick note of those children who are lacking in confidence or those who are very confident can be invaluable, particularly when considered alongside work in books. This will inform the content, support and structure of the following day's lesson.

Finally, the end of the lesson should look to praise and celebrate the children's learning achievements. Learning is specific as success criteria for a reason, to recognise success. Therefore children explicitly understanding why they have been successful with a particular activity and celebrating this in the classroom are essential. Celebration of success can take many forms in the classroom: a smile and a 'well done!' goes a long way with us all; sharing the achievements with the rest of the class or with a child's parent at the end of the day; team points or stickers; displaying children's achievements in the class or across the school; publishing a class anthology or creating a class library of excellence or Hall of Fame. There are many ways to celebrate children's learning successes and these are vital in reinforcing self-esteem and children's sense of belonging to their class.

Classroom organisation

As a student, the classroom in which you find yourself will probably have been set out by the teacher and the children may well already have their own fixed places but, through negotiation, it may be possible to rearrange places or even furniture and resources. Hastings and Wood (2002) argue that the physical arrangement of the children in the classroom does make a difference to learning for some pupils and that the key is to match the organisation to the learning activity.

Classroom layout is a skill which requires the teacher to be able to visualise the children in action and the movement and resource requirements of the planned lesson. When the lesson is planned, it is a good idea to talk yourself through it and even walk through the use of space and resources. The following questions might help:

- Will the children feel comfortable and safe?
- Are the children arranged to support speaking and listening, where appropriate?
- How does the layout impact on behaviour?
- Do the children need to work as ability groups or mixed ability groups and do their places support this?
- Are the children able to access resources or do they need to be pre-prepared and set out on tables?
- Will anything need to be moved during the lesson and are the children used to safely moving equipment or furniture?
- Will the children need to move and how can this best be organised?
- How will adults in the room be deployed and where do they need to be positioned?
- Are all children able to see any demonstrations, board notes or focal points?

Display

Displays are a significant element of the learning environment. They can make the space vibrant and interesting; they can inform, support, stimulate and celebrate. Although teachers are no longer responsible for actually putting up displays, they need to have a vision for the learning environment and to be very clear about the intended audience and impact of each display. Table 6.1 provides some possible purposes and audiences together with some associated tips.

Drake (2009) identifies some key points for good practice in display in the foundation stage. These points, we would suggest, are transferable to any key stage. She suggests that displays should have an objective and be planned, that they should celebrate individuality and respect development, and that they motivate children, inform parents/carers and make creative use of space and resources.

Use of resources

Using the interactive board and visualiser to support learning

Most classrooms now have an interactive whiteboard which can be invaluable when setting up lessons in advance with imaginative resources. Presentation programs can be used to set up flip charts to help structure the lesson with key questions, images and prompts. This can be very supportive for the teacher and enables the lesson to flow smoothly without the need for the teacher to constantly refer to their lesson plan. These resources will be interactive and directly involve the children in using the board. It is important to stress this interactivity as a means of implicitly using ICT to further learning. Ensuring this interactive approach in delivering key learning points really helps to

Table 6.1 Guidance on display

Purpose	Audience	Tips
As a stimulus to inspire, intrigue, engage and/or inform the children about a topic being introduced, e.g. a display of objects associated with a story or a display of scenes from the Second World War.	This is likely to be a classroom display associated with a new theme and the main audience is the children.	This type of display often needs a flat, horizontal space to accompany it on which artefacts and books can be placed. Add questions to engage the children and create a space where they can pose their own questions. Make the display interactive with things to do, e.g. wires to connect, flaps to lift, pictures to link to words. This display can grow as the theme develops so plan spaces where the children can add resources they have found and their own work.
To provide support for learning, e.g. a display of adventurous vocabulary and phrases for story writing.	The audience is the children while writing but this type of display can be used as a teaching aid to refer to during lesson introductions and plenaries.	These displays are often semi-permanent so find ways to preserve them, e.g. by using good-quality paper and by laminating them. Refresh the display by changing the backdrop and some of the features every so often. Leave space where the children can contribute their own ideas and learning.
To allow for specific feedback on lessons, e.g. a talking wall where the children can put Post-its explaining issues they have had with a particular aspect of learning.	The audience is usually the teacher and/or LSA but the children need to be aware anyone can read their notes so confidential notes about sensitive issues need to go elsewhere – perhaps in a sealed box with a slot for posting.	The backdrop for feedback displays needs to be at child height and a supply of Post-its needs to be kept nearby. The teacher needs to ensure they respond either by picking up on common issues in lessons or by approaching individuals.
To celebrate achievements, e.g. a display showing different elements of learning related to a theme such as art, writing and photographs of a drama lesson about the rainforest or different children's responses to the same piece of learning, e.g. paintings of the rainforest.	The audience is the whole class and parents. If outside the classroom other pupils can enjoy and learn from the display.	Try to ensure all children have their work displayed at some time during the term. Add labels to show the skills that have been addressed through this learning. The children are also always pleased if someone from the senior leadership team adds a comment to respond to the display.
To reinforce the learning process, e.g. a display showing the whole process of a design and technology project from research notes and first designs through to finished products and evaluations.	The children in the class and visitors to the school.	Involve the children in putting this display together – it does not have to be neat and beautifully arranged as it is a record of the emerging learning.
To model effective learning, e.g. a display of question starters.	The children in the class.	See the section on questioning.

weave together both children and the teacher through the teaching process and will lead to greater understanding for the children. Be wary of simply providing children with a 'cinema show' that they only end up watching as it will result in less effective learning for all pupils. Also, writing on an interactive whiteboard can take some practice for adults and children alike, so take time to familiarise yourself with it well before you intend to begin using it in your lessons. However, the facility to save all your board notes for future reference is helpful in reminding the children of the learning journey, even across days, weeks or longer.

Many classrooms also have a visualiser which is an excellent resource for instant classroom feedback as it instantly projects images from books or 3D objects such as a Petri dish with salt crystals as part of a science investigation. Children's work can also be projected and this is a highly effective assessment for learning tool as positive examples can be shared with the class for the children to discuss and give feedback and, if sensitively handled, offer suggestions for improvement. With the appropriate software, visualiser pages can also be written on and saved for future reference (e-learning is discussed more fully in Chapter 12).

It can also be useful to have access to a normal whiteboard for quick notes and for information that needs to remain visible throughout the lesson or, alternatively, this can be done on a large piece of paper.

Physical resources

Every classroom will have access to a range of physical resources; some will be consumables such as art materials and others non-consumables such as books or science equipment.

When planning a lesson it is important to talk to the class teacher about the availability of consumables as these can be precious commodities, some of which may have been earmarked for special projects later in the year. It can be very frustrating to plan a lesson in detail, only to find that the resources are not available and cannot be provided in time or that they are not accounted for in the budget. While students are often tempted to provide their own resources, this can be a costly affair when providing for a whole class.

It is also vital to find out about the range of equipment available and to think about the following questions:

- Are there enough pieces of equipment to carry out a class activity or will the activity need to be carried out in groups?
- Is the equipment shared by the whole school and will it need to be booked out in advance?
- Will the children be familiar with the equipment or will they need to develop the skills before undertaking any practical task?
- Are there any health and safety considerations with any of the equipment?

Using a variety of teaching materials can keep the children interested and the learning fresh. For example, visual materials can include books, DVDs, images from ICT, online blogs or short films, images from magazines and newspapers, photographs (including those taken by the children) and 3D models. This links to VAK (visual, auditory and kinaesthetic) learning which is explained in a separate section within this chapter.

Deployment of adults in the room

When planning the lesson, it is vital to consider how any adults might be deployed. LSAs (learning support assistants) will know the class and are an important classroom resource. The lesson plan should show their role in the lesson and it should be shared with them before the lesson commences. Be aware that LSAs may have specific responsibilities for certain children; the classroom teacher would be able to provide this information. It may be usual practice for the LSA to have a specific role during introductions and plenaries. For example, it could be that they are asked to sit alongside a particular group of children using a mini-whiteboard to support with explanations and check understanding or to extend thinking.

LSAs can also be very supportive in monitoring behaviour and supporting classroom routines. They can act as a barometer for the normality of the situation, for example whether a child generally works at a higher standard or whether an individual usually finds it hard to stay on task. LSAs are also often tasked with running intervention programmes and being aware of any comings and goings for such activities will be important in ensuring the smooth flow of the lesson and the continuity of learning for the children (see also Chapter 16).

As a student it is important to have an understanding of the school's policy for deploying other adults such as parents or work experience students. It is helpful to plan for these adults/students so they are clear about their role and you, as the student teacher, are aware of any safeguarding protocol. Parents are often happy to read with children or to support practical activities such as sewing or cooking. They often naturally engage the children in positive speaking and listening about a task but it is also often helpful to arm them with some key questions.

Some schools have a policy whereby parents do not work in their child's class but if this is not the case, it can be beneficial to plan to deploy parents in a group which does not include their child. Some are happy to read stories to a group or a whole class and if fathers or grandfathers can become involved in this way, it can provide an excellent role model for boys. Nowadays many schools have sessions where parents stay and play or where they engage in family learning. These sessions are rich opportunities for children to see adults as learners and to see the whole school community as a learning engaged community.

Where parents have particular experiences or cultural knowledge to share, they may be invited to talk with the children and to answer their questions. Talking to the class in advance about the kinds of questions they may have, will make for a more productive session and ensure their contributions are appropriate. Such sessions are often most effective if they are kept within reasonable time limits and involve artefacts, visual stimulus or practical activities.

Involving and engaging parents in the children's learning can really enrich and extend the experience but it is always best to discuss your intentions with your class teacher prior to inviting additional adults into the classroom (see Chapters 2 and 16).

Questioning

Teacher-led questions

A key part of planning is thinking through differentiated key questions that you want the children to be able to answer by the end of the session. Alongside this, it is crucial to plan carefully phrased questions throughout the lesson which are responsive to the children's level of understanding and help to move their thinking forward. Personalising your questions to the different ability levels in the class may mean that you need to ask carefully differentiated versions of the same question. You may want to check the understanding of a particular child and so direct a question personally but this can also be done in a less threatening way by asking all children in a particular group or the class as a whole to respond, for example, by putting a response on a mini-whiteboard. This approach encourages the children to be actively listening at all times and provides you with an effective assessment opportunity to inform your next steps.

Consider the types of questions you are using and whether there is a balance of open and closed questions. It can be threatening to children if it they feel that there is only one correct answer and they don't know it. Questions phrased to suggest that there are many answers such as 'How many different words/numbers can you think of that ...' or 'What words could you use to describe ...', 'what materials could _____ be made of ...' etc. enable all children to respond at their own level.

When asking any questions, particularly if addressing one particular child, remember to always give an appropriate amount of thinking time before expecting an answer. If a child is unable to respond within that time, try rephrasing the question and telling them that you'll come back to them in a couple of minutes for an answer.

CRITICAL ISSUES

Shirley Clarke (2008) suggests that teachers' responses to questions are vital in terms of building pupil confidence. She also suggests that it is not appropriate to leave pupils with misconceptions and so proposes responding to children as if they were adults in a staff meeting.

Read Shirley Clarke's views on this (see Further Reading at the end of the chapter) and consider:

- How might framing answers as if in response to adults make a difference to the classroom climate, the willingness of children to contribute and the modelling of appropriate communications?
- What are the challenges in speaking to children as if they are adults?

Child-led questions

Encouraging children to think of and ask their own questions is invaluable for many reasons. It requires them to organise and think through their own thoughts, can demonstrate their level of understanding, provides opportunity to practise and develop their questioning skills and can give them ownership of the direction of their learning.

Although young children often have a natural instinct to ask 'why?' it is usually necessary to explicitly teach a wider range of questioning skills appropriate for the school context. This is often best achieved through modelling and structuring. It can be useful to have a display on your wall with question starters, e.g. What, Why, Where, When, Who, How, If ... then ..., Should, Could. The teacher can then model questions with a particular starter which the children can practise themselves. It can also be used as a means of differentiation by expecting more able children to use the more challenging question starters of 'If', 'Should', 'How', 'Could', 'Is', 'Has', etc. These question starters require the children to hypothesise and to develop their own ideas of what the answers might be.

Opportunities for the children to ask their own questions may arise from the use of talk partners, hot-seating a character or at the start of a new area of learning. Using children's questions at the start of a new topic can be particularly effective as they can direct learning by demonstrating what the children want to find out and can also be recorded and revisited as their learning progresses to assess what they have learnt.

Asking children to pose questions on a picture related to a new area of learning can also be an effective way of engaging them, for example asking questions around an illustration from 'The Lady of Shallot' before then starting to read the poem. Questions arising might range from 'Who is the lady and why is she in a boat?' to 'Is the lady in the boat escaping from something?' 'If she is escaping, what is she escaping from?' This allows children to be actively involved at all levels, fires up their imagination and leaves them keen to find out if their initial thoughts and ideas are along the right lines.

Finally, children asking the class teacher questions provides an excellent opportunity to model and praise the process rather than the end product. We want children always to contribute their thoughts and answers in lessons without a fear of 'getting it wrong' or that there is only one correct answer. As a trainee teacher, if you are ever asked a learning-related question that you do not know the answer to immediately, be honest with children. A useful phrase to use at this point could be. 'What a good question, I don't think I know the answer to that one but I know how to find it out.' This provides an excellent platform upon which to model how we wish our children to approach difficult questions, valuing the process of seeking an answer as well as reinforcing the children's perspective of you both as their teacher as well as a learner yourself.

Creativity

Although a teacher's creativity may be seen as a natural attribute, it can also be developed as a skill. This can be linked to flexibility and adaptability and to encompass 'thinking on your feet' which teachers often develop with experience. These include the moments when, for example, there is a power cut and your beautifully prepared interactive flip chart cannot be accessed. Coming up with a plan B while thirty expectant children look on can be daunting but one way forward can be to involve the class in thinking of creative solutions. Children will often respond positively to such a challenge and, again, it models the teacher as a learner, open to new ideas.

Children can also respond very well to creative spontaneity where an opportunity is spotted by the teacher and the moment seized. This is highly effective with moments of awe and wonder such as a sudden storm or snowfall. Here the confidence to be spontaneous is based on the relationship with the class and class teacher. It would be important to ensure such a diversion does not throw the rest of the week's learning off schedule. One of the safest and most effective forms of spontaneity is simply taking the learning outside. This provides a new dimension and helps the children to engage positively with their environment. There is more space and often children can feel happier and more relaxed outside. As a teacher you may also feel less constrained by concerns about noise disturbing other classes. However, it is important to acknowledge that being outside can bring some additional challenges. Wind and traffic noise can make it harder to gain the children's attention and fewer physical boundaries can make it harder to gather the children together. This can be overcome by telling the children they are responsible for being able to see and hear you at all times and to come together at a prearranged signal.

But creativity can also be fostered by seeking out and trialling innovative ideas. Teachers often look forward to the input of a student or a newly qualified teacher to bring fresh ideas to the school and will be keen to offer support. Innovative practice can fall flat if the children do not have the necessary 'learning to learn' skills to support the activity. For example, bringing role play into a lesson when the children have no experience can result in them feeling uncomfortable and behaviour deteriorating. Consider the skills the children will need in order to make the pedagogy successful and ask about their prior experiences. It is also wise to try some bite-size activities before basing a whole lesson on practice that may not be successful. For example, if using drama as a basis for writing, try some five-minute drama activities each day until you are confident the children will buy into your planned activity.

Time management

When carrying out teaching practices, some students find time management a challenge. Here are some check points for consideration:

- What might your timetable look like and what non-contact time will you have for preparation and marking? Can this be negotiated?
- Are you able to vary the type of outcomes and feedback so marking is balanced with verbal responses and peer evaluation?
- When might it be appropriate to engage children in self-assessment or self-marking, for example checking their own calculations with a calculator?
- How can children be engaged in classroom routines and tasks such as setting out resources?
- Are daily activities paced so the children are challenged but demands on your and their energy levels are reasonable?
- Are types of lessons timed to allow for appropriate setting up and clearing away?

Children often sense when a teacher is not managing time well and the sense of anxiety can be transferred from teacher to children. When there is more to do than will possibly fit in the time, the teacher must prioritise. We have always found it helpful to consider the following when prioritising:

- What must be done to ensure pupil safety?
- What must be done to follow school policies and procedures?
- What will make the most difference to pupil learning?

When there just is not enough time to do everything, a set of beautifully marked books may not have as much impact on learning as picking out some key issues to feed back to the class and then spending the time on a really well prepared lesson for the next day.

Some teacher tasks are very time-consuming and they may have value but it can be helpful to consider the task as an equation: the amount of effort and time required against the value added to pupil learning. If the answer is lots of effort and time resulting in major impact then the task may be worth undertaking. But if it is lots of time and effort for little impact then the task may not be so valuable. Of course, as a student, you may not have the luxury of making such decisions and there may be national or school policies which override your views. But using this mental check for time management has served us well over the years and resulted in more effective practice. Certainly it can be argued that teachers who manage their time well in and out of school while maintaining a healthy work/life balance can be fresher and more creative in their role than someone who devotes every spare moment to work with some tasks having little impact on the core purpose of classroom learning.

Summary

The most effective teachers model lifelong learning:

- They continuously reflect on their practice and hone their own skills as part of a classroom learning community.
- They talk explicitly to other professionals and to their pupils about the development of skills, some of which are organisational and related to lesson structure, environment and resources and others which are personal and interpersonal and related to human interactions and qualities such as creativity.
- They open and strengthen channels of communication for feedback on the impact of their skills.

Issues for reflection

- On the next visit to your school, reflect upon the relationships the class teacher has with their children, parents and other staff. How does the teacher gain their respect, confidence and trust? What is their body language like during lessons or with others around the school? How do others respond to the class teacher?
- When observing lessons, specifically focus on the structure of the lesson, how it begins, develops and ends – what is the teacher doing at each of these given points within the lesson? Do all lessons start the same?
- Discuss the classroom skills the class teacher thinks are most important with the particular class you will be teaching.
- Look at the use of a class teacher's time throughout the school day. What, if any, implications might your findings have for your own professional practice?
- You might find it helpful to reflect upon what requires the most time, how the class teacher manages time and how they react creatively when a change needs to be made.
- Undertake lesson observations specifically focused upon questioning. Try to note down the different types of questions the class teacher uses by example, noting the children's responses for later reference.

Further reading

Clarke, S. (2008) *Active Learning Through Formative Assessment.* London: Hodder Education. This is a very readable and practical book which provides advice on how to engage children as active learners. It covers broad issues such as creating an ideal culture but also discusses specific issues related to lesson planning.

Dean, J. (2009) *Organising Learning in the Primary School Classroom,* 4th edition. London: Routledge. This book has a chapter about developing the role of assistants (ch. 4, pp. 35–44) which contains practical advice on assistant deployment.

DfES (2005) *Excellence and Enjoyment: Social and Emotional Aspects of Learning: Guidance.* London: DfES. This series of documents provide a comprehensive curriculum for social and emotional aspects of learning. We think the teacher's resources are easy to use or adapt and can be effective learning tools.

Kyriacou, C. (2009) *Effective Teaching in Schools: Theory and Practice,* 3rd edition. Cheltenham: Nelson Thornes. This book considers the importance of developing good relationships between teachers and pupils and discusses the balance between respect and rapport (ch. 7, pp. 101–19).

CHAPTER 7

THE UNIQUE CHILD: APPROACHES TO DIVERSITY AND INCLUSION

Melanie Foster, Graham Handscomb and Elizabeth Cornish

Chapter overview

As a teacher you are there for every child in your class. This can be quite daunting! Personalising the educational experience for each child is challenging, particularly when some will have specific special educational needs. In this chapter the authors explore the issue of inclusion, provide practical guidance and demonstrate how inclusion is everyone's business.

So you want to enter the teaching profession? What an exciting career! It is one which will allow you to explore your own creativity and inspire a new generation to believe in their own self-worth. And yet, what challenge in taking such a responsibility. For the most part young people only have one chance in education and the relationship they hold with you as a teacher will influence their view of themselves and their ability to learn and can impact on their aspirations for their future. You play a great part in shaping their career path and their whole outlook on life.

If there is one key message that we wish to be taken from this chapter it would be for you to continue to challenge yourself throughout your career by asking 'are your expectations of *every* child in your class high enough?' We all progress at different rates, have our own learning styles and can *all* achieve when teachers have a clear understanding of what we really can do. As a teacher it is best if you establish a baseline (that is where the child is starting from) and then work out meaningful next steps in children's learning. You will, in your career, teach children who have barriers which inhibit their learning, whether these be social, emotional or educational. Never be influenced by first impressions. All children can learn, but you may need to challenge your own views and really go out of your way to understand a child's strengths and needs in order to plan an effective and meaningful education – a necessity and right for every child!

Beginning to understand how a child with social, emotional or learning difficulties feels and sees the world will be a lifelong learning experience for you. The more you learn the more you will realise that there is always more to learn. However, never despair! Taking the time to understand individual needs is a great step forward and will support you in becoming an outstanding teacher for *all* children.

What is inclusion?

This chapter is about the need for all teachers to gain an understanding of and take responsibility for inclusion. So what do we mean by the term inclusion? Well, there are lots of definitions. Some of these focus on the important dimension of facilitating the learning of children with special educational needs: 'For many people inclusion in education is thought of only as an approach to serving children with disabilities within general education settings' (Ainscow et al., 2006, p. 2). This is a key feature certainly, which we shall address in this chapter, but is not the whole picture.

For others inclusion is an even broader concept dealing with fundamental issues about the value of human beings and the rights of the individual (UNESCO, 2000). So within this wider perspective the aim of inclusion is significantly expanded: it is 'to reduce exclusion and discriminatory attitudes, including those in relation to age, social class, ethnicity, religions, gender and attainment, (Ainscow et al., 2006, p. 2). For you as a teacher, it goes to the heart, or the core moral purpose, of your teaching and your role as an educator. It is about adopting an outlook which regards each child as being unique and an individual, and understanding the implications of this. These include recognising that all of these individuals have their own set of learning and emotional needs.

This poses the considerable challenge of how can you serve these often diverse needs in classes of 30 or more? The fundamental imperative of inclusion for you and your colleagues is: 'How can schools ensure they are meeting the needs of all their children?' (Ekins and Grimes, 2008, p. 9). As you set out on your teaching career this can be seen as a daunting and forbidding task, but do not be dismayed! The purpose of this chapter is to show that this is not only entirely manageable but also that making inclusion your business is actually what makes teaching such a fulfilling and rewarding profession.

Chapter overview

We begin with our exploration of inclusion thinking and practice by first emphasising that you are there for all the children in your class; this means ensuring learning is personalised for each child. Then we will address some of the specific challenges posed by children with special educational needs. This will involve looking at the SEN Code of Practice guidance, followed by examining in some depth four specific examples of SEN and practical strategies for how you can meet these needs. We will then explore the very rich dimension of teaching children from minority ethnic groups who may be learning English as a second or third language.

In all this you are not alone and so we will look at processes and mechanisms that are likely to be in place in your school to support you with this aspect of your work. This includes the role of the Special Educational Needs Coordinator (SENCo) and adults who support you in the classroom. Finally we conclude by showing how inclusion and school success and improvement go hand in hand. We emphasise above all that good inclusion practice is dependent on establishing a whole culture that recognises and values diversity.

Personalisation of learning

Personalised learning is high on the educational agenda. The personalisation of learning recognises that pupils have different 'starting points' in terms of early promise, interest, aptitude and ability. It is now accepted that, in order for children to make progress, it is vital to set challenging personal objectives in addition to following a group lesson objective. We can use the analogy of a journey made from different points of origin and taking different routes but arriving at the destination with shared knowledge, skills and experience.

This learning concept applies to all pupils, including those with defined barriers to learning or special educational needs. In fact this way of approaching lessons allows individuals to understand and appreciate that each fellow learner is different and will learn differently, without particular children feeling embarrassed or stigmatised about receiving additional support.

This means that each pupil's 'pathway' through a lesson, the tasks set for them or the tasks they choose, the style in which they learn, the form of expressing understanding and the form of assessment applied may be different according to the needs of that pupil. There are huge implications for planning and delivery for the teacher; it is a major steer away from the lecture style 'one-size-fits-all' lesson towards the creation of an offer of a wide range of learning opportunities in which the learner is an active partner. The crucial issue is to foster an environment in which the focus is on learners and their individual needs: 'When classrooms create a thoughtful and learner-centred climate, achievement is high' (Watkins, 2010, p. 6).

Special educational needs

The 2001 SEN Code of Practice (DfES, 2001a) sets out guidance on policies and procedures which aim at supporting pupils with special educational needs to reach their full potential within their school community (developing skills to support a successful transition into adult life). For many children who have additional emotional, social or learning needs their education will be met by you within a mainstream environment. The SEN Code of Practice recommends that schools adopt a graduated approach. This includes support described as 'School Action' and 'School Action Plus' so that where necessary you should receive specialist support to enable a child to make meaningful progress.

It also provides advice on carrying out a statutory assessment of a child's SEN and of making and maintaining a statement of SEN for children with severe and complex needs, and carrying out annual reviews of statements and planning for young people with SEN to make the transition to college, training and employment. The Code emphasises the importance of involving children and parents in decision-making and of effective multi-agency working to combine services around the needs of the child and their families.

True inclusive educational practice, where you as a teacher can provide evidence of progress for every child in your class, can only happen by recognising each of your children as a person first, with their individual interests and needs. We cannot go into great detail about the rich variety of needs you will meet in your teaching career, but we have tried to provide a taster from a child's perspective to support early identification.

In the following sections we will cover four specific areas of special educational needs that you are likely to encounter: dyspraxia, autism, dyslexia, and children with speech and language difficulties.

Dyspraxia

As a person who had a real sense of dread in PE lessons, Melanie, one of the authors, has a personal empathy with those who find motor coordination activities a real challenge. We very much believe that it is important for you as a teacher to be equipped in the early stage of your career to meet the needs of such children. You will at some time have young people in your classroom with motor coordination and perceptual difficulties, often referred to as dyspraxia.

What is dyspraxia?

Dyspraxia is often referred to as the 'hidden handicap'. While a child in your class may be perceived as having 'normal intelligence', they may experience difficulties with physical activities, legible handwriting, organisation in the classroom and/or visual processing of information in relation to reading and numeracy. Poor coordination can impact on eating and dressing skills. Children in your class may be seen as messy eaters or present with an untidy attire. Many will be aware of their needs and see themselves as different which in return results in low self-esteem and low self-confidence. This can have a profound effect on their ability to succeed in school, and you as their teacher, have a real part to play in identifying, planning and meeting their needs. Always remember, however, you are not on your own. There should be systems in your school that will support you.

Alerting behaviours

It is important to recognise that every child is an individual and will develop their skills as they progress through primary school. However, as a beginning teacher, the following indicators, although not a comprehensive list, may help you recognise a child displaying needs which can then be further investigated:

- difficulty in judging spaces accurately and poor spatial organisation – this may result in a child bumping into objects or even missing their chair when attempting to sit down
- difficulties in PE activities relating to hopping, jumping, balancing and ball skills
- anxiety in the playground or on apparatus
- difficulties with threading, manipulating Lego bricks or poor drawing
- inability to coordinate dressing and undressing
- poor written content even though through discussion you know the child has a good knowledge of the subject matter
- poor handwriting with many reversals and poorly formed letters
- frustration when several things happen at once
- children with verbal dyspraxia may know the names of their letters but experience difficulty in sequencing them or forming words
- poor organisational skills.

What can you do in the classroom?

We would not give you, nor suggest there are, prescriptive strategies to meet the needs of a child with dyspraxia. Indeed, our first suggestion would be for you to speak to your SENCo and ask for an observation checklist to help you gain a better understanding of the child's motor skills, reading ability and manual dexterity. However, the following classroom modifications may support you:

- use story boards to help structure writing
- encourage the child to use a pencil grip to help develop handwriting skills
- introduce cursive writing as soon as possible. This will help the spacing of letters and words
- use coloured lines when creating grids or shaded squares as a tool to encourage the child to leave spaces between letters and words. Children with dyspraxia can be sensitive to colour contrast. Pale colour contrast is less sensitive to the eyes and can help a child focus and make progress

- vary your teaching approaches. A child with dyspraxia benefits through demonstration and hands-on activities
- support the child with organising their work, breaking instructions down into small steps
- during any art activities, give the child a photograph rather than asking them to copy a 3D image
- provide guidance about spatial concepts, e.g. top, bottom, inside, front, left, right. Many children may have a poor sense of position of space yet their understanding of spatial concepts is good.

Autism

What is autism?

Autism isn't something a person has, or a 'shell' that a person is trapped inside … autism is a way of being. It is pervasive. It colours every experience, sensation, perception, thought, emotion and encounter, every aspect of existence. It is not possible to separate the autism from the person – and if it were possible, the person you would have left would not be the same person you started with (Sinclair, 1993). Children in your class may see a child with such social and communication needs as being 'odd' or different. In addition, such complex needs can sometimes be interpreted by some staff as a behaviour issue. To really plan and teach effectively, it is important to recognise these needs and understand them from a child's perspective. Do not assume you understand their view of the world.

Alerting behaviours

Children on the autistic spectrum are seen to display a range of needs focusing on difficulties with social communication, social understanding, flexible thinking and social imagination. A child with autism in your class may:

- have difficulty in understanding social behaviour which impacts on interaction with children and adults both within the class and playground
- focus on irrelevant features
- have a fear or anxiety over something other children in your class accept as 'normal'
- show excessive focus on details with limited ability to prioritise
- have difficulty in understanding rules and have limited awareness of what is socially acceptable
- develop routines and rituals
- have good language skills but have problems with the give-and-take nature of conversations, may repeat what is said to them or talk incessantly on a topic of their own interest
- understand what other people say to them but may prefer symbols, pictures and signs
- not speak or have fairly limited speech

- have difficulty in switching focus from one activity to another
- have difficulty in understanding that other people have a different point of view
- display concrete thinking and have difficulty in combining ideas
- have difficulty in developing play skills with others.

What can you do in the classroom?

- Provide structure and task-orientated programmes, both academic and social
- Be very visual
- Sign and zone the classroom
- Create low arousal work areas
- Establish visual routines for personal space
- Make use of social stories.

Social stories are a highly effective teaching tool and will support you in teaching social skills to children with autism and related disabilities. They provide children with accurate information about those situations that she/he may find difficult or confusing such as lining up for assembly, playtime activities, running down the corridor. They focus on important social cues and actions and reactions that might be expected to occur and why. The goal of the story is to increase the child's understanding of what they are expected to do in a situation, what to say and to make them more comfortable. An adult will work with the child to build up a framework of expected behaviour and outcomes. Each phrase can be accompanied by photos or pictures of the child in the situation.

A sample social story
Situation: lining up

- At school, we sometimes line up.
- We line up to go to the assembly, to go out to play and to go to lunch.
- Sometimes my friends and I get excited when we line up because we're going someplace fun, like out to the playground.
- It is okay to get excited, but it is important to try to walk to the line. Running can cause accidents and my friends or I could get hurt.
- I will try to walk to the line.

CRITICAL ISSUES

We are not born to suffer. We are born to thrive. If you live in a dry area and your garden receives little water, you plant plants which like dry soil. But when you are given a plant that likes wet soil, you don't kill it, you water it, you spend one of your 1,440 minutes each day watering that plant. Because you know that, given the right care, that little bit of effort can produce spectacular blooms. And so it should be with children like us. (*Joshua Muggleton*, age 17)

This was said in the context of bullying being experienced by this young person when he was at primary school several years ago. How would you go about using Joshua's experience to tackle attitudes to difference within the group of children in your class? Drawing on the reading in this chapter what arguments would you use to help develop the understanding of a colleague who sees inclusion as just being the concern of the SENCo?

Dyslexia

What is dyslexia?

For children with dyslexia, there is often a discrepancy or mismatch between reading, writing, spelling and/or numeracy difficulties and their general level of ability and achievement. Such children may be highly articulate or achieve a high standard in some areas of their learning, but their reading ability may be below their chronological age. Again children who experience such difficulties often know they are different from their peers. This in turn can lead to low self-esteem and behaviour can suffer as a result. Children can be great actors and will take on another role to hide what they see as their disability.

Alerting behaviours

- Difficulty in remembering a list of instructions
- Problems getting thoughts together coherently for story or essay writing
- Sequencing problems so may need to be taught strategies to cope or find alternative ways of remembering
- Difficulty in organising work
- Answering questions orally but unable to write the answers down
- Limited written work (pupils find that the less they write, the less trouble they get into for making mistakes)
- Very poor handwriting
- Difficulty in copying accurately
- Spelling the same word several different ways
- Visual memory difficulties.

What can you do in the classroom?

There are a range of things you might do but remember no single one will result in a magic solution. These strategies are often most effective when used in combination and in relation to each other. Remember of course the most important factor, that any strategies used depend crucially on your knowledge of the children and the quality of relationship you secure with them. Given these caveats, useful strategies include the following:

- build trust
- use a specifically targeted programme for developing literacy skills including:

  - a multi-sensory approach
  - use of word families
  - carefully taught phonics and blends
  - lots of repetition and over-learning.

Speech and language difficulties

Although not addressing this in detail, we did want to highlight the areas of speech and language difficulties as they can affect children's social, emotional and educational development. Research studies suggest 5–7 per cent of our children could experience such difficulties in understanding or using speech and language, meaning one or two such individuals may be in your class.

What are speech and language difficulties?

There is an array of terminology associated with speech and language difficulties and within your teaching career there may be children in your class identified with:

- specific language impairments
- speech and language delay
- speech and language disorder
- speech, language and communication needs.

In addition, it is important to know that such difficulties can be associated with a broad range of disabilities including hearing impairment, cognitive/learning disabilities, physical disabilities such as cerebral palsy and young people on the autistic spectrum.

Alerting indicators

Even for experienced class teachers it can be difficult to identify a child with speech and language needs. Specific speech problems resulting in poor intelligibility where a child may substitute one sound for another or have problems with clustering sounds may be easy to identify. There are, however, many children who have learned to be adept at an early age in using visual and contextual cues to support their understanding. It is not until curriculum demands increase that the fragility of their language skills are evidenced through poor educational progress, sometimes accompanied by poor behaviour. As a teacher you may be alerted through your child having difficulty with:

- attention
- following instructions
- expressive language difficulties
- social use of language and how they interact with friends
- poor use of eye contact in conversations
- difficulty in understanding and interpreting gesture and facial expressions and tone of voice.

What can you do in the classroom?

Your SENCo may provide you with specific checklists to help you identify specific problems. However, the following suggestions detail general good teaching strategies that you as a class teacher may use to support children with speech and language needs:

- ensure you have the child's attention before you start talking or giving him/her an instruction. Saying 'everybody' may not necessarily get your child to focus
- where possible, give the child a warning of what may be happening next, e.g. 'In five minutes we will be finishing our writing and going to assembly
- summarise key points and support with visual information
- teach the child to be alert to key phrases and explain what they mean and what you expect from the child when they are said
- check the child has understood key messages before moving onto the next point
- be aware of particular times of the day that cause difficulties. Remember, good planning by you as their teacher is often a key to a child's success.

Supporting children from minority ethnic groups

School context

It is a very positive aspect of group learning that some learners will come from minority ethnic groups and perhaps be learning English as a second or third language. The 'rich mix' of different languages and cultures is cause for acknowledgement and celebration. However, this aspect of inclusion can be a sensitive area and can initially feel overwhelming. As with all aspects of inclusion a lot depends on your school's strengths and experience in the particular area of provision. Some schools will have a truly multicultural ethos with systems in place to support you being effective. Others will be less familiar with receiving students with English as an Additional Language (EAL) and will be developing effective procedures. Your school should be mindful of the national statistics relating to the attainment of minority ethnic groups and the importance of monitoring key groups against their counterparts. The important action for you is to ensure you know the particular profile of your school in relation to minority achievement and then to look at the make-up of your group in order to plan inclusively for different languages, cultures and religions.

The provision and strategies for learners with EAL should be considered separately to special educational needs provision. There is a fundamental difference between these needs and they require a very different approach. It would be a mistake to expect the same rate of progress from a learner with EAL as a learner with SEN; if a learner has not been identified with SEN, progress should be rapid. Of course this does not mean that you should not be on the lookout for additional needs; if an EAL learner does not move from step to step at the expected rate the influencing factors need to be examined.

Assessment

It is vital to complete a full assessment of pupils with English as an Additional Language. You would not be expected to complete this assessment yourself. The likelihood is that there will be a designated EAL coordinator in your school who will probably tap into an additional EAL service for specific expertise. It is likely that a 'beginner' learner in English might be assessed in their first language or 'mother tongue' to ascertain their educational background and their likely rate of progression in English. Students who have recently arrived from overseas will have had very different experiences. There is a possibility that schooling may have been interrupted or of a very different nature. There is also a possibility that they may have experienced a traumatic or at least unsettled time if their family are asylum seekers or refugees. However, this should not be assumed some children will have had a thorough education in their first language and some exposure to the English language and British culture. Again, do your research – never assume.

Ideally you will receive a copy of the full assessment which, in addition to information about language proficiency and a learning profile, should contain details of the learner's history and feelings about the recent changes in their lives. As with every learner best practice would be to focus on strengths and key interests so that learning has a positive flavour from the beginning. 'New arrivals' should all benefit from a short induction programme to help them adjust and orientate themselves around their new school. The involvement of other children in this process will make it much more effective whether it results from a formal 'buddying' system or enriched opportunities to socialise and learn together.

It is important to note that the levels used to describe the degree to which learners are able to 'function' in English are different to SEN stages. There is an 'extended scale' for speaking and listening strands which come before Level 2 of the national curriculum levels for English. 'Beginner' English speakers are assessed in listening and speaking skills and given a descriptor as follows: Step 1, Step 2, Level 1 Threshold, Level 1 Secure and then Level 2 onwards of the standard National Curriculum descriptors in speaking and listening.

For a full description of assessment levels and strategies it is very useful to refer to *A Language in Common: Assessing English as an Additional Language* (QCDA, 2000).

School inclusion policy and practice

We recognise that teaching, although exciting, is hard, but an optimistic teacher can bring so much hope to young children. You will have difficulty planning specific interventions for some young people and specialist teachers, and may indeed require specialist training.

The next part of this chapter discusses a general overview of systems that may be found in a school. You are part of a team. However, as a non-specialist class teacher, it is essential that you take responsibility for identifying those children who may require additional or specialist support. Your optimism in seeing all children flourish is vital. Do not give up at the first hurdle and seek out the SENCo to ask for support. They are there to support, but you are there to inspire and support the learning of all pupils in your class.

Familiarise yourself with the processes and mechanisms at your school. You can do this by asking the following questions.

What are the expectations of your role in terms of inclusion?

You will have a twofold responsibility in terms of inclusion. First, there is a duty to uphold and positively reinforce the values of the school's inclusion policy. This means becoming familiar with the policy and keeping current with changes and being able to communicate the principles of the policy to other stakeholders in an appropriate way.

Second, you will be expected to enact the values and objectives of the policy through your teaching. This means that one of your main aims will be to be aware of the needs of the learners in your class and to plan and deliver creatively so that they can be included in every learning experience and opportunity. This is a tough call and an issue which is high on the national education agenda as well as at your school. You will not be on your own with this one: school leaders have a responsibility to ensure you receive the right level of support and training to enable you to work inclusively. You should also receive guidance and support from key school personnel who will also link with other professionals.

The most important action point for you is to prepare by knowing how, when and from whom to gain the pertinent information about inclusion priorities at your school and the school policies set in place to address established and changing needs.

What is the SENCo's role/what are the SENCo's responsibilities?

Each school has to have a defined role the holder of which oversees additional provision; their title may vary from school to school but the most common term is Special Educational Needs Coordinator (SENCo) or Inclusion Manager. Their key responsibilities in school are:

- putting in place a graduated response system to meet children's needs at the earliest opportunity
- ensuring liaison between parents and carers
- working with other agencies, including the educational psychology service, medical and social services and voluntary bodies

- advising other staff about SEN and having a school policy for dealing with SEN children
- most importantly, having in place a mechanism to ensure those pupils identified with SEN make progress.

So you can see this role is a pivotal one. However, beyond the key responsibilities listed above, their role in whole-school inclusion in its widest sense may differ from school to school. Your school may have other key workers who contribute to aspects of inclusion such as behaviour and attendance, ethnic minority achievement, English as an Additional Language and SEAL. So it is very important to be clear about the following issue of key people to contact.

Who/when/where is your key point of contact? What are the lines of communication?

Each school will have its own system for ensuring you are equipped with the necessary information with which to plan fully inclusive lessons for your children. As a class teacher, you may meet with the SENCo (or other key personnel) to exchange concerns and receive updates and guidance. Other effective systems involve publishing regular bulletins about inclusion issues, keeping an up-to-date 'provision map' and ensuring inclusion issues are on the agenda at regular staff meetings.

How is provision organised and administered?

Be aware of the particular ways in which your school creates a programme to accurately match the child's needs with appropriate interventions – the organisation of provision varies from school to school. The national drive towards personalisation is helpful in that it should be common practice to explore the nature of educational provision planned for each learner. In the past problems have arisen for pupils who were withdrawn from lessons as a matter of course because of an identified additional need without there being a sound rationale for that withdrawal from the main group, or indeed for reintegration. It is now seen that children might follow different pathways through a lesson or even the school day in order to achieve positive learning outcomes. The big difference is that this is a planned pathway with a specific goal in sight rather than an ad hoc withdrawal.

Provision management is a strategic tool which gives an overview of all provision that is being made which is 'additional to' and 'different from' a school's differentiated curriculum offer. As well as mapping all provision, schools should be able to set expected progress outcomes for all SEN/LDD (Learning difficulties and disabilities) provision and track the progress made by individual pupils and groups of pupils. As a class teacher this will support you in evaluating the effectiveness of the provision for children and young people with SEN/LDD and where necessary take action to improve it.

Working with other professionals

Your school SENCo or inclusion manager will hold the main responsibility for coordinating multi-agency provision by external providers. However, you will still have an important role to play in providing accurate and up-to-date records/observations which will serve to support the formative work between the child and the professional. Once qualified you would naturally be included, in person or through documentation, in professionals', meetings discussing the strengths, needs and planned way forward for the child in your class. The partnership with the professional and the school works both ways; you might be a major contributor to their assessment and formative work but you should also expect to receive incredibly useful help with developing strategies to support your planning and the child's learning.

Who might these professionals be?

Just as the breadth of children's needs is extensive, so are the range of services, agencies and individuals that might work with the school. There are many colleagues that may work in partnership with the school but key players in the SEN field, who you may at some time work with, include the educational psychologist and the speech and language therapist.

What are protocols for professional working?

The SENCo or inclusion manager would have the responsibility for making and maintaining links with appropriate professional and voluntary services; they would also be responsible for making referrals and arranging assessments. So it is very important not to bypass the established protocols or key personnel because they hold the overview of provision for the school and will need to rationalise how resources are allocated and monitored. This key person will also be well informed about how to handle sensitive information and when and how to update/engage parents and carers. We cannot stress enough the importance of sensitive communication with parents and carers. They are your most influential partners in ensuring success for a child. If you are unsure what to say, speak to your SENCo who should provide guidance.

Planning for inclusion

The following gives some basic guidance when planning for inclusion (see also Chapter 11 on planning in general). It is important to start with a close look at your group/class profile, noting particular highlighted pupils with defined needs. Best practice would be to talk through the available data with the SENCo and/or the previous class teacher; in this way you can gather important background information about individuals and the make-up of the group. All teachers become familiar with the group dynamics eventually but this is a good opportunity for you to influence these in a positive and formative way through careful planning. Small-group work, seating plans, use of space, creative pairings and use of adult support in the classroom can be more effective if background details are considered at the outset.

It is natural to focus on existing barriers to learning when considering lesson planning. However, we remind you of our key message at the beginning of the chapter – are your expectations high enough for every child in your class? Simply making the work easier is not the solution. You need to identify the key skills you wish the child to develop and work out the small steps to help them achieve. You may then need to generalise this skill in different situations. It is then that real progress will occur. Focus on the child's strengths and involve fellow classmates in helping to meet learning objectives across the group. Fostering and celebrating difference and skills will promote a wider under-standing of learning in your class: this best practice benefits all children in the group, not only those with identified additional needs.

You may find in Figure 7.1 the summary of key elements to bear in mind when planning a useful aide-memoire.

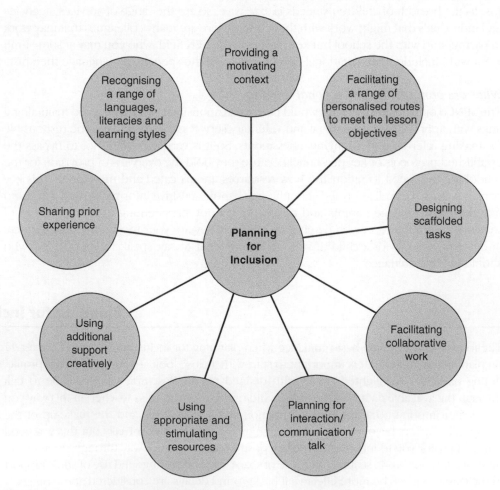

Figure 7.1 Planning for inclusion

Using additional in-class support for inclusion effectively

It is likely that, in order to provide an inclusive learning environment and to enact the strategies that have been devised to support individual and group needs, you will be working with additional adults in the classroom. For example, children with a statement of SEN may have allocated 'learning support assistant (LSA) hours' and specific objectives to work towards with their allocated LSA. Your school may well have a policy of attaching teaching assistants (TAs) to classes in order to support their learning and the school's inclusion policy in general. There may also be a wide variety of other supporting adults sanctioned to support learning such as parent-helpers, student-teachers, work experience placements, etc. (see also Chapter 16).

Additional support may come from a variety of volunteers and professionals and for a variety of different reasons but there are some general rules you can stick to in order to make the most of this support.

- Introduce your colleague to the class and present a united approach. Your children may be curious as to who the additional adult is; it is best practice to introduce your colleague to the group and not to leave them feeling unsure and like a 'spare part'. Agree details such as how you both feel your colleague should be addressed, e.g. Mr Cornish or Tim (your school may have a policy about this so do check), and explain their role briefly and in very positive terms. Avoid mentioning specific children who may well be the object of support. They could be sensitive about their need for extra help. A good example might be: 'We are very lucky that Mr Cornish is here to help us learn and to do really well in our lessons.' Make it clear that your colleague is to be given the same respect and courtesy that you expect from pupils for yourself.
- Make firm arrangements about when and where important communication will happen – this is vital in making support as seamless and effective as possible. Decision-making about the precise role of your colleague in terms of managing behaviour for learning, on-the-spot decision-making, etc. will engender a helpful clarity.
- Model good working behaviours with your colleague – children will pick up on the commitment and enthusiasm displayed between their teacher and their colleagues.
- Communicate, in advance, the learning objectives underpinning the lessons. Ideally, share as much as possible about the learning objectives and content of the lesson in advance. If your colleague has to work 'blind' this will diminish their ability to suggest/plan supportive strategies and to address the particular needs of individual learners in meeting learning objectives. Also there may be pertinent information to share about the group/an individual which will impact on the children's learning.
- Plan collaboratively. This is a vital part in making support effective. A shared understanding of the additional need of individuals and the group will shape decisions about lesson planning. It is good practice to share lesson plans in advance but best practice to actually plan collaboratively.

- Deliver creatively. Avoid your support colleague becoming a 'silent partner'. From the start plan for their active involvement in a manner appropriate to their role. An experienced LSA or TA might take a team-teaching role whereas a parent-helper might feel more comfortable reading aloud to the group or even modelling to the group. Pupils receiving additional support generally find it easier (and more enjoyable) to accept extra help from a figure who is accepted and valued by the whole group. It also avoids the 'joined at the hip' syndrome, a criticism of support which becomes too focused on one student and detracts from the learners' motivation to progress independently.

Balance of support and independence

Additional support is most effective where desired outcomes are crystal clear and where strategies have been planned in advance. It is important to consider the balance between providing extra support to a learner and nurturing independent learning skills. This should be a key aspect of consideration when planning with your colleague. A close relationship between a child and their support worker should not discourage independence and planning should involve developing strategies to encourage the students to move towards independence.

Independent learners develop the attitudes, knowledge and skills needed to make responsible decisions and take actions dealing with their own learning. Independent learning is fostered by creating the opportunities and experiences which encourage motivation, curiosity, self-confidence and self-reliance; it is based on the child understanding their own interests and valuing learning for its own sake.

In summary, teachers and colleagues providing additional support can foster independent learning by:

- using a variety of ways to gain understanding of their child's abilities, needs and interests
- making education relevant to the child's needs and interests
- teaching and modelling independent learning skills
- providing children with choice in assignments and topics within a range of choices, increasing students' responsibility for decision-making in the independent learning process
- utilising collaborative instructional techniques.

A culture of inclusion

One of the key messages of this chapter has been the importance of each individual's learning needs. You will also have understood that in achieving this you will rely upon working with others and on there being a clear commitment to inclusion within the whole school community. The one cannot be fully achieved without the other:

> It [inclusion] does not only focus on a response to individuals but on how settings, policies, cultures and structures can recognise and value difference. (Ainscow et al., 2006, p. 2)

Ekins and Grimes (2008) see this in terms of the need to take fundamental positive action by all if the prize of inclusion is to be genuinely won:

> We believe it is the duty of all teachers and schools to actively work together to identify and remove potential barriers to the participation, engagement and achievement of all students in their school setting. (p. 7)

Through their research they have fashioned a programme of 'Inclusion in Action' which 'encourages the development of joined-up thinking in schools which sees all children as complex individuals with the right to fully participate and achieve' (Ekins and Grimes, 2008, p. 7).

Where a culture of this kind flourishes it forms a fundamental part of how the school goes about examining its success and is woven into its whole approach to self-evaluation and school improvement (Ekins and Grimes, 2009). So, you will find that such commitment to inclusion pays great dividends because it helps not just those children with specific special educational needs, but also drives up standards for everyone and, most crucially, transforms relationships positively between all members of the school community.

Summary

- It is important to ask yourself, are your expectations of *every* child in your class high enough?
- You will teach children who have barriers to their learning – social, emotional and educational. Be ready to understand their strengths so you can plan a meaningful education for them.
- Inclusion relates to fundamental issues about the value of human beings and the rights of the individual. Within this context inclusion facilitates the learning of children with special educational needs.
- A commitment to inclusion aims to reduce exclusion and discriminatory attitudes.
- In your teaching you need to ensure learning is personalised for each child, recognising that pupils have different starting points and varied needs.
- It is helpful to become familiar with the SEN Code of Practice.

(Continued)

(Continued)

- It is important to become familiar with the specific educational needs you are likely to encounter and practical strategies to address them. These include dyspraxia, autism, dyslexia and speech and language difficulties.
- Children from minority ethnic backgrounds bring a diversity to be celebrated.
- Strategies for EAL need to be considered separately to SEN provision.
- You need to familiarise yourself with school inclusion policy and practice.
- The support your SENCo or inclusion manager can provide will be crucial. There will also be other specialist professionals and adults working in the classroom to provide support.
- Aim to develop an inclusion culture in your classroom ... and remember inclusion is everyone's business.

Issues for reflection

- How will you foster positive and formative relationships with parents of pupils with SEN? Think about effective ways of offering and explaining useful strategies.
- Think about how you will review your own practice on an ongoing basis. How will you know you are making a positive difference for your pupils with SEN?
- How will you keep abreast of current educational thinking? Reflect on how you will continue to learn about, and explore, developing SEN issues. Consider referring to:

    - http://www.education.gov.uk/schools/pupilsupport/SEN
    - http://www.teachingexpertise.com

- With a group of colleagues, discuss which element of planning and delivering SEN provision prompts the most questions for you personally. Explore possible next steps to improve your knowledge and expertise around the defined areas.

Further reading

Gross, J. (2008) *Beating Bureaucracy in Special Educational Needs*. London: David Fulton. This book aims to help you spend more time improving the quality of teaching and learning for pupils with SEN and disabilities rather than focusing on the paperwork that many systems can generate. It contains practical strategies that can be used within everyday teaching.

Long, R. (2007) *The Rob Long Omnibus Edition of Better Behaviour*. London: David Fulton. Long aims to improve your understanding of children's behaviour difficulties and why they arise and suggests positive ways of dealing with challenging situations. He describes good practice that can pre-empt and alleviate problems.

Lorenz, S. (2002) *Effective In-class Support: Management of Support Staff in Mainstream and Special Schools, Resource Materials for Teachers.* London: David Fulton. This publication offers guidance in a series of checklist-style bites, ideal to revisit in terms of planning and reviewing the impact of support staff. The dual approach to mainstream and special school contexts is helpful in that there are a wider range of strategies and applications to explore.

NALDIC (2010) *National Association for Language Development in the Curriculum Supporting EAL Learners*. Online at: http://www.naldic.org.uk/ITTSEAL2/teaching/Workingwithnewlyarrivedlearners.cfm. The NALDIC site is kept current through pertinent research projects and therefore never goes out of date in terms of best practice and national expectations. The site has a comprehensive menu covering multiple elements of language acquisition in a user-friendly format.

Wilmot, E. (2006) *Personalising Learning in the Primary Classroom: A Practical Guide for Teachers and School Leaders*. Bancyfelin, Carmarthen: Crown House. This is a very 'hands-on' guide which will offer you some useful practical strategies in addition to explaining the rationale behind them from a school leadership point of view and giving a clear illustration of how classroom provision contributes to whole-school policy.

CHAPTER 8

POSITIVE ETHOS: MOTIVATION AND BEHAVIOUR

Anne Cockburn and Paul Parslow-Williams

Chapter overview

Seeing things through children's eyes is very important in helping you understand their motivation and behaviour. This chapter gives clear and grounded guidance on how to achieve high expectations of children through a range of strategies. This includes the use of praise when it is genuine, specific and unqualified, and a carefully thought through approach to routines, rights, rules and sanctions. In all of this the authors stress that you are not working in a vacuum but within the context and support of your school.

Introduction

By the time they start school, children have learnt a vast amount. From being crying babies squirming in their mothers' arms they have become articulate individuals who can run, jump and dance about. They can reason, make decisions, sing songs and so the list goes on. How did they learn so much in such a short space of time? The answer is multi-faceted and complex but, briefly, comprises modelling others' behaviour, trial and error as they attempt to master a new skill and what some might consider innate programming.

Think about your own learning. What can you remember from ten, twenty, thirty years ago? Can you remember first riding a bicycle, making a cake, learning to read? How did you acquire these skills? Did you learn to write using the same, or similar, techniques to learning to sing? We suspect not: different skills often require different learning strategies.

Skills acquisition is one branch of learning but what about, for example, understanding and attitudes? How did you acquire your understanding of yourself or science or the English language? It would be an oversimplification to suggest that you learnt to talk through imitation alone for that would not explain why young children produce words such as 'goed' instead of 'went' or 'sheeps' instead of 'sheep'. Such mistakes signal a powerful understanding of how language works and how rules may be applied, albeit wrongly in these cases but nonetheless intelligently. Humans are generally very quick and effective learners: your role as a teacher is to capitalise on this fact but, to do this, you need insight into schools, schooling and, of course, children as intelligent and thoughtful recipients of your teaching.

Motivation

Schools are rather odd places: they can be ranked with prisons and mental institutions as the only places people are compelled to attend. If you stop to think about it, it is hardly natural for 30 children to be cooped up in a small room, often with only one adult, for hours on end, day in, day out. As some of our Masters students commented: 'Children are expected to be together seven hours a day possibly with people they don't like: why should they learn?' (Eve); 'If you want someone to learn something, would you put 30 people in the same room?' (Sandy).

These are good points and ones we should not ignore. As teachers of the twenty-first century, however, we need to recognise that, to date, putting 30 people in a room day in, day out seems to be the most cost-effective and efficient way to educate them. Indeed, millions of teachers all over the world do an excellent job but it is not through sheer luck or an abundance of good intentions. A multiplicity of skills and attitudes are required, many of which are described and discussed in this book.

As a beginning teacher it is highly understandable that, having taught a lesson, one of your main concerns will be your own performance in the classroom. At the end of a session you may find yourself thinking, 'How did I do?' rather than 'What sort of experience was it for the children?' (Haydn, 2007). We all think like that from time to time particularly when we feel under pressure such as when our teaching practice is being assessed by a tutor, colleague or Ofsted. Here, however, we would like to encourage you to turn your attention away from yourself and towards the unique collection of other individuals in your classroom. Right from the outset we would argue that it is important to think about the particular needs of your pupils. This will be discussed more fully in Chapters 7, 10 and 11 but, in brief, we recommend that *you drive through the lesson as a child* once you have prepared a session but before you commit yourself to it.

In Chapter 5 a clear case is made for observing children closely in classrooms whether you, or someone else, are teaching them. Much vital information can be gained in this manner including a considerable amount which you might not anticipate! We know, for example, that teachers have considerable influence on their pupils but it can be easy to forget that children spend much of their time trying to interpret their teacher's behaviour so that they can do their utmost to please them. Peter, a Masters student, recalled a conversation he had overheard. A small group of juniors were examining some work they had just received back from their teacher: they were convinced that those with a dot after their ticks (that is, '✔.') had performed better than those without. The challenge was then to see how many of them could achieve dotted ticks.

On hearing the above tale, two other Masters students immediately came up with examples of how some children will blindly follow their teacher's commands. Alison reported that, on being told to give themselves 'a mark out of ten' some of her pupils literally wrote, 'A mark out of 10'. Similarly two of Colin's pupils, having heard 'Just write Joe Bloggs' next to the space requiring 'Name' wrote 'Joe Bloggs'. These children were not, we hasten to add, trying to be difficult; they were, however, doing what their teachers asked without making any effort to process their requests. In other words they were not engaged in the spirit of what was being asked of them.

Lest you conclude that it is only more sophisticated, older primary pupils who respond in this way, consider Ward and Rowe's (1985) observation:

> Several 4-year-olds working round a dough table. Each was working independently of the others. And each worked on his or her unique project. One made a ring and offered it to the play leader. She said, 'how lovely' and kept the ring on her finger. All the other children immediately abandoned their projects, made dough rings and presented them in the same fashion. (p. 3)

There will, we are sure, be many other more recent examples in the literature where learners have – as Doyle (1977) so succinctly put it – 'exchanged performance for grades' but, rather than take our word for it consider:

- your own reactions when you are asked to produce a piece of assessed work
- how children respond when you – or someone else – asks them to do something.

In both cases we would predict there would be an element of, 'What are they after?' 'How can I achieve the best result?' It *may* be that, as you undertake an assignment, you suddenly realise you are enjoying the process and that you have become *intrinsically motivated* or, in other words, so engrossed in the topic that you want to continue the work because it fascinates you. Or you may simply do assignments in order to pass them in which case you are *extrinsically motivated.* People who are extrinsically motivated often achieve very high marks usually through sheer hard work and determination but, we would suggest, it may be with gritted teeth and little pleasure. One of the major challenges you face as a teacher therefore is to encourage intrinsic motivation. Our observations suggest that people learn most successfully and with the greatest enjoyment if they engage in an activity for its own sake. When was the last time that proved to be the case for you? What lessons can you learn from it to enhance your own professional practice?

Creating a positive learning environment

So how can you provide the most effective environment for learning? In order to create a positive classroom climate, we have found that it is important to ensure there is an emphasis on noticing and talking about what is going well rather than focusing on the negative. Interestingly, research shows that we tend to focus on the negative while taking positive behaviour for granted. Take a moment to think about your everyday life: how often do you compliment your friends, partner, children, colleagues or even complete strangers on what they have done? Might there be opportunities for you to do it more often without it seeming artificial and false? Now take a second or two to reflect on how you react to a smile or a word of praise. Some of you may feel slightly surprised or even embarrassed but we can guarantee with almost 100 per cent certainty that you will feel better and more positive than when faced with a scowl or even the mildest of criticisms. Indeed, in our experience, you can lavish someone with praise but, if you insert one hint of criticism, the former will be ignored while the latter will be remembered.

In classrooms spanning the full early years to adult age range we have observed the following:

- Introducing a concept by praising learners for things that happened in the previous session is effective because (a) it gives a sense of continuity from session to session and (b) it ensures a positive start to the current session.
- Praise needs to be genuine and specific. In school (as we are not sure that our university students would appreciate it!) referring to classroom rules and routines helps to make the praise specific and helps those rules and routines to lodge in the children's minds. Specificity is important as it acts as a reinforcement and reduces misunderstanding.
- Consideration needs to be given to when and how praise is given, for example whether someone will respond better to public praise or a private word. Having said that, recognise that most children (and we have never encountered one who did not) like their parents/carers to hear positive things about them: a short positive note or a quick call to the child's home can work wonders.
- It is important to be persistent, even if someone appears unaffected by your praise. It may, for example, take those who are unused to praise a while to become accustomed to the idea and realise that your praise is a direct and real response to something

specific that they have done. Others may feel that responding to praise from you as their teacher might appear to be a sign of weakness, especially if they are more familiar with a culture where bad behaviour is rewarded by apparent admiration and cheering from peers. Overcoming this reaction is not easy and is something that will be addressed below but suffice it to say here that, eventually, persistent praise does pay off in the vast majority of cases.

- Occasionally, children will reject direct statements of praise, usually for one of the reasons outlined above. A comment such as, 'That's a very imaginative poem you have written there, Jamie' may be met with, 'No, it's not, it's rubbish'. One way to counter this is to use an 'I statement' as this moves the focus from the child to the teacher while still recognising the quality of the work. For example, in the situation above, a teacher aware of the child's particular needs might instead choose to use a phrase such as 'I really like the way you have used metaphors to create poetic images. I can clearly see what you have written in my head'.

- It is most effective if you can be generous and avoid qualifying your praise. How often, for example, have you felt great when someone has said something like, 'I really like the way you did X' only to be deflated two seconds later when they add, '... but it would have been even better if you had done Y'? We suggest therefore you avoid remarks such as: 'You came into the room very sensibly just then. It's a pity you don't do it more often.' Such a strategy, as you will see at the end of the chapter, raises some important and challenging issues for reflection.

- Looking out for and praising children's effort rather than just their achievement is vital. Not all of us are destined to be another Einstein and yet many of us work extremely hard and endeavour to do our best. Such persistent effort can become demoralising if it is never recognised and rewarded. Indeed, over time, some people adopt an attitude that it is better for their self-esteem if they do not put the effort into a task because, should they fail, they can claim that it was because they did not do any work rather than face the possibility that they were not clever enough to achieve full marks. Teenagers are particular prone to such behaviour but the seeds from which it develops can be sown at a very early age.

- Finally, where possible, praise what matters to the learner as well as what matters to you as a teacher. To illustrate this we would like you to consider an extract written by Anne Cockburn in the previous edition of this book:

... Shona immediately went off to ask her class of 5-year-olds why they thought they learnt about numbers. Their answers were as follows:

So when you're older you know about numbers.
So we know what adding up and taking away is.
To learn how to count to high numbers.
So we know everything when we're grown up.
So when we're older we know all the answers.
When we grow up we'll be really clever and gets lots of money.
So we will learn to count up to 100.

We come to school to learn numbers so when we grow up we'll be clever. So we know how to count. To do sums.

When we grow up and our teachers ask us we'll get it right.

'Cos when we come to school we have to learn things.

It did not appear to matter to the children that learning sums, to them, was a means to an end in accomplishing school work rather than something that would be more use to them in later life. They saw it as a job to be done and they did it. (Marshall, 1988, goes so far as to liken this approach to a production-line model where the product is of paramount importance.) (Cockburn, 2006, pp. 77–8)

What can we conclude from the above cameo? Did Shona praise her pupils? If so, for what? How do you think she altered her classroom practice as a result?

CRITICAL ISSUES

In 1968 Rosenthal and Jacobson's seminal book entitled *Pygmalion in the Classroom* explored whether,

... a teacher's expectation for her [his] pupils' intellectual competence can come to serve as an educational self-fulfilling prophecy. (p. vii)

Since then the book has been cited over 2,000 times. Search the Internet and your library catalogue to find some of the more recent of these citations and, having read them, discuss your conclusions with your colleagues. What are the implications for *your* professional practice?

Establishing appropriate expectations for classroom behaviour

In this section we will explore how we can establish classroom routines, rights and rules and consider their value in creating positive conditions for learning. It is vital to plan how you will do this from the outset for, however well you motivate your pupils and provide a positive learning environment, there will come a time when someone will test your boundaries. It may not be your first day in class or even the first week but it will come wherever you are and whichever age range you teach. These words are not intended to put you off but, if you establish appropriate expectations for classroom behaviour early on, you will be prepared and able to respond with the necessary confidence when the need arises.

Firstly it is very important to establish routines within your classroom. As discussed elsewhere in the book this will help you organise yourself and manage the myriad of demands on your time and attention. Crucially in the context of this chapter, it will also help your pupils feel secure and confident. As adults we all have our own routines which help our lives run more smoothly. Occasionally they are interrupted which can prove unsettling and tiresome: searching for your toothbrush after a few days away might be a minor example or encountering an empty cereal packet as you are about to embark on your breakfast.

As someone learning to be a teacher we suggest that you adopt the routines of the classes you work with when on teaching practice. Take note of as many of these as possible for, once qualified, your task will be to establish your own routines. These may range from how you give out resources to the class to your expectations as to how they behave in the event of a fire. It is worth taking into consideration what the children might have done in the past – especially if they are encountering school for the very first time – and, particularly in the case of the latter, whether the school has specific routines which they expect you to follow.

Next let us turn our attention to rights and rules. Consider Galvin et al.'s (1999) caution:

> Behaviour can be an area where we expect so much and teach so little. (p. 23)

Reflecting back that the most effective and enjoyable learning takes place when individuals are fully engaged in the process, a remark made by a child and cited by Rogers (1990) seems very apt:

> I think that the rules should be made by the kids and the teacher, then it would be fairer and the kids couldn't complain about the rules. (p. 124)

A good starting point we have found is to ask the class. 'What type of classroom would you like to work in?' This opens up the opportunity to discuss with the children the basic fundamental non-negotiable rights that they should expect to enjoy at school. How this is done depends on the age, experience and maturity of your pupils. It may be that, from time to time, you will need to nudge the conversation along to ensure that key topics are aired. This needs to be managed sensitively as you do not wish to give the impression that the children's involvement in such a decision is a token gesture on your part. In our view fundamental issues – such as noise levels – are best agreed upon as part of a calm, reflective, and genuine dialogue rather than a unilateral decision by you as their teacher. Commitment from all parties is key.

The rights you explore with younger children might include the rights to feel safe, to be heard and to be treated fairly. If you are in an upper primary situation you might find it useful to consider with your class some of the rights produced by the United Nations. For example, Article 12 states that every child has the right to say what they think in all matters affecting them, and to have their views taken seriously, and Article 28 maintains that every child has the right to an education.

One of the consequences of rights in a society is, probably inevitably, the creation of rules to ensure they are upheld. Again, in our view, it is important to involve your pupils in deliberations and agreements relating to class rules. Once a list of proposals has been drawn up in appropriately child-friendly language you could then ask everyone to sign it and post it on the wall for all to see.

There may be a temptation when producing such a list to make it fully comprehensive and wide ranging: avoid it! Too many rules can make life unduly cumbersome and may encourage unnecessarily long discussions in the future on who did what to whom, when, where and why. Rather it is better to have a few, clearly specified rules which everybody understands. You should also aim to present the rules as a collection of 'dos' rather than 'do nots' since they will then act as a reminder to pupils as to how they should behave in a given situation. The rules you decide upon may change according to circumstance. Thus, for example, you and the children may conclude that the definition of acceptable noise levels varies depending on activity. As a result the class may devise an adjustable noise meter such as shown in Figure 8.1.

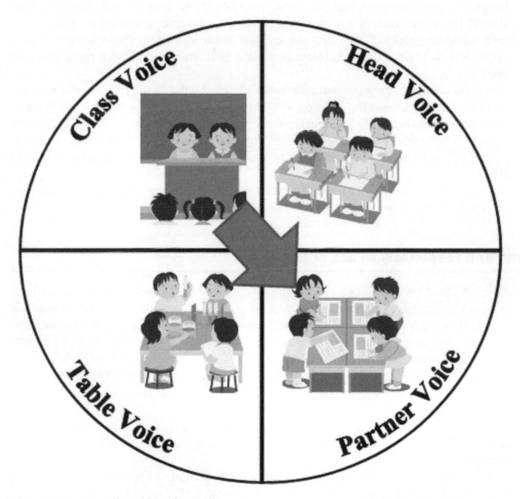

Figure 8.1   An adjustable noise meter

To summarise our thoughts on the creation of class rules based on many years of experience across the early years and primary age range we suggest that you:

- involve the children
- keep the rules simple and use child friendly vocabulary
- make them positive
- limit yourselves to a small number
- have them on display and use pictures to help reinforce them
- refer to the rules regularly
- arrange class meetings or 'circle time' to review them from time to time.

Finally, having created the rules, you and the children need to consider what will happen if they are breached. As far as possible these actions and consequences should be as well matched as possible. Thus, for example, if someone deliberately says something unkind that hurts the feelings of another pupil then the agreed consequence of their action might be to spend time in at break writing a letter of apology.

It is important to recognise that sometimes you can be the victim of your own success: you may have motivated the children so well that, in their excitement but entirely unintentionally, some begin to call out in response to your questions. Here, having previously agreed in principle on the strategy with your class, you might adopt a 'one warning' policy: you indicate that the behaviour is unacceptable (see below) but allow a second chance.

As will be discussed in the next section, however, you may not always decide to respond immediately to minor, or sometimes even quite major, infringements.

Actions and responses: to act or not to act

When a child breaks a class rule it may not always be entirely straightforward for you as the teacher. As above, when a child makes an unkind comment to another pupil, they take responsibility for their actions (see below) and pay the penalty. Occasionally you may find yourself acting instinctively if a child is in a potentially life-threatening situation and, for example, about to run in front of a car. Often, however, a certain amount of professional judgement is called for. This will develop with experience. You may sometimes *feel* indecisive – that is only human – but try not to show it!

Teacher indecision when it comes to managing misbehaviour makes some children feel insecure while opening up a range of opportunities for those with potential to take advantage of you.

As soon you as you detect a hint of possible infringement of the class rules you might run through the following:

- *Am I being oversensitive?* If it is very noisy, for example, it might simply be that the children are taking a minute or two to settle down: this is not unreasonable if you have given them a stimulating challenge!
- *What have the class been doing in the last hour?* If you have been sitting quietly for a long time do you find it easy to remain still? Why should children?
- *What have I asked the children to do?* Have I given them enough information? Might it be too easy? Too hard? Too boring?
- *Have I provided appropriate opportunities?* The response to this may overlap with the answers to the above but you might also consider whether you have given the class, for example, a chance to fully engage in a quality discussion before asking them to commit their thoughts on a controversial topic to paper.
- *Is something unusual going on?* You cannot be privy to everything that is going on in your pupils' lives but it can be helpful if you know friends have recently fallen out or someone is having a birthday party later in the day or a child is finding home life difficult. In this last case you might well be wise to seek advice from a more experienced colleague.
- *Is there anything I can do to avert potential misbehaviour?* If you are a parent you may find this easy to answer. If you are not, I suggest you find time to watch experienced parents with a baby: we would be very surprised if, within a short space of time, you did not find them diverting the child's attention to stimulate their interest, prevent tears, etc. Praising something a child is doing well may prove to be a very effective diversion strategy: telling Jana she is sitting beautifully might stun a very talkative child into silence for a few seconds while you call the class to attention.
- *If I take action what are the likely consequences?* This can be a particularly tricky question if one is new to teaching so it is worth taking time to reflect on it now rather than first confront it within a busy classroom environment. It is also worth discussing the matter with more experienced colleagues having observed them closely working with a class. We shall discuss this further below.

Having observed hundreds of beginning teachers over the years a common reaction to misbehaviour is to respond to it immediately with a sharp command such as, 'John stop that at once!' Occasionally this is the best course of action as it leaves little room for doubt. It may, however, be rather an unnecessary overreaction and it will certainly interrupt the flow of your session. An alternative is to adopt a non-verbal strategy. The most common of these are listed in Figure 8.2. How many have you tried or observed?

You might be surprised that we include ignoring somebody's behaviour as a strategy but, if you stop to think about it, sometimes people behave in a certain way to attract attention. It might be because they are spoilt and used to being in the limelight. It might be because they are bored and wish to liven up the proceedings a little bit. Tactical ignoring can prove highly effective in these and a range of other situations. It might not, however, work if a child is unusually unsettled and they wish to alert you to the fact that,

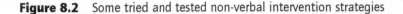

Non-verbal interventions

- Tactical ignoring
- Proximity – stake out your territory!
- Pause
- The stare
- Facial expressions
- Gestures and signals

Figure 8.2 Some tried and tested non-verbal intervention strategies

for example, there is a wasp in the room. The best option in such situations is to calmly open a window, guide the wasp gently through it if you can and carry on.

Simply moving closer to someone who looks as if they are about to start up a conversation with their neighbour can enable you to continue a session while sending a very clear signal to the potential offender! Be overt if you are choosing to do this, nothing is gained by stealthily sneaking up behind pupils.

We have used all of the strategies listed in Figure 8.2 when working with children and adults: in your next class at college see if you spot any of them.

On other occasions (or, if the above do not have the desired outcome after a few minutes) you may find it more effective to make a comment and, in so doing, de-escalate a situation (Figure 8.3). (For further exploration of these issues read Rogers, 2011.)

Some of these will be familiar and have been touched on above. Often they can work well in combination. So, for example, if you notice that Sally is chattering away in the corner you might begin, 'Well done for working so quietly Zack.' If this does not have the desired effect on Sally's behaviour you might calmly say, 'This is a quiet time thanks Sally' in a tone that assumes she will respond appropriately. The use of 'thanks' adds weight to your assumption. If there is still no suitable response, move closer and employ the broken record technique. Almost without exception children will respond after three such reminders. Using humour is a powerful strategy that has the potential to diffuse confrontational situations by allowing both sides to retreat with minimal damage to egos. It is, however, a risky approach that demands that the teacher has a detailed knowledge of all the children in the class as it will not work with everyone. Imagine you are waiting for the class to settle on the carpet and you spot a boy in a world of his own flapping his arms and buzzing around the back of the class. Rather than admonishing him for holding you up, you might choose to call out, 'Come on Mr Bumblebee, come back and join the rest of the bees in the hive over here.'

Partial agreement allows the teacher to show empathy with the pupil while also making expectations clear. For example, you may say to a pupil, 'I understand that you are upset because you had an argument at break but you need to get on with your work now and we can talk more about what happened at lunchtime if you wish.'

Verbal strategies for de-escalation

- Descriptive praise of desired behaviour
- Use names to 'jolly along' (learn them all)
- Humour: exaggeration, funny accents (but *never* at expense of child)
- Rule reminder
- Broken record – give instruction, pause for take-up time and then repeat it
- Partial agreement

Figure 8.3   Tried and tested verbal strategies for de-escalation

What to avoid if you can and what to do if you can't

Although – in the tenor of much of this book – we do not wish to dwell on the negative, we want to take a couple of paragraphs to discuss some of the common mistakes we have observed. Before we do, however, take a moment to think about the following, 'Would you mind passing the butter please?' If someone said that to you what might you do and/or say? We suspect you would almost certainly pass the butter (assuming it was within reach!), possibly adding a polite comment as you did so. Over the next few days you might take the opportunity to observe how adults make requests of each other. We think you might be surprised to note how often it is done in the form of a rhetorical question. In such cases a verbal response is not really expected but an action is: 'Would you like to sit over there please?' 'Can I squeeze past you please?' 'Would you mind turning out the light when you leave?' In essence these are all requests rather than real questions and, indeed, you might be somewhat surprised if a colleague turned round to you and said, 'No I will not turn out the lights when I leave!' It would, however, be a legitimate response to a seemingly legitimate question – albeit rather a rude one.

When you would like a child to do something tell them directly! You might find this more difficult than you anticipate at first. Asking even your politest pupil, 'Would you like to sit down over there please?' runs the risk of a negative response as they are likely to interpret it as a genuine question rather than, to put it at its bluntest, a command. As you might imagine, questions such as, 'How many times do I have to ask you?', 'Are we going to have to wait all day?' and 'Do I look like an idiot?' run an even higher risk of an unwelcome response!

As we said earlier in the chapter, you are likely to experience a honeymoon period when you first start working with a new class. In time – and this could be hours, days or possibly weeks – even the most placid and well behaved children will start to test your boundaries. It is entirely natural and something that humans do in common with other members of the animal kingdom. When it happens do not think the worst and then overreact. In the previous edition of this book Rob Barnes (2006) warned readers of the dangers of

… being aggressively 'manic' in your vigilance. The manically vigilant teacher treats each infringement of attention or pupil disruption as a personal threat, barking at pupils in return … Two effects … [of this] are you will shift the focus towards pupils' behaviour (rather than concentrating on your teaching and pupils' learning) and you will invite pupils to try you out. (p. 128)

The idea of children 'trying you out' is not a pleasant one but, if you are cognisant of the possibility, you can avoid it by providing them with something far more interesting – such as your fascinating lesson – to engage their attention. Should you find, however, that the session which looked fantastic on paper is going down like a lead balloon, do not be afraid to change course *even if you are being assessed by your mentor or teaching practice supervisor.* Even those of us who have been in the profession for many years have to alter direction mid-session from time to time: trust your professional judgement in these situations as a lesson which is not taking off in the way you had hoped is unlikely to spring into life if you carry on in the same vein. The main reasons why some sessions are less successful than others is considered further in Chapter 11.

Below we discuss a range of other strategies often employed by beginning teachers which prove, almost invariably, unsuccessful. Before we do, take a few minutes to picture yourself teaching an ideal session. What do you see? A room filled with animated children? You relaxed and in control? Is everybody on task, behaving beautifully and enjoying the experience of being in your classroom? Now imagine if someone shouts a command across the room at the top of their voice. What happens? The atmosphere is broken. All too often inexperienced teachers tend to talk over their pupils. Sometimes nobody hears them as the noise levels are simply too high. At other times they may have been heard but disregarded. And frequently on such occasions a teacher may give the impression of being someone slightly out of control. Thus we advise you wait until the class is quiet before you talk to them as a group. This may take some time but we strongly recommend that you sit it out calmly and with every appearance of being in control (even if you do not feel it!). If you wish to speak to someone while the class are engaged in individual or group work move beside them rather than bellowing across the classroom in the hope that they will hear. Alternatively, or as a first step, you might catch their eye and try one of the non-verbal techniques listed in Figure 8.2 above. *Very occasionally* in your career you might have to shout at a child who is some distance away from you and at risk. Under such circumstance we recommend a short, sharp command such as, 'Stop!' or 'Sandy stop!' That should gain everyone's attention and it is at that point you can add further instructions. *Do not*, however, use this strategy unless you feel you absolutely have to: used more than once in a blue moon it will soon lose its potency.

There may be times when you are so angry that you want to shout at someone: resist it. It is a mistake to discipline a child when you have lost control of your temper. It is fine for you to appear angry on occasion but it is far from fine if you are not in control of your emotions. Sometimes – and we hope this is rare – you may find that you are at the end of your tether and it is as well to consider what might be the best strategies for you to adopt under such circumstances. Possible options are to:

- ask a responsible child to take a note to another teacher requesting help. Even the most experienced teachers do this from time to time and it is an entirely professional strategy: being human we all have days when it is all too much
- recognise you are angry and take a few seconds to calm yourself down: a few deep breaths can often help
- accept that you are not feeling as in control as you might like and switch to a simpler, probably more routine, activity. This might, for example, be reading the class a story or taking a break to do a quick game you all enjoy before, possibly, reverting to the original activity.

Next time you are in school ask colleagues about strategies they use. This is a good way to pick up tips and it also gives you an idea as to what is common practice within a school. Before we move on, it is also worth taking a few minutes to dwell on what tends to trigger *your* temper. It may be that you are a very calm and placid person and that it is not easy to unsettle your equanimity – lucky you! If you are prone to losing your temper though you would be wise to consider the catalysts and whether you can do anything to alleviate the potential pressures.

If a child is being persistently difficult some resort to frequent threats but do not take any action until it is too late. Try therefore to avoid 'If you do that again I'll do X' and then not do X when it happens again. We shall discuss sanctions towards the end of the chapter but suffice it to say here that if you say you will do something then do it.

A similar pitfall is to become so exasperated by a child's behaviour that you are too harsh. Undue severity can also be an issue for inexperienced teachers if they are very nervous and anxious to establish their authority: scared children do not make willing learners.

Being human it is only to be expected that you will like to be liked: we all do. As a teacher this is not your prime concern. We are not, of course, proposing that you encourage your pupils to dislike you. Rather we suggest you avoid being unduly worried about what someone might think of you if you tell them off. Perversely, if you let a child know their boundaries, they are more likely to feel secure and respect you.

Very occasionally you may find yourself disliking one of the pupils in your class: *never* let them know. And, whether you like a child or not, *never* criticise a child for being who they are: tell them you do not like their behaviour but never say you do not like them.

CRITICAL ISSUES

Galton (2007) argues that:

> From the pupils' perspective, the messages relating to learning and to behaviour in many primary classrooms are ambiguous. This is because

(Continued)

(Continued)

different rules appear to operate when the class is engaged in regulating their thinking and when they are concerned with regulating their behaviour. (p. 114)

What do you think? Why? To reflect on your answer more fully we suggest you compare some of the most prominent learning theories including, in particular, B. F. Skinner's philosophy. Also take the opportunity to reflect on your own classroom practice and that of more experienced teachers.

Sanctions and repercussions

In this chapter we have talked a lot about what you should and should not do to discourage misbehaviour but, if it persists, what can you do? Our first recommendation is to consult the behaviour policy of any school you are visiting. Every school should have one. Of course, realistically, this is not always possible before you find yourself in the classroom and therefore our second piece of advice is that you observe other teachers *and* discuss their strategies with them. Both are important as not everyone follows their own counsel!

Throughout this chapter we have tried to convey that you and your pupils are in a learning partnership. You might be in charge ultimately but you all have rights and responsibilities. If someone contravenes the rules of the group it is important – and indeed effective advice – to ensure that they maintain their dignity. The implications for your practice are threefold. The first is that you provide them with a simple choice: you might say, 'If you complete your maths quietly and sensibly now then you can go out at breaktime. If you don't, you will have to stay in with me while the others go out to play. Which is it to be?' Fortunately most opt for the former of these. If they opt for the latter we suggest that they do at least some work during the break after which they have a few minutes to run around outside so that they have some fresh air and expend some of their pent-up energy before returning to class. Should you find that a child persistently opts to stay in at breaktime with you we suggest you make a few enquiries: it might be, for example, that they are being bullied in the playground or that they are having a challenging time at home and yearn for a bit of extra adult attention.

The second implication for your practice if you have to sanction a child is to help them take responsibility for their own actions. Use this opportunity to guide the pupil through their decision-making processes that led to the rule-breaking in order to help the pupil make a better choice should they find themselves in a similar situation

Non-verbal	Verbal
• Tutts and teeth sucking • Pouts • Sighs • Tears • Exasperated arm-folding • Glares • Kicking desk	• 'It wasn't me!' • 'I was only ...' • 'They were ...' • 'Mrs X lets us ...' • 'I hate this ... school'

Figure 8.4   Some pupil responses to guidance from the teacher

in the future. Some will find this very difficult but, not only is it an effective way to discourage repeat bad behaviour, it is a very important life skill which we might all do well to remember!

As you endeavour to guide a child in the art of maintaining their dignity you may encounter some of the behaviours listed in Figure 8.4: ignore them.

If all else fails, you will need to employ an exit strategy. Schools will have a routine for dealing with pupils who are persistently disruptive as part of their behaviour policy. This might involve the child working in a different class, with the head teacher or in a designated 'time-out' area. You will almost certainly need the assistance of another adult to ensure the child arrives at the correct destination and is appropriately supervised. Do not feel that you have failed if you need to call in the cavalry, these systems have been established for a reason. Your authority and the learning of the children in the class will both be compromised if a seriously disruptive child is left unchallenged.

The third implication for your practice, once the dust has settled, is to rebuild bridges. This is best done before the end of the school day and, especially with very young children, we recommend that you do it as soon as possible once they have calmed down. A cooling-off period is essential as it recognises a child's need as a human being to regain control of their emotions. It also means that your follow-up actions are likely to be more effective. One simple – but tried and tested way – to build bridges is to praise a child for some specific good behaviour following their misdemeanour. This provides them with a clear signal that all is well again as well as reinforcing what you consider to be appropriate behaviour. Another longer-term strategy is to discuss with them how, together, you might tackle their persistent poor behaviour pattern. This is likely to include exploring what triggers their actions. So, for example, if sitting next to Fred sets them off you might discuss where they might work better. You could also consider whether a reward scheme – such as a star chart – might help them manage their behaviour. Involving a child in such decisions helps them feel more aware, grown up and responsible which, in turn, enhances their self-esteem and diminishes their need to act immaturely.

Final thoughts

In this chapter we have tried to provide ideas and strategies which will suit those of you visiting classrooms as part of a teaching practice and those of you embarking on your first post as a newly qualified teacher. Obviously the two situations are rather different. As a visitor you have the advantage of being able to take on someone else's rules and routines. They will not be your own and they may not entirely be in accord with your own philosophy but you and the children will probably find it easiest if you continue the class teacher's regime. It will also provide you with the opportunity to try out strategies that you might not otherwise have considered.

As a new teacher it may feel as if you have to start from scratch. In some ways this might appear straightforward as you are freer to adopt your own ideas. Remember though that you will not be working in a vacuum: use your colleagues and the school's policy as guides. Indeed, as will be discussed further in Chapter 18, make sure that you ask about your prospective school's behaviour policy. If it seems in accord with your own philosophy then great! If it does not you might seriously wish to reconsider whether you would take the job if offered.

Summary

- Dedicate time at the start of the year to making pupils feel welcomed and included in your classroom. This, along with establishing rules, routines and responsibilities, will help lessons to run smoothly over the year.
- Try to focus your attention on what children are doing well. A positive approach that 'catches children being good' will result in a friendlier working atmosphere for all.
- Inevitability of a sanction is more important than the severity.
- Management of children's behaviour in a school is a team effort. Don't feel afraid to ask for help when situations become challenging.

Issues for reflection

- Observe a teacher and note what they praise. What else could you praise? In your experience, including what you have read above, why is praise so important?
- What do you do when you are not motivated during a lecture? Why? Does a lack of motivation necessarily relate to the content of a lecture or the quality of the lecturer? What are the implications for your own professional practice?

(Continued)

(Continued)

- In your experience, what is the most effective way to get you to improve on the quality of your work? Might your response influence how you interact with your pupils? If so, in what way?
- What classroom routines do you hope to set up? How will these be conveyed to (a) the class and (b) adults who work in your classroom?

Further reading

Barnes, R. (2006) *The Practical Guide to Primary Classroom Management*. London: Sage. This book was written by an experienced teacher educator and is based on his many years of working with beginning primary teachers as they develop the skills of behaviour management.

Brophy, J. (2010) *Motivating Students to Learn*. 3rd edition. New York: Routledge. In this book Jere Brophy successfully combines theory and practice in a very thoughtful and accessible manner.

Rogers, B. (2011) *Classroom Behaviour: A Practical Guide to Effective Behaviour Management and Colleague Support*. 3rd edition. London: Sage. Bill Rogers has a very amusing writing style and, over the years, we have observed our students implementing his suggestions very effectively.

CHAPTER 9

REFLECTIVE PRACTICE

Jenifer Smith

Chapter overview

Reflection is about slowing down, thinking more deeply, asking questions, being willing not to have complete answers, learning to live with uncertainty, seeing patterns, making links between experience, reading, writing and talk. This chapter considers why reflective teaching is important and ways in which you might begin to reflect on practice, and suggests ways of focusing reflection in the classroom.

Do you swim? Can you ride a bicycle? Do you improvise with other musicians or use a screwdriver? Could you tell someone else how to do any of these things? You can give them pointers, you can tell them the rules or how things work, you can demonstrate, but they must get the sense of *how* to do it themselves. They have to hold the screwdriver and feel how it is in their hand. They have, somehow, to let go while taking note of how the successful moments feel. And they must carry that sense with them so that they can use that knowledge again. If you were to think in too much detail about how you ride a bicycle as you ride, the chances are that you would fall off – or never get started. You can help others learn to do these things, but it is hard to find the words to describe just what the knack is. Swimming, riding a bicycle, wielding a screwdriver are activities which depend heavily on knowing through the body, in relation to a machine or tool. Improvising in music demands not only the skills of playing an instrument and knowledge of harmony, melody and rhythm, but also an awareness of others and the sounds they are making, or even about to make, a sensitivity to what is going on around you and the effect that you are having on your surroundings. As you are in the midst of cycling or improvising you may not be thinking consciously about what you are doing, but you can take time outside that activity to reflect upon your actions. Teaching is a highly skilled activity which requires us to anticipate and respond to the complexities of the classroom, to make judgements and to act upon them and to be aware of the con-sequences of our actions. Others can talk with us and share their experience of teaching and we can learn from practical advice. However, becoming a teacher and the process of teaching itself, is something we must each grow to understand and know for our-selves. As we learn to teach and continue to develop our skills, we respond to the many, many tiny events of the classroom and we draw upon an intricate web of knowledge and experiences to help us. (For a fuller exploration of classroom skills see Chapter 6.) It is not always easy to articulate this complex activity, and sometimes advice given or theory proposed does not match, or seems too easy by comparison, with the messiness and unevenness of the experience itself. Reflection helps us to make better sense of our teaching and learning and in so doing grow in skill and understanding.

Knowing-in-action

We learn about teaching by teaching, by learning how it feels and what the signs are. But we also learn by reflecting on our thoughts and actions, and by relating our thoughts to the advice, written and spoken, of experts and to other analogous experiences of our own. When we are in the midst of the situation we do not necessarily think consciously about what we are doing, particularly as we become more skilled. It is what Donald Schön (1983) describes as knowing-in-action.

> Our knowing is ordinarily tacit, implicit in our patterns of action and our feel for the stuff with which we are dealing. It seems right to say that our knowing is *in* our action.

> Similarly, the workaday life of the professional depends on tacit knowing-in-action. Every competent practitioner can recognise phenomena – families of symptoms associated with a particular disease, peculiarities of a certain kind of building site, irregularities of materials of structures – for which he cannot give a reasonably accurate or complete description. In his day-to-day practice he makes innumerable judgements of quality for which he cannot state adequate criteria, and he displays skills for which he cannot state the rules and proce-dures. Even when he makes conscious use of research-based theories and techniques, he is dependent on tacit recognitions, judgements and skilful performances. (pp. 49–50)

Skilled teaching calls upon every aspect of our being, the whole person: physical presence and action, physical awareness of the activities and actions of the classroom, smell, sight, sound, intellectual understanding, emotional and moral awareness, and social consciousness. As we gain experience in the classroom we learn to read the signs. We also need to think about the context in which we work and which we create. A teacher is making judgements about how to act every moment of the day, and planning is based upon a range of understandings. When you begin teaching there seem too many things to hold in the mind at one time. In the moment, in the classroom, the teacher calls upon their own unique experience, knowledge and understanding. You will notice that some things 'work' and others can lead to horrible, toe-curling disasters. Some things are just 'OK'. As you respond to children, adjust your actions in the classroom and think consciously about your presentation or the way you are asking questions, you are drawing on any number of sources to inform your action. A memory of a piece of advice or of the actions of a teacher you have observed may come into play as you deal with the events of a lesson. You may be consciously trying out an idea or you may find yourself drawing on your own experience of the last time you were in a similar situation. In the classroom, you must act. Later, with a little time to reflect, you are able to begin to see patterns and to articulate what you are doing or might do.

Putting reflection to work

Professional practitioners do not merely act without thinking. They reflect on their actions both in the midst of acting and later. Reflection can help us to identify the strengths and shortcomings of our actions so that we can make changes or capitalise on a success. Reflection can help us solve problems, and reflection can offer us a moment of stillness in a job which is never finished, where there is always something more that could be done. Schön suggests that 'thinking-in-action' is sparked by surprise. Indeed, our surprised pleasure at things that go well is one thing which prompts us to look back and consider how that success was achieved. Why did we judge it successful? What were the conditions? What did we do? What was our thinking and our intention? Teachers also reflect on the curiosities and the discomforts of the classroom. How will I respond to what this child's actions are telling me about her understanding of pattern? What is preventing this child from making progress in reading? Why is the class so unsettled after lunch – and what shall I do about it? How might I engage more children when I introduce a new topic? And they can choose to reflect on the everyday happenings of the classroom, perhaps the actions of a child who often goes unnoticed, to help them learn about teaching and about learning. A class of children constantly presents the teacher with intriguing puzzles. It is one of the real pleasures of teaching to engage with these puzzles. Indeed, I would suggest that a careful awareness of what children tell us through their speech and actions and our subsequent reflections on that knowledge is central to the act of teaching. Children are not the only presence in the classroom.

There are other adults, both within and powerfully on the fringes of the classroom: other teachers, classroom assistants, parents, governors, other professionals (see also Chapter 2 and Chapter 16). Sometimes you may wish to reflect on the roles they play and upon your relationship with them. However, the other key presence in the classroom is you, the teacher or student teacher. Teaching is a part of who we are, and our actions in the classroom are informed by our beliefs, our understandings and our prejudices. Reflection has an important part to play in helping us resolve the part the self plays in teaching and in helping us to identify the blind spots and troublesome areas which make our teaching less effective for some children.

CRITICAL ISSUES

Some practitioners believe that teachers should derive their own theories from reflection on their own practice alone while others take the view that reflection on practice can be informed by reading and that the interplay between observation, reflection and existing theory is a fruitful way of developing one's own conceptual frameworks. Consider these two points of view. Decide to which one you are most drawn and identify the arguments which support your point of view.

The teacher we might be

It is quite likely that you have some sense of the kind of teacher you want to be, although this picture may change with experience. It will be drawn from any number of images. We are shaped, as teachers, by our own experiences of teachers and of learning. Thinking about teachers, those who have taught us and others whom we have observed, can help us think about some of the ways we behave when teaching, and about our beliefs and assumptions. There may be others who are not teachers in schools but who have, nevertheless, taught us about ways of being with children and about teaching. It is worth reflecting on such influences, attempting not only to recall and describe carefully how these people behave and how you feel about them, but also to think about what it was in particular that made them so effective or so destructive, and how that is present in some of the ways you behave or aspire to behave.

We can also draw upon our own experience of childhood. Reflecting on our learning in different contexts can help us think about ourselves as learners and as children experiencing school. There are two main reasons for reflecting on our history as learners and on our learning processes. Reflecting on our own processes of understanding can be helpful in finding ways of explaining something, setting up a series of activities or creating a context for learning. It can help us to place ourselves in the position of learners. It can also help us to remember and recognise differences and extend the possibilities we offer in our classroom. We need to be aware of different styles of learning, to know that we are likely to favour our own preferred style and to be able to think about planning for a variety of approaches.

Knowing ourselves is important in a classroom. Knowledge of ourselves can help us to be more open to others and be open to other ways of thinking and behaving. Look back over your history as a learner. Think about the rhythms and impulses of that history. What were your passions? What have you found easy and why? What did it feel like to be able to run fast? Write a beautiful script? Make others laugh? What fostered those things? What hindered you? Have there been changes in enthusiasms and feelings of success? Think about the images and stories which stay with you. Make a list of the stories which you tell, or could tell which you think help to define you as a person, as a teacher.

It can be interesting to write a history of yourself in some particular area of learning: as a writer or reader, or mathematician. What is your history in relation to physical exercise and sport? Art? Music? Science? Often teachers, when writing about their history as readers, find that they are missing some of the most significant experiences from their classrooms; others, recognising real difficulties or prejudices, are able to think about how to prevent those from spilling over into the experiences of the children they teach.

Contexts for reflection

Reflection is a way of thinking about things which pushes beyond the superficial and beyond incapacitating worry, although it cannot be guaranteed to be a comfortable process. Of course, one way of reflecting is in your head as you walk or drive or do household chores. But there comes a point when we need something more. We might want to read something, to talk with others, try our ideas out, or we might wish to write them down, to stop them slithering about, forcing us to engage thoroughly rather than leaving difficult things on one side.

Conversation

The act of speaking, and of writing, can offer the opportunity to move beyond the surface and beyond nagging worry. It helps us move into reflection, exploration and action. Talking with others can be crucial to reflection, and it is worth finding colleagues, fellow students and teachers with whom talk can go beyond the initial sharing of adventures and letting off steam. Letting off steam and the recognition of similar problems and pleasures remains hugely important throughout your teaching career, but the very best conversations are those which allow you to take a broader view of what is happening or to engage more deeply in what concerns you. During the year you are training, some of the best reflective conversations will be with the class teacher with whom you are working. Sometimes the teacher will have been present when events have occurred that have intrigued or frustrated or really pleased you. They know the children you are working with very well, and it is often a pleasure and a help to them as much as it is to you to talk about these things at the end of the day or during breaks. Not all teachers wish to talk in this way, and many are busy with other commitments in school. However, teachers are often glad to talk to students about what is going on in the classroom. When we are first learning we are more likely to be self-conscious about what we do and to reflect on it. Sometimes teachers do not have the opportunity to talk with others about the business of teaching and find that having to articulate practice for a student teacher is helpful to them as well as to the student.

If you work with a teacher who is willing and who enjoys reflecting on the day's events, enjoy and appreciate the opportunity this offers. Talking forces you, as does writing, to formulate your ideas, though, perhaps, with more allowance for gaps and incompleteness than writing. As you describe a situation you are forced to think about it again, and the very presence of a listener can make you aware of what you saw, your perceptions of it and how you are presenting it (what are you hiding, what exaggerating?). A conversation can allow you to test your hypotheses and to try out different approaches. The teacher's experience and particular knowledge of the children you are teaching can give you a deeper insight into their learning. They can offer you a different way of looking, and can give you more information which you can use to adapt and develop your thinking. Try to be open and contemplative, rather than rushing to solutions, and be aware when talk becomes a way of avoiding thought or action.

It is possible to plan reflective conversations with both teachers and tutors on the basis of focused observations of your teaching. When you know that you are to be observed, you might identify an area of teaching or class management that you would like the observer to take particular note of. This may well be an area that you have been thinking about already. The perceptions of an observer can bring a new perspective to your thinking and understanding. This opens up the possibility of professional conversation about shared concerns. You may have specific questions to ask teachers or tutors. Try not to want a definitive answer to some of the more complex questions. See how your own experience and the observations and thoughts of others can weave together with your thinking to make something that you, personally, can work with.

Apart from the experienced practitioner, perhaps the most influential, lifelong partner in conversation can be a fellow student. You share the experience of learning together. You are faced with similar challenges in terms of practical teaching and getting to grips with new curriculum areas and teaching theories. You will have your own ideas and understandings of education, and you are in a position to support and challenge each other on an equal footing. You may be lucky enough to get to know someone well enough to be able to talk openly about each other's qualities and blind spots and to test out new ideas without fear of embarrassment.

Talk opens possibilities and, like the experience itself, is mercurial. Writing can hold the moment so that you can return to it.

Writing

We can write something down and then return to it when the heat of the moment has cooled. Writing forces us to find words, to slow down, to look at the situation more carefully and in greater detail. During school placements, whether you are observing, working with a teacher, with small groups or teaching the whole class, it is helpful to make notes of things that you notice, that you do, that raise questions for you. There is so much going on in a classroom that it can sometimes be difficult to know what to note down. For that reason, you may find it useful to have a focus for your written notes and I shall return to that later in the chapter. When you are teaching, whether it be small groups or a whole class, the kind of notes you make should help you to think about your practice. You need to make useful notes that do not feel to you as if you are simply fulfilling a requirement made of you by the course. The notes should help you to consolidate and develop your own practice. Writing evaluations of your teaching can be very time-consuming. Sometimes students feel that they are a distraction from the job of planning for the next day and marking children's work. They need to be a part of that thinking and planning.

There is a real value in writing down notes during the day and at the end of the day before you go home. These may take the form of an aide-memoire or questions or a description of something that happened which puzzled you or which you think may be part of an emerging pattern. Notes written during the day can be useful because they catch that moment and can serve as a reminder of how you felt and of things you want to think about at leisure. Notes written on teaching plans are helpful because they relate directly to the lesson and can be used when planning. Often, these notes will refer to a child or group of children, or to a response by the class to something that you have done. It may be something you wish to replicate or which you hope will never happen again! Either way, your noting it down gives you a chance to think about it later. It is surprising how easily we forget things that seem very memorable in the classroom. Things move so rapidly. There can be many remarkable moments in a single day.

You may wish to choose a focus for what you write down so that you have some aspect of teaching or learning uppermost in your mind while you are working. You can look back over a week or more of such notes and see how things have changed, or consolidated; see whether there is a pattern to what you are writing, to your preoccupations, to things that you are noticing about the ways in which they respond and the ways in which they reveal what they are learning. It is worth writing things down because our feelings and perceptions change, and it is useful to be reminded of how we saw things at different stages in a day, week or school placement. A record of observations and your responses to events can chart your progress. It can also help you to celebrate success, or see that things are not as bad as you thought they were at the time!

Journals

A teaching journal can become a powerful part of a teacher's continuing professional development. It can provide a space for reflection, an opportunity to make sense of what is happening in the classroom and in your teaching life, and to move beyond the surface, to acknowledge things and to make connections. 'The journal holds experiences as a puzzle frame holds its integral pieces. The writer begins to recognise the pieces that fit together and, like a detective, sees the picture evolve' (Holly, 1984, p. 8). It is a place for reflecting, speculating, wondering, worrying, exclaiming, recording, proposing, reminding, reconstructing, questioning, confronting, dreaming, considering and reconsidering. It is a space for thinking. (See also the section on 'enquiry and research' in Chapter 2.)

A journal is usually a personal document. There are no hard and fast rules about how it is kept or what is written there. Some people like to use a special notebook that can be carried around. Others prefer a loose-leaf folder or the computer. One student really began to find writing useful when he began a blog. A journal usually combines a written record of events with a record of thoughts, feelings, ideas and questions. It can include drawings and other visual ways of recording and thinking, although I believe that extended writing in a journal can be of enormous value professionally and personally. Mary Louise Holly suggests that a journal is something like a cross between a log and a diary.

> Journal writing can include the structured, descriptive, and objective notes of the log and the free flowing, impressionistic meanderings of a diary. That is, it can serve the purposes of both logs and diaries. It is a more difficult and perhaps more demanding document to keep – indeed, it is more complex. Its advantages are also greater: it combines purposes and it extends into other uses. The contents of a journal are more comprehensive than those of either a log or diary, has both objective and subjective dimensions, but unlike most diaries, there is a consciousness of this differentiation.
>
> In a journal, the writer can carry on a dialogue between and among various dimensions of experience. What happened? What are the facts? What was my role? What feelings and senses surrounded the events? What did I do? What did I feel about what I did? Why? What was the setting? The flow of events? And later, what were the important elements of the event? What preceded it? Followed it? What might I be aware of if the situation recurs? This dialogue, traversing back and forth between objective and subjective views, allows the writer to become increasingly more accepting and perhaps less judgmental as the flow of events takes form. Independent actions take on added meaning. (1984, p. 6)

How might I write in a journal?

Write in a way which pleases you. Don't worry about formal language conventions; abbreviations, incomplete sentences, lists, lots of exclamations are all fine. Take risks with the writing, explore your own voice. Write long entries as often as possible to develop ideas fully. Sometimes try and write in great detail. Toby Fulwiler (1987) believes that quantity is the best measure of a good journal. Sometimes you need to write your way into understanding or insight.

What might I write in my journal?

Write to record. Write to remember the detail. Write to explore and to discover. Write speculatively, analytically, imaginatively. Write in immediate response to something, capturing the moment. Write later, reflectively. When you are working in the classroom, you react in the moment. When you have the opportunity to step back and view the same events from a distance your perceptions can change and you are able to consider other possibilities and to probe a little, challenging and affirming one's actions, considering the behaviour of children more tranquilly. Mary Louise Holly says:

> Once we move beyond perplexing events, we often dismiss them until they recur (sometimes in a slightly different format), and as they often relate to the same underlying problem, we are likely to continue to cope with our circumstances on an *ad hoc* basis. This sometimes solves the immediate problems; sometimes it does not. If we could freeze our perceptions *at the time of our action*, we might be able to identify and understand better the underlying problems and contributing factors that are ordinarily only vaguely 'felt'. And we could prevent many problems from recurring – we could learn from our experience.
>
> Keeping a personal-professional journal allows us to do just that. (1984, p. 18)

Writing to evaluate

As student teachers, you are likely to be much more rawly conscious of your actions than a more experienced teacher who has much experience to draw on. A journal can bring a sense of perspective to some things that can feel potentially overwhelming as you begin to work in a classroom. A journal can also help you to begin to formulate and clarify some of your underlying beliefs about teaching and learning, and to relate the theory you are learning to the practical experience of the classroom. One of the most difficult things to think about is our overarching aims in teaching. These and underlying principles are often the hardest things to identify when preparing plans for teaching placements but reflective teaching suggests an approach which goes beyond simply becoming competent in certain techniques. Writing about the events of the classroom gives you the opportunity to consider why you did certain things. This kind of reflection, rooted in the events of the classroom, can help you identify aims and principles. These in turn can be drawn upon effectively when you are planning.

Keeping a journal can also play a significant part in self-evaluation. During training and then as a member of the teaching profession, you will be evaluated by others, and their observations and insights can make a significant contribution to your development. However, ultimately, the responsibility for your growth as a teacher lies in your hands, and a journal can provide the opportunity for you to think about your practice. I often think of reflecting in teaching as a bit like the growing of fertiliser crops. You grow clover, high in nitrogen, and plough it back into the ground. You take note of actions, feelings, responses, failures, successes. You think about them, try and make sense of them. Then that experience can be ploughed back into your teaching.

When I introduce the idea of a journal, I often use the notion of a 'disturbance' as a starting point, at which point students often laugh ironically. I have tried using other words to avoid the negative connotations of disturbance, but keep returning to it, because I think that the things we are drawn to reflect on are often those which have disturbed our view of the world in some way. These need not be negative things so perhaps another useful image is that of the grit in the oyster, the tiny thing that nags at us and becomes a pearl. When a child acts with unexpected success, or suddenly makes a breakthrough in some way, there is often the element of surprise and then the puzzle of how that success was achieved. Sometimes there seems no rhyme nor reason to it. Sometimes we have a hunch as to why it might have happened, but we want to know more, to explore the conditions and actions which contributed to that happening. So a disturbance might be a surprise, a moment of great pleasure, a nagging worry about why a child does not seem to be making progress, the sneaking feeling that, although they are all sitting quietly and answering the questions, nothing much seems to be happening in the way of learning, the horrible feeling when a class just won't settle or the moment when anger catches you unawares. When you begin writing a journal you might begin with a moment such as one of these. Begin by describing that moment. Tell the story. Recall the detail. And then let the pen go. Write whatever comes into your mind as you think about the event you have described. Later, come back to the writing, and write again.

There are any number of ways of writing about teaching which may or may not be a part of your journal. Some people like using a journal very much, others feel less comfortable with it. Reflective writing can be very fruitful, but you may not always wish to write. Sometimes things which you wish to reflect upon can be represented in different ways. Reflection is about slowing down, pausing. Drawing can be helpful. You may exclaim, 'but I'm no good at drawing!' You do not have to be a consummate artist to make a visual representation of various aspects of your classroom practice.

You might try maps, drawings or diagrams of:

- a lesson
- something you are reading, relating it to your classroom experience
- children in the class you are teaching
- your feeling through a lesson or series of lessons
- you and your relationship to the class
- the way the classroom looks at different times of the day, or at the moment of one particular event you would like to think about.

Using photography

Digital cameras can also provide the focus of useful reflection that can come both at the point of composition and then, later, on examining individual images and sequences of images. These may remind you of a moment or train of thought, or help you see patterns and preoccupations that you were not aware of in the busyness of the classroom. If you choose to use photography, try to choose images thoughtfully. Think about capturing something more abstract and elusive than a documentary record (though this can be useful). Photographing children can be problematic, and I have found that in choosing not to include people in my photographs, I have discovered ways of capturing the events of a classroom that are highly evocative. Sometimes I create a composition, so that a combination of objects will tell a story that relates to my thinking, teaching or actions. You can photograph children's work, equipment, a desk and all its accoutrements, the light falling through a sunny window. Later the photograph will give you a starting point for thinking and may draw your attention to patterns and details that you had not considered before. You can also choose to take a photograph at one or more set times during the day, say 8 a.m., 12 p.m., and 3 p.m. I know a student teacher who took a photograph of herself every morning before she set off to school. I tried it myself, and it provides an intriguing insight into much more than your choice of outfits over a period of time. Another student combined his own notes and drawings with related images and found texts. Images can provide a powerful starting point for reflection.

Although I have suggested that a journal is a personal document, there is also real value in sharing your thoughts with others. By doing so you broaden the professional conversation and bring other perspectives to bear on your experience. I am not suggesting that you share everything that you write in a journal because there can be a real value in the sense of privacy it brings, but there are aspects of a journal which can be very useful in focusing conversations with other teachers, with your tutors and with peers. You may choose to use the journal in an extremely personal way, and touch on things that you do not wish to share. However, a professional journal can make a significant contribution to your evaluation of your progress and assessment of your learning.

CRITICAL ISSUES

There are many ways of becoming a reflective practitioner. I think that writing should play some part in reflection, but the kind of writing that one chooses to undertake is likely to be different. Think about yourself as a reflective practitioner. How would you characterise yourself at the moment? What elements of reflective practice might enhance what you do? Consider your own next steps, either alone or in discussion with a colleague or supervisor. Plan how you would like to develop and what support you need to achieve your aims.

Reflecting on lectures and workshops

Lectures and workshops often occur before you have had a great deal of experience of teaching. They should support your classroom practice. However, you may find that you need to return to lecture notes with the knowledge and questions that you have once you have begun to teach. Sometimes work outside the classroom can seem irrelevant to you as you grapple with the practicalities of managing a large class. Reflective practice involves making links between theory and practice. Lectures should raise questions for you. You may begin lectures with particular questions in mind, and more will be raised. Discuss these with colleagues and with the tutor. Relate these to your reading. Try and respond to the lecture as well as recording information. Think about what it is that is raised by the lecture which prompts you to find out more when you go into school.

Responding to reading

On a PGCE course, reading may seem like an impossible demand, or even a luxury. You are more than likely to limit your reading to texts which will answer the immediate demands of the course. However, reading can help you make the best possible use of your school placements. Reflecting on experience is crucial to one's development as a teacher. Making links to the experience and theories of others enriches, broadens, affirms and challenges your thinking. Ask others, especially tutors, about books and articles which might help you think in greater depth and with finer purpose about the issues which are engaging you.

Whatever you choose to read, make links between your own thinking, your experience of teaching and what you are reading. Theory on its own is hardest to deal with. The challenge is to make sense of it in terms of what you are learning through experience and to translate the theory into the practice of the classroom or use it to help you interpret what happens there. Always be prepared to test ideas out, to test them against your observations and experience, and to challenge your own perceptions. Books which are full of practical ideas for teachers can be really useful, but if you like an idea suggested, be prepared to think it through and decide what its purpose is and why you want to use it. Sometimes books which emphasise experience, which may be autobiographical, strongly narrative or even fictional, can help you think around situations and get a sense of them. Sometimes they can help you picture yourself in similar situations or aiming to achieve similar outcomes. Talk with others about what you are reading. Use writing to help make sense of it, to develop it into a shape you can use and make your own. Many books about teaching tell some kind of story. More often than not it is a smooth and successful story. Rarely do books and articles reveal the messy reality of a classroom, the unsatisfactory ragged nature of much teaching. Sometimes such smoothness can make even experienced teachers feel inadequate or guilty. Stories can be useful touchstones. Records of successful practice have embedded in them ideas which are useful to practitioners. Always, though, trust the reality of your experience, make links with what you read and keep moving between the two. Especially useful is to identify themes, questions and interests which arise directly from your practice and seek out the books and articles which will help you to explore these further.

Although, at first, you may feel that your emphasis is on the *how* of teaching, reflective teaching implies an active concern with aims and with what happens as a result of your actions. When planning, the underlying question of why you are choosing any course of action or sequence of activities is fundamental. When teaching, and when observing the classrooms of others, you may find it useful to have particular questions in mind. Mary Jane Drummond (1996) refers to six 'deceptively simple' questions suggested in the Open University publication, *Curriculum in Action: An Approach to Evaluation*.

1. What did the children actually do?
2. What were they learning?
3. How worthwhile was it?
4. What did you (the teacher) do?
5. What did you learn?
6. What will you do next?

To these six questions, I would add: 'How did you know?' Think about the evidence that is leading you to draw certain conclusions. Check whether you are seeing what is there, or what you would like to see! In her article 'Teachers Asking Questions' (1996), Mary Jane Drummond goes on to say:

> A simple question about classroom things may tell you something about people; a question about children may tell you a lot about teachers; a question about learning may tell you more than you wanted to know about teaching. Linked to this proposition is my belief that children are expert witnesses in our search for evidence of teaching and learning. (p. 12)

While you will learn a great deal from the practice of other teachers, the close observation of children and reflection on their actions seem to me to be central to the art of teaching. Learning from children's behaviour and from their responses to the activities you prepare for them is closely linked to the everyday assessment of children and to your day-by-day adaptation of your plans for individuals and groups. David Hawkins, in his essay 'I, Thou and It' (1974), talks about the notion of a 'feedback loop'. The teacher provides a context, materials and an activity for children to explore and work with. Children's actions and responses can tell you about what they already know and what they are interested in, and can give you clues as to what you might offer them next in order to build on that. At its simplest, you may notice that some children still have difficulty dividing by ten, so you make a mental note that that is an area you must continue to focus on for them. However, you may want to look beyond the surface and think about what a child is telling you through what they say, write and draw, and how they do those things. Listen carefully to what children say and what you notice them doing. When you are observing, assisting in the classroom and working with small groups, take as much opportunity as you can to find out more about children, what they know and how they set about tasks in different subject areas. You will have opportunities to learn in much greater depth than you are able when working with the whole class. Ask children to try and explain to you their think-ing and the processes which they are using to inform whatever activity they are engaged in. Such close attention to what children have to say can be significant in your assessment of children.

Michael Armstrong (1980) suggests that we can think of children as apprentices, who behave as writers, artists, mathematical thinkers, scientists. He argues that they use their limited experience and knowledge to its maximum, using the same processes as an adult practitioner. His detailed observations and analysis of children working in the classroom offer a way of looking at what goes on in the classroom which invites reflection. When looking at children's work it is always worth asking the question: 'What does this tell me about what the child knows?' 'What is their achievement?' And then, 'Did the task set give the child the greatest opportunity to reveal their knowledge and understanding?'

During your training you are learning about classroom skills and about ways of behaving with children, both socially and as a community of learners. At the beginning of the year you are likely to be very conscious of yourself as a key player in the classroom. As you become more experienced, awareness of the children you are teaching will become increasingly important. However, you remain, always, a significant figure in the classroom. Part of learning to be a teacher is knowing how and when to intervene, when to act and when to stand aside. Self-knowledge, self-awareness, is a fundamental part of creating the context for children's confident growth as learners and as people. Reflection is partly about moving away from the self. It is not always comfortable, but nor should it be negative.

Reflection is, or can be, an integral part of teaching. The way we reflect and the focus of our reflections can change as we change. Reflection at the beginning of your training is likely to be different from reflection at its end, as you start your career and later as you continue to gain experience. Teaching is a complex activity. It is full of uncertainties and indeterminacies. The more we write and reflect, the more we learn about our teaching, and the more comfortable we become with the uncertainties of the classroom.

Summary

- Teaching is a highly skilled activity which requires us to anticipate and respond to the complexities of the classroom, to make judgements and act upon them, and to be aware of the consequences of our actions.
- Reflection helps us to make better sense of our teaching and learning and in so doing grow in skill and understanding.
- We learn by reflecting on our thoughts and actions, and by relating our thoughts to the advice, written and spoken, of experts and to other analogous experiences of our own.
- Talking with colleagues, reading, writing and reflecting on photographs are all effective ways to stimulate our thinking and, potentially, enhance our professional practice.

〜〜   **Issues for reflection**

- What opportunities for reflection could you build into your week?
- How could you use a journal – and what forms might it take?
- Think about a recent success you have had as a teacher or as a learner. Why did you consider it a success? What can you learn from the experience?
- Think about the kind of learner that you are and the teacher you hope to be. What implications might that have on the children you teach? How might they benefit and what might they miss out on?

Further reading

Bolton, G. (2010) *Reflective Practice: Writing and Professional Development*. 3rd edition. London: Sage. This excellent book is one that you are likely to return to throughout your career. It explores the nature of reflective practice and provides a wide range of practical suggestions for reflecting on practice. It is a very accessible text which can be used according to your preferences and needs.

Drummond, M.J. (1996) 'Teachers asking questions approaches to evaluation', *Education 3–13*, October. In this useful article Mary Jane Drummond focuses on how asking questions can contribute to evaluation and development and includes a health warning about the potentially unsettling nature of asking questions.

Holly, M.L. (1989) *Writing to Grow*. Portsmouth, NH: Heinemann. A useful guide to writing reflectively using a journal. It includes a rationale for using a 'personal-professional journal', examples from teachers' journals and practical suggestions for keeping a journal.

CHAPTER 10

ASSESSMENT

Ralph Manning

Chapter overview

Let's test the children! But why? Assessment can range from being a very simple task to a surprisingly complex process. It also generates lots of heat and controversial debate. In this chapter Ralph Manning tackles all the issues head on. He explains why it is important to be clear about the purposes of assessment, what you are measuring and what is provided by different types of assessment. This comprehensive guide shows how assessment can be used as a tool to inform your teaching and improve children's learning.

Introduction

The chapters on assessment and planning should be seen as a unit. These two areas of a teacher's professional skills are complementary and dependent on one another, and neither should be considered in isolation from the other.

It can argued, simply, that assessment is just the measurement of learning and that it is important to know this to report a child's attainment. However, what is the purpose of reporting children's attainment? There are many possible reasons: governments and authorities which hold schools accountable for the education of children need some means to assure the taxpayer that schools have used public money well and that the nation's children are being well-educated. They use children's attainment to make judgements about the quality of schools and the teaching within them. On the other hand, parents and teachers want to know their children are making good progress and celebrate their achievements. In either case, there will be an expectation for attainment, or a plan, that the child has either satisfied or exceeded in some recognisable way. So in these cases the nature of the *assessment is dependent on planning*.

However, there are further, more valuable, purposes for assessment: for one thing, it is impossible to plan a suitable course of learning for a child unless you know the child's starting point. If you are unaware of a child's existing knowledge, understanding and skills in any area of the curriculum, then your plans for that child's learning may have incorrect assumptions about their ability to engage with and develop the new learning. The child may either be bored by an apparent repetition of what they already know or they may lack prerequisite skills without which it is impossible to understand the new material you are planning to teach.

Another valuable purpose of assessment is for you to evaluate the effectiveness of your teaching. How well was the intended learning developed? What problems arose in the child's learning and how should you deal with these in subsequent teaching? Is there anything you can learn that will change your plans when you next come to teach this aspect of the curriculum? This is often referred to as *evaluation* of teaching, but it relies on accurate and effective assessment of children's learning to make conclusions about your teaching and how to improve it. This reflective practice, properly informed by evidence, is an intrinsic skill of good teaching (Pollard, 2008).

In the last two cases, *good planning is inextricably dependent upon assessment*. So we find that assessment and planning are equally necessary for the success of both.

There are, of course, some broader uses of assessment in our society. Qualifications are a means of assessment used to determine entry to a particular job or course of study for those who meet appropriate criteria. However, once again, this is usually to ensure that entrants have specific prior knowledge, understanding and skills which are necessary for that job or course of study, i.e. because a *plan* for their work is dependent upon the prior attainment of these criteria. You will not be employed to drive a heavy goods vehicle unless you have a licence which authenticates that you know what you are doing at the wheel of such a potentially dangerous machine because your future employer has plans for you to actually drive the vehicle somewhere. In other cases, when a number of candidates are assessed as meeting the entry requirements, further assessment may be made in order to choose the most talented or highest achieving candidates. This may be because their additional skills and knowledge may bring added longer-term benefits, whether it be that they may be able to work more quickly, provide new ideas, move on to take more responsibility or, in the case of undertaking a course of study, they may be easier to teach or their performance could bring more prestige to the teaching organisation. In either of these situations, assessment is still linked to plans and expectations, albeit with perhaps less clearly defined outcomes.

CRITICAL ISSUES

Originally, reaching level 4 in the National Curriculum Attainment Targets for the *core* subjects of English, mathematics and science was considered to be the *average* attainment for a child at the end of Key Stage 2. According to the results of the Key Stage 2 national tests in 2009 (DCSF, 2009b), 80 per cent of children attained level 4 in English, 79 per cent in mathematics and 88 per cent in science. Was it accurate for the Chief Inspector of Schools to assert from similar results that ' ... *20 per cent leave primary school without a solid foundation in literacy and numeracy'* (Clark, 2007, p. 2)? How has the assessment evidence been used here?

Assessment of learning

Effective assessment should enable you to identify a number of pieces of significant information, all of which are crucial to completing your understanding of a child's present and future learning:

- *A measure of a child's attainment in some specific knowledge, skills and understanding.* This may be the exercise of a particular skill, the child's understanding of a new concept or perhaps simply the recall of a memorised fact. In identifying this, you are concerned with the quality of the evidence you will actually look for, otherwise known as the *assessment criteria* or *success criteria*, not just the means by which you will find it. The way you determine success criteria varies according to the *order of cognitive processing* and the *learning situation* (see below), and some situations offer more tangible or quantitative criteria than others. Nonetheless, there are always some criteria by which we establish attainment, since attainment is intrinsically defined with respect to a wish, an ideal, an expectation, a goal or a standard of some kind with which you compare the actual evidence.
- *Misconceptions or errors in the child's knowledge, skills and understanding.* This is where the evidence reveals, often through an error, that a child misuses a skill, misunderstands a concept or inaccurately recalls some prior knowledge. This aspect of assessment is often forensic in nature: you are trying to establish the *root cause* of the problem and it requires a diagnostic approach to what a medical doctor would

call the 'presenting problem': the evidence provides us with symptoms – clues to the underlying problem. However, you must be careful not to jump to conclusions about the reasons for a particular presenting problem. It is very important to talk to the 'patient' too, for example asking a child to recount what they did, how they did it and why they did it in a particular way. This is especially important when you have not been able to observe the child working and only have their 'finished' product, e.g. a piece of written work, as the presenting evidence. As teachers, we need to investigate the symptoms to determine what help the child really needs.

- *Potential next step(s) in the child's learning.* This is one of the most important and complex skills of the teacher – to identify, given the child's current attainment, what you consider to be a reasonable progression in their learning. This needs to be sufficiently challenging to engage them in learning, but not too large a step at any one time that they are overwhelmed and unable to cope with the next learning situation.
- *Barriers to the child's further attainment or understanding.* Assessment should also uncover potential inhibitors which must be removed or overcome in order for a child to make progress. For example, when learning to swim, fear of getting your face wet will limit your ability to develop a good swimming stroke. Effective instructors take great pains to help learners overcome this fear, devising games which encourage children to put their face into the water in non-threatening, enjoyable situations.

A hierarchy of learning

It is a common and simplistic view of learning and its assessment that every instance of learning can be treated in the same way. In fact, there are different types of learning experiences and different *orders* of knowledge, skills and understanding encountered within them. This distinction between levels of *cognitive* learning was modelled helpfully in a *Taxonomy of Educational Objectives* (Bloom et al., 1956, revised in Krathwohl, 2002). For over 50 years, Bloom's work has been used very effectively and reliably by educators to plan and examine learning intentions and the success or otherwise of teaching to meet these. The taxonomy developed a progression of learning from lower-order skills, knowledge and understanding upwards through successively higher-order levels of learning which require more complex cognitive processing.

For example, recognising or recalling facts, such as multiplication facts, or matching the phoneme (a phonetic sound) to its grapheme (a written letter or sequence of letters) would be attributed to the lowest order, *factual knowledge*. Reproduction of a simple procedure, such as how to measure and cut out a specific shape from a piece of card, or phonetically decoding the sound of a written word would rank a little higher, but would still be a fairly low order of factual knowledge and skill. In all these cases the outcomes could be achieved with little understanding of what was taking place: a child does not need to know the name of the shape they are cutting out, nor its intended purpose; similarly, they do not need to understand the meaning of a word before they can accurately decode and say aloud the sound of that word.

A higher order of learning, *conceptual knowledge* or *understanding,* occurs where a child understands a concept behind a procedure and can use this to self-correct if necessary: for example, a child uses a method to subtract one number from another, knows how the method works and can go back to correct a step which they made in error. A child with a higher understanding than this recognises the relationship between addition and subtraction and can construct an appropriate addition to check the answer of their subtraction.

A higher order of learning, *procedural knowledge*, is demonstrated when a child encounters a task, can *apply* the steps to carry out the task and can *analyse* the order in which the steps are needed. Most problem-solving requires us to do this. Think of the different skills you apply from art and design, technology, mathematics, physical education and other areas of learning. A still higher order of cognitive processing enables us to *evaluate* a plan carefully to determine if it is or is not feasible.

Our highest order of thinking enables us to find novel ways of combining knowledge, skills and understanding from different areas to generate alternative solutions to a challenge; then to plan how to carry out those solutions in order to synthesise or *create* new knowledge, skills and understanding to tackle unusual or more demanding challenges.

In our assessment of children's learning, it is important to assess learning in *all* levels of cognitive processing. You must therefore plan for learning to take place at each of these different levels at appropriate and regular points in your teaching. Assessment of lower-order learning is generally more straightforward than higher-order learning, because in the former, the learning can be in discrete steps and we are usually able to identify specific, tangible evidence which demonstrates accurate recall of knowledge or use of the lower-order skills.

Low-order skills can often be observed in the firm evidence of children's outcomes from a lesson – how to calculate, write a sentence, read a compass, join two pieces of wood at 90° and so on – specific knowledge, skills or understanding which they can copy and reproduce. For this reason they are sometimes referred to as *hard* or *firm skills* (Corder, 1990). *Firm* is a preferable term, as 'hard' can also mean 'difficult', which is not what we mean here. High-order skills, by contrast, are referred to as *soft skills* because the learning is usually difficult to quantify unambiguously and is often built upon combinations of knowledge, skills and understanding. Soft skills are difficult to assess directly from tangible products and are more usually revealed through a child's *process* during an activity rather than their products at the end of the activity.

If children are to develop high-order thinking, they need to be provided with experiences where 'soft skills' are the expressed learning intentions of the teaching and activities they undertake. To do this the teacher needs to provide high-order and carefully situated learning experiences where the child has to apply, analyse, evaluate and create their own solutions, make decisions, communicate them to others, etc. in the process of their activities. This is just as important as teaching the child the 'firm skills' they need. Those in primary teaching situations can spend a disproportionate amount of time teaching and assessing low-order learning, which is easiest to measure, at the expense of children's higher-order development, which is often much more difficult to assess. This is to the detriment of their learning as in low-order situations some children may appear to attain very well but they cannot apply or combine their skills in other ways when faced with new or more demanding situations.

Learning situations

Every instance of learning takes place within a context, or a *learning situation*. The choice of learning situation has implications for assessment too. There are basically two types of learning situation: *constrained* and *unconstrained*.

Unconstrained

An unconstrained learning situation is one where the teacher has planned and prepared for a very wide range of engagement by different children, where the actual learning experience may vary quite markedly according to the interests of the child. This type of situation is typical and frequently used in Early Years Foundation Stage settings. For example, the teacher may have buried a number of articles in a sandpit. There may also be some spades and different-shaped buckets for children to use. The teacher may have in mind that this could develop children's knowledge and understanding of the world, following a book they have been sharing about how we find out about the past from discovering and finding out about buried artefacts. 'Excavating' the 'dig' may be an activity that a child takes up. However, other children may have a range of different valid learning outcomes across the curriculum from engaging with the same resources in different ways: one child may be more interested in pouring scoops of sand through their fingers, another may be hiding their feet, still another using the buckets to form sandcastles and perhaps even one child comparing the amount of sand held in the different buckets.

All of these markedly different activities and the different learning outcomes they produce are possible from the same learning situation and set of resources. The means of assessment will need to gather evidence through close observation, or snapshots at different points during the time period, and/or through conversation with the children themselves during or soon after their activity.

In this kind of 'child-initiated' activity, identifying assessment criteria is often after the fact, depending on how the child engages with the resources, because it is not obvious which learning outcomes may be (albeit unwittingly) pursued by each child. Nonetheless, once the child does demonstrate some aspect of learning, it is usually then possible to compare the child's achievement with a range of potential expectations in that area of the curriculum.

Constrained

A constrained learning situation is where the expectations of learning are more constrained by the formal curriculum and we say that they are 'teacher-initiated'. For example, a child's learning situation may be constrained in order for them to practise adding different numbers to a total of 5. The teacher has identified that the child needs to develop these skills and so will engineer the learning situation to provide specifically for this outcome. The child may simply wish to arrange some counters in an interesting layout but the teacher will need to intervene and work with the child to establish the intended learning outcome. A child may wish to bang their shoe on different surfaces to hear the noise it makes but the teacher may intend that the child uses the shoe in order to learn how to tie a shoelace! Constrained learning situations become much more the modus operandi, even from Key Stage 1 upwards, as the formal body of knowledge, skills and understanding in the curriculum becomes more detailed. It is this content which children have a statutory entitlement to learn and which schools are expected to teach. However, it is always helpful to enable the child to have some say in their own learning and to lead with their own interests where possible, as this is helpful in developing children's motivation for learning (see Chapter 8).

Note that there is no direct correlation between the order of cognitive learning which takes place and whether the learning situation is constrained or unconstrained. The development of higher-order skills often requires much greater flexibility in the means and resources by which children reach particular outcomes, but the outcomes themselves may be very well-defined.

Types of assessment

There are three types of assessment. Each is conditioned by the period of time to which it refers, but the difference between types is more concerned with their effect on learning than their timing.

- *Summative assessment.* Looking back at the end of a period of learning, perhaps one week, or completing a unit of work over several weeks, over one term, or even over a year, what has the child achieved? The longer the period, the more detail may be known, though if the evidence is actually accumulated over too long a period rather than in one 'snapshot' some of it will have been superseded by later progress (or lack of retention!). It is helpful to celebrate a child's achievements and useful for evaluating your effectiveness in teaching, but it is not immediately useful in identifying learning needs without further analysis of the detail.
- *Formative assessment.* At the end of a lesson or the conclusion of a sequence of lessons, understanding the child's present attainment, difficulties and misconceptions enables you to plan appropriately for their learning needs in future. The important

thing here is that the purpose of this assessment is focused on developing learning, so the focus of the evidence to be found is aimed clearly at this.

- *Dynamic assessment.* This is the immediate assessment you make of different learners' progress and difficulties as they arise during a lesson. An experienced teacher does this instinctively, every time a child asks a question or as they observe a child's work or play, to decide how best to respond in order to move the child on in their learning. It is another of the most important and complex skills of a teacher, and it is exercised many times each day in a multitude of interactions with different children. It requires you to repeatedly switch context from one child to another, and while it makes teaching fascinating, constantly challenging and fast-paced, it can also make it very tiring!

Summative assessment is also sometimes described as 'assessment *of* learning' to distinguish it from the other two types, which are used to inform further planning and teaching. Formative and dynamic assessment are sometimes described as aspects of 'assessment *for* learning'. However, in recent years, research and development in how to use assessment more effectively to help learners understand and take ownership of their own learning has developed a much richer vision of the latter term. While *formative assessment* is very important in *assessment for learning*, these two terms are not synonymous.

Assessment for learning

Over the past twenty years, great progress has been made in the development of assessment *for learning*. Seminal work by Sadler (1989) questioned the nature of assessment at that time and argued for two significant improvements. Firstly, the teacher should share with the learner the teacher's *formative* assessment of them. The common conception of the teacher–student relationship is that the student's responsibility is to respond to learning situations designed by the teacher and that assessment of the learning and what should happen next is the responsibility and domain of the teacher. Sadler argued that students made more progress if they themselves understood their own formative assessment in specific terms. The student

> ... has to (a) possess a concept of the standard (or goal, or reference level) being aimed for, (b) compare the actual (or current) level of performance with the standard, and (c) engage in appropriate action which leads to some closure of the gap. (Sadler, 1989, p. 121)

In other words, the student has to understand what they are aiming for, the difference between that and what they know now, and how they can succeed in getting to their target. This may not sound like rocket science, but consider your own learning or working life. Can you recall times when you have completed something but not really understood the objectives or what the criteria for success would be? This situation persisted in schools (and still does in some) where children are expected to learn because they are following the teacher's instructions, while to the child who does not understand what they are learning they are simply doing something that the teacher has told them to do. I remember a D&T lesson once when I was a pupil at secondary school in which I was required to shape a piece of metal, presumably for practice in using some specific tools or technique though this was not evident to me at the time. Instead, I saw little point in producing a clearly useless, twisted piece of mild steel just for it to be thrown in the scrap bin!

Secondly, Sadler argued that the teacher should also enable the student to develop the ability to make their own assessment of their learning together with the skills to plan their future learning experiences:

> Part of the teacher's responsibility is surely, however, to download that evaluative knowledge so that students eventually become independent of the teacher and intelligently engage in and monitor their own development. (Sadler, 1989, p. 121)

This second notion is effectively summarised in the old Chinese proverb: 'Give a man a fish and you feed him for a day. Teach a man to fish and you feed him for a lifetime.'

Sadler's work was taken forward by others in the field, including members of the influential *Assessment Reform Group (ARG)*, who mobilised educators to reconsider the purposes and means of assessment to meet the needs of present-day and future generations:

> The awareness of learning and ability of learners to direct it for themselves is of increasing importance in the context of encouraging lifelong learning. (ARG, 1999, p. 7)

The argument here is that the teacher's ultimate purpose is not just to teach specific knowledge, skills and understanding, but also to develop the student's capacity for independent learning, by teaching them the skills necessary to do this. It was very effectively applied to the development of Assessment for Learning in secondary schools (Black and Wiliam, 1998a, 1998b; Black et al., 2003a, 2003b) and then to primary education, particularly by Clarke (2001, 2003). The research has amply demonstrated that learning is more effective when even young children understand what, why and how they are learning. In this way children are encouraged to take ownership of their own learning rather than simply carry out activities because they have been told to do so.

In the course of this, *Assessment for Learning* has become something of a 'brand name', and has often been borrowed and sometimes misused by government departments and other interested parties in their reports, so be careful that those you read really mean the same thing when using this title.

To put Assessment for Learning to work, the teacher needs the set of six key strategies illustrated in Figure 10.1. We are going to look at each of these strategies in turn.

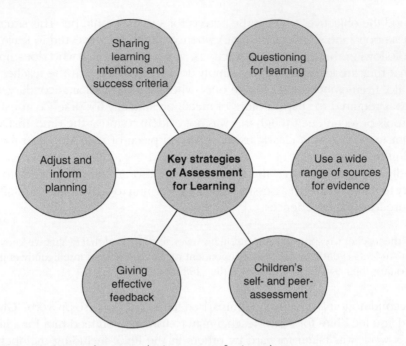

Figure 10.1   Key strategies to use in Assessment for Learning

Sharing learning intentions and success criteria

The research shows that it is very helpful for children to understand what they should be able to learn from a given situation. Teachers can often concentrate on describing to the children what they will *do,* e.g. 'We are going to make moving birthday cards', rather than what they want the children to *learn,* e.g. 'We are going to learn *how to use levers* in birthday cards to make them move.' There is a careful and crucial distinction here. If the focus is on learning how to use levers, other activities could be substituted instead of making birthday cards, but the lesson remains focused on the learning intention. If you are not clear about the real learning intention, the child may well make an interesting birthday card but learn nothing about how levers work! Sharing the learning intention with the children does not mean it must be displayed up on the whiteboard (though it may be) or that it must be announced, like a ritual, at the start of every lesson. Sometimes, as an element of surprise or to create interest through a narrative, the learning intention may be made clear later in the lesson. However, at a suitable point in the course of the lesson, it should be possible to ask a child what they are learning or have learned from an activity and to get a reasonably appropriate answer.

Learning intentions may be framed and expressed differently in different learning situations, but they are still important to the assessment process. When the learning intention has been planned, the assessment criteria or *success criteria* can be decided. Success criteria enable you assess *the degree* to which a child meets the learning intention. This is a question of *what* evidence you will look for. Sometimes when asked how they will assess a child's work, a student-teacher might say, 'I'm going to read their story', or 'I'm going to look at their work', or in the example above they may say, 'They're going to make a card'. These are not *criteria,* simply a statement of *where* the teacher might look to find evidence. Success criteria describe the *qualities* of the evidence you may expect to see, for example: 'There will be at least one feature which moves through the use of a lever.' There can now be no doubt that unless the card has at least one feature which is worked by a lever, the learning intention has not been met, no matter how attractive the birthday card!

However, we must remember that because children progress differently, the degree to which they meet a learning intention will vary. This will depend on a child's prior attainment – their existing knowledge, skills and understanding. In any class there will be a range of likely attainment, so it helps to consider a range of success criteria. However, it is usual that a number of children will be able to meet the same criteria, so a helpful way of managing this is to think of up to three (or at most four) levels of expectation for the success criteria – something that *all children* in the class could achieve, something that *most children* would be able to do and something that *some children* may be able to go on to achieve. In our example, these might be:

- *All children* 'will produce at least one feature which moves through the use of a rigid lever.'
- *Most children* 'will produce at least one feature which moves using a hinged lever.'
- *Some children* 'will combine different levers to provide a combination of features.'

The idea of *all, most* and *some* allows for different children to succeed in different and more progressively creative ways, but should be chosen to reflect the potential attainment of groups of children within the lesson. It is important that these success criteria are shared with the children. Children normally want to be pleased with the outcome of their efforts and when they know exactly *how* they can succeed, they will try harder to do that. We will return to this idea in Chapter 11, but it is important for children's ownership of their learning to help them decide for themselves which is an appropriate level of challenge to aim for in each new learning situation rather than labelling the child by fixed 'ability groups' and always assigning them the same level of expectation regardless.

It is worth noting that there is still some flexibility in how the child may meet the criteria in each case. The 'rigid lever' could be one straight piece of card, or it could be an L-shape or other variation. The 'hinged lever' could be just two pieces of card loosely joined with a split clip fastener, or the child could make this more elaborate.

Notice that the *some children* criterion also has the facility for a child to display some high-order skills in their decision of which different types of lever to combine. This is a typical way to assess *soft skills*: enabling a qualitative judgement to be made about the child's decision-making process. It may require asking the children to explain why they chose the mechanisms they did. The teacher is then analysing children's statements such as 'because it looks the best', 'because it is easier to make than …', and so on. Such judgements are difficult to quantify, because different reasons can be equally valid. The same soft skills may be assessed again and again throughout a child's development, because the nature of the skills are such that they continue to develop. For example, how do you measure 'creativity'? When could you say that a child 'completely achieved' this? It is a continually developing skill which is very hard to assess. It depends on the resources available, the nature of the discipline in which they are working – creativity in mathematics is demonstrated differently from creativity in visual art – and, ultimately, creativity depends upon the range of prior learning (some of which may be 'firm skills') which the child already knows and they can bring to bear. For example, if you know only one procedure for multiplying two numbers, it is not a measure of your creativity that this procedure is the only one you use every time.

Another related aspect is that of *motivation*. It helps enormously if we can stimulate children's interest in learning, and wherever possible it is useful to provide a motivation for their learning. Understanding what we are trying to learn and how we can succeed is a great motivation in itself, but it also helps to provide other intrinsic reasons for wanting to succeed. For example, in the case above it may be because 'you are going to make your own moving birthday card to give to someone you love' (see also Chapter 8).

Questioning for learning

A second strategy which research identified, particularly through Clarke (2001) and Black et al. (2003b), is to change the focus of questioning which the teacher uses (see also Chapter 6). It is common practice among teachers to begin a new topic with some assessment and revision of what children already know about it through questioning the class. However, teachers often ask closed questions, requiring a small number of specific answers. This reduces the number of participants to only those who are confident of providing the answers which the teacher expects. For example, a teacher may ask a straight mental arithmetic question: 'What is 51 – 29?', and one child will answer '22'. The teacher has only learned that one child can carry out this calculation; they do not know who else can or can't, nor *the means* by which they may arrive at the answer. In another example, in opening up a discussion on the water cycle, a teacher may ask, 'Does anyone know what we call it when a puddle dries up?', when they are trying to find out who knows something about 'evaporation'. Sometimes it can turn into a guessing game: 'What's on teacher's mind?' as children desperately endeavour to provide the word which will end the teacher's quest:

First child: 'Is it condensation, Miss?'
Second child: 'No, it's' "evacoration".'
Third child: 'Evacuation!'

The danger here is that the thinking required of the children is really quite limited – they either know or they don't. The level of thinking is typically attributed to the lowest order. The cognitive process is simply the recall of facts, or at most a limited demonstration that the child has *a process* or technique as in the case of the mental arithmetic question. There is little scope for children to contribute something that they do know unless they have one of the limited number of possible answers to the question.

To engage more children, and with a higher order of thinking, more open questions need to be chosen for the initial assessment, such as: 'How could we calculate 51 – 29?' In this example, the teacher is inviting the children to describe the strategies they could use to carry out the calculation. By saying *How could we…?* the teacher is establishing that the class together is trying to construct an answer and they are not seeking to test one child. The teacher can, with the rest of the class, analyse and evaluate a child's given strategy, for example *counting back* from 51 to 29. The teacher can then (sensitively) invite others to help in gently correcting any misconception or error, before asking for alternative strategies and encouraging children to suggest why some strategies might be more helpful than others for this particular calculation. Another child may suggest using *addition and bridging*, say add 1 from 29 to 30, then add 20 from 30 to 50, and finally add 1 from 50 to 51. In this way, a higher order of learning has taken place, the teacher has involved more children and they have helped correct, compare and evaluate the strategies they are using. If in the next stage of the lesson the teacher intends to extend or expand the children's calculation skills, they have already begun to establish children's motivation for their learning intention.

In the example of the water cycle, a number of more open questions could be asked, such as: 'How do you think we get rain?', 'Where does the water go to when puddles disappear?', or 'Why do clouds form?' The questions would be intended to solicit a range of different contributions which the teacher can link together, being careful to celebrate every helpful contribution, even though the children may not use the correct vocabulary or be able to describe more than a few aspects of what happens. Clarke (2001) insists that saying *Do you think …?* is important as it shows the teacher is not asking for certainty. In this case, the assessment provides the questions for which the children do not have answers, which in turn help to frame further learning intentions.

Higher-order questioning stimulates the children towards higher-order thinking and helps to generate the motivation for their learning too, as the children think about what they hope to learn, or try to make sense of the 'missing' pieces in their existing understanding.

Use a wide range of sources for evidence

In the short term, the evidence gathered to make an assessment must be capable of enabling you to learn the key pieces of information described in the earlier section

'Assessment of learning'. The evidence sought may vary as needed according to the learning intentions, success criteria and learning situations, and may need to be combined from the different sources listed below.

To build up as complete a picture as possible to have a well-informed understanding of each child, it is essential to gather a rich range of different types of evidence:

- *Products*. These are tangible 'end-results' of a child's activity, for example a page of written work, which has been completed in response to the learning intentions; alternatively it could be something a child has designed or made, for example a junk model or a short animation produced on a computer.
- *Observation*. It is very useful to use some periods of lessons to observe an individual or small group of children very closely as they undertake a learning activity. This is imperative in order to understand how well a child understands a *process*. You cannot fully assess this without observing the child putting the process into effect. (See also Chapter 5.)
- *Questioning*. This may be questioning an individual in a formal or semi-formal interview with a set of prepared questions designed to test and probe the child's learning; alternatively it could be questioning the child in *ad hoc* interactions in the course of the lesson, or as a means to learn more about the way they completed a piece of work or why they arrived at particular results. You will also use plenary sessions in lessons in a semi-formal way to address questions to the whole class, both to 'open' areas of learning and also to test and confirm children's learning, to identify and engage with difficulties and misconceptions as a larger group.
- *Other means of recording evidence*. This could include, for example, digital or video camera, audio recording or screen capture of a computer session. Observation and questioning need focused time to work with children, so it is useful if it is possible to turn some of these into 'products' by finding ways to record and later play back the child's process. This is also useful to share the assessment evidence with the children themselves (see below).
- *Children's self- and peer-assessment*. It is helpful to get evidence from children's own understanding of assessment. This will be discussed in the next section.

Children's self- and peer-assessment

A significant strategy in educating children about the process of assessment and its importance in their learning is to encourage the children to share in assessing their own outcomes. This helps to develop their understanding of the value of assessment in their learning, helps them to recognise their own success in learning and their needs, and helps them to become more focused on the learning intentions and success criteria in the work they do.

Engaging children in their own assessment can begin simply with everyone in the class 'marking' their own or their partner's products under the guidance of the teacher, sharing in feedback and follow-up where learning points arise. The success criteria need to be well understood to do this. It is simple enough for children to assess firm skills such as after a spelling or 'times tables' test, but more complex for them to assess the completed birthday cards in the example above or to assess the performance of a piece of drama. In these kinds of situations the success criteria need to be clearly established by the teacher, who should encourage the children to direct their comments to what has worked well or how work can be improved within the criteria.

Self- and peer-assessment needs sensitive, careful but clear direction from the teacher. It requires you to develop the classroom culture of being *a community of learners* who support and help one another. As a teacher, you need to *model* to the children that you are always a (lifelong) learner too. Your children need to be encouraged that the aim of the process is to recognise what has been done well and to help everyone to do even better in future. This is sometimes very hard for children at first, and you will need to be very diplomatic in channelling children's criticism constructively.

For 'performance-based' work, say for a drama or PE sequence, it can be very helpful to make a video recording and watch this together. You can stop and replay aspects for further examination. Keep directing the children to identify successes and where and how specific things could be improved.

For other pieces of work a questionnaire can be devised which helps the child to identify how they think they have fared with a learning intention in a particular activity. For younger children, and to reduce the dependence on written assessment, a simple selection from one of ☺, ☺ or ☹ is helpful, while for older children space for a more considered assessment is very helpful. There is a simple example questionnaire for design technology on the 'Birthday card' in Figure 10.2.

Notice that the child is being directed to focus on the success criteria in the first four statements. However, the last statement requires them to explore their learning in more

I can make a lever from card:	☺ ☺ ☹
I can make a lever with a hinge:	☺ ☺ ☹
I can include different types of levers:	☺ ☺ ☹
I work accurately and neatly:	☺ ☺ ☹
Where I had problems and how I overcame them:	

Figure 10.2 An example self-assessment questionnaire

depth. This is potentially the most helpful item of feedback to you as a teacher, in helping the child to understand where they are in their learning and the higher-order learning they have achieved.

It is important not to rely *only* on the children's assessments! For you, their self- and peer-assessments are helpful but not decisive. As their teacher, you are far more experienced and skilful in assessment than the children, and you cannot abdicate your responsibility for maintaining an accurate and complete picture of each child's attainment.

Giving effective feedback

Both the quality of the feedback we provide to children and the way in which we provide it have a huge impact on their learning. The quality of our feedback must be such that it helps them to develop their knowledge, skills and understanding. Simply writing 'Good work!' and awarding a 'house point' or a 'smiley face' has no educational benefit for the child beyond simple reassurance for their self-esteem; it continues to make the child reliant on you to know what is 'good' about a particular item of work. On the other hand, we have probably all known the experience of working really hard and being very engaged in producing something, only to be devastated when it was returned to us covered in a sea of red ink! This had the double-whammy of lowering our self-esteem while also not telling us anything helpful educationally because there was too much information to absorb! The result was that we simply felt like failures rather than learners.

For feedback to be helpful towards a child's learning, it needs to be clearly focused on the learning intentions. It is very easy for a child to become gripped by the thrill of developing an exciting character in their story if this is the learning intention, so it is not helpful for the teacher then to point out every spelling mistake or mistake in punctuation. If you want your children to experiment with different types of lever, the resulting birthday card may be a little messy, cluttered or incomplete. Is that important compared with the learning intention?

Clarke (2003) advises being very focused on providing feedback which expressly addresses the success criteria. After all, if you have taken pains to ensure that the children understand the learning intentions and know how to succeed, it is only fair that you assess them on these grounds and do not suddenly introduce 'alternative' or 'hidden' criteria upon which their work is to be assessed. It is easy to think, 'Yes, but they should already know this too.' However, it is hard to remember everything else when you are a young learner, enthusiastic in your work and learning something new. Other strategies may help here. Teaching the children to review their completed written work against a checklist before they finish can reduce their careless errors but can also leave the piece looking like a battlefield of hasty corrections.

When assessing a 'product', look for some places where the success criteria have been met and celebrate these. Then identify one or two places where the child has not met the success criteria and invite them to correct or reflect on these. If the child has been very successful, identify a suitable next goal for them to think about and challenge them to have a try at this.

How you give this feedback is just as important as the feedback itself. It is most effective to have a conversation directly with the individual child. When this is possible, it can also save you effort in annotating their work and writing feedback. It is also essential if you need to explore misconceptions and errors further in order to identify how to help the child. However, when it is not possible to speak individually, make sure that you provide an opportunity to explore common points of feedback with groups of children, or even with the whole class. If you have written feedback, make sure you provide time for the children to read and act upon this. Unless you do this, children will quickly look for some reassurance that they have 'done alright' but are likely to ignore the rest of what you have taken the effort to write!

Adjust and inform planning

The final strategy of effective *Assessment for Learning* is to ensure that what we learn about children's attainment and their resulting learning needs is used to inform our planning for subsequent teaching. It is pointless to continue with a sequence of lessons in their present planned form if our assessment of the last lesson shows that some children are having great difficulty in their understanding and will not be able to engage with the next steps in the learning intentions. We will need to change our plans, adapt or introduce one or more different lessons with modified learning intentions and/or success criteria to help these children (see Chapter 11).

It is also important to note that assessment has to be timely or you cannot use it for this purpose. Delaying the assessment has the same effect on subsequent teaching as not assessing their learning.

CRITICAL ISSUES

Look at the way experienced teachers are using assessment in your placement school(s). Read *Inside the Black Box* (Black and Wiliam, 1998a). How effectively have its findings been applied? Are all the strategies of *Assessment for Learning* used within the school?

What to record and when

It is important to record only what is actually useful when assessing learning. Much day-to-day formative and dynamic assessment is transient. The child moves on so quickly that recording every detail of their learning is not only tedious but of no value in the longer-term picture of their learning or for adapting your planning. From lesson to lesson it is most helpful to record just the *exceptions* to your lesson's success criteria. That is, note which children were unsuccessful in meeting the success criteria and those who surprised you in the way they exceeded the success criteria. This is helpful to inform you when you adjust your planning for subsequent lessons, and useful in identifying any patterns of evidence in under- or higher-than-anticipated attainment for individuals.

Beyond this it is helpful to make more formal records of how every child in the class has met success criteria for significant, overall learning intentions at appropriate points in their learning. These would be times such as the completion of a topic or the end of a sequence of lessons comprising an identifiable unit of work, e.g. at the end of a week-long focus on developing calculation skills. The aim here is threefold:

1. to build up the *summative* picture of learning for reporting an individual child's achievement;
2. to use this record formatively to identify the significant next steps in learning for this child whenever teaching returns to develop this particular area of topic further in future;
3. to evaluate and improve your teaching.

Determining levels of attainment

Establishing effective expectations for attainment, and hence standardised criteria for summative assessment of learning, is possibly one of the most vexed aspects in education in England and Wales in the past 20 years. Similar debates have taken place in Scotland and Northern Ireland. The establishment of a National Curriculum for England and Wales brought with it a graduated set of expectations for assessing learning. The curriculum was subdivided into different strands of learning, known as *Attainment Targets*. Each Attainment Target described a progression of learning within that strand of the curriculum, set out over a number of *Level Descriptions*, where level 1 was the lowest level of attainment and level 8 the highest (DfEE, 1999). When these were established, the national average would be to reach the expectations for level 2 by the end of Key Stage 1 (year 2) in the Attainment Targets for English, mathematics and science, while at the end of Key Stage 2 (year 6), the average attainment would be to reach expectations for level 4. However, the level of detail needed for making judgements about children's achievement has led to considerable debate about how progress should be interpreted between level descriptions. Attempts to interpret progress at this finer granularity have begun with the National Strategies work on 'Assessing Pupils' progress' (DCSF, 2010a), but following the change of government in May 2010, this work is under review at the time of writing.

Modes of reference

There are also three *modes* of reference which can be used with assessment data. Which one is used depends on the purposes of the assessment.

- *Criterion-referenced.* These are assessments made against objective standards, such as the Level Descriptions for Attainment Targets in the National Curriculum. Another criterion-referenced assessment is a driving test. GCSEs and other examinations are also set against criterion-referenced data.
- *Norm-referenced.* These are assessments made against peers, such as the kind described earlier to find the 'best' candidates for job or university selection procedures. There are also plenty of unhelpful examples of *criterion-referenced* assessment being reinterpreted in *norm-referenced* ways: for example, *'School exams: have standards really fallen?'* (Baker, 2010).
- *Ipsative.* This is probably one of the most encouraging modes of reference to use with children in a primary school. It is an assessment made against the child's own previous attainment. Hence it is truly a measure of *achievement* rather than simply attainment, and can be used to celebrate the extent of progress a child has made independently of their actual level of attainment. Athletes use this kind of measure all the time in trying to improve on their previous 'personal best' time or score. Celebrating some ipsative progress shows the child that their efforts are producing results. It is often possible to observe some improvement, even if the child is not yet meeting established expectations.

Summary

This chapter has established the important interdependency between the teacher's skills in assessment and planning for learning. Significant developments in making assessment more effective for learners have been highlighted, especially how to undertake assessment *for* learning, rather than just assessment *of* learning. Key strategies of Assessment for Learning are:

- sharing learning intentions and success criteria with children
- developing the use of questioning to open up higher-order learning and motivate children
- using a rich and wide range of evidence to inform assessment
- involving children in self- and peer-assessment to build their skills in using assessment and understanding their own learning

(Continued)

> *(Continued)*
>
> - providing effective feedback which informs children about their learning
> - using assessment to adjust and inform your planning.
>
> Finally, we have looked at some of the ways in which expectations for attainment have been developed and used.

Issues for reflection

Look at the *Ten Principles of Assessment for Learning*, published by the Assessment Reform Group (2002). Are you applying these principles in your own teaching practice? How? Try to list some examples of what you have done. Compare your experiences with your colleagues.

Further reading

Alexander, R. (ed.) (2010) *Children, Their World, Their Education: Final Report and Recommendations of the Cambridge Primary Review*, London: Routledge, chapter 16 'Assessment, learning and accountability'. This summarises the recent findings of the Cambridge Review on the current issues in the purpose, nature and means of assessment.

Clarke, S. (2005) *Formative Assessment in Action: Weaving the Elements Together.* London: Hodder-Murray. This book builds on and develops Clarke's earlier books, superseding the superficial implementations in many schools, bandying terms such as 'WALT' and 'WILF' without really applying the principles of Assessment for Learning. It is probably the best treatment of the subject applied to the primary school.

And, for the 'Critical Issue' task you will require:

Black, P. and Wiliam, D. (1998) *Inside the Black Box: Raising Standards Through Classroom Assessment.* London: School of Education, King's College; see also *Phi Delta Kappan,* 80(2) pp. 139–48.

CHAPTER 11

PLANNING

Eleanor Cockerton

Chapter overview

Making lessons work? It's all in the planning. Much great teaching relies on the bedrock of good planning. While acknowledging that schools and teachers plan in different ways Eleanor Cockerton provides some fundamental principles and guidance on how to plan effectively. She demonstrates how personalising your own planning to the needs of the children you teach can make all the difference.

Introduction

Planning needs to be considered in close partnership with assessment. Reading the previous chapter alongside this one will give you a better view of the process. Planning is a vital part of teaching and it is well worth spending time and effort getting it right. It can be an invaluable teaching and self-assessment tool and it will ensure that you have thought through exactly how the lesson will work for you, the children and any supporting adults. You will then be able to look back and see if it worked as you imagined, whether the children learned what you had intended and anything you did to improve or detract from their learning experience. It takes practice and can be a highly individual process, so do not despair if it takes a while to make it work well. When you are able to plan effectively it will put you in a stronger position in the classroom. You will have a clear idea of where you are going, the timing of different elements and what the learning should look like by the end. It will make you feel more prepared when you are in front of the class, a little like a sophisticated security blanket, and will make your thought processes evident to anyone supervising your progress. It is very difficult to help a prospective teacher improve their teaching when the planning and thinking behind it are difficult to unravel.

Depending on the way your placement school plans, you will be given long- and/or medium- and sometimes short-term plans to work from. This is rather a 'swings and roundabouts' situation as the more the school has done for you, the less you will need to do but the less you will learn about the whole planning process and your individual needs. It is important therefore to make the planning your own. I have always found it extremely difficult to teach effectively using plans which I have not personalised taking into account my children, my teaching style and my resources. You also lose some of the excitement from planning your own learning opportunity or taking a bit of a risk because you think a particular activity will grab your children's interest.

Elements of your planning are likely to be dictated by preset curricula (such as the National Curriculum, Early Years Foundation Stage Guidance or school documentation) but there will be some elements you will be able to make your own. Some schools also use commercial schemes of work as a basis for planning. There may be opportunities to plan cooperatively with colleagues in a parallel age group or you may be teaching more than one age group in your class. Your training establishment will also have its own views on what should be included although these tend to be fairly standard. So, as you can see, there are many variations before you even start to think about how and what might work best for you.

The Early Years Foundation Stage (EYFS) planning takes on a quite different guise from that undertaken in Key Stages 1 or 2 as the children take much greater control over their learning. Long- and medium-term plans will contain ideas, possibilities and a balance between the subject areas devised by the teacher(s) but short-term and lesson plans will have a much greater emphasis on the children's needs and interests. Activities will not necessarily have predetermined learning outcomes and there is a much greater emphasis on observation. The whole process needs to be extremely fluid and adaptable.

In this chapter I aim to help you through the maze of what you might be presented with and how to turn the planning process into an invaluable personal learning resource. I have chosen not to include specific examples of plans as there are so many ways of doing this. Your training institution will have formats of the kind of thing they expect and adapting what you are given using this advice is going to be easier than trying to juggle several different systems.

Long-, medium- and short-term planning

These terms are used within schools and training establishments but can mean a variety of things. They are used to describe the various stages of the planning process but may not all be used in your particular placement school.

Long-term plans

These are generally discussed and planned as a school, or possibly with a subject leader, and may reflect a whole year's teaching or possibly a term's. They give an overview of the learning expectations of each class or age group and enable individual teachers to plan more specifically within these.

They ensure:

- all aspects of a subject are covered
- skills and processes have a logical progression
- equipment and resources, which may be limited, are not being used at the same time in two different areas of the school
- where there are two or more classes of the same age group the children have an equitable experience
- if necessary, they take into account something specific to that school such as a special event.

Long-term plans will contain varying amounts of detail. Some schools will use the same long-term plans from year to year while they remain appropriate, and some will change them on a yearly basis. Schools with mixed-age classes usually consider this stage of the planning in some detail to ensure that all children receive good subject coverage without unnecessary repetitions. Long-term plans may also be formulated where cross-curricular links are identified. This type of learning approach is becoming more common and is explored in detail in Chapter 14, 'Making sense of the curriculum'. Whatever you receive will be individual to the school's needs and ethos.

For younger children long-term plans are usually based around topic areas and possible activities which would meet the Guidance for the Early Years Foundation Stage (DfES, 2007) or other National Curriculum needs for this age group. Visits and visitors as well as any special events would be planned here too.

Medium-term plans

These may be for the length of a topic, a term, half a term or a week depending on the school's or teacher's views and needs. They put more substance into the long-term plans and are usually individual to the class teacher. In a school where there is more than one class of a parallel age group these can be undertaken jointly, or occasionally one teacher will plan one subject area such as maths and another English and ideas are then shared. Almost invariably these will need to have enough room for you to teach in an appropriate way for your own children.

Medium-term plans for you may initially be a week of maths or English lessons where your concerns will be to show appropriate progression with learning objectives, teaching and activities all building gradually on learning from the previous lessons.

Medium-term plans in the EYFS would use information from the long-term plan but would start to incorporate ideas from the children.

Short-term plans

For an experienced teacher these may be presented as a week or a group of lessons but each will have been planned with specific learning objectives, teaching input, activities and assessment criteria in mind. They should be fluid in that the children will not necessarily have reached the point you predicted by the end of the lesson and therefore the next session will need to reflect this.

Short-term plans for the EYFS would set out in detail any adult-led activities with expected outcomes, the deployment of adults, continuous provision, a guide to what might be set out initially in different areas of the classroom and outside area, and observation opportunities, and would be open to change and adaptation according to the children's needs.

As a trainee you will need to plan each lesson you teach in some detail. This will be discussed later.

What do your plans need to show?

Your training establishment will have set out requirements for what you should include but you will undoubtedly be required to provide more details than your class teacher's plans in order to demonstrate your thought processes in a clear and ordered way.

Long- and medium-term planning

Initially you will not need to be part of this process as your individual lessons will build on your class teacher's planning but very soon you will need to consider the bigger picture. What you are given as a starting point varies considerably from school to school and sometimes medium-term plans are devised by a group of teachers during holiday periods, so if your placement stretches across a half term you may find there is nothing in place when you start for a later part of your placement. Try to see this as a positive learning opportunity and offer to join in the planning process. This will give you a chance to see how the other teachers operate and to put forward some thoughts and ideas of your own. If you are working in a paired placement (where you have another student teacher working alongside you in the same class) this is something you can work at together.

However, you may find that very little has been done in this area and it is entirely down to you. This sometimes happens in a summer term placement in year 6 where the testing has finished and the curriculum requirements have already been met. This can also be turned to your advantage. It gives you a real opportunity to embrace the subject knowledge and skills required to teach a topic and although it may not initially be as successful as adapting someone else's plans, you should end up with a much sounder understanding of the whole planning process.

You may have a class teacher who presents you with very full medium- and/or long-term plans from which you can plan very easily.

Whatever you are presented with at this stage I would advise you to talk to the class teacher (and maybe the subject coordinator) about the needs of your children and possible difficulties, what they have covered before, any available resources and how you might obtain them, as well as considering how you might add to the process with your own expertise, materials and preferences. You will undoubtedly need to put more thought and detail into these plans at this stage. You will be more focused about where the learning is going if you think about learning objectives. (What exactly do you want the children to learn in each lesson?) Some possible activities would be helpful although these should not be set in stone and can be changed later. Looking at the available resources or searching the Internet at this stage could give you some real help in deciding what the best activities and teaching resources are which would help the children meet your learning objectives. You could then think about how you might assess learning. (What will it look like at the end of the lesson?) The more thought you put in at this stage the less work you will need to do at the lesson planning stage. I find this part of the process really exciting but have often found that my ideas need a little taming when it comes to writing the lesson plans. If this part of the process is planned effectively it gives you real chance to prepare all manner of things such as collecting equipment or organising a visit or visitor or borrowing a resource from a friend or the library or museum service. The more you put in the more the children are likely to gain from the experience, so it is really worth spending some time and effort at this stage.

Medium-term plans need to be fluid as the process of learning can be unpredictable and areas may need to be revisited or the children may learn more quickly than you thought. I have always found it useful to annotate my plans either in a different colour pen from the original or making handwritten comments on a computer-generated one. This ensures it is really clear to you or anyone else looking at your plans how you have adapted your teaching according to the children's needs. If you find yourself teaching the same topic at a later date this information can be really useful to refine the plans and give you sensible starting points. From your point of view as a trainee it is immediately obvious to your class teacher and/or supervisor that you are reflecting on how your teaching and the children's learning relate to each other.

In the Early Years Foundation Stage you need to show how you intend to implement your ideas for topics by outlining possible activities and how these fit with the EYFS Guidance in the six areas of learning. You also need to suggest how the different areas of the classroom might be used and possible resources. Here again it is a question of reaping what you sow and more time spent on developing ideas here will save you time later.

CRITICAL ISSUES

One of the recommendations of the Cambridge Primary Review is to:

Work towards a pedagogy of repertoire rather than recipe, and of principle rather than prescription. (Alexander, 2010, p. 511)

What do you think of this statement? Read further about these ideas in the chapter on 'Re-thinking Pedagogy'. Reflect on the pedagogy of your school and your own views. How will this influence how you plan for the needs of your children?

Lesson plans

These need to be detailed and show your thought processes. They certainly need to have enough information so that another teacher could use them to teach from if you were suddenly called away or were ill. As I said initially, it is difficult to help a student improve their teaching if their planning documentation is muddled or too brief. Once completed it should act like a written shopping list – even if you leave it on the kitchen table you generally remember what you need to buy because you have reinforced the thought process by writing it down. It is helpful to have it nearby (as with the shopping list) while you are teaching to refer to occasionally, but it should be embedded in your mind firmly enough so that you do not have to hold it in front of you throughout the lesson.

Your lesson plans should include details such as date, time, number of children, year group(s), subject (and maybe the topic this falls within) and length of lesson. They need to set out clear learning intentions or objectives (what they are going to be learning today) and how you are going to assess that learning (assessment or success criteria). Success criteria are discussed in more detail in the preceding chapter on 'Assessment'. Sometimes you may overlap with other curriculum areas, such as in a lesson on writing instructions for making an Egyptian mummy which may be taught as an English lesson but would have developed out of a history topic, and it is helpful to note this. Key vocabulary is useful as a reminder for you and also any other adults in the classroom. Resources and anything else needing preparation beforehand is a part I always tried to write carefully as realising you have forgotten to locate the bead strings in the middle of a maths lesson can be really disruptive. A little bit of forethought here helps to make the lesson run smoothly. You also need to think about how the children are going to access any resources such as whiteboards or art materials. It is well worth observing how experienced teachers manage this and trying some different approaches (see also Chapter 5). I always favoured giving children responsibility for equipment but letting 30 children get up to find whiteboards at once is never going to be an efficient use of time. I had daily monitors and made sure that any regularly used equipment was easy to access. This helps when tidying too.

If we move on to the actual lesson content, the detail needed here is really a matter of personal preference but you do need to ensure that you have thought about every stage of your teaching and the resources required, the way the children are going to be organised, how the other adults are going to be deployed, and how the lesson will begin and end. You will also need to consider the differing abilities and levels of understanding among the children and any children who have other particular needs such as language, behaviour or physical. Although you need to provide for different abilities you should not need any more than three activities, so do not make life more complicated than it needs to be. You may have children for whom these activities do not work but often they can be amended slightly to be appropriate. Sometimes differentiation by outcome will be your preferred option where, for example, the more able children will have done the task in more depth. Your class teacher will be the best source of information initially although as you get to know the children you will soon find you will develop your own ideas. You will also need to consider whether, when and how you might use a plenary session. This is generally used to gather together or assess the learning at the end of a session but can be at any time. The word plenary means 'full' or 'all together' so is purely something the whole class engages in. To begin with it is helpful to have timings for the various parts of the lessons. One of the most common difficulties beginning teachers have initially is overrunning the allotted time and therefore not reaching the concluding part of the lesson – often the 'plenary' where the learning is evaluated or reinforced or skills learned are to be used in a real-life context. There are so many different facets to teaching a lesson, the potential for things to go wrong is great. Even experienced teachers do not escape this although practice and evaluation limit the potential for failure. Every time you begin with a new class you will go through the process of developing plans and activities which work for that group of children, so it is a continual learning process.

The final requirement of your plan will be a space to evaluate your teaching and the children's learning which will be further discussed later in this chapter.

In the Early Years Foundation Stage your lesson plan might be for a short whole-class lesson or a group activity. This could be with just a few children for whom this activity would be appropriate, with the whole class in rotation or with children who choose the activity. Whichever it is, at this stage you will need to include your learning objectives and possible success criteria. These are more problematic with small children as they often take an activity in a different direction from that which you had planned and it can be counterproductive to try to change their course. You soon learn when you can persuade children back to your course and when it will not work.

You need to have a list of resources and equipment so you are fully prepared before you begin and an outline of your activity. Key questions and vocabulary are useful reminders and you need to have considered how you intend to assess the outcome. The key difference from Key Stage 1 and 2 planning here is thinking about the 'next steps'. This gives you the opportunity to note down where you think particular children need to go next with their learning. This will then be carried forward in your general planning. Again, noting down your successes or otherwise is good practice for improving your teaching. Some teachers find that planning in this way for their teaching assistants works well as there is likely to be a much clearer understanding of what you intended than you could establish in a quick chat about sowing seeds or making play dough. As you can see this type of plan is only going to apply to some of the learning for some of the time so more thought needs to be spent on the bigger picture which I will explain in more detail in the next section.

Planning a sequence of lessons

This may seem a daunting prospect to begin with but view it as an opportunity to really take responsibility for the children learning something at a deeper level of understanding.

Begin by looking at the expectations of the learning. This may be outlined in the medium-term plans but you may need to look at documents such as the National Curriculum or other government documentation. Ask you class teacher to help here. You will also need to ask him/her to tell you where the children's expected starting point might be. This will be an approximation as even if the topic is building on work covered as little as a term ago there is no guarantee that the children will have remembered all they had achieved at that point. A little revision or consolidation of skills is therefore good in order to establish current understanding as well as to act as a reminder to the children.

You then need to divide the learning into lesson-sized chunks within the number of sessions your sequence allows for. Consider what your learning objectives will be for each of these stages. Do not make them unnecessarily complex but do make sure they are specific enough to indicate what you are expecting the children to learn during that lesson. 'To name and understand properties of 3D shapes' is a little too vague to be helpful. 'To be able to classify 3D shapes using the terms faces, vertices, edges and curved surfaces' would be much clearer. You might also want to think about how you would explain that to the children in language which would be clear for them. Having established what you want the children to learn you then need to think about what direct teaching, modelling or revision you will need to do and how you will deliver this. In the context of the 3D shape-learning objective you might demonstrate what the terms mean and then play a game to reinforce the learning, or you might have a range of regular and irregular 3D shapes for the children to investigate and sort and then teach the terms that they would need to describe what they had done. There are as many ways of delivering a lesson as there are teachers. Use ideas from what you have observed or ideas from your tutors to begin with and gradually adapt and add to these to suit your particular needs. There is also a wealth of ideas on websites but be careful that what you select meets your learning objective. You do not need to reinvent the wheel for every lesson in your sequence. Often, if you have taught the children a game, it can be easily adapted to move the children on to the next stage. After each lesson an instant evaluation of your teaching and the children's learning will give you an indication of whether the next lesson in your sequence will work or whether you need to adapt it. You need to be reflective and critical but the sooner after the lesson you review the teaching and learning the more detail you will remember. Do not be afraid to go back and teach a concept again. If the children have not understood it will be counterproductive to try to move them to the next stage – *even if it means you will not get to your planned end stage!* No one will thank you for leaving the children in a state of confusion.

I have concentrated rather on a maths context here but in an English lesson it would look much the same. If your end point is going to be 'To write a traditional tale' then you need to consider all the skills the children will need to have in order to do this. Your first lesson might include a chance for the class to tell you what they know already about traditional tales and how they work, although again your class teacher will be a good source of information about prior learning. You might spend time on characters, good beginnings and possible endings. You might use film, drama, still photography, cartoons and animation as well as books as input and to practise the necessary skills. All the time you need to be building up the children's skills so they can reach the end point successfully.

You will need to devise some way of assessing whether the children have met your learning expectations. This is often produced as a written piece of evidence. From the school's point of view this means that there is a collection of written work which shows progression and is usually kept in an exercise book. Parents can see these easily and the results can be discussed. From a child's point of view, producing the same kind of evidence all the time can become tedious and flat and for some children the writing process is a difficulty in itself so you will not see an accurate reflection of their learning. In these days of technology, evidence can be kept as a photograph, a photocopy of notes on a whiteboard, notes taken by a scribe, etc. This was really brought home to some PGCE students I was teaching a history session to. They had spent a while researching their given topic and when feeding back to the rest of the group I asked how they would prefer to present their findings. Out of four groups of 30 students none of them chose to produce a written account! Assessment of learning has been covered fully in the previous chapter.

Planning in EYFS

In the EYFS, planning for continuity, good coverage and individual needs is an area where many students become confused about what is and what is not important. I will outline what you *do* need to have on record. The other adults need to be able to see what is in your mind, as do your class teacher and your supervisor, and you need a record of what was planned and what happened in practice.

1. Starting with your medium-term ideas, on a weekly basis you need to consider the whole teaching space, inside and out. Using what the children have previously shown you, plan for each area and consider what equipment and possible additions

or substitutions could happen during the week to keep these spaces exciting and fresh. Devise a simple planning format which has sections for each of the areas and systematically think through each area. These can and should change as the children use them and demonstrate interests and needs. You may have planned to have mini beast cutters and related extras with dough which you have made, but if the children decide on baking cakes and discussing tea parties instead then you need to provide something for them to cook in and possibly plates, birthday candles, etc. Ask them what they need and involve them in their learning. You can even involve them in the planning process such as in designing a new role play area. When this happens your plans need amending and doing this in two colours, one for your changes and one for those suggested by the children, will give you a clear picture of how much control the children are taking and what they are showing you about their learning needs.

2. A timetable for general responsibilities and activities for the week is also valuable. You need to indicate where direct teaching is to happen and where an adult is there to support rather than lead. Deployment of adults is a key factor and making sure that all the children are adequately supervised while still being able to take control of their play and learning is important. Make sure your adults feed back to you any observations of the unusual, the surprising or general trends so that these can inform your future plans. You also need to allocate some time for observation. Watching closely how children play will help you immensely in planning appropriately for them. The key is to remain flexible. *You will not have achieved everything in your medium-term plan if you have really taken notice of what the children are telling you about their learning needs.*

Using plans to improve teaching

Evaluation

I have always found that evaluating my plans was one of the best ways of improving my teaching. I annotated them at the first available opportunity and encouraged my teaching assistants to make notes either directly onto my plan or on Post-it notes which could then be attached to the plan. Do not do this on a fresh plan on the computer. It is much more helpful when you look back to see what you changed from your original plan while you were teaching;

- any activities which were a real success or failure
- whether particular groupings of children worked well or not
- whether the resources were adequate
- any areas of difficulty
- classroom management points
- uses of any other adults.

It is also useful to have an immediate assessment of which children really struggled and any who achieved beyond your expectations. This is not the same as a considered formative assessment process but will give you an indication of how you might need to change the next lesson for those children. Ask your teaching assistant to make notes of any surprises during whole-class teaching. You may think you will remember but chances are that you will not. Once noted on your plans they will be in the context of your teaching and they can then feed into more detailed lesson evaluations as soon as you have the time.

One of the most effective ways of moving your teaching on is being able to reflect on these findings and consider what it is that you may have done to influence them (see also Chapter 9 on reflection). This is a skill which all good teachers do throughout their careers. I still do this in the context of my PGCE teaching and adjust my plans accordingly to improve the outcome and ease of understanding or to ensure individual needs are met.

What you do not want to do in this process is sink into deep depression because you will never 'get it right'. There will always be room for improvement and the better you get to know your children the more likely you are to feel you have not quite met their needs. If, like me, you have a tendency to focus on your failings, make a list of the good points first and highlight any breakthroughs. These are really important and sometimes one child understanding a concept they have found really difficult is reward in itself.

In the Early Years Foundation Stage evaluation works in much the same way and there will be days when you seem to have achieved nothing you set out to do but there will have been achievements! Ask your teaching assistant to help you here.

Reflection is more fully discussed in Chapter 9.

Refining your planning to enhance learning

Your teaching will be much more effective if you plan to use your strengths. You may find that these change slightly as you progress through your training but consider how you might include the skills you gained before embarking on this course.

Be adventurous. Try some of those suggestions which your tutors have suggested and give them a fair go. Think about the times you remember from when you were at school. There were probably visits or visitors or something different which happened and although you cannot be all singing and dancing every day, variety is going to keep your teaching and the children's learning fresh.

Useful resources

ICT can offer wonderful learning opportunities but using a slide show for every lesson is not going to improve your teaching. What I have often seen happen is that the student teacher is sidelined by the slides which then dictate how the lesson will run. Any text you show needs to be minimal and of a font size which is easily readable. And do not assume that because you have put your learning objective on the interactive whiteboard (IWB) that the children have read and understood it. Many student teachers are hampered by the fact that the IWB is often the only board available to write on in a classroom and there is an expectation that this expensive piece of equipment will be used as much as possible. This is a real difficulty and needs to be considered carefully when planning. Many children spend most of their waking day with a screen of some sort in front of them, especially if the IWB is in use most of the time. Before using the board think whether it will help the children meet your learning objective(s) and what the other options might be: plan for technology failure! What will you do if the Internet is down or you cannot calibrate the board? (see also next chapter on e-learning).

Although *you* are an amazing teaching resource consider what other options there might be. I have used a parent who was a vet to come in with her dog and demonstrate the sort of care he needed. She even clipped his toenails. That was a far superior experience than using a video or a book and the role play and understanding of caring for animals was greatly improved. On another occasion we wrote to the local council when investigating our locality with concerns and ideas for improving road safety outside the school and they sent their road safety officer to discuss our suggestions. This gave a really clear meaning to the children's work. The local religious minister is often willing to come and baptise a doll or bring artefacts. Visiting local places is relatively easy to organise and well worthwhile provided you have given it enough thought at the planning stage. It is surprising what children do not know about their neighbourhood, so do not assume because it is on their doorstep it will not be interesting. These options need to be considered at the medium-term planning stage so that you can plan to maximise the experience and organise it well.

Encouraging independence

The temptation when you begin teaching is to 'float' so that you are able to deal with difficulties before they escalate. Try to gradually wean yourself off this. Plan to focus on one particular group of children to really move them on. This can be in stages at the beginning. Settle the children and deal with any immediate needs, then sit with your focus group. Then, near the end of the session, you could circulate again and check on general progress. The children will soon get used to the idea that you are not always available and such a strategy will enable you to spend more time with a group.

You need to help all your children become independent learners and the way you plan can either help or hinder this. Often the lower achievers sit with a teaching assistant so that they have instant access to help when they need it. This strategy does help with immediate classroom management needs but these children will not learn important independence skills if this is their only working experience. All children need regular opportunities to work independently and the tasks or activities need to be ones which they can access with no help. As you get to know the children better you will be able to work out appropriate opportunities and activities. One of the worries student teachers have with this is how to keep the children engaged while they are working with others. Make them accountable so by the end of the lesson they will need to have achieved something specific which they know you are going to ask them about or maybe they will need to report back to the rest of the class. If they know there will some immediate comeback it will give them more incentive to be successful. You can also give them independence strategies so that they do not bother you at the first difficulty such as 'If you get stuck, think about the instructions, ask the person next door to you, ask a designated reader/helper to help you read the instructions/sort out what you do next' etc. The other side of this is that *all* the children deserve some quality time with you.

Planning opportunities for talk

You also need to plan for opportunities to talk. I always refer to my ability to negotiate around Norwich in a car when thinking about this. I have a vague idea where different parts of the city are in relation to each other but it is not until I am trying to give someone directions that I really get it sorted out. Verbalising your learning really reinforces it, and this needs to be a consideration in your plans: how you might include talking partner opportunities in your whole-class teaching or plenary and what opportunities there might be in group or paired work where this kind of discussion can take place. Sitting and listening is something that none of us do efficiently for very long at a time so breaking up your teaching with opportunities for the children to discuss, reflect and consolidate like this will add to their learning potential.

Using support staff

Planning for your extra adults can initially be quite difficult and there are several things to take into consideration. Find out your support staff's strengths and preferred ways of working from them and/or the class teacher and build on these. Remember that working with the same group of disillusioned or disruptive children is not going to be a fulfilling task day after day so ring the changes. If possible ask them to feed into your planning and help to make them a part of the process. Ask the support staff to feed back to you on how the children achieved but also on the strengths or weaknesses of the activity. Use them to support children in whole-class teaching or to observe for you. Make sure they are really clear about what you intend in your lesson by giving them a clear copy of the plan and explaining which parts they will be responsible for. Some classes have a communications book if teachers and teaching assistants do not have a chance to speak to each other before the day begins. However you do this, do bear in mind that teaching assistants are paid a fraction of a teacher's salary and therefore your expectations must not be unreasonable: remember that, on the whole, they are dedicated, positive and have the children's interests at heart. Working with other adults is discussed more fully in Chapter 16.

Catering for different ages and abilities

Most Key Stage 1 and 2 classes will have some sort of ability grouping already in place (usually for English and maths but sometimes for science) to aid differentiation and help teach the children at an appropriate level. While these groupings have their place there are other ways of organising the children when planning tasks and activities. Where children are conducting an investigation or the outcome is a joint effort, mixed-ability pairings or groups can work surprisingly well. This requires some knowledge of the children as the pairs or groups need to be supportive. Giving a poor writer a more able writer as a scribe to record views or thoughts, especially at a planning stage, can free a child from the constraints of writing so that they can concentrate on thinking and developing ideas. This is certainly worth trying and you may be pleasantly surprised at the results.

Planning for a class where there is more than one age group can be difficult. Your class teacher will be able to offer you guidance here. One of the difficulties is that these children will often be in the same class for more than one year, so it is important that they do not repeat the same curriculum. If there are two year groups together quite often they will focus on the specific subject areas for one of those year groups. What the teacher then needs to ensure is that the teaching covers the skills that both age groups need to acquire. This is really no more than a greater spread for differentiation. I have taught in mixed age classes for many years and have really enjoyed the mix of abilities and the potential to move more able children on and support those who are having difficulties. Mixed ability groupings in this context have the potential to really move the younger children on whilst reinforcing valuable learning for the older ones. In some very small schools you may find reception and Key Stage 1 in one class and all of Key Stage 2 in another. The numbers of children in each class are usually quite small so planning will focus much more on individuals. Again, your class teacher will be in the best position to advise you and there will be as many benefits as disadvantages in the experience.

Planning Independence at Early Years Foundation Stage

In the Early Years Foundation Stage many of these points are also applicable. You need to be imaginative and involve the children as much as possible in planning and organising their environment. If they feel they have ownership of their setting in this way they will then use it more effectively as well as seeing the need to look after it. It is important to foster independence skills at this stage too. Make sure that children can access equipment easily and ensure that they take responsibility for their environment and learn to tidy up. Talking skills can be introduced here. Start simply by getting them to talk about a picture they have drawn or a model they have made so they have some visual prompts. Listening is also a key skill if this is going to work well. The attention span of 3, 4 and 5 year olds is extremely short so even if you manage to keep them sitting on the carpet for 30 minutes do not assume they have absorbed all your words of wisdom. Plan for short sharp whole class sessions with changes in activity and if they are having a day when they cannot do it do not push it! They will however concentrate for quite long periods of time when involved in their own play so also make sure that they have chances to do this.

CRITICAL ISSUES

The Teaching and Learning Research programme identified that,

> A chief goal of teaching and learning should be the promotion of learners' independence and autonomy. This involves acquiring a repertoire of learning

strategies and practices, developing positive learning dispositions, and having the will and confidence to become agents in their own learning. (Alexander, 2010, p. 303)

How did you develop these necessary skills? Observe how other teachers foster independent learning dispositions. How independent are the children in your class? Decide what your priorities would be for planning to improve independent learning opportunities.

Final thoughts

According to *Children, Their World, Their Education* (Alexander 2010),
Good teaching:

- Is well organised and planned
- Is reflective
- Is based on sound subject knowledge
- Depends on effective classroom management
- Requires understanding of children's developmental needs
- Uses exciting and varied approaches
- Inspires
- Encourages children to become autonomous learners
- Facilitates children's learning
- Stimulates children's creativity and imagination.

(p. 281)

If you have captured these elements in your planning then your teaching is going to be heading in the right direction!

Summary

- Be clear and focused in your planning. Remember someone else will need to be able to read it and understand your thought processes.
- If learning objectives are used then make them simple and ensure your teaching and any activities or tasks feed into achieving them.
- Use your long- and medium-term planning to think about exciting resources and start to prepare them.

(Continued)

(Continued)

- Be clear about how you are going to be able to tell if your plan was successful.
- Record any observations as soon as possible and use them to inform future planning.
- Try something new. If you stick to the same mould you will not progress to be an exciting and inspiring teacher.

Issues for reflection

- Observe teaching in a different key stage from that you have chosen. What are the different planning implications for this age group? What could you use from this to incorporate in your own planning?
- From time to time (maybe at the end of each placement) look back at your planning notes and evaluations. What were your key breakthrough moments? Is there anything you tried and rejected which you think you might be ready to try again? Are there any continuing areas of difficulty which you really now need to sort?
- Think about all the children in your class. Choose one or two who you really feel you are not reaching and plan some lessons with their needs particularly in mind. Did this make a difference? What have you learned from this about your teaching and the children's learning?

Further reading

Alexander, R. (ed.) (2010) *Children, Their World, Their Education.* Abingdon: Routledge. This is the final report of the Cambridge Primary Review which is a comprehensive examination of English primary education based on extensive, recent research. The chapters on 'Children's Development and Learning' and 'Re-thinking Pedagogy' give particularly interesting information related to the planning process.

Fisher, J. (2008) *Starting from the Child,* 3rd edition. Maidenhead: Open University Press. This looks at the needs of very young children but is a very useful starting point for teachers of any age of child. Especially relevant is the chapter on planning for learning.

Pollard, A. (2008) *Reflective Teaching,* 3rd edition. London: Continuum. This has a very comprehensive chapter on planning as well as useful web links.

CHAPTER 12

E-LEARNING

Helena Gillespie and Abigail Williams

Chapter overview

We live in a digital age that has the potential to transform the life opportunities of the children you teach. Yet the power and influence of technology within and beyond the classroom can feel overwhelming. This chapter will help you overcome such forebodings through showing how technology can be learning-led, teacher managed and brought to serve the aims of the curriculum.

An introduction to e-learning in the classroom

There are many things about a twenty-first-century primary school classroom that a time traveller from a Victorian classroom would recognise – the teacher's desk, tables facing the front, books available to pupils and even the slates to write on (although the slates are now mini whiteboards!). However, one thing which the Victorians couldn't even have dreamt of is the technology in classrooms. The range available is widening all the time: desktop computers, wireless laptops, digital cameras, camcorders and microscopes, mobile phones, hand-held sensors and, perhaps the most ubiquitous of all, the interactive whiteboard. The Victorian time traveller, marvelling at these objects, might very well ask how these amazing devices have changed the way teachers teach and how children learn. The answer to this question is varied and complex. Assessing the real impact of technologies in our classrooms is notoriously difficult. Where technologies do make an impact, they are so closely linked to other positive factors such as a good teacher, a creative approach to the curriculum and well motivated pupils that it is impossible to say that it is the technology that has made the difference. Nevertheless, over the past 20 years, millions of pounds have been spent on equipping classrooms with a range of technologies, and good teachers make use of them in ways which improve the quality of teaching and learning.

As a teacher setting out on their career, you may be familiar with some of the technologies you encounter in the classroom, like digital cameras and laptop computers. However, some technologies, like the interactive whiteboard, might be unfamiliar. Through your training and induction and as your career progresses you will need to develop your skills in using these technologies to facilitate learning electronically. The term 'e-learning' refers to this electronic learning, that is learning that uses any type of electronic device. On the one hand, it is necessary to learn how the devices and software applications work. On the other hand, you need to learn when, how and crucially *why* you can use technology in your teaching. At first the former may seem more daunting but in fact the latter is actually a much harder task. The solutions you find will depend on the way you teach in general, but if you succeed both in learning to operate the technology and in using it effectively, your teaching, and the learning of the children in your class, will be enhanced. This chapter focuses, for the main part, on the 'when, how and why' of using technology in the classroom.

Curriculum design and learning technologies

When to use meaningful and fit-for-purpose technology

In January 2008, an independent review of the primary curriculum began under the leadership of Sir Jim Rose. His final report considered 'learning technology' and included the recommendation that it be placed at the heart of the primary curriculum, both as a discrete 'skill for learning and life' and embedded through all aspects of learning. He commented: 'Used well, technology strongly develops the study and learning skills children need now and in the future … and it will become increasingly important to command ICT skills to prepare for technologies of the future …' (2009, p. 12).

Before you accept the Rose review recommendation of when to use technology, you will need to consider what it means to place technology at the heart of the primary curriculum, what it means to teach technology as a discrete subject or skill and what it means to embed technologies through all aspects of learning within your context. Can you clearly identify when the use of technology is meaningful and fit for purpose?

Rose emphasises the crucial importance of ICT

> To argue against the importance of ICT in the primary curriculum is to ignore the increasing digitisation of information worldwide … Information required for leisure, work, finance, communication and citizenship will be mediated electronically. In all branches of knowledge, all professions and all vocations, the effective use of new technologies will be vital. (2009, p. 71)

As a teacher, you cannot ignore the prospect that our daily lives and those of our learners are becoming 'digital lives' and that we are continuously influenced by the introduction of new technologies and the reinvention of the old. These life changes will be influenced from far beyond the school boundaries as technological advancements are made, worldwide technology consumption increases and political and economic requirements change. But how do you know that you are using technology appropriately and not just for its own sake? To help avoid this you will need to use reflective practice to be fully aware of when it is appropriate to use technology to enhance your teaching and your learners' learning. It is critical to understand the desired impact that the technology will have on raising the achievement of the children and young people that you teach.

You also can't ignore the prospect of the evolving 'digital school' where technology is embraced in the school vision and strategy in the manner that Rose describes. In such a vision technology will be integral to day-to-day school practices. These characteristics are easily recognisable through the following examples of technology enabled:

- lesson planning, resource creation and sharing of resources
- recording of learning impact, Assessment for Learning, monitoring and evaluation
- communication and collaboration within school, across schools and with the community
- reporting to parents and carers
- administration and information management
- professional development.

How to place technology at the heart of the curriculum

The focus for the following section of the chapter will be on how to place technology at the heart of the primary curriculum and embed it within all aspects of learning with specific examples of when technology is meaningful and fit for purpose. Caution needs to be observed when planning the design of the curriculum as this can often fall victim to the technology that is available or limited to what is understood. Having resource constraints can be very challenging and requires you to be creative in your approach. The examples below draw upon a range of creative solutions.

Digital images, digital video and digital audio recording through the curriculum and all aspects of learning

Digital photography is a quick and easy tool to support a vast array of learning and teaching activities. Where there is a digital camera, there is likely to be a digital video function, so capturing events, stimulating role play and developing a creative curriculum can be achieved at a low cost. Digital cameras can exist in a range of formats and can appear where you least expect them, e.g. built into laptops and game consoles. Mobile phones are a handy source for cameras, but be sure to check your school policy before encouraging pupils to bring digital cameras, game consoles and mobile phones into school for use in the classroom.

Some examples of classroom application of digital cameras are as follows:

- *Scientific reporting*. Photographs and video recordings can be taken of each stage of a science experiment. This is a useful tool to support scientific report writing. Images can be easily transferred to a document, presentation, slide show, film or blog. Each image can be used in a sequence to show the events that took place, for example a melting ice cube or a plant growing.
- *Storytelling*. The creation of storyboards for supporting storytelling within a variety of literacy activities including creating comics and animations may be supported by cameras. Digital cameras enable 'real-life' stories to be captured in real time and beyond the school boundaries.
- *Geography*. Cameras can be used within geography lessons for pupils to compose and film news reports, weather reports and documentaries and record daily events using video logs. This can be the pupils' first experience of journalism and broadcast media.
- *History*. Moments in history, stories being told by members of the local community and changes within the local environment can be captured on film.
- *PE and sport*. Both still and moving images are useful for recording, playing back and analysing performance in PE and sport.

To achieve greater inclusive classroom practice and to meet a wide range of needs of visual and auditory learners, combining text, digital images, digital video and audio recordings (to create podcasts and vodcasts) will provide improved access for all learners to a wider range of activities across the curriculum. For example,

- *Mathematics*. 'Mental maths' podcasts can be recorded by staff and pupils to give pupils experience of listening to oral problems as well as viewing written problems.
- *Modern foreign languages and English as Additional Language learning*. Podcasts can support pupils when learning new vocabulary, e.g. combining digital images and the spoken word.

As with digital and video cameras, podcasting and film-making software also promotes the active participation of children in learning and develops a wide range of skills in the creation of content. For example, these can support revision activities, as children produce their own aides-memoires to listen to and watch rather than traditional reading or writing revision activities.

For learners with additional needs, beyond developing the ICT skills, the creation of content focuses on the pupils' ability to apply literacy, numeracy and subject knowledge. These tools are also very important in promoting pupil voice activities that can be recognised beyond the classroom, such as in BBC School Reports broadcasts.

How to teach ICT as a discrete subject or skill

Teaching primary and early years' technology as a discrete subject can often be challenging. One significant area of weakness in teachers' subject knowledge was identified in March 2009 by Ofsted. They showed the findings from a study of 177 schools between 2005 and 2008. It found: 'The pupils observed generally used ICT effectively to communicate their ideas and to present their work, but they were less skilled in collecting and handling data and in controlling events using ICT' (2009b, p. 4). The report continued to state: 'Teachers' subject knowledge was weakest in data logging, manipulating data and programming.' So, it is important that you identify your strengths and weaknesses in ICT subject knowledge and skills and, where possible, undertake professional development. This can often be daunting and you may want to start your professional development with more familiar technologies, such as Lego™ which offers a familiar and wide range of opportunities to explore control technology, and undertake more familiar ways of e-learning via online resources, such as software tutorials and Youtube video tutorials, and follow guidance documents that can support you on a day-to-day basis.

We also can't assume that the current and future interpretation of the ICT curriculum as a discrete subject and ICT learning outcomes will remain static. In the past, for pupils to 'use text, tables, images and sound to develop their ideas' (QCDA, 2000, p. 16) the output would have taken the form of simple word-processed documents with a picture inserted or a presentation with a voice-over. The output today could be interpreted as a film, a blog, a wiki, social networking or the development of a website. So it is important that you keep abreast of new technological innovations and are aware of how aspirations for learning outcomes can be raised as a result.

Learning with technology

In many ways, the presence of technology is now so widespread in schools, it seems pointless to question how it supports learning; rather it is just a part of everyday school life. However, when we look at different technologies, we can see that they are best suited to supporting learning in different situations. Some technologies support learning in effective ways that could not be replicated without those technologies and in some cases the technology allows learning to take place in a new and sometimes novel context. However, sometimes technology is planned as part of lessons but actually it adds very little to the learning experience. When you decide to include ICT as part of your teaching, you should make sure that the learning is authentic and worth the effort of including the technology in the lesson. You may also consider the ways in which technology can appeal to different groups in the class, thinking about the activity and how different groups will best learn. Table 12.1 gives some examples of how different technologies can be applied, and shows the range of effective, and not so effective, ways of encouraging learning in lessons.

As the range of available learning technologies increases, teachers need more and more to ask questions about how they can affect learning for the class or groups within the class. Here are some of the things a teacher should ask themselves when planning to use technologies:

- What is the main purpose of the technology in terms of added benefit to learning? Therefore is it worth the effort of including the technology in the first place?
- Does the technology offer access to resources or encouragement to learn which appeals to specific groups or individuals in the class? And so should the technology be targeted at groups or individuals for maximum effect?
- How can technology promote a variety of approaches to learning in the classroom, for instance problem-solving or collaboration?

Table 12.1   How different technologies can be applied

Technology	Example of possible application	Description of learning
Interactive whiteboard	Displaying information, watching video, whole-class teaching, recording ideas	Mostly passive for learners; appeals most where children learn well by seeing and listening
Digital cameras	Taking photos and video	Instant replay of pictures means learners can interact with the product and respond. Encourages discussion and engagement where learners have control of the camera
Using the Internet to search for information	Using websites or search engines/directories to search for information about keywords	Inconsistent and unpredictable; searches can result in a variety of outcomes, only some of which are accessible to learners
Using programmable robots or cars	Making shapes with Roamer, the programmable robot, or negotiating a maze with a remote control car	Problem-solving skills are employed and the physical engagement suits more active learners. Can encourage collaboration where learners work well together
Educational 'games'	Providing an opportunity to rehearse knowledge/skills or use it in a new situation; examples include mental maths games and keyboard skills programs	Existing knowledge and skills can be practised and honed; can often provide 'instant' feedback to learners about their achievements

New contexts for learning

One of the best reasons for including technology in lessons is that it enables learning to take place in new and creative ways and that it is inclusive of a variety of learning approaches. One example of technology that can fulfil this brief is computer games. Computer games are a contentious issue. Some view them as an undesirable aspect of children and young people's lives, and perhaps even a danger to them. The Byron Review (2008) discussed at length the impact of computer games on children's social development, pointing out that:

> It is imperative we consider how children learn throughout their development, especially given the ongoing debate in the research evidence and the need to think about probabilities of risk rather than conclusive harms. A major concern relating to video game playing is whether children learn anti-social or violent behaviour from the games they play. How much could children learn from inappropriate content or behaviour online or in video games? (p. 31)

In addition the review considers how cognitive development might be affected by long periods playing computer games:

> In order to cope with the enormous amount of input information into the brain, there are ways of short-cutting our processing of information. One way we do this is to set up expectations that affect how we perceive information – this is where the brain abstracts the structure of experienced events, and sets up expectations about what will happen in the future; this is called Neural Statistical Learning. The implication is that if a child has had frequent experiences of playing a game, it is possible that the brain will set up an 'expectancy' to act in the real world in the same way that they act in their virtual world. This could be either positive or negative to the child. (p. 32)

Despite these issues, Byron cautions that we should try to manage the risk of computer games rather than reject their use altogether. Given this, teachers need to consider whether computer games could or should have a place in classrooms at all. Considering the risks identified in the Byron Review, teachers should have a compelling reason for including them. Some of these are discussed in the study published by Futurelab into computer games, schools and young people (Williamson, 2009). A survey was undertaken as part of the report and showed that 35 per cent of teachers have already used computer games as part of their teaching and a further 60 per cent would consider doing so. This is not to say that classrooms are braced for an influx of Wii and Nintendo DS consoles (to name but two examples!) but that gaming is increasingly being experimented with or considered by teachers. The report explains that the most commonly cited reason for teachers to consider using computer games in their teaching is pupil motivation and engagement, although teachers also recognise that games can support cognitive development and higher-order thinking skills as well as technological development. However, the report goes on to note teachers' concerns about the dangers of computer games, including those mentioned above by the Byron Review. There are also some significant barriers to effectively including computer games in the curriculum, such as cost and lack of professional knowledge. The report concludes that computer games can support defined educational objectives in the classroom, and that computer games are more than 'just for fun'. To what extent future teachers can expect to be using computer games in their teaching is debatable; however, teachers beginning their careers should make sure that this is one aspect of learning technology that they do not overlook.

The internet and virtual learning environments

Learning opportunities online – an introduction

In January 2009 (2009a), Ofsted published an evaluation of virtual learning in schools and colleges. Their inspections found that, on the whole, development of virtual learning was at an early stage in the primary sector. However, this doesn't mean that new teachers don't need to consider virtual learning – in fact it's a very important part of young children's lives.

The best way to start exploring what teachers need to know about virtual learning is to define it. In essence the 'virtual' part means any learning opportunity which takes place over the Internet. The 'learning' part should have a wide definition too, taking into account not just the school curriculum but all sorts of other knowledge and skills too. We also need to remember that the Internet is now accessible via a wide range of technologies, including mobile devices and the television as well as desktop or laptop computers. All of this means that children can engage in virtually learning many things in many places, at any time. Some typical examples are:

- a 4-year-old singing along to their favourite song on the CBeebies website
- a 7-year-old showing their grandparents pictures of the school play on the school website
- a 9-year-old picking up the instructions for the homework from the school's own virtual learning environment (VLE).

These examples show the range of places a child might engage in virtual learning. It might be a mass media website such as the BBC, or the school's public website, or, for an increasing number of primary schools, their own secure VLE and online space where teachers, children and parents can engage in teaching and learning inside and outside the classroom.

School virtual learning environments

In their report, Ofsted (2009a) found that teachers and learners were making use of the tools available to them via a VLE in a variety of ways. The tools and uses vary widely, but here are some common examples of the tools (sometimes referred to as learning objects or applications) which are available:

- *Assignments* – these can be long or short tasks set by the teacher for learners to do in or outside the classroom.
- *Gradebook* – this is a way that teachers and learners can record and access marks for work.
- *Calendar* – a way of recording and sharing useful dates and timetables among the community.
- *Survey/choices* – this is a way of collecting and collating the views of the users.
- *Attendance and monitoring* – teachers can use statistics created by the VLE to see which learners are using the VLE, for what and when.
- *Quizzes/tests* – online assessments that can be formal or informal.
- *Forums/discussion boards* – a space where teachers and learners can communicate via text. More complex VLEs might also offer 'synchronous' communications tools such as instant messaging or talk/video links.
- *Weblinks* – links to online resources outside the VLE itself.
- *Files* – links to files such as photos or text files which can be downloaded by teachers or learners.
- *E-portfolios* – spaces created by learners where they can link together various electronic resources (pictures, text, links) to provide a record of their learning.

Not all schools would use all of these tools but the potential for using them is substantial. There is more on ways to use VLEs in Gillespie et al. (2007) who found that VLEs were not being used consistently by all teachers in a school or college, rather that there were pockets of good practice. Interestingly the teacher responsible for the good practice was not always an ICT enthusiast in other ways, but was more likely to be a confident teacher using the medium to support their teaching (Ofsted, 2009a, p. 12).

Worries about virtual learning and what to do about them

As technologies have developed that allow children to learn and interact online, many parents and teachers have become concerned about the dangers and problems which might arise. These range from computer use encouraging children to be more sedentary, to children encountering inappropriate material, to stranger danger online. As teachers we must be sure that we have considered all the risks of using these new teaching tools and how to manage them. Also, and perhaps more importantly, we must encourage children to think about the risks and manage them for themselves. One of the most important things that we do for children is to help them become active and responsible citizens, and this applies to citizens of virtual places and spaces too.

In 2008 Byron published her report into keeping children safe in the digital world. She recommended that children, parents, government and technological industries share the responsibility for safeguarding children when they are in the digital world. The report recognises that there are many opportunities afforded to children when using the Internet (and when using computer games) but that children's critical evaluation skills are less well developed than their confidence in using technology, and that many parents do not necessarily feel well enough equipped to help them develop ways of using technologies responsibly because of their own lack of confidence in this area. The same could apply to many teachers, who feel that children are often 'one step' ahead of them in using the latest online tools and spaces. However, as beginning teachers, we should not worry too much about this, as there are some simple steps we can take as teachers and as part of a school community to help children use virtual spaces safely. These include the following:

- Developing and regularly reviewing an ICT policy that has safety as a significant dimension. A shared understanding of the issues and an open discussion among school staff is important in building a culture of safe use of technologies.
- Including safety issues as part of day-to-day ICT teaching, encouraging children to consider the issues of using websites, browsing and talking online. Children need to think about the content of what they are accessing and talk to an adult if it makes them uncomfortable.
- Setting up teaching rooms so that all the children's screens can be easily seen by the teacher and making children aware that they will be monitored. It should be clear to them that while they are at school they should be focusing their computer use on school work.
- Discussing the issues openly with parents, explaining the benefits of technologies and how the risks are mitigated within the school; for example, many schools access the Internet through a filtered service which blocks any 'unsuitable' material.

CRITICAL ISSUES

In the key recommendations of her report, Byron (2008) states that:

> One of the strongest messages I have received during my Review was about the role that schools and other services for children and families have to play in equipping children and their parents to stay safe online. To empower children and raise the skills of parents I make recommendations to Government in the following areas: delivering e-safety through the curriculum, providing teachers and the wider children's workforce with the skills and knowledge they need, reaching children and families through Extended Schools and taking steps to ensure that Ofsted holds the system to account on the quality of delivery in this area. (p. 8)

In your placement school, find out more about the school's policy on e-safety. Consider how this impacts on your own practice when you use the Internet in your teaching and make sure you model 'good Internet behaviour' in your lessons. When evaluating a lesson that includes the Internet, review your approach to e-safety in that lesson. Find out more about this topic by reading the full text of the recommendations of the report.

Social networking, commercialisation and learning

The latest phenomenon in virtual learning is social networking via the Internet. At the time of writing, there can be few children and young people who are unaware of sites like Facebook, Bebo, Twitter and MySpace which allow users to set up profiles and communicate with friends and the wider world. These sites are designed for older teenagers and adults, but many young teenagers and even pre-teens know about and even use the sites. Even if they do not, primary school-aged children would benefit from using some of the tools they provide in a 'safe' environment to develop the skills they may need to use social networking sites in the future.

Such sites have also been held responsible for several high-profile and tragic cases of what the press call 'cyber bullying'. While it is possible to argue that bullying is a social and not a technological issue, we must bear in mind that online environments present particular opportunities for bullying behaviour to take place. Teachers should be aware of the possibilities for bullying in this context in the same way that they are aware of the possibility in face-to-face contexts in school.

Teachers should consider that in many online learning areas and virtual learning environments, commercial products are not advertised. So most 'educational' websites do not have a commercial aspect, and what children encounter through school VLEs and the BBC website does not overtly promote commercial goods and services. However, if children move away from these two sources the online world is littered with overt and covert advertising and promotion of particular products and services.

In their recent paper Carrington and Hodgetts (2010) discuss the BarbieGirls™ website. While this site has high-quality graphics, parental involvement and engaging activities, Carrington and Hodgetts caution against some of the site's values. Based upon a consumption culture and communications with other like-minded girls, social and gender stereotyping is a danger with such sites, as well as the obvious links to a commercial product. The question that parents and teachers must ask is whether the benefits of using such a site outweigh these dangers. As teachers we may choose to avoid using such sites, but it is an important part of children's online socialisation to begin to make decisions about what they access themselves.

Another website teachers might use is that of Milkshake. This website has games and activities relating to many children's favourite characters that promote reading, matching, listening and many other skills. The question teachers need to ask themselves in using this website is whether the benefits outweigh the risk that using the website promotes consumerism in children. Is it OK to do Peppa Pig matching even if it risks the children wanting to go out after school and buy the latest Peppa Pig toy, book or T-shirt?

CRITICAL ISSUES

In *Toxic Childhood* (2006), Sue Palmer argues that:

> There is gathering evidence that noise impedes children's educational progress (for instance, schools on airport flight paths tend to have lower than average test scores) – this appears to apply in homes as well, as children from homes where the TV is on all day are less likely to read at the age of six. (p. 112)

> What evidence can you find that Palmer is right about the problem of noise? How does this affect the way you might use technologies in your classroom? What are the implications for parents?

Learning opportunities online – some conclusions

There is not enough space in this chapter, or indeed this book, to thoroughly discuss all the learning opportunities that are offered to children online, and in any case, by the time you read this, more will have been developed. But as teachers we need to consider this aspect of children's life carefully. In school, using school-based websites and virtual learning environments we have a lot of control over what children see and do online, but we must be aware that we are preparing children for an unpoliced online environment. One of the most important things we can teach them in this context is how to be safe and responsible online, and those lessons cannot start too early.

Final thoughts

Few people would dispute that technology is a part of everyday life in the twenty-first century, and that that is especially true for children and young people. However, as teachers we should be aware that there are many problems related to engaging with technology, including the way the curriculum is designed, cost-effective training and concerns about the possible dangers of too much screen-based learning or entertainment. It seems unlikely that the importance of technology will diminish, and if we are to fully prepare the children of today for work and life in the future we must engage, where we can, in fruitful and constructive ways with computers, cameras, games, mobile devices and the whole range of technology which we are offered.

Summary

- This chapter has helped you consider the when, how and why in terms of using technology as part of your teaching.
- Remember that issues about using technology are still fundamentally considerations about learning.
- E-learning refers to learning which utilises any electronic advice.
- Using technology effectively can significantly enhance teaching and learning.
- Placing technology at the heart of the primary curriculum can strongly develop study and learning skills.
- It is important that you consider the implications of teaching technology as a discrete subject on the one hand, and embedding technologies in all aspects of learning on the other.
- Be alert to the dangers of using technology just for its own sake. Instead address what will be the desired impact of technology on raising the achievement of the children you teach.
- It is useful to think through the range of applications of digital devices to areas of the curriculum.
- Consider ways in which technologies can promote variety of learning and learning in creative ways.
- It is important in your teaching to think through the issues involved and the opportunities promoted by virtual learning.
- You need to encourage children to address issues and risks related to Internet learning and how they can manage these themselves.
- You need to be fully aware of and able to manage the benefits and the dangers of social networking as part of learning.
- Above all, be confident and positive about working with children on the great contribution technology has to make to learning.

Issues for reflection

- Using technology is an expensive and risky business. Equipment is costly and sometimes prone to breakdown at crucial times. If a teacher chooses to include technology in their lesson it should be in ways that justify this expense and risk. What would be your criteria for effective use of learning technology?

(Continued)

(Continued)

- The use of technology needs to be carefully organised in lesson planning so it gives maximum benefit to the group or individuals in the class. Consider how technology can facilitate inclusion.
- Teachers need to keep up with the latest developments in learning technology and should think about how to make this a focus of their professional development.
- You will need to be able to identify what learning outcomes you require your learners to achieve and identify the technology that will best enable this outcome to be achieved.

Further reading

Facer, K. (2009) *Educational, Social and Technological Futures: A Report from the Beyond Current Horizons Programme*. London: DCSF and Futurelab. This report reviews the potential futures for education that might emerge from social and technological change over the next two decades. It will give you an inspiring insight into the potential contribution technologies have to make to education.

Ofsted (2009a) *Embedding ICT in Schools – A Dual Evaluation Exercise*. London: Ofsted. This is a research report which reviews the extent to which ICT is embedded within primary, secondary and special school practice. You will find it useful to help inform how you can go about integrating ICT into your teaching across a range of subject areas.

Section 3

MANAGING THE CURRICULUM

Managing and developing the curriculum your pupils will experience is a very important part of your professional responsibilities. This section helps you gain a clear understanding of the background to the shaping of the curriculum over the years and to the current national and school contexts. We provide guidance on how to be in command of statutory requirements while also maintaining flexibility to ensure curriculum experiences are creative and dynamic. You will discover very practical approaches to designing and organising the curriculum. This includes not only making sure that it is joined-up and coherent between subject areas but also between each of the stages of primary education. All of this we hope will help you ensure that children experience a curriculum which is vibrant and relevant to their learning needs and interests.

CHAPTER 13

THE DYNAMIC CURRICULUM

Fiona Dorey and Graham Handscomb

Chapter overview

What determines the kind of curriculum that the children you teach will experience? Is this all laid down by government statute and guidance or is there scope for individual teachers to put their stamp on the curriculum? Fiona Dorey and Graham Handscomb explain how, within the framework of government and school policy, you have the flexibility to keep the curriculum creative and dynamic.

Introduction

As adults, when many of us think back to our own school experiences, we cast our minds back to secondary school where we were taught discrete subjects. Depending on where or how we were trained as primary practitioners, this image of the curriculum can often be reinforced, as subject specialists are employed to ensure we have the necessary subject knowledge and teaching approaches to enable us to teach our pupils effectively. However, the curriculum is more than a collection of subjects and it does not take anyone long before they realise that schools approach the design and delivery of the curriculum in different ways. The best schools are continually reflecting on how and whether their curriculum meets the needs of their pupils and make small but subtle changes on a term-by-term or year-by-year basis. In this way the curriculum can be described as dynamic. The purpose of this chapter is to explore how you as a teacher in your school take statutory curriculum requirements, as laid down by government and in law, and design and develop your own curriculum and translate that into the classroom. Hence, no two schools have the same curriculum despite an extensive set of statutory requirements. Successful schools and teachers understand that the 'curriculum' is more than a set of statutory requirements of content, but rather is a combination of content (what we want the children to learn), pedagogy (how we are going to organise the learning) and assessment (how we will know we have been successful).

This chapter therefore has a liberating message! Yes, you will be working within the context of an extensive set of statutory requirements. However, at the heart of you becoming an accomplished professional is the way you take control of the curriculum in your school context and relate it to the needs of the young people you teach.

Background

A good start is for you to gain an understanding of the basic national framework for the primary curriculum. In this chapter we will concentrate on outlining and thinking about the requirements for England. Although part of Great Britain and the United Kingdom, Scotland, Wales and Northern Ireland have their own curricula and this is also true of the majority of European countries, whose statutory curriculum requirements can be sourced via the Internet. Wherever you are planning to work and teach, there will usually be some form of curriculum requirement, whether these be of a national statutory nature or an independently drawn up set of requirements by the individual institution or organisation, and it will be your responsibility to familiarise yourself with that framework.

At the time of writing, the two documents which set out the statutory requirements for the curriculum for children aged 3–11 are the Early Years Foundation Stage (EYFS) and the National Curriculum. The former sets out the requirements and expected development for children from birth to 60 months and the latter sets out the same for children from their fifth birthday, the point at which all children should receive a formal education, to the end of primary school, the academic year in which they have their eleventh birthday.

The EYFS has been in place since 2006 and is based around four themes:

- A Unique Child
- Positive Relationships

- Enabling Environments
- Learning and Development.

Each theme is linked to an important principle. These principles are outlined in Figure 13.1.

A Unique Child

- Every child is a competent learner from birth who can be resilient, capable, confident and self-assured.

Positive Relationships

- Children learn to be strong and independent from a base of loving and secure relationships with parents and/or a key person.

Enabling Environments

- The environment plays a key role in supporting and extending children's development and learning.

Learning and Development

- Children develop and learn in different ways and at different rates and all areas of Learning and Development are equally important and interconnected.

There are six areas covered by the early learning goals and educational programmes:

- Personal, Social and Emotional Development
- Communication, Language and Literacy
- Problem Solving, Reasoning and Numeracy
- Knowledge and Understanding of the World
- Physical Development
- Creative Development.

None of these areas of Learning and Development can be delivered in isolation from the others. They are equally important and depend on each other to support a rounded approach to child development. All the areas should be delivered through planned, purposeful play, with a balance of adult-led and child-initiated activities.

Figure 13.1   Principles of the Early Years Foundation Stage from the Statutory Framework for the Early Years Foundation Stage
Source: DfES (2007, pp. 7 and 9).

The National Curriculum has been in place for longer than the current EYFS and was brought on to statute in 1999. It is a result of a review of the previous National Curriculum and is often referred to as National Curriculum 2000. The two broad aims for the school curriculum are reflected in section 351 of the Education Act 1996, which requires that all maintained schools provide a balanced and broadly based curriculum that:

- promotes the spiritual, moral, cultural, mental and physical development of pupils at the school
- prepares pupils at the school for the opportunities, responsibilities and experiences of adult life.

The National Curriculum sets out the Programmes of Study for the eleven statutory subjects at Key Stage 1 and twelve subjects for Key Stage 2, with the appropriate Attainment Targets known as level descriptors. The Programmes of Study outline the knowledge, skills and understanding for each subject which should inform and be addressed in the curriculum.

In addition, under the Education Act 1996, schools must provide religious education for all registered pupils. Schools, other than voluntary aided schools and those of a religious character, must teach religious education according to the locally agreed syllabus. Primary schools must also provide and keep up to date a written statement of their policy on sex education and make it available to parents and pupils. Since September 2010 it has also been a requirement that all children in Key Stage 2 are taught a modern foreign language. The introduction of Academies and Free Schools in 2011 has meant these institutions do not have to follow the National Curriculum if they so choose.

We hope this quick review gives you a clear picture of how the present framework for the curriculum has come about. Now we will look at some of the other developments that have influenced the curriculum.

Other influences on the curriculum

Alongside the statutory aspects of curriculum provision are a whole host of recommended strategies, initiatives and related resources to support you with curriculum planning, predominately for Key Stages 1 and 2. Included within the National Curriculum documentation is the guidance for Personal, Social and Health Education and Citizenship. There is also the Primary Framework which is probably the most influential in informing teaching and learning for English and mathematics in the Primary Phase. Other resources and guidance include SEAL (Social and Emotional Aspects of Learning), Assessment for Learning (see Chapter 10), and the Assessing Pupils' Progress materials. The Primary Framework is the result of a review of the National Literacy and Numeracy Strategies which were introduced to all schools in 1998 and 1999 respectively. The rationale underpinning the two strategies was designed to raise standards in reading, writing and mathematics by the end of Key Stage 2, as well as provide teachers with a framework to plan for progression in learning from ages 5 to 11, resulting in consistency and entitlement of provision for all children. With the implementation of the strategies into the majority of primary schools came the introduction of the daily literacy and mathematics lessons, which take up a substantial amount of the teaching time and, therefore, have had a significant impact on the rest of the curriculum. It is worth noting that the National Curriculum was introduced after the implementation of these two strategies and it still aims to provide a broad and balanced curriculum. So schools have had to think creatively about what that means for them, while still striving to meet targets and ensure children are able to perform in the 'high-stakes' tests which inform the accountability system for our primary schools.

We think this is a very important tension or dynamic for you to consider as you begin your teaching career. How do you put your own creative 'stamp' on the curriculum you facilitate for your children, ensuring that they have a broad and balanced range of experiences, while at the same time fulfilling the demands of the national agenda and standards requirements?

Schemes of work

This interesting professional dilemma is certainly reflected in the issue of the national support materials that have been provided for teachers. Shortly after the publication of the National Curriculum, the Qualifications and Curriculum Authority (QCA) began to publish a series of schemes of work to support teachers. These are detailed plans broken down into lessons with relevant objectives, activities and expected outcomes. Many teachers and schools embraced these at first in the primary phase and schools drew up their own curriculum map setting out when each unit of work would take place. However, the negative aspect of using these schemes of work was that they encouraged discrete subject teaching, much like a secondary school approach, and this often resulted in a weekly timetable with lots of shorter lessons for each subject. The primary school day came under a lot of pressure to deliver, and with the introduction of initiative after initiative there was soon not enough time to do everything. Many teachers also became disenchanted with the activities and focus contained within the QCA schemes of work and wanted to move away from using them.

Some schools began to start thinking more creatively about how to organise and deliver the curriculum by blocking work and using more cross-curricular links. With the publication of the Primary National Strategy (DfES, 2003) and its accompanying continuing professional development (CPD) resources entitled *Excellence and Enjoyment: Learning and Teaching in the Primary Years* (DfES, 2004a), schools and teachers were encouraged to rethink their curriculum provision, redesign their curriculum map if necessary and become more creative with their learning and teaching approaches. In addition *Excellence and Enjoyment* highlights the role assessment for learning plays in successful learning and brings to the fore again the skills which are included in the National Curriculum and Early Years documents but which sometimes were missed in the drive to ensure subject knowledge was covered.

Assessment for learning

So having given a basic summary of the national framework for the curriculum we now look at how this has been complemented by the Assessment for Learning (AfL) initiative

Assessment for Learning is the process of seeking and interpreting evidence for use by learners and their teachers to decide where the learners are in their learning, where they need to go and how best to get there. (Assessment Reform Group, 1999, p. 7)

Seven key characteristics of Assessment for Learning identified by the Assessment Reform Group:

- AfL is embedded in a view of teaching and learning of which it is an essential part.
- AfL involves sharing learning goals with learners.
- AfL aims to help pupils to know and to recognise the standards for which they are aiming.
- AfL involves pupils in self-assessment (and peer-assessment).
- AfL provides feedback that leads to pupils recognising their next steps and how to take them.
- AfL is underpinned by the confidence that every student can improve.
- AfL involves both teacher and pupils reviewing and reflecting on assessment data.

Figure 13.2   What is Assessment for Learning?

(see Figure 13.2 – see also Chapter 10, Figure 10.1 for a diagrammatic representation for learning in practice). Assessment for Learning has become a driving force in education at all levels in the past few years.

With the publication of *Inside the Black Box* (Black and Wiliam, 1998a) practitioners have reflected on what it is they do to help children make progress in their learning. It was not long before others, notably Shirley Clarke, took up the gauntlet and began to support primary teachers with strategies to support pupil progress. The Primary Strategy intiative also produced guidance and materials within the *Excellence and Enjoyment* resources. The National Strategy (for both Primary and Secondary) also carried out pilots in the use of resources to support periodic teacher assessment, which resulted in the publication of the Assessing Pupils' Progress (APP) suite of materials. These are a set of paper and web-based resources to guide teacher assessment of pupils' attainment in reading, writing, mathematics, speaking and listening, and science (but only for AT1 – scientific enquiry) which are designed to be used diagnostically on a periodic basis to identify gaps in learning. The materials received a mixed reception from practitioners and professionals: on the one hand they were embraced wholeheartedly and teachers understood that this approach to teacher assessment could ultimately replace the existing testing regime; on the other hand they were seen as yet another set of summative assessment sheets which duplicated or added to the workload.

Assessment for Learning (AfL) is integral to learning and teaching at all ages. For early years teachers it is woven through their daily practice. The use of a high proportion of child-initiated activities allows the teacher to assess on a daily basis where the children are in their learning and where to take them next. The careful planning and provision of a fine balance of direct teaching, teacher-led activities and child-friendly resources allows the children to develop their learning through play and independently. We recommend that you aim to see AfL in practice in the hands of an experienced and effective teacher during a visit to the early years classroom. Then take a walk through all the classes from reception up to year 6 to look at how the same strategies are being used should result in being able to see Assessment for Learning in action, but perhaps looking slightly different. The use of child-initiated activities becomes rarer as pupils are more directed in their learning, but you should still be able to see independence and choice in the way children undertake some activities. How is the teacher using small-group or guided-group work to develop the learning and assess progress? How much do the teachers rely on formal testing on a regular basis, including times tables and spelling tests, as opposed to informal assessment strategies such as questioning and discussion or the application of learned skills?

Tailoring the curriculum

When looking at the publications which set out the statutory requirements of the curriculum, it is important to remember that they all set out *what* has to be taught but not *how*. It is the '**how**' that gives you the flexibility to tailor the curriculum to meet the needs of the children and for teachers to use their professional judgement as to which aspects need more or less time or more or less emphasis. The first step is usually the drawing up of a curriculum map for the whole school, which draws together an outline of what children will be taught and when. In the early years this is often organised under theme titles drawing together the various objectives from the areas of learning. A similar approach can be taken in Key Stage 1 and Key Stage 2, but usually these decisions will have been made before you start work in the school and your role will be to translate the curriculum map or long-term plan into medium- and short-term planning and thence into lessons for the children. (see also Chapter 11).

Many teachers and schools have moved towards developing a skills-based curriculum with less emphasis on the core subject-related knowledge. By 2003, with the publication of the Learning and Teaching CPD materials, there was a growing feeling that the National Curriculum is too prescriptive in terms of knowledge acquisition. However, just remember that skills are threaded throughout the National Curriculum (DfEE, 1999). In the section entitled 'Learning across the Curriculum' it clearly lists and expands on the Key Skills and Thinking Skills which should be taught to children:

Key Skills

- Communication
- Application of number
- Information technology
- Working with others
- Improving own learning and performance
- Problem-solving.

Thinking Skills

- Information-processing
- Reasoning
- Enquiry
- Creative thinking
- Evaluation.

In addition each subject's Programme of Study sets out the subject-related skills which should be taught through the knowledge and understanding children gain. In subjects such as science and mathematics these are called 'Scientific Enquiry' and 'Using and Applying', but they are also present in other subjects such as History: 'Historical Enquiry', 'Historical Interpretation', 'Organisation and Communication'.

The move towards providing a skills-based curriculum has resulted in schools adopting a variety of approaches, with the best schools creating a curriculum which pulls on the best elements of each, adapted to suit their needs. These approaches include the following.

- *'Mantle of the Expert'* – a dramatic enquiry-based approach to teaching and learning invented and developed by Professor Dorothy Heathcote at the University of Newcastle upon Tyne in the 1980s. The big idea is that the class do all their curriculum work as if they are an imagined group of experts.
- *Enquiry-based learning* – similar to 'mantle of the expert' but not as open, presenting a scenario, intended outcome or question and pulling the learning together under that banner, using the children's prior knowledge and experience as the guide and motivation for the unit of work.
- *Theme-based learning* – organising objectives and learning under a banner title. In this way teachers develop the subject skills with the subject knowledge linked to the theme.
- *Developing the whole school curriculum* – in line with the six areas of learning as set out in the Early Years Curriculum.
- *Commercial providers and publishers* – several of these exist and provide the school, for an annual fee, with a complete curriculum including medium- and short-term lessons, usually based around a theme. Some examples are given in the Further Reading at the end of this chapter.

This is by no means an exhaustive list, rather just a snapshot of what is available in terms of guidance, support and approach. Do remember that schools will have spent years rather than days or months drawing up their curriculum, continually adapting it and reviewing it on a regular basis to ensure that it meets the needs of the children – personalised learning at its best. As the on-entry profile of the children changes through societal change and changing government guidance schools will continue to adapt their curriculum accordingly. Indeed it is because our thinking and approach to education is continually part of political, social and professional debate that you will find teaching is such a dynamic profession.

Reviews of the curriculum

As part of this debate you may be aware of two major reviews of the primary curriculum which have taken place in the past few years. The first was carried out by Sir Jim Rose and was commissioned by the Labour government. The second, the Cambridge Primary Review, was directed by Sir Robin Alexander and funded by the Esmée Fairbairn Foundation. Both of these reviews produced their final reports close to each other and, for that reason, their outcomes and recommendations were widely compared. You will find that it is often the case that such major reviews do not always get fully implemented because of other prevailing social and political trends but they do powerfully affect the educational landscape in which you operate and inform your professional perspective.

Rose Review of the Primary Curriculum (DCSF, 2009a)

This review was part of the Labour government's World Class Primary Programme the aim of which was to improve standards in primary schools in England. The central questions for the review were: what should the curriculum contain, and how should the content and teaching of it change to foster children's different and developing abilities during the primary years? The review took 12 months and included wide consultations with a range of stakeholders. The final report made 25 recommendations which were based on evidence from this broad range of research. These recommendations were taken forward by the Qualifications and Curriculum Development Authority which published the New Primary Curriculum, due to be implemented by September 2011. However, this curriculum was removed from the statute in the run up to the general election in May 2010 and the new Coalition government discarded it.

The New Primary Curriculum was represented by a circular diagram at the centre of which were the three aims: Successful Learners, Confident Individuals and Responsible Citizens. The next layer was the Essentials of Learning and Life which were a set of skills to be incorporated into and developed throughout the planned curriculum. These were similar, but more detailed, to the existing skills in the National Curriculum. The final layer was the six areas of learning. This was where the detail of the content lay together with the subject skills to be taught and the breadth of the learning. The objectives were set out across three phases: early, middle and later. These were not designed to be delivered at certain times or ages but rather showed a progression in learning across the primary phase.

The New Primary Curriculum was, broadly speaking, received positively. Many teachers did not feel they would need to make many changes as they had already been reorganising their curriculum along the same lines. It must be remembered that part of Rose's research was based on the good practice already happening in primary schools. For others it was an opportunity to revisit and rethink their curriculum models.

The Cambridge Primary Review: *Children, Their World, Their Education* (Alexander, 2010)

This review was wider reaching and investigated more than just the curriculum. Consequently it took longer than the Rose Review – six years. It looked beyond the curriculum into the changing shape of society and what the world looks like to children, thus coming to recommendations for schools and the curriculum which reflected the changing backgrounds of pupils and their needs. The starting position for Alexander's Review was as follows:

> Our system of primary education was created on the basis of a particular view of society and people's places within it – or rather the place of those children and families who did not want or could not afford private education. But today's Britain is less sure of itself, and the inequalities between rich and poor are no longer assumed to be the way things inevitably are and forever must be. (Alexander, 2010, p. 15)

The recommendations in this review addressed more than a simple view of what should be taught and how it should be taught, but also dealt with school funding and teacher education among other things. It also presented a set of twelve aims to drive the curriculum which are interdependent and which interplay with eight domains of learning.

Essentially, despite all the press coverage when the two reviews were published and the different reactions to and presentations of their findings, both reviews found in favour of a national curriculum which would set out a minimum entitlement for children to learn. Both are driven by a set of aims and both looked to reorganise the content into domains or areas of learning, thereby linking together common themes and taking local issues into consideration. Both were designed to develop skills learning as well as content learning.

CRITICAL ISSUES

Rose v. Alexander?

Some commentators have seen the positions taken in the Rose and Alexander Reviews as being polarised with regard to each other. Do some further reading on the issue and reflect on what you see as the main differences between them. Where would you place yourself in relation to these views? How does this reflect your current thinking?

From the page and into the classroom

The starting point for you as a teacher in deciding how to arrange the curriculum is to consider the needs of the children and the locality in which the school is based. What facilities are easily accessible on the doorstep? What external support or visitors can be accessed? What is the socio-economic background of the local area? What sort of experiences will the children probably have had prior to starting in the school or your class? Planning the curriculum provision for children in a small country village school with only three mixed-age classes and which is surrounded by fields and animals as opposed to a large two-form entry primary school in a seaside town is a different ball game altogether, even though all those children will be assessed against identical criteria and should all be learning about the same subjects during their school life. Also, take care about making assumptions about the experiences children will have received. Just because a child has travelled widely, e.g. a services child, does not mean they know what is beyond their immediate surroundings. We cannot assume that children have had the same experiences that we had when we were young – many have never been on a bus or a train or visited their own main town or city, and many young children have never handled actual money. However, they may have experiences we did not have linked to the developments in technology and the way we live nowadays. Consider what has changed in your lifetime.

Curriculum themes

So, having ascertained the level of need of the children and what is available to support learning and teaching, the next step is for you to consider what to teach, when and how the curriculum looks to the child. There has been a tendency among many practitioners to adopt a cross-curricular approach to learning as opposed to teaching discrete subjects each week. There are several reasons underpinning this move, some of which are logistical and some of which are in the children's interests. With the introduction of more and more directives from government and recommendations of what should be taught to children in addition to the statutory elements of the National Curriculum, the school day has become more and more squeezed for time. Children are not staying in school longer so a quart is being fitted into a pint pot! In addition presenting children with a 'bitty' week where everything is taught on a weekly basis for a short space of time does not allow learners to fully engage and immerse themselves in their learning, and the younger the child the harder it is for them to retain and progress in their learning in some twelve different subjects. For this reason many teachers organise their objectives together within a theme. This is usually an overriding title for the unit of work under which objectives from different subjects which naturally link together can be grouped together. Very often the theme will have either a scientific or a humanities focus allowing a different slant to the learning with each unit. The theme can vary in length of time depending on how much is going to be taught. Some themes can be as short as a week or two, whereas others can take up to the whole of a half term or even a term. An example of a theme could be the Olympic Games covering objectives related to data handling (Mathematics), locations of countries and physical geography, chronology (History), weather (Science and Geography), biographies (English) and athletics (PE).

It's learning that counts

When using this approach to the curriculum, it is important for you to remember that the learning objectives should be first and foremost at the front of our mind – what is it you want the children to *learn* as opposed to what you want the children to *do*. The former keeps us focused on the learning and in this way we ensure that we cover the breadth of the curriculum throughout a certain timescale. The latter is an activity-based approach and can lead to over-repetition of certain aspects of learning and some objectives being missed altogether. The overriding principle of the Early Years Foundation Stage and the National Curriculum is the provision of an entitlement to all children and that the curriculum provision is not dependent on the strengths and whims of individuals. Having decided which objectives link together to the theme and to each other, your medium-term planning can expand this to include the teaching approaches and activities which will be undertaken to engage children in their learning.

There are different learning and teaching approaches which you can use on a daily and weekly basis. For English and mathematics the National Literacy and Numeracy Strategies developed the structure of the three-part lesson with a focused teaching input, including modelling and demonstration by the teacher of new concepts or skills, followed by individual or group work, and then finishing with a plenary session to review and consolidate learning. This approach quickly became the norm for many lessons but, with the restructuring of the Strategies into the Primary Framework, a more flexible rationale for learning and teaching was encouraged using different approaches and strategies. The use of guided work or guided learning, as opposed to group work, was developed further so that teachers can bring a small group of children together with the same learning need and address that need within the whole lesson as part of the independent learning session.

A range of approaches

You will soon come to realise that the same approach or lesson structure does not match every subject or activity. Hence alternatives may be tried and used successfully. The National Strategies (2009) produced the following as part of their CPD programme to schools to explain some pedagogical approaches:

Modelling	The teacher as expert demonstrates both the process and the internal dialogue that a learner might go through.
Direct instruction	Explaining and demonstrating how something works or how to carry out a process; giving instructions to prompt or inform the next steps in children's learning.
Dialogue and discussion	Using planned opportunities for focused talk, teachers develop an understanding of children's thought processes and ideas.
Problem-solving	Planned opportunities for children to apply their learning, pose further questions and develop and test hypotheses.
Apprenticeship	Planned opportunities to learn alongside another more expert learner (adult or child).
Practising and rehearsing	Repeating learned facts or skills to develop automatic recall or to internalise the process.
Questioning	Using questions to identify prior learning, scaffold understanding and extend thinking for learning in order to create new meaning.
Self-directed learning	Planned opportunities for children to decide what and/or how they learn.
Use of symbols, images and models	Planned opportunities for visualisation and representation to secure and aid understanding.
Inductive learning/enquiry	Planned opportunities for pupils to sort, classify and re-sort data to begin to make hypotheses that can be tested in future work.
Tutoring	Addresses errors at the point of misconception. Supports the child in articulating their thoughts as they learn. Can occur in formal and separate tutoring sessions or as individual support to children in the course of independent work.
Scaffolding	A Vygotskian term (Vygotsky, 1978) referring to all pedagogical techniques that consciously use the learner's existing knowledge, skills or understanding as a starting point, recognise what is within the Zone of Proximal Development for that learner (what they will be able to achieve with help), and move them towards that point.

Whichever approach you decide to use will be decided upon by considering the key questions of what it is you want the children to learn and what is the best approach for you to use to teach and for them to learn that particular objective.

You will also find there will be some aspects of the curriculum which do not lend themselves to a cross-curricular approach easily. You may need to tackle these areas via some discrete subject teaching. There are several subjects which are often taught discretely, PE, music and modern foreign languages being just a few examples. This is not to say that there can never be links made but some schools have found that it is easier to employ specialists to teach some subjects. With the implementation of PPA (planning, preparation and assessment) time for all teachers, some schools use these specialists to cover classes during that non-contact time.

This brings us neatly to the two main subjects which are judged in the accountability system: English and mathematics. The performance of primary schools tends to be judged according to the outcomes of the oldest group of pupils by Ofsted and the Attainment Tables (known as the league tables) as published on a yearly basis by the government. Schools have to set targets for how many children will attain a certain level for the end of each Key Stage, some of which are statutory and some of which are not. So the accompanying assessment and testing regime overshadows the breadth of the curriculum and these two subjects, consequently, often have a greater share of the time allocation than the other subjects. You may come to reflect, with many other teachers, that the testing regime has a significant influence on curriculum provision. It is likely that in the schools where you are employed that, regardless of how the curriculum map provides for cross-curricular teaching and learning, most teachers choose to have a separate English and mathematics lesson on a daily basis. This was reinforced by the National Literacy and Numeracy Strategies and by the subsequent Primary Framework for Literacy and Mathematics. This web-based Framework provides a comprehensive breakdown of objectives and planning with associated resources for English and mathematics and is an extensive scheme of work to meet the National Curriculum requirements for English and mathematics.

This imbalance between English and mathematics versus the rest of the subjects is a constant source of debate and you need to decide your own position. Some teachers include other curriculum subject knowledge through their English and mathematics lessons and there are obvious links to be made, e.g. data handling and measuring in science and design technology, research skills and note making in history, diagrams and labels in science or geography, to name but a few.

How do you know you have been successful?

It is too easy for us to answer the above question by saying: we can test them! And although assessment is the key word for knowing how you have been successful there are many different ways of carrying out this assessment and of gauging pupils' successes. As the third element of the curriculum (content, pedagogy and assessment) and as a new teacher it is important to understand the role of a test, usually written, and the limitations of a test in the field of assessment. Ultimately we have a statutory duty to report children's outcomes against the Foundation Stage Profile and National Curriculum Level Descriptors which are a snapshot of ability and progression but these descriptors do not cover every aspect of a child's learning.

Chapter 10 deals with assessment in detail, but we pose some thoughts about assessment here with specific considerations about the curriculum in mind. It is useful to reflect on a range of strategies you can use to assess learning, e.g. the use of a carefully thought out question which develops the children's thinking and reasoning skills can bring things to light that you did not previously know. For each lesson ask yourself what will the children say, do or write to show they have learnt something today. When planning your lessons or series of lessons consider what opportunities are you building in for the children to choose how to complete a piece of work, what opportunities there are for you to observe them working, and to capture how often the children work independently. Are you involving the children in the strands of assessment for learning? By doing so you will find out more about pupils' achievements than just using a paper-based stand-alone test. This is the difference between assessment *of* learning (summative) and assessment *for* learning (formative).

The use of peer- and self-assessment is also immensely powerful and not to be underestimated. Although good practice will need to be modelled by the teacher in the first instance, children quickly become skilled and honest in their reflections of their learning and understanding of what they need to do to improve. This is complemented by your feedback which can be instant and verbal, especially important for the younger children, or written down for reflection and action at a later time, more appropriate for older children. Remember, though, it is the quality of the guidance not the quantity that is important, and one or two pertinent prompts can be more effective than a half page of evaluation.

This is not to negate the fact that children need to be taught and this is usually considered to be most important in English and mathematics, but by careful linking of subjects together and using the skills from one lesson in another, it is possible to assess pupils' learning against more than one objective and more than one subject at a time. A science investigation can allow children to show how they have developed in their scientific skills (carrying out a fair test and drawing conclusions), their data handling skill in mathematics (presenting results in tables or graphs) and their writing (presenting their findings, writing instructions, writing for a purpose, using appropriate vocabulary). All this in one piece of work!

It is also important to consider children's engagement and enjoyment. These aspects are difficult to measure but are the key to learning. If the curriculum you provide results in the class being engaged in and enjoying the activities they will be more motivated to learn and the results will speak for themselves in the outcomes.

CRITICAL ISSUES

Reflect upon a lesson which you consider to be successful. What was it that made it such a success? What did you do as a teacher and what did the children do and learn? How can you use this occasion to influence your future approach and work with this group of children?

What next for the curriculum?

If we reflect on what the curriculum is and accept the three main components of content, pedagogy and assessment, then we will understand that the 'curriculum' must be an ever-evolving piece of work. A balance will always need to be found between the prescriptive elements, as set down by statute and government, and the flexible elements, those which we can influence in our daily work in the classroom – the pedagogical approaches and assessment practices. The Early Years Foundation Stage and the National Curriculum set out the prescriptive elements for us alongside the statutory testing regime, and they have a very clear purpose: to ensure an entitlement for all children; to establish expected age-related standards; to promote continuity, coherence and a framework for progression; to provide for and promote public understanding. As a professional teacher you will need to keep in mind a view of what constitutes a balanced curriculum for the children you teach. Within the constraints or framework of the school setting and current government policy, how do you continue to keep the curriculum creative and dynamic? With changes in government and national policy guidance the curriculum will change but one thing is clear: there will be a National Curriculum. The Coalition government has announced its intention to restore the National Curriculum to its original purpose – a minimum national entitlement for all our young people organised around subject disciplines. The continual message is that a 'slimmed down' curriculum will be the result. Whatever the outcome it will be for schools and teachers to decide how best to deliver this curriculum and how to make it work for their children.

The great message is that you are entering a profession where there will always be renewed thinking and recurring challenge about the heart of your work – teaching, learning and the curriculum you provide:

> ... the curriculum itself cannot remain static. It must be responsive to changes in society and the economy, and changes in the nature of schooling itself. Teachers, individually and collectively, have to reappraise their teaching in response to the changing needs of their pupils and the impact of economic, social and cultural change. Education only flourishes if it successfully adapts to the demands and needs of the time. (QCA, 1999, p. 13)

Summary

This chapter has covered the following key messages:

- Aim to gain a good understanding of the basic framework for the primary curriculum.
- To ensure the curriculum you teach is dynamic, you need to translate the statutory curriculum requirements in the context of your school and the needs of your learners.
- The framework for the primary curriculum includes the Early Years Foundation Stage Guidance and the National Curriculum.
- Assessment for Learning is integral to learning at all stages. Be clear about the distinction between assessment *of* learning and assessment *for* learning.
- Statutory guidance sets out *what* has to be learnt, not the *how*. It is the how that gives you the flexibility to tailor the curriculum to the needs of the children you teach.
- There are a variety of approaches to a skills-based curriculum.
- When developing your approach to the curriculum be sure to take account of the school context and its locality.
- Remember it's learning that counts – what children will learn rather than what they do.
- Government guidance and professional thinking about the curriculum will continue to change and it is important that you keep aware and are engaged in this evolving debate.

Issues for reflection

- Aim to visit an early years' classroom/setting and consider how the balance of direct teaching, teacher-led activity and use of child-friendly resources could help to inform how you shape the curriculum in other primary stages.
- Are you using the flexibility to tailor the curriculum to the needs of your children sufficiently?
- Consider the different approaches to providing a skills-based curriculum outlined in this chapter, and reflect on what type of approach you find attractive and why.

(Continued)

(Continued)

- How will you address the issue of the potential imbalance between English and mathematics verses other subjects?
- Consider how you will determine which of the range of pedagogical approaches listed in this chapter you will use in your teaching and why.

Further reading

Alexander, R. (ed.) (2010) *Children, Their World, Their Education*. Abingdon: Routledge. The final report from the Cambridge Primary Review. A short overview of the report, entitled 'Introducing the Primary Review', can be downloaded from http://www.primaryreview.org.uk/.

DfES (2004) *Excellence and Enjoyment: Learning and Teaching in the Primary Years – Professional Development Materials*. Nottingham: DfES Publications. A set of six booklets and three videos providing guidance and CPD resources on the main aspects of primary teaching from curriculum design to planning to assessment for learning.

Rose, J. (2009) *Independent Review of the Primary Curriculum: Final Report*. Nottingham: DCSF Publications. This is the final report from the Rose Review of the Primary Curriculum.

Websites which give information about different commercial curriculum providers and/or approaches (this is by no means a definitive nor an exhaustive list but is suggested as a starting point):

http://www.creative-partnerships.com. The Creative Partnerships programme brings creative workers such as artists, architects and scientists into schools to work with teachers to inspire young people and help them learn.

http://www.creativelearningjourney.org.uk. This resource has been developed by teachers for teachers to deliver a valuable personalised curriculum meeting individual, school and community needs.

http://www.internationalprimarycurriculum.com. The International Primary Curriculum is a theme-based approach to planning and teaching originally developed for international schools.

http://www.mantleoftheexpert.com. This is useful to teachers, students and school leaders interested in using and developing MoE as an approach to teaching and learning for the twenty-first century.

CHAPTER 14

MAKING SENSE OF THE CURRICULUM

Paul Parslow-Williams and Michael Pond

Chapter overview

How do you make sure the children you teach have an enriching, broad and balanced curriculum experience? This chapter takes you on an investigation, exploring different approaches to the design and organisation of the curriculum and the strengths and weaknesses of each.

Introduction

Planning the curriculum of a school is a very contentious and complex matter. It will, depending on the views of those of different political and/or educational philosophies as well as available resources, have inconsistent and, at times, contradictory priorities. Lawrence Stenhouse, as early as 1975, captured the essence of this, we believe, when he wrote the following.

A curriculum is rather like a recipe in cooking. It can be criticized on nutritional or gastro-nomic grounds – does it nourish the students and does it taste good? – and it can be criti-cized on the grounds of practicality – we can't get hold of six dozen larks' tongues and the grocer can't find any ground unicorn horn! A curriculum, like the recipe for a dish, is first imagined as a possibility, then the subject of experiment. The recipe offered publicly is in a sense a report on the experiment. Similarly, a curriculum should be grounded in practice. It is an attempt to describe the work observed in classrooms that it is adequately communi-cated to teachers and others. Finally, within limits, a recipe can be varied according to taste. So can a curriculum. (Stenhouse, 1975, p. 4)

Here Stenhouse identifies the key challenges of curriculum design and in this chapter we shall investigate some examples of how schools have adopted various curriculum models which they believe meet the needs of their community.

If a Victorian teacher were to find themselves magically transported to a typical modern primary school, they would almost certainly be initially surprised by the advances in technology they saw, but after a cursory glance at the timetable on the wall, they would be reassured to discover that in a century relatively little had changed. The days would be organised into discrete blocks of subjects, dominated by the traditional '3 Rs': *R*eading, w*R*iting and a*R*ithmetic, which are most likely taught in the morning when the children are considered to be 'fresh and alert', while the remainder of the cur-riculum, which includes subjects such as history, geography and the arts, would take place in the afternoons. Interestingly, should this same teacher travel around the world, they would find the range and hierarchy of subjects to be common to primary curricula in the majority of countries visited, with language and mathematics at the top, science and humanities in the middle and the arts at the bottom.

Many of these similarities, will, of course, be for good reason, since, for example, few would dispute the prominence awarded to the English language in our schools. Moreover, some would also argue mathematics and science deserve their status in rec-ognition of their merits as languages of quantity and reason respectively. Nonetheless, the relentless focus on the core subjects of English, mathematics and to a much lesser extent science (which has lacked a national strategy or framework), has, some would claim, been to the detriment of the other subjects. Alexander (2010) describes the primary curriculum as being divided into a two-tier system: Curriculum 1 'the basics' a school's performance which is seen as an indicator of its success (determined through rigorous assessment) and which are prioritised in terms of time, training and resources; and Curriculum 2 – 'the rest'; which are rarely assessed and are given a low priority in terms of timetabling and provision for continuous professional development (CPD).

The initial promise – and achievement – of a broad, balanced and rich curriculum has been sacrificed in pursuit of a well-intentioned but narrowly conceived 'standards' agenda. The most conspicuous casualties have been the arts, the humanities and those generic kinds of learning, across the entire curriculum, which require time for thinking, talking, problem-solving and that depth of exploration which engages children and makes their learning meaningful and rewarding. (Alexander, 2010, p. 237)

Even as this chapter is being written, which happens to be at the time of the publication of A-level and GCSE examination results, yet again the rhetoric being used by various media journalists is full of phrases such as 'soft and hard subjects' as they indulge in their annual debate on grade inflation.

Over the years, some educationalists have warned that an overemphasis on the basics is in fact counterproductive and that a broader curriculum offers meaningful contexts for children to use and apply the very skills that are so valued. For example, over 30 years ago it was said:

> … there is no evidence in the survey to suggest that a narrower curriculum enabled children to do better in the basic skills or led to the work being more aptly chosen to suit the capacities of the children. (HMI, 1978, p. 114, para. 8.28)

Furthermore, there are many schools that are able to achieve a balance between maintaining standards in the basics and providing children with a rich and varied experience in school. The Ofsted (2002) report *The Curriculum in Successful Primary Schools* acknowledged this:

> The schools in this survey achieve what many others claim is not possible. They have high standards in English, mathematics and science, while also giving a strong emphasis to the humanities, physical education and the arts. (p. 7)

When looking closely at how the curriculum was organised in these schools, it was noted that while subject-based teaching was the most common approach, teachers capitalised on the links between areas of the curriculum and in doing so they:

- strengthened the relevance and coherence of the curriculum for pupils
- ensured that pupils applied the knowledge and skills learned in one subject to others, thus reinforcing their learning and increasing their understanding and confidence
- made good use of longer blocks of time, enabling pupils to undertake sustained work in themes covering two or three subjects.

Ofsted returned to take another look at the most successful schools in England and Wales six years later in their 2008 report *Curriculum Innovation in Schools*. Their findings were similar and they organised the innovations made by surveyed schools into four categories:

- curriculum delivery through themes or interdisciplinary links rather than discrete subjects
- flexible use of curriculum time
- alternative curriculum pathways
- a concentration on developing learning skills.

This trend continued and more recently the Rose Review (2009) of the primary curriculum went a step further by explicitly drawing attention to the value of cross-curricular teaching in organising teaching and learning and recommending that it be used more widely in schools. Although the report was interpreted by some as heralding the return of topic-based teaching and the end of subjects in primary schools, Rose clearly called for a combination of approaches stating:

> High standards are best secured when essential knowledge and skills are learned both through direct, high-quality subject teaching and also through this content being applied and used in cross-curricular studies. Primary schools have long organised and taught much of the curriculum as a blend of discrete subjects and cross-curricular studies in this way. It is the best of this work that has informed the recommendations of the review. (2009, p. 2)

Encouraged by such pronouncements, there is at the time of writing a growing movement in primary schools towards teaching in a cross-curricular way, drawing together a range of subjects under the umbrella of a theme or project. This has not always been the case, however, and cross-curricular teaching has seen its status in the primary schools wax and wane. Over the decades some reports such as Hadow and Plowden have very much supported it.

> It is essential at this, as at later stages, to give meaning and content to the child's studies by relating them to living interests; to appeal to and cultivate his imagination; and to encourage him to develop, in his small way, habits of independent thought and action. (Board of Education (Hadow Report), 1931, p. 40, para. 37)

> One of the most important responsibilities of teachers is to help children to see order and pattern in experience, and to extend their ideas by analogies and by the provision of suitable vocabulary. Rigid division of the curriculum into subjects tends to interrupt children's trains of thought and of interest and to hinder them from realising the common elements in problem solving. These are among the many reasons why some work, at least, should cut across subject divisions at all stages in the primary school. (Central Advisory Council for Education (Plowden Report), 1967, p. 197)

Others were reported as taking a different view; for example, in what came to be famously known as the 'report of the three wise men', it was stated:

> ... much topic work has led to fragmentary and superficial teaching and learning ... [and] ... conversely that, teaching focused on single subjects benefits primary pupils. (Alexander et al., 1992, para. 3.4)

Critics of cross-curricular approaches worry about a lack of intellectual rigour resulting from tenuously linked topics and fear a watering down of traditional subjects such as history and science whereas those in the other camp claim that subject-based teaching is rigid, lacking in creativity and not attuned to how young children think. As we are sure you will have gathered from this chapter and others by now, politics and education have had a long and troubled relationship, particularly where the curriculum is concerned.

You will often hear veteran teachers exclaiming 'we've been here before' at the launch of a supposed new initiative, talking of 'going full circle' or describing a pendulum that has swung back and forth between the demands of successive governments. In a reply to a letter enquiring about the status of the primary curriculum, a spokesperson for the newly elected coalition government stated within a year of the Rose Report:

> The Government has decided not to proceed with the new curriculum proposed by Sir Jim Rose under the previous government. The Government believes that such a curriculum would be too prescriptive and bureaucratic and there is a concern that a move away from traditional academic subjects could lead to an erosion of standards in our primary schools. (DfE, 2010)

These tensions and seismic shifts in state educational philosophy are unhelpful and different teaching approaches should be thought of as being complementary rather than mutually exclusive. Alexander (one of the 'wise men') has since clarified in the Cambridge Primary Review (Alexander, 2010) that while there were deep concerns about what he described as the unnecessary complexity of classroom organisation with groups of children pursuing multiple areas of the curriculum simultaneously, the key message of the 1992 report was 'repertoire, balance and fitness for purpose' (p. 293) which included a plea for teachers to consider *all* teaching approaches available to them and to make professional and principled decisions about which to use and when. We shall keep this very much in mind in this chapter as we look more closely at the ways in which schools organise and approach the curriculum.

CRITICAL ISSUES

The Hadow Report was a document published in 1931 that explored the educational needs of infants and young children and discussed the implications of the findings on schooling. Although the report was published 80 years ago many of the issues debated are the same as those that educationalists wrestle with today. Read the report or search for a summary online (e.g. Gillard, 2007) and reflect on the recommendations in light of your own values and principles about curriculum design and organisation. How does the Hadow Report compare to more recent documents such as the Rose Review (Rose, 2009) or the Cambridge Primary Review (Alexander, 2010)?

Approaches to the curriculum

When teaching in a cross-curricular style, teachers may well adopt a particular approach which has been developed either commercially, e.g. *International Primary Curriculum*

(International Primary Curriculum, 2011) or *Creative Learning Journeys* (Creative Learning Journey, 2011), or by passionate practitioners within various institutions, e.g. *Mantle of the Expert* (Bolton and Heathcote, 1995) and *Take One Picture* (National Gallery, 2011). On the other hand, such projects may have been developed by a teacher him/herself from a particular enthusiasm or interest and these may then become the focus of a year group's work within the school. They may also be taken up by the rest of the staff team.

If you have observed teachers working in this way, you may well have been impressed by the results such undertakings achieve in terms of the learning in which the children participate and the commitment they give to the project. As with many things you will see in schools, such successes are arguably as much the result of the drive and enthusiasm of the teachers as the particular method – it is often said that anything works in the hands of the right person. However, if you are to achieve similar success then you will need to become more than just the 'technician' who presents someone else's ideas to your class. In order to ensure that you are the true professional, you will need to have a ready understanding of the underpinning which should support the particular pedagogical approach adopted so that you can ensure there is more than lip service paid to the essentials of continuity and progression and a broad and balanced curriculum.

There needs to be a principled approach to curriculum planning when drawing together the skills and the content of what have been traditionally seen as separate subjects into a linked area of study. To do this, you will need to consider the distinct 'way of knowing' (known as the epistemology) of each subject and the skills which it is presupposed the children have or will need in order to make sense of what they are doing and are learning. A starting point when considering linking subjects together to tackle a project or theme is first to recognise the aspects which actually separate the subjects and make them distinct ways of coming together to understand the world in which we live. You may find it helpful to think of the subjects as different lenses to look at the world through.

> The curriculum of a subject should be determined by the most fundamental understanding that can be achieved of the underlying principles that give structure to the subject. (Bruner, 1962, p. 31)

There is a danger that if we artificially clump together subjects into one 'area of learning' within the curriculum we will fail to see that, epistemologically, these subjects are distinctive intellectual ways of finding and establishing knowledge. Science, for example, is essentially empirical, i.e. it operates by following a systematic process of testing a hypothesis using observable and measurable evidence. History, on the other hand, requires looking at what remains of a particular time and recreating the best account of the events. Because history, by definition, refers to things that have already happened, it cannot be tested in the way that science can. There is also a danger that some concepts lose meaning when they are part of a cross curricular unit. 'Force', for example, has vastly different connotations depending on whether you are thinking in a scientific, historical/political or spiritual domain.

If this is accepted, then what must be recognised is that when any cross-curricular project is being undertaken that involves a science element, then this should, where possible, be approached using the 'cognitive toolkit' from that subject, in this case the scientific method. Similarly, when the project considers some aspect of the past then the child must approach it using the conventions of a historical investigation. These are discrete ways of study and you as a teacher must ensure that the child has the skills and resources to tackle the particular aspect of the project in the appropriate way, even if it takes place in the domain of a multidisciplinary project or topic.

For example, David, a Year 3 teacher, is looking to plan a cross-curricular unit of work around the theme of Ancient Egyptians. This theme obviously has a strong historical focus and when the children weigh up carefully different sources of evidence to determine who they think built the pyramids he is confident that they are both developing their skills of historical enquiry and building their knowledge of an ancient world society. Nonetheless, David also wants to bring in aspects of science since he feels that the topic provides a motivating context for some investigations. From past experiences, he knows that children are intrigued by the mummification process and so he plans to provide the resources for children to investigate this practically (using oranges instead of people you will be relieved to read). Since the children will be encouraged to generate lines of enquiry and follow them through practically he can be sure that the children are working in an authentically scientific manner.

What we wish to avoid is a subject losing rigour in order for it to fit in with the theme. As exciting as it might be for your pupils to build chariots in design and technology to match your topic on the Romans, if they are greatly restricted in their design choices and the mechanisms they can explore because you feel a lack of authenticity would ruin the class display, there is a risk that the very essence of design and technology will be lost and it becomes simply 'making'.

Thematic and topic-based approaches

The cases given above are relatively simple examples of teachers combining a couple of subjects together. The degree to which schools have adopted cross-curricular teaching varies greatly. At the most basic level, teachers continue to teach in discrete subjects and some incidental cross-curricular links are made where appropriate. Some teachers might go further and shuffle the order of subject focuses around so that groups of lessons that take place in a half-term are united by a common theme but are still taught as separate subjects. An example of this might be a teacher deciding to teach about rocky shore and marine habitats in science at the same time as she teaches about coasts in geography and explores seascapes in art, all of which are strengthened further by a school trip to the beach (see Figure 14.1).

Here is a more detailed example. Sameera is looking forward to working in Year 5 and before she starts she is handed a curriculum map (Figure 14.2), which offers a very brief overview of what will be taking place in each subject across the year.

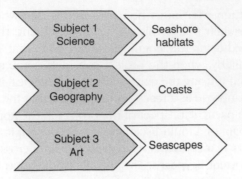

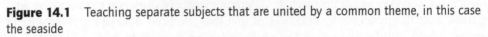

Figure 14.1   Teaching separate subjects that are united by a common theme, in this case the seaside

Subject	Autumn term	Spring term	Summer term
English	As set out in Literacy and Numeracy Frameworks		
Mathematics			
Science	Electricity and magnetism	Sorting and classifying materials Changes in state (water cycle)	Light and sound Microbes
History	Victorians	Aztecs	
Geography	Should the high street be closed to traffic?	Water	
Design & Technology	Moving toys making use of cams	Bread	Purses and pencil cases
Art	Representing people in action	Goldsworthy and the use of natural materials in art	Sculpture and the work of Henry Moore
Music	Class orchestra: arrangements	Soundscapes	Singing
PE/Dance	Swimming	Gymnastics	Dance composition
Games	Invasion games: touch rugby and netball	Striking games: cricket	Athletics: track and field
ICT	Vector drawing	Databases	Digital video
RE	Hinduism	Sikhism	Buddhism

Figure 14.2   Curriculum map

At first glance, the curriculum map looks very crowded. As you might expect, having to juggle a dozen different curriculum areas, not including additional aspects such as primary languages, PSHE (Personal, Social and Health Education) and citizenship, is very demanding for teachers and it is a tall order to expect children and teachers to follow all the different strands of learning in one week. Weaving the threads together by organising subjects into themes is one way of managing this load although it is not the only strategy. For example, many teachers do not attempt to teach all the subject areas in the same week and may block periods of time to complete a sequence of learning. This might include alternating which of the non-core subjects, say either history or geography, is taught each half term or even completing a sustained run of one subject area over several afternoons or as a dedicated themed week. This helps to build a momentum and is particularly effective when teaching practical subjects such as design and technology projects.

Returning to Sameera, she decides that after looking across the whole year, there are some areas that can be consolidated around an organising theme. After consulting the National Curriculum documentation, one of the key messages she wants children to take away from studies on the Victorians is that highly motivated individuals can have a lasting impact on society. She also wants children to appreciate how the drastic changes in lifestyle during this time had huge implications for public well-being. Many of the social and health problems in this period resulted from overcrowding and the consequential limited access to clean water and poor sanitation. Sameera notes that this links to planned work in geography on water and aspects of the science curriculum such as sorting materials, micro-organisms and the water cycle. She also intends for children to use historical sources such as the online census data and would like the children to present their research as a dramatic documentary, being able to see how this links to expectations in ICT. With this in mind, she plans a cross-curricular unit of work based around the orientating question 'How and why did public health change over the Victorian period?' and comes up with the outline plan shown in Figure 14.3.

Sameera hopes that the strong and relevant links that exist between the different parts of the curriculum will help to deepen understanding in all areas. While children may be working in different modes as they use the tools from each subject domain, such as looking at documentary evidence of the impact of individuals such as Lord Shaftsbury (history), creating a digital film (ICT) or investigating experimentally how dirty water can be cleaned (science), the context will be the same for each of these activities, adding some much needed continuity and relevance to their work (see Figure 14.4). Furthermore, discoveries in one area will help to deepen understanding in others.

Another approach is to take a central theme from which different subject areas branch out and use this to 'flavour' the curriculum. While this certainly helps to frame all of the learning in a similar context, there is a danger that the links made between subjects are superficial. Stimulating as it is to search for connections, if you find you really need to think about them or they are becoming abstract, then this is a warning sign that you are in danger of creating shallow and tenuous links. This tendency to overextend ideas and approaches in teaching, particularly with respect to cross-curricular teaching, was noted in the Hadow Report 80 years ago.

Subject	Lines of enquiry
History	• What was life like for Victorians, particularly children? • How healthy were they? • How do we know? • How did changes in lifestyle, scientific understanding and public policy influence health?
ICT	• How can we use digital film to make historical documentaries? • What can we learn from census records and how can we retrieve information? • How can databases help us to manage information efficiently?
Geography	• What is our relationship with water? • How does this compare to other parts of the world? • How can we use water in a more sustainable way? • What impact does water have on public health?
Science	• Why is dirty water dangerous? • How do we clean water? • How did scientists and doctors use evidence to make changes in order to improve health?

Figure 14.3   Outline plan

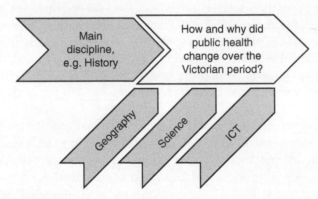

Figure 14.4   A multidisciplinary unit of work consisting of a leading subject and several other different subjects in support

In the first place, there is always some danger that a new method, particularly if, within its proper field, it is a strikingly useful one, may be forced beyond its proper limits. (Board of Education, 1931, p. 103)

Although most teachers are rarely short of ideas for overarching themes or topics for cross-curricular study, it can be intimidating for even the most experienced to design an organising framework and ensure that there is academic rigour as well as continuity and progression over the year and across the year groups. Simply organising serendipitously under an 'umbrella' is not enough and further consideration is necessary to determine the key issues, problems to investigate and concepts. In order to do this it is your responsibility as a teacher to prepare and present a project so that it is possible to see where relevant links can be made that strengthen the learning experience for children. A starting point to your planning would be the recognition of what might be termed 'orientating concepts'. These are in effect the essential ways of approaching or even thinking about a topic and are used to generate lines of enquiry. Many of the cross-curricular projects of past decades, such as the Schools' Council 'Place, Time and Society' (Blyth et al., 1976), were based on these. Figure 14.5 shows the seven orientating concepts in this case.

These types of question are qualitatively different from other aspects of any topic because they do not focus so much on facts but seek ideas, higher concepts and explanations. You can

Orientating concept	Explanation We need to encourage children to ...	Example lines of enquiry
Similarity and Difference	• Ask how something compares with or differs from what we already know • Appreciate the need for a point of reference in order to be able to note areas where things are the same or different	*In what ways are Bedouin homes similar or different from ours?*
Continuity and Change	• Realise that people, places, objects and relationships can and do change. • Look for the inheritance of the past and innovations which signal new directions	*How has our town changed in the past 100 years?*
Cause and Consequences	• See what has brought about a state of affairs or what could be/has been the result of certain actions	*What caused the Great Fire of London? What effects did this have on the city and its people?*
Conflict and Consensus	• Note that causes and effects do not always fit together harmoniously • Explore if a happy state of affairs exists or not	*Explain the good and harm done by motor cars.*
Values and Beliefs	• Consider what people involved think is important and why they hold those beliefs	*What did the Ancient Egyptians believe about the afterlife?*
Power	• Determine the structure and direction of the power relationships in a situation	*What was Henry VIII's relationship with the Church?*
Communication	• Study how information is shared in a system	*How was propaganda used by the Allies in the Second World War?*

Figure 14.5   Orientating concepts in Blyth et al. (1976)

Geographical enquiry and skills

3. Knowledge and understanding of places

Pupils should be taught:

a. to identify and describe what places are like [for example, in terms of weather, jobs] ...
d. to explain why places are like they are [for example, in terms of weather conditions, local resources, historical development]
e. to identify how and why places change [for example, through the closure of shops or building of new houses, through conservation projects] and how they may change in the future [for example, through an increase in traffic or an influx of tourists]
f. to describe and explain how and why places are similar to and different from other places in the same country and elsewhere in the world [for example, comparing a village with a part of a city in the same country] ...

Figure 14.6   Extract from the 1999 National Curriculum

find examples of these encapsulated within the programmes of study in the current National Curriculum. This is more evident in some areas, e.g. geography, than others and can be seen in the extract in Figure 14.6 taken from the 1999 National Curriculum (DfEE, 1999).

It is only when a clear foundation in thinking and questioning skills has been established that teachers should begin to look at the key areas of content within cross curricular studies.

Some teachers plan the whole term or half term of learning around an overarching theme and individual lessons may feature learning objectives from more than one subject. This type of teaching tends to be more common in the Early Years Foundation Stage and Key Stage 1. A popular example of this used with young children is the organising theme based on 'minibeasts' (a word which only ever seems to be used in primary schools and, much to the annoyance of zoologists, is used by children and teachers as an unscientific catch-all term that includes insects, crustaceans, molluscs and indeed any small animal). In lessons centred on this theme you might expect to find children developing their vocabulary through labelling parts of insect bodies, investigating habitats, looking closely at shape and number patterns in minibeast anatomy and exploring related literature such as Eric Carle's Angry Ladybird and Hungry Caterpillar. Figure 14.7 provides a diagram showing a curriculum organised in a similar way focusing on toys.

International Primary Curriculum

There are a now a number of companies that produce ready-made cross-curricular themes that schools can purchase. Popular examples include the *International Primary Curriculum* and *The Creative Learning Journey*. The former has produced eighty different thematic units including topics such 'Chocolate', 'Earthquakes and Volcanoes' and 'Mission to Mars'. On their website, they describe how each unit is structured:

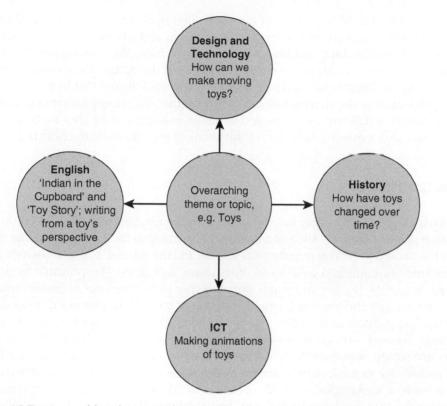

Figure 14.7 Overarching theme used to contextualise curriculum across several subject areas

Each unit of work is launched through an Entry Point which introduces the theme to the children in an exciting and memorable way. The learning process is then continued through a Knowledge Harvest, Explaining the Theme, Individual Learning Tasks, and finally an Exit Point.

For the unit based on Chocolate, they suggest that eight weeks of curriculum time could be organised as follows:

- 1 week on the Entry Point, Knowledge Harvest and Explaining the Theme
- 1 week on art
- 1 week on geography
- 1 week on history
- 1 and a half weeks on science
- 2 weeks on technology
- half a week on 'international tasks'.

When discussing her experiences with teaching this unit in a teachers' magazine ('Sweet like chocolate', *Junior Education Plus*, March 2008, pp. 33–6), a teacher described how the different areas of the curriculum slotted together into the theme: in art the children explored the aesthetics of packaging and advertising; in geography the focus was on sustainability and fair-trade issues surrounding the growing and distribution of the cacao crop; in history the children researched the Aztecs, their encounters with Cortez and the impacts of chocolate being brought back to the Old World; in science, using chocolate as the starting point they investigated the energy contents of food and the demands of different exercises; and in design and technology, they made their own snack bars after exploring different combinations of ingredients with chocolate.

Take One Picture

In 2001, The National Gallery in London developed a teaching approach based on using a single piece of artwork, such as a painting, as a stimulus for a cross-curricular theme. This has proved to be very popular with schools and the scheme has now been extended to include museums and galleries in other towns and cities. The principle behind the project is that the teacher and pupils work together to explore lines of enquiry that have been inspired by children's encounters with one of the famous pictures displayed at the gallery. The pictures used in the scheme are carefully chosen and have a rich cultural heritage that makes them captivating focal points for class themes. While art is clearly the principle subject, other curriculum areas are also involved depending on the context of the picture. For example, when Turner's *Fighting Temeraire* was chosen in 2009, themes explored by schools included the life of Nelson and the Battle of Trafalgar, recycling (after learning the ship was to be broken up), how the River Thames has changed over time, exploration of coloured lighting techniques to create different moods and effects and even traditional carpentry skills to recreate authentic furniture from the period. Films and images of their work can be found on the gallery's website (National Gallery, 2011).

Project-based and problem-solving approaches

Children enjoy working towards shared goals and seeing tangible outcomes for their accomplishments in the classroom. Cross-curricular projects endeavour to exploit this by giving children a purpose for their studies and the opportunity to apply their acquired skills in a real-life situation.

Imagine, for example the following scenario, the chair of governors is pleased to have secured funding to develop the outdoor area of the school. She wants children to be included in this project and recognises that this is an ideal opportunity for children to gain valuable experience of improving their own environment. She links up with a class teacher so that children can be consulted throughout. Drawing mainly upon the science and geography programmes of study, the teacher is able to ground the project firmly in the curriculum and soon the children are fully involved in planning a wildlife garden, after researching conditions for habitats and completing a baseline wildlife census of school grounds, designing

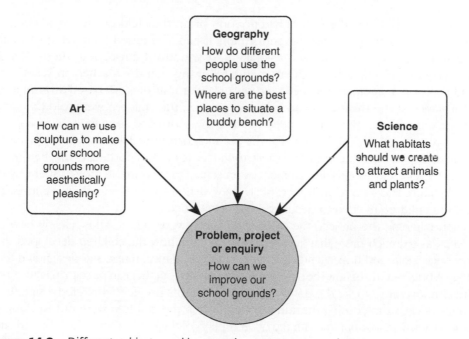

Figure 14.8   Different subjects working together to support a project

and situating the new 'buddy bench' based on surveys and interviews of younger pupils, and even work with a local sculptor to produce works of art to decorate the area. A project such as this would encompass many areas of the curriculum (see Figure 14.8), reward children with a sense of civic pride in their achievements and foster a sense of camaraderie.

This is an example of a 'one-off' event. As a teacher, you have to be constantly vigilant for similar opportunities that make learning relevant and current. As you become more experienced, your teacher 'radar' will improve and you will be better able to spot potential starting points for curriculum enrichment. You will, however, need to learn to switch this off at times, as partners, family and friends will soon become irritated if social outings turn into scouting missions for school. The vignette below describes a more sustainable cross-curricular project carried out in one of the author's schools.

A national opera company contacted the school and asked if the teachers and children would like to be involved in the production and performance of an opera planned to be presented at the local theatre in a few months. The school has a strong tradition in the performing arts and jumped at the opportunity. Once in school, the company, consisting of performers, songwriters and choreographers, worked in partnership with the teachers and Year 5 and 6 children, and together they took the *Barber of Seville* as a starting point and adapted it into an opera of their own with unique songs, dances and costumes, all of which children played a part in. Not surprisingly, the sell-out performance was a roaring success and had a huge impact on all concerned, so much so that the teachers in the school wished to sustain the project for future cohorts. The teachers involved observed how the project had not only given the children an exciting context and audience for their writing and performing, it had also raised their self-esteem and increased levels of confidence and risk-taking were noticed throughout the remainder of the year. To maintain the momentum, the following year the teachers in Years 5 and 6 and senior management planned a cross-curricular unit of work based around a real performance at the theatre. On arrival in September, the children were told the venue was booked and that they would need to write the script and song lyrics, choreograph the dances as well as design and make the set and costumes. They were even given the responsibility of working with the theatre effects team to coordinate the lighting to create the different moods and ambiences on stage. To recoup the money spent by the school to hire the theatre and any experts they wished to employ such as a choreographer, the children needed to calculate a fair ticket price.

When planning the project, the teachers involved were able to show clearly how the project was so much more that 'just a school play' and how the children developed their knowledge, skills and understanding in literacy, drama, dance, music and design and technology. A brief outline of how the different subjects fitted together can be seen in Figure 14.9.

It is important to make the point here that while this project demanded a significant amount of class time during the autumn term, when the children were not working on the play they were continuing with the other aspects of the curriculum, which by and large

Curriculum subject	Lines of enquiry
English	• What traditional stories are of local cultural importance? • How are traditional narratives translated into plays, TV programmes and films? • What makes a great play script and how do we write one? • What makes an effective song and how do we write lyrics? • What are the most effective ways of communicating with our audience? • How do we publicise our play? • What am I like as a performer? • How effective was our play and how do we know?
Design and Technology	• How can I design and construct theatre costumes and stage props that are realistic, durable enough to be transported and able to be seen by the audience in a large theatre? • How can we use theatrical lighting to enhance what is taking place on stage?
Dance (PE)	• How can I communicate narrative in the form of a dance as an integral part of a musical production in front of an audience?
Music	• What makes a good song structure and how can we use music to enhance our play? • What would be appropriate music to dance and perform to? • How can we compose our own music to create mood and ambience?

Figure 14.9   Project outline

were taught as separate subjects. For example, while the children used mathematics and ICT (spreadsheets) to calculate costs and organise seating plans, this was a peripheral aspect of the project and as such the teaching for these subjects followed discrete, relatively unrelated programmes of study.

'Mantle of the Expert'

Some schools use dramatic simulations to create meaningful and relevant contexts for learning that pupils feel they have a real stake in. The most widely known approach used in primary schools is 'Mantle of Expert' and is based on the work of Dorothy Heathcote at the University of Newcastle upon Tyne. The rationale of this teaching method is that drama is used to create a fictional situation in which children are behaving as if they are the 'experts'. By taking on this 'mantle', the children are situated in the centre of the learning situation rather than observers looking in. Through thinking and working from this perspective, they are able to interact with imagined characters and situations from any time or place and it is hoped that, when doing so, the children will use and develop the same types of knowledge, skills, understanding, vocabulary and behaviours as the experts in the real world would. Moreover, this form of 'process drama' helps children to empathise with different points of view and appreciate the complexity of situations. These scenarios aim to use powerful narratives to capture children's imagination and create a sense of urgency known as a 'productive tension' (Bolton and Heathcote, 1995) that gives momentum and pace to the work. Although the scenarios may be focused on one particular subject area, they are usually multidisciplinary and when planning the teacher needs to think carefully about the types of knowledge and skills that the imagined experts would possess and how these might link to the aims and goals for the children's learning. Typically, the teacher uses a 'client' to interact with the pupils and shape the narrative. Using this approach, realistic challenges can be set for pupils indirectly through letters and e-mail or in person by a volunteer in role (usually another teacher or teaching assistant). The 'Mantle of the Expert' website that promotes and supports the use of this approach (Mantle of the Expert, 2011) includes many examples of dramatic contexts for learning and is well worth a visit. These include:

- a mountain rescue team that battles against time to save a climber stranded after a fall and who is threatened by deteriorating weather conditions
- a marine engineering company that faces the combined challenge of rescuing a whale trapped in fishing nets and retrieving valuable artefacts from a Tudor merchant ship
- the discovery of a hidden Roman strongbox that may hold the secrets of the rebellion led by Boudicca.

It could also be said, that although any topic will be centred on certain content, many cross-curricular projects are very much skills led. This being the case, not only must you have a ready understanding of what the subject entails, you must also be able to analyse and understand the key skills that are required by the children to undertake the planned activities.

As a minimum, an analysis of research skills suggests that the following are involved: the ability to

- find information
- evaluate information
- organise information
- communicate
- generate questions for lines of enquiry.

Indeed, all these skills and others are set out in what in our experience is the often under-used preamble to the National Curriculum documentation (DfEE, 1999, pp. 20–3). Not only this, however, if we intend children to be able to take on projects of the type that require role-play then it is necessary to foster certain positive attitudes and behaviour. It is essential that in any role-play scenario children will be able to cooperate with one another; they will be open-minded and prepared to listen to others and consider new evidence and opinions; they will be prepared to be independent and take responsibility for organising their own programme and progress to some measure. Again, it cannot be assumed that children already have these positive attitudes so you must be prepared to encourage a classroom environment and ethos that ensures these develop. Before one can use any skill, it must first be acquired and indeed this may in some cases necessitate specific teaching. Thus time must be built into any project to achieve this.

The examples shown above take a central theme, narrative, project or even a picture and then use the various subject disciplines to investigate it from multiple perspectives, each revealing a different piece of the puzzle. This adds coherence and purpose to children's work and illustrates to them how different subjects work in concert to deepen understanding.

CRITICAL ISSUES

Visit the Take One Picture, Mantle of the Expert or International Primary Curriculum websites. Find an example of a cross-curricular unit of work and consider the following:

- How are subject-specific knowledge and/or skills strengthened through the links made?
- What other aspects of the child are developed through the approach taken?
- What challenges do you think that teaching in this way might present?

Final thoughts

It is a significant challenge for teachers to assess children's progress in the different subject areas as they navigate their way through topics and themes such as 'Dinosaurs', 'Homes' and 'The Seaside'. Teachers need to think carefully about the particular knowledge, skills and understanding developed within each area and plan a route map through that ensures that children aren't treading *unnecessarily* over old ground and are receiving an increased level of intellectual demand as they progress. Cross-curricular themes may be made up of several subjects but they will not necessarily be included in equal weighting. Often themes will be led by one subject such as history for example, with the others complementing effectively but in secondary positions. This being the case, the teacher will need to ensure that subsequent themes offer new experiences such as moving from one with a science and technological focus to another based around the performing arts. Since many schools that adopt cross-curricular approaches tend also to give the children a significant role in generating lines of enquiry and directing the projects, they often develop systems that track carefully which skills and concepts children encounter so that future scenarios can be designed to build on areas that haven't previously been addressed and present fresh challenges.

Summary

- Different approaches to curriculum design pass in and out of fashion as governments change and the educational zeitgeist shifts back and forth from subject to thematic and project-based teaching.
- Whichever method of organising the curriculum is adopted – and each has their inherent strengths and weaknesses – it is important that a principled approach is taken. Indeed, they are not mutually exclusive and schools do not need to choose between them. Teachers should feel confident enough to make professional decisions as to when they feel a particular approach is most appropriate.
- Local projects and significant events (both real and imagined) can be used to add authenticity to teaching and learning.
- Stimulating projects, topics and themes can be created by blending several curriculum subjects together. When doing so, teachers and curriculum organisers across year groups and phases in schools need to work together when planning to ensure that children have a broad and balanced educational experience.

〜〜   **Issues for reflection**

- Why are some subjects considered to be more important than others? Should the subjects that help prepare children for the 'world of work' take priority over those that facilitate creative expression and healthy living?
- When you are in school, look over planning documentation. Can you identify areas where cross-curricular links could be made?
- 'Walk a mile in another man's moccasins' by occasionally reading the education sections of national newspapers that you do not normally choose to read. What are the differences in how the school curriculum is reported? What are the implications of these alternative points of view for curriculum designers in school?

Further reading 📖

Alexander, R. (ed.) (2010) *Children, Their World, Their Education*. Abingdon: Routledge. In chapters 13 and 14 (pp. 203–78) of the final report from the Cambridge Primary Review, Alexander and other members of the team explore in great detail with reference to key reviews, the dynamic history of the primary curriculum in England and discuss the principles that should underpin any new curriculum.

Barnes, J. (2011) *Cross-Curricular Learning 3–14*. 2nd edition. London: Sage. This accessible book discusses examples of cross-curricular themes and explores the underlying principles of teaching in this way.

National Advisory Committee on Creative and Cultural Education (NACCE) (1999) *All Our Futures: Creativity, Culture and Education*. London: DfEE. Although published over a decade ago, the report, written by a committee led by Sir Ken Robinson, is as relevant now as it was then as it explores the continuing tensions between teaching 'the basics' and creativity. Sir Ken Robinson is an inspirational, humorous and poignant public speaker. Many of his presentations are world famous (some have been downloaded over a million times) and are essential viewing for anyone involved in education. Two of his most notable talks given at the TED (Technology, Entertainment, Design) conferences include the following examples.

Robinson, K. (2006) 'Schools Kill Creativity'. Available online at: http://www.ted.com/talks/lang/eng/ken_robinson_says_schools_kill_creativity.html.

Robinson, K. (2010) 'Bring on the Learning Revolution!'. Available online at: http://www.ted.com/talks/sir_ken_robinson_bring_on_the_revolution.html.

CHAPTER 15

CONTINUITY AND PROGRESSION FROM 3–11

Alan Pagden

Chapter overview

Educating 3–11-year-olds is a complicated business. At least part of what is involved takes place in institutions called schools. These come in different shapes and sizes based, at least in part, on assumptions about how children's needs change as they get older. Alan Pagden discusses these, together with similar assumptions that underpin the prescribed curriculum. He invites you to consider a possible future in which the child experiences increased 'continuity' across their primary years (e.g. in relation to such matters as 'pupil autonomy') as well as clearer 'progression' (e.g. from spontaneous play to systematic investigation). Understanding this bigger picture is essential if you are to make the most of your career in primary education.

Introduction

The aim of this chapter is to help you to develop an understanding of the big picture. You might well intend to spend most of your teaching career working with a particular age group – Year 3/4, for example. However, even with this narrow focus, in order for you to do your job well you will need to know about the characteristic experiences of teachers and children throughout the primary age range.

The twin themes that run through this chapter are 'continuity' and 'progression'. For a child to succeed there are some things that should stay the same throughout their time at school: most obviously, the combination of physical and social factors that ensures the child's right to feel safe and cared for. Other things should change progressively in order to support the child's growing competence and maturity: for example, the complexity of texts designed to foster the development of literacy skills. The term 'continuity' applies not only to the child's experience across the time they spend in school but also to the degree of consistency that they experience between life at home and life at school. Although it is difficult to separate these two kinds of continuity, this chapter concentrates mainly on the former while Chapter 16 focuses on the latter. Furthermore, in looking at how schools might provide for 'progression' from 3–11 the chapter makes little reference to the important matter of planning in the long, medium and short term since this is dealt with in Chapters 10 and 11. As a teacher of Year 3 children, for example, you need to have a good understanding of how your colleagues in adjacent years work if you are going to offer your children an experience that incorporates relevant aspects of both continuity and progression.

More generally, all teachers in a school should have a good understanding of the child's whole experience. At one level this obviously refers to the experience of the children you teach directly, that is, in most cases, your class. A 'complete' knowledge of the learning experiences on offer to the year group or groups in which you teach is essential if you are going to provide balance and coherence in your planning, and take full advantage of opportunities to build links between different experiences. At another level, however, it is also important for you and your colleagues to know about the experiences of the 'average' child as they progress through possibly eight continuous years in the same institution. This is a far more limited demand than that placed on teachers in Austria, for example, who follow a cohort of children from year to year through their entire time at primary school.

In the following two sections I describe aspects of the situation you will find yourself in as a trainee and newly qualified teacher (NQT) in terms of some of the constraints and possibilities that primary schooling currently presents in England and Wales. To begin with I look at how schooling is organised, giving us schools of different sizes that cater for different age ranges, and how organisation in this sense interacts with the prescribed curriculum which also rests on certain assumptions about what is best for children of different ages. I then consider the idea that your principal task as a teacher is to nurture the disposition to learn. These matters are connected since your ability as a teacher to pursue this crucial task is constrained and supported by the kind of institutional framework within which you work. The chapter looks briefly at the role of parents in relation to the child's disposition to learn and then in conclusion it invites you to consider the notion of continuity and change in relation to your own teaching career.

The curriculum and the organisation of schools

The curriculum

The intention here is to discuss in general terms the 'prescribed curriculum', remembering that the quality of what actually happens in the classroom will always depend on how you as the teacher bring the official documents to life for your particular group of children at any one time. Typically you will be aiming to qualify as a teacher of 3–11-year-olds, specialising in either the 'lower' (3–8) or 'upper' end of the age range. There are clearly enormous changes that take place in a child's development through the seven or eight years they spend in primary school. Individuals, of course, will develop at different rates in different areas of learning, but schooling as a system, through the statutory curriculum, is organised into phases which structure provision in a way that is designed to meet the characteristic needs of different cohorts. At the time of writing two documents – the National Curriculum (DfEE, 1999) and the Statutory Framework for the Early Years Foundation Stage (DCSF, 2008) – set out the statutory entitlement to learning for 3–11-year-olds in England. Although the second of these has effectively extended the former 'foundation stage' to include children from birth to 3 the age range encompassed by primary schooling (i.e. 3–11) can still be described in terms of three phases: the Foundation Stage, Key Stage 1 and Key Stage 2. While it is inevitable that further changes will be made to these arrangements in the near and/or distant future, these are unlikely to negate the general points that I make here.

Built into the statutory curriculum are ideas about the progress that the average child will make as they move through the three phases (in Wales the term 'Foundation Phase' is used to refer to the 3–7 age range). During the latter part of the 'Early Years Foundation Stage' (from around 3 to the end of the Reception year) the curriculum is organised around six 'Areas of Learning' and expectations are described in terms of 'Early Learning Goals'. There is a great deal of flexibility at this stage as regards the kinds of experiences that might be planned. In Key Stage 1, comprising Years 1 and 2, teachers must follow the much more tightly prescribed National Curriculum in three core and seven foundation subjects. They also have an obligation to teach RE, and will normally have a Personal, Social and Health Education (PSHE) programme to follow. The emphasis in Key Stage 1 is on the core subjects, particularly English and maths, and there is little prescription in terms of content across the foundation subjects. In Key Stage 2, the same subject areas are followed and children begin to learn a modern foreign language. The programmes of study are more prescriptive in terms of content than they are in Key Stage 1, although the current version of the National Curriculum is much better (that is, thinner) in this respect than previous versions. The general pattern, then, is for the content of the curriculum to become increasingly prescribed as children move from 3–11. This inevitably has a bearing on children's experience of freedom vis-à-vis what and how they learn.

You will notice that, although they are officially called key 'stages', I prefer to use the word 'phase' which is familiar in professional discourse. It is appropriate also because the idea of a 'stage' of development has played a key role in developmental theories (notably Piaget's) and it is important not to confuse the way a system of schooling is structured with ideas about how individual children develop and learn. As you are no doubt aware, in other countries the structure is different and most start their children on a 'formal' school programme later than we do. Although the debate about an ideal start date, addressed for example by the Cambridge Review (Alexander, 2010), is relevant and important it is not discussed here in any depth. Whatever advantages different systems might have, it is invariably the case that a system designed to cater for the majority will not suit everyone. The Foundation Stage, for example, covers the first two years of schooling (nursery and Reception classes), during which time children in the 3–5 age range are ostensibly taught through a play-based curriculum. Some of the children who enter Year 1 classrooms at the age of 5 (that is, move into the next phase – Key Stage 1) will not be ready to take advantage of the learning experiences that are typically organised for children in this phase where there is a strong emphasis on the acquisition of 'basic' skills. Ideally, for these children, teachers should continue to draw on the ideas and resources of the Foundation Stage, that is they should sustain a play-based curriculum. Difficulties arise where there is a particularly strong disjunction between the educational values that underpin the curricula of consecutive key stages. Arguably this is what happens at the transition from Reception to Year 1 where teachers have a particularly difficult task in reconciling the needs of many of their children with the demands of the curriculum. This issue is touched on again below.

The key stages of the National Curriculum for England and Wales were initially defined along with an assessment system that was deliberately designed to avoid the creation of a testing culture in schools (DES and Welsh Office, 1987). This is why the levels of achievement are very broad and the average child is expected to progress through each of them in two years. The original idea was to keep testing to a minimum (that is, at the end of key stages) and to ensure that the curriculum was not assessment led. Unfortunately, high-stakes testing (e.g. with target setting and league tables) has come to dominate the curriculum, especially in the final year of primary schooling, Year 6. This undermines some of the key principles that the National Curriculum embodies such as the importance of breadth and balance. At the time of writing the government has just commissioned a review to look at the negative effects of the assessment system and this will hopefully lead to improvements. A general principle for you to draw from this account, however, is the importance of understanding exactly what your overall statutory responsibilities are, so that you will be able to make judgements in your planning and your teaching in the best interests of the child. In recent years, in England, teachers have sometimes been led to believe that they 'have to' undertake practices (e.g. excessive testing) when in fact they are under no statutory obligation to do so. As with planning the full implications of different approaches to assessment cannot be explored here (see Chapter 10). The key point, as regards the child's experience of continuity and progression, is that assessment should be more about the individual and less about making comparisons among the members of a given cohort (consider the concept of 'ipsative assessment').

Different kinds of school

There are a number of important ways in which schools differ that may determine, to some extent, the possibilities that are available to you as a teacher. There are, for example, schools with religious affiliations, independent schools, and other schools such as 'academies' and 'free schools' that do not fall under local authority control. Here two dimensions along which schools vary are looked at. The first is age range and how systems of schooling carve this into chunks that are then ascribed titles such as infants, junior or middle. The second is size. So far, I have described the national system for primary schooling in England as comprising three phases defined in terms of the requirements of the school curriculum (including the National Curriculum). Alongside this curriculum structure schooling is organised into different age-based types of school through two- or three-tier systems, not all of which coincide with the key stages of the National Curriculum. In the past across the country we had a wide range of different systems for staging children's progress through school. School transfer could occur at virtually any age, depending on where the individual lived. Children might have moved from 3–9 primary schools to 9–13 middle schools (for example, until recently, on the Isle of Wight), or from 3–8 first schools to 8–12 middle schools (for example, until recently, parts of Norfolk). In recent years, however, many local authorities have reorganised in order to align their times of transfer with National Curriculum defined phases. On balance this is a positive development, but it should not lead us to forget some of the reasoning that informed the development of alternatives such as the middle school system, which is strongly associated with a particular educational rationale (see Hargreaves, 1986). The experience that children have of their schools as institutions can be profoundly different. Some will move through two or three separate schools/settings, even if they don't move home, while others will stay in the same school from nursery to Year 6. The main reasons behind the decisions that lead to different arrangements for schooling in different areas are economic and demographic. There are, however, educational reasons why some arrangements might be better than others, and it is a good idea to consider some of these.

An advantage of schools that encompass all three phases is their potential to ensure a high degree of continuity and to plan for progression through the whole age range. By contrast it is arguable that every time a child changes school they are faced with challenges and potential discontinuities that could set them back. Most schools prepare children for their move to a new class at the end of the school year by introducing them to their new teacher and by giving teachers time to talk about members of their new class with the previous teacher. This is obviously supported with transfer records of various kinds. Even more important is the need for liaison between teachers across the years of transfer from one school to the next, and for children to be made to feel welcome at their new school. Some schools put a great deal of effort into making the experience of transfer positive, but even when this happens there is often a markedly different culture that children have to get used to when they move, for example from an infants to a junior school. It seems likely that separate schools (e.g. infant and junior) generate stronger age range-specific 'cultures'. These are built partly on the value systems that underpin different curricula but also on other things including the possibility that certain sorts of people are attracted to working with children of a given age range.

There is an important difference between infant schools and junior schools that should be noted. Whereas the latter enjoy an uncomplicated match between the age group that they cater for (i.e. 7–11) and a particular key stage (i.e. Key Stage 2), the former embrace two key stages (the Foundation Stage and Key Stage 1). The so-called 'infant' age range is 5–7 (Years 1 and 2) but infant schools invariably include Reception classes and they might also include a nursery. Hence, one way or another, these schools have to support children in making the transition from the Foundation Stage to Key Stage 1 and, as indicated above, this can be difficult. The advantage of a nursery class attached to an infant or primary school lies in the possibility, under the framework of the Foundation Stage, to develop a coherent programme for the 3–5 age group. This is difficult, however, because Reception classes are generally regarded as part of the main school, a presumption normally reinforced by a common basic timetable that is out of sync with their feeder nurseries even when these are part of the same school. Furthermore, where nursery classes have been built onto established infant, first or primary schools, they have typically not been integrated with Reception classes, and are often built as completely separate units, sometimes a significant distance from the main school building. Nursery schools, which are separate institutions in their own right, often with two or three classes, are even less open to integration with the Reception classes that they feed, which are often in more than one school. They do, however, have the freedom to concentrate all their efforts on early years' practice and some have become centres of excellence, providing a model, not only for nursery classes in primary schools, but also for the many other settings where young children find themselves. The Foundation Stage offers a framework for a coherent approach to learning and teaching in the 3–5 age range. However, there remain significant physical and temporal obstacles to nursery/Reception integration, and whether you work in a nursery school, a nursery class or a Reception class you will need to make a special effort to coordinate your efforts with colleagues across the nursery/Reception year divide.

Another key factor determining the character of a school is its size. Possible educational advantages of large schools include increased opportunities for grouping children in different ways (including setting/streaming), access to more/better resources and a wider range of possibilities for staff deployment (e.g. vis-à-vis specialist/team teaching, school-based CPD, creative management structures). The success of a school in making good use of these opportunities will obviously depend on many things, chiefly, I believe, the quality of leadership and the degree of collaboration among staff. A major challenge in large schools encompassing all three phases is the need to ensure that the interests of certain age groups (typically the oldest) are not given special attention at the expense of others. This often comes to the fore when attempts are made to plan for continuity and progression throughout the school. For every advantage that a large school has there is a corresponding disadvantage. Very small schools which encompass all three phases are perhaps the best placed as regards their potential to provide continuity of experience for individual children. Teachers and other key adults can establish supportive relationships with all the children in the school and maintain them through a number of years – sometimes up to eight. This is the firmest foundation that a young learner could ask for but again it does depend on the quality of leadership and collaboration within the adult team. For most children in primary schools their class teacher quickly becomes the most important adult, and this is especially true when the individual concerned exhibits the qualities that, in the children's view, make a good teacher: which is not to say that children shouldn't be taught by more than one person. Indeed, it can be very beneficial for them to have regular contact with a number of adults, as they typically do in an early years' setting (see also Chapter 16).

So what is the ideal primary school? I am tempted to say one that encompasses all three phases without being too big or too small. In my view, two-form entry, 3–11, schools are about as big as any school should get. With over 500 pupils they are, in some respects, too big; the head teacher cannot realistically get to know all of the children individually. On the other hand, they are big enough to ensure that no teacher works in isolation and this, for me, is crucial. The very best years of my teaching career have been spent working closely with like-minded colleagues in teams, the most supportive being the year team or partnership. Having said this, it is important to acknowledge that it is only in the context of current English primary schooling that I make this assertion. Because there is an inextricable link between the organisation of a curriculum (e.g. the degree to which it is prescribed) and what might be considered 'best' working practices, the question of school size will vary according to the particular curriculum in place. Small schools with mixed-aged classes are in a better position to develop ongoing educative practices that are passed down from one generation of children to the next with very little input from the teacher. In Roth and Lee's (2006) terms it is these schools that offer the potential for the creation of genuine 'learning communities' (see also Chapter 2). Arguably, since the inception of the National Curriculum in England, small schools have been at a disadvantage since they have been unable to take advantage of some of their inherent attributes such as mixed-aged classes.

The generalist teacher

Running alongside the persistent drive to push up 'standards' there has been an emphasis on the importance of subject knowledge. Large schools are more likely to be able to appoint subject coordinators for each subject with specialist knowledge and enthusiasm for their subject, whereas small schools have to rely on individuals to take on multiple subject responsibilities. Specialist subject teaching is also more likely to take place in large schools where, even within the year team, there is scope for varying degrees of specialisation. However, in most primary schools, even large ones, you will be a generalist class teacher and your responsibility will be to teach most, if not all, subjects to your class. You will be supported in this by documentation of different kinds (for example, the programmes of study, school policies and schemes of work), by various other resources and by colleagues (for example, subject coordinators, teaching assistants), but what actually happens at the chalk face is your responsibility. Does this mean that you should be an expert in every subject? Or does it mean that as long as you have enough expertise to teach the 'basics' you'll get by, since all you need to do in relation to the other subjects is trust the plans that you are given? I say no to both of these questions.

From their inception in the nineteenth century, primary schools have always had at their core the basic structural unit of class teacher and class, one teacher responsible for the delivery of the whole curriculum (however impoverished that might be) to a number of children (for example, 30), normally for the duration of a year. The main reasons for this form of organisation are probably economic. The case for the generalist teacher, however, can be made on a number of grounds. I have already intimated that class teachers are in a position to achieve an acceptable degree of balance and coherence in the curriculum offered to their class or year group, especially where the prescribed curriculum is fundamentally imbalanced. When you are intimately acquainted with the whole, through teaching every subject, you are obviously better placed to do this. Also, through careful and creative planning you are in a position to exploit the potential of cross-curricular work. I also referred above to the importance for children of supportive interpersonal relationships and the key role that the class teacher has to play in establishing these. Perhaps the greatest potential of generalist teaching, however, lies in what Edwards and Mercer (1993) refer to as the formation of 'common knowledge'. The classroom is a social interactive context in which the teacher can play a pivotal role by establishing routines, referring back and forward to key events, making conceptual links between diverse learning experiences, and so on. Through their interactions with the class as a whole over a period of time the teacher is able to establish and develop a unique shared culture that provides a basis for much of the learning that takes place. This potential is greater in countries such as Austria and Italy where class teachers follow a particular cohort/class of pupils throughout their primary years.

In my opinion, as a primary school teacher you should think of yourself, first and foremost, as a generalist. This might appear to be a rather old-fashioned claim. In the past primary teachers would say 'I don't teach subjects, I teach children'. While secondary colleagues identified themselves with their subject, and enjoyed a degree of status from their evident expertise, primary teachers would claim that their own expertise lay not in subject knowledge but in knowledge of child development. This, I believe, was a cop-out. Knowledge of how children grow and learn is very important and it is unfortunate that you are unlikely to cover it in depth during your training. However, you do need a certain amount of subject knowledge in order to teach effectively and this too should be seen as an essential part of your professional expertise. Problems arise, I think, when subject knowledge is reified (that is separated from the context in which it is put to use) and you are led to believe that once you've acquired it, that's all you need to do.

This can lead in one of two unfortunate directions. In areas where you lack confidence, you become too reliant on other people's plans and fail to engage with the children at their level of interest and understanding. In areas where you are confident, you present yourself as a resident expert, the fount of all knowledge, a role that many young children readily cast you in, and the children come to rely on you for all the answers.

Both of these scenarios can be avoided. A good generalist teacher has the confidence and enthusiasm to research areas in which their knowledge is lacking before they are required to translate this new learning into ideas for the classroom. This is part of the planning process, but it often goes further and deeper than the children would be ready to go themselves. You will always be able to teach better if you have engaged with the subject material yourself at your own level, which in primary teaching is invariably at least two or three steps ahead of the children. As Blyth et al. (1976) argues, your job is to use the disciplines (e.g. geography and history) as resources, which you bring, along with your life experience and that of the children, to the task of 'curriculum making' (see Chapter 14). The ability and willingness to learn when new knowledge is needed is, arguably, more important than subject knowledge per se. In this regard, the generalist teacher represents an ideal role model for today's children who are growing up in an ever-changing world where, we are told, they will need to learn new skills and adapt to new work practices on a continual basis.

Nurturing the disposition to learn

In this section consideration is given to the idea that a 'disposition to learn' is something that should be nurtured throughout a child's primary years and that this presents a significant challenge, in particular for teachers of older children. Katz (1993), the person most clearly associated with the idea of dispositions as educational goals, argues that dispositions such as curiosity, playfulness and perseverance should be planned for, with the same level of commitment that goes into the planning of knowledge and skills. One of Katz's (1993) examples is of the child who has the skills of a reader but not the disposition to read, her argument being that skills training can be introduced too early resulting in the disposition being thwarted. Although the Early Years Foundation Stage curriculum is not explicitly organised in terms of dispositions it is, arguably, more amenable to such an approach than the National Curriculum of Key Stages 1 and 2. Indeed Katz's (1993) argument focuses exclusively on early years' practice. Dispositions such as playfulness, curiosity and perseverance along with others that are more tightly focused, like Katz's (1993) example of reading, can be construed as components of the more general 'disposition to learn'. Taking as read the proposal that dispositions should be planned for in the early years, this section looks at how such an approach might be followed through into the later primary years. Although some dispositions such as 'perseverance' have obvious relevance throughout the primary years, even if they are not explicitly planned for, others such as 'playfulness' are more strongly associated with early childhood and might be seen as having no place in curriculum planning for older children. In order to unpack the complexity of this scenario two interconnected aspects of early years' practice are looked at with a view to explicating the threads of continuity and progression that might, in an ideal world, follow through into Key Stages 1 and 2; these aspects are the importance of encouraging 'independence' and the recognition of the learning potential of 'play', both of which contribute to the child's sustained 'disposition to learn'.

The independent learner

Chapter 11 noted the importance of recognising the different requirements for planning that characterise the curriculum at each of the three phases. Even a cursory comparison of an early years setting and a Year 6 classroom reveals enormous contrast. Consider, for example, the balance between child-initiated and teacher-directed activities, a key dimension of planning in an early years setting. For large parts of the day or half-day in a typical setting most, if not all, children will be engaged in self-initiated activities, many of which could be described in terms of some kind of play. Play, in its various forms, is regarded as an essential vehicle for learning in young children (DCSF, 2008) and for the most part it can be regarded as child-initiated. By contrast, in Key Stage 2 play is generally regarded as a leisure activity – something reserved for break time. Furthermore, in a typical Key Stage 2 classroom, children spend most of their time engaged in tasks that have been set by the teacher. Of course in the early years context the nature of children's activity in play will be determined to a large extent by the quality of the environment that has been created by the adults, so there is a sense in which it is not entirely child-initiated. The children, nonetheless, exercise a far greater degree of autonomy over what they do than their counterparts in Key Stage 2. On the face of it then there appears to be a disjunction between two radically different approaches whereby children move from an environment in which their independence is encouraged and play is rewarded to one in which, at least as far as the curriculum is concerned, children's independence is curtailed and play is sidelined.

This, however, is a gross simplification of what might be involved. To begin with, giving children freedom to choose, and encouraging them to do so thoughtfully, is only part of the business of promoting 'independence'. As well as being motivated by their desire to exercise control over the environment, including the other human beings in it, young children are driven to participate in the social life that surrounds them. Hence, in addition to being given the chance to exercise their autonomy, children need opportunities to act responsibly as participants in the social world, and there is no doubt that the classroom, at least potentially, provides a context for them to do just that. The child who is maturing as an 'independent learner' does not only show increasing awareness of their learning needs and an ability to make sensible decisions in relation to those needs; they also show a growing understanding of their responsibility within the learning community, with all that this entails. Of course, in order to encourage a growing sense of responsibility, children should be offered structured opportunities to contribute in different ways to group endeavours including, for example, opportunities to support the learning of peers. In light of this social dimension the distinction between child-initiated and teacher-initiated activities need not imply an individual child acting autonomously; young children often initiate activities collectively through play and in so doing they generate a 'peer culture' (Corsaro, 2009). Although part of what is involved here is in opposition to the adults' agenda it nonetheless represents a potential seedbed for the development of pro-social collective action in the long term. The challenge for teachers of older children then is to create space for 'child-initiated' activity of this kind. Complementing the role of the generalist teacher in orchestrating the generation of 'common knowledge' the peer group should be given the opportunity to develop themes of shared interest that are worthy of serious study; in other words, at least part of the curriculum content that is on offer should be negotiated. This obviously raises questions about how time is managed in primary classrooms.

Learning through play

Closely connected to the principle that children should exercise a significant degree of autonomy in the early years, is the idea that play is intrinsically educative. Vygotsky (1978) famously described the child in play as behaving 'beyond his average age, above his daily behaviour; in play it is as though he were a head taller than himself' (p. 102). Unlike Piaget, Vygotsky (1978) believed that socio-dramatic play in young children was foundational since it is through play that they learn how to create imaginary situations (the foundation for abstract thought) and it is through play that they learn how to subordinate themselves to rules. It is not possible to explore the full implications of these ideas here or to look at the evidence (see Smith, 2010). It is interesting, however, to consider the essence of Vygotsky's argument, which points to a line of progression through which the principles that govern play in the early years continue in later years to underpin different forms of activity – rule-based games and traditional school learning. It is, furthermore, important to acknowledge, with Vygotsky (1978), that this is only true of development in advanced industrial societies. Recent cross-cultural research on play suggests that its potential as an educative process is far greater in societies like our own than it is in traditional societies (see, for example, Gaskins et al., 2007). This is because, whereas children's play in traditional societies consists mainly of the acting out of familiar adult roles, in advanced industrial societies children also engage in fantasy play where they create imaginary situations inhabited by invented characters and/or ones taken from the media. This, arguably, helps them to develop the kind of thinking (abstract, hypothetical) that is required in a world that is full of uncertainty where enormous importance is given to science and the arts.

From the foregoing, while there does seem to be a line of progression along which the kinds of 'play' activity that children engage in should be expected to change as they move through their primary years, there is good reason to believe that the essence of what makes play a worthwhile activity in the early years remains important in later years. Although it is beyond the scope of this chapter to give a full explanation of what that 'essence' is, it is possible to trace connections between the play that young children engage in and certain ways of learning that are quite explicitly valued during the later years of primary schooling. What I have in mind here are such things as investigation, creativity, problem-solving, drama and the ability to work in teams. Taking Vygotsky's (1978) focus on socio-dramatic play as a starting point, while it is, in its purely spontaneous form, clearly most prevalent among 3–6 year-olds, it is nonetheless not the case that as children mature and their preoccupations change they inevitably lose their ability to play – to act out a role within an imaginary context. Neither is it the case that they lose the complex set of skills that accompany this ability. If the value of socio-dramatic play in the early years lies, as it might be argued, in the processes of identity formation that it permits children to engage in, then there are good grounds for assuming that older children will continue to gain from equivalent experiences. These can be provided through a range of drama techniques applied across the curriculum; two approaches that are of particular interest are 'Forum Theatre' and 'Mantle of the Expert' (see Chapter 14). While work of this kind is normally used as a vehicle for one or more extrinsic learning objectives and is therefore seldom seen as an end in itself, for the participants it is invariably highly motivating, partly because the option of being a bystander simply does not exist. The 10 year-old who becomes fully immersed in role as a First World War combatant or climate change scientist experiences a form of emotional engagement that is carried over into other modes of learning such as reflective writing and research.

Another aspect of play where lines of continuity and progression can be traced through the primary years is that of 'investigation'. Although this term is not being used here in a very precise way it usefully draws attention to a certain kind of learning process, exemplified in the young child's exploratory play (for example with sand, blocks and other material resources) that also occurs, in ideal circumstances, across a range of curriculum subjects throughout the primary years. Another way of talking about the investigative approach as it might be applied with older children is in terms of 'enquiry-based learning'. In principle children can undertake investigations in any curriculum area or within a cross-curricular theme; the degree to which investigations are open-ended and/ or focused on genuine problems (i.e. where the teacher doesn't have the solution) will vary accordingly. Consider, as an illustration, the classic investigation in primary science, typically referred to as 'sinking and floating'. Few children in our culture enter an early years setting or start school without having explored this phenomenon to some degree at home, typically through water play in the bath or paddling pool, where they witness for themselves objects sinking and/or floating. Some will have had more experience than others both in terms of the kinds of materials that they have had access to and the quality of mediation from adults. Virtually all children continue to enjoy water play in early years settings where opportunities to explore different tools (e.g. for squirting or pouring) and materials (e.g. for mixing or making bubbles) are offered by thoughtful adults. Later, possibly in Key Stage 1 and again in Key Stage 2, children explore the phenomenon of sinking and floating in the more formal context of the science lesson.

Obviously children bring with them to these lessons ideas about the behaviour of materials and objects in water that they have developed through previous experiences. Here the teacher's goal is to elicit the children's current levels of understanding and to move them on towards a more 'scientific' way of thinking. Typically this involves drawing their attention to such things as the difference between the properties of a given material (e.g. plastic) and the properties of objects (e.g. a hollow ball) since both are factors in determining whether or not something will sink or float. In contexts such as this the teacher needs to strike a balance between exposing the children to new ideas (e.g. Archimedes' Principle), which might simply confuse them, possibly in the long term turning them away from science, and grounding the discussion in the children's current understanding, based as it is on their concrete experience. A sensitive teacher here is not only well enough informed about the science to know what the next conceptual steps might be, they also know how to challenge children (e.g. by introducing novel materials) without confusing them; if necessary, they stay clear of 'key concepts' (e.g. density) that for some children would be perceived as impenetrable jargon. There is good reason then to retain a good measure of the element of play in Key Stage 2 science investigations – a good measure of learning by doing. This argument is reinforced by the fact that every classroom contains a mix of individual biographies and many children come into such lessons without having had sufficient experience of water play in their early years either at home or in a setting. This also raises the question as to whether older primary school children should be given opportunities simply to play with water and other materials – for example, in a well designed 'outdoor classroom', possibly during break times.

Most children come to school with a disposition to learn, and if they don't then this should be regarded as a matter for concern. Arguably, our first duty as educators is to nurture this disposition. In practice our success rate is not very high, as demonstrated by the large numbers of demotivated 10 and 11-year-olds currently in our schools – children who do school work only because they have to. By implication I have suggested that this is, at least partly, due to our failure to build progressively on good early years practice. If we are serious about promoting such things as creativity, independence and the ability to work in teams, we must recognise the implications that this has for teaching and curriculum organisation. In Key Stage 2 the curriculum should be organised differently from how it is organised in the early years, and the change from one form of organisation to the next should be gradual – it should exhibit elements of both continuity and progression. There is evidence to suggest that in this country a particularly abrupt change occurs when children move from their Reception class to Year 1 (e.g. Anning and Ring, 2004). In particular, in this section, I have picked out two aspects of early years practice that support the disposition to learn and I have argued that measures could be taken to build progressively on these so that children continue throughout their primary years to exercise a degree of control over the content of their learning and they continue to enjoy the pleasure of learning through play.

Part of what is needed here requires change that is beyond the capacity of an individual teacher; for example, a better balance could be struck between teacher-initiated and child-initiated activity by allocating at least part of the content of the curriculum for teachers to negotiate with their pupils in the medium term. However, a lot can be done within current constraints by teachers who recognise the value of play in all of its forms. Without straying too far from the prescribed content of the curriculum, approaches can be developed that encourage children to be 'playful' and these are not limited to the drama contexts and science investigations illustrated above. I will now explore the idea that part of our responsibility as primary practitioners is to work closely with parents to nurture in their children the disposition to learn and thereby to lay down the foundations for 'lifelong learning'.

CRITICAL ISSUES

Taking Vygotsky's analysis of play as its starting point the journal article 'Using the transformative power of play to educate hearts and minds: from Vygotsky to Vivian Paley and beyond' by Nicolopoulou et al. (2010) demonstrates how systematic educational practices can be devised that incorporate a 'play element'.

Read the article and consider how Vivian Paley's storytelling/story-acting practice might work in classrooms with older children. Can you think of other ways in which a 'play element' might be integrated into routine classroom practices?

Working with parents

Early years practitioners have long regarded parents as the child's 'first educator', an idea that is acknowledged implicitly by the framework for the EYFS (DCSF, 2008), which regards the birth of the child as the start of a lifelong learning journey. In this section I explore the idea that, in ideal circumstances, parents play a pivotal role in supporting that journey by providing continuity between home and 'school' and through the many changes that occur in the child's educational career, perhaps even into adulthood. Crucially, parents have the capacity to bolster their child's self-esteem in the face of the many challenges that school presents and they have a very direct impact on the child's developing identity as a learner. A full exploration of 'learner identities' is beyond the scope of this chapter, although a lot of work has been done in this area (see, for example, Stables, 2003). Suffice it to say that children who have a 'disposition to learn' tend also to have a positive image of themselves as learners. It is important, however, not to lose sight of how complex this matter might be. Dweck (2000), for example, has done some very interesting research that draws our attention to the relationship between the child's beliefs about what it means to be clever (e.g. whether intelligence is fixed or not) and their orientation towards learning (e.g. whether they persevere or give up when the going gets tough). According to Dweck (2000) teachers' feedback plays an important role in sustaining or challenging different orientations. The influence of parents, however, must be as significant, if not more so, especially when account is taken of their role during the child's pre-school years. Acknowledging the importance of the parents' role in sustaining continuity for the child, it is interesting to look at how the relationship between parents and teacher changes as the child makes their way through primary school (see also Chapter 16).

Recognising parents as the child's first educators, early years practitioners invariably invest a lot of energy into forging close links between school and home. This usually begins well before the child's first day, with visits by teachers and other workers from the setting to the child's home. The majority of parents take advantage of the opportunity that the home visit offers for them and their child to meet the staff in an environment where the child in particular feels confident. From the practitioner's point of view, seeing the child in context is an ideal way of gaining an insight into their young lives, and this enables them (the adults) to respond appropriately during the child's initial settling-in period. Even when home visits don't occur there is normally more direct contact between parents and teachers in the early years than there is later on. As a teacher of younger children you will have face-to-face contact with parents on a regular basis. Mainly through informal discussion, you will establish and develop relationships with parents which have the potential to provide a foundation for future positive relations between home and school. As children get older and move through the system, direct parental contact becomes less frequent, although formal mechanisms for liaising with parents are maintained and developed, such as reporting, conferencing and school events. Arguably, this is appropriate since many children regard it as a mark of their growing independence that their parents no longer see them into school, and some increasingly view school as their space, keeping their parents in the dark as regards what they get up to. However, the importance of working with parents does not diminish as children get older.

As a teacher of older children it is crucial that you recognise the significance of parents by building on the positive relations that hopefully have been established by your early years colleagues. Every parent has ideas about educational concepts such as 'learning', 'intelligence' and 'the curriculum', to a large extent formed through their own experience of the education system. In combination with the information about their child's achievements that they are provided with, this 'understanding' determines the ideas they develop about the child as a learner, which in turn impacts on the child's own self-concepts. Some parents, for example, form views about how 'academic' their child is fairly early on in the child's school career, and this narrows their view of the child's full potential. Through informal communication throughout the year, conferences and written reports you will provide and mediate information about how the children in your class are getting on at school. A school that sets or streams and where great emphasis is placed on the importance of test results will give very different messages to parents as compared with one which is more concerned with the whole child where difference is seen as a resource and something to celebrate rather than a problem and/ or justification for the 'inevitability' of competition. In your discussions with parents, you are in a position to put things in perspective, and to support each parent in finding a way to value the unique achievements of their child.

Not all parents feel comfortable coming to school, essentially because as children school let them down by failing them academically, by failing them socially, or both. Such parents are often ill equipped to get the most out of a meeting with you the teacher; they might be verbally aggressive, over-compliant or simply stay away. Some schools have developed strategies to encourage such parents to participate more fully in their children's education, for example by offering adult literacy classes run during school hours. While programmes of this sort are worthwhile, it is important to consider how better relationships with parents might be developed and sustained into the future. Parents, who are now reluctant to come into school even though they care about their children and want them to have the best education possible were themselves once pupils in primary schools. The children we are teaching now are parents of the future, and if we nurture their disposition to learn, their self-esteem and their sense of well-being then we will be laying good foundations for the success of their children and grandchildren.

Continuity and change: your career

It is true that you cannot be a good teacher without being a good learner. Teachers who look at each new class in September, at the potential of a chance event (a snowstorm or a local building initiative) and at each individual achievement of their pupils, with fresh eyes, will over the years acquire a store of immensely valuable experience. This is the kind of knowledge that will serve you well even when you move on to work with a different age group, in management or in an area of specialisation such as learning support. Some teachers follow very varied career paths in terms of the age groups they teach and the kinds of schools they work in, while others stay with the same age group in the same school for a much longer time. Whichever approach you take to your career, you will need to be able to adapt to changes that are beyond your immediate control. Since the late 1980s primary schools have been subjected to a continuous barrage of change initiated by central government and it has been difficult for teachers to retain a sense of control over their work. Hopefully the balance of control will shift back to the profession, but this will not mean the end of change. If you enter the profession with a sense of moral purpose this will stand you in good stead; some things will always be worth fighting for. If you are starting your career as a young teacher you might well still be in the 'classroom' in 2040 or 2050. Hopefully then you will look back to the present and be able to recognise significant improvements that have been made for children in the 3–11 age range. Following the main threads of this chapter these would include a greater recognition of the generalist class teacher and, particularly for older pupils, a marked increase in learner autonomy together with increased opportunities for 'play'.

Summary

In this chapter I have invited you to think about the three phases of primary schooling, covering the 3–11 age range, as a whole. I have highlighted issues of continuity and progression through a discussion of the curriculum, the organisation of schools and the child's 'disposition to learn'. Issues discussed include:

- the optimal size and structure of primary schools
- the advantages of generalist teaching
- the potential for building on good early years principles pertaining to pupil autonomy and the value of play
- the role of parents in relation to the child's developing image of themselves as a learner, and how teachers might mediate this process.

As I hope I have made clear, the system we currently work with is far from perfect. However, this will not necessarily stop you from having a positive impact on children's lives or from playing your part in shaping the profession of the future.

Issues for reflection

- Some subjects you will be teaching you will already know a lot about. Others you may well feel less confident about. How will you fill in the gaps in your knowledge?
- Take some time to observe one of the youngest and then one of the oldest pupils in one of the schools you are visiting (half a day for each child would be ideal). Ideally you should focus on equivalent activities – e.g. in 'science'. What similarities and differences do you see in the type of activity, the degree of choice and the mediation of adults?
- Find out about the strategies your school uses to support children in making transitions: (a) within school from one class to the next; and (b) between the school and other institutions.
- Try to envisage the child's journey through one of the schools you are working in from their point of view. Consider how the teachers communicate their expectations at the various stages of the educational journey. How do you think the differences and similarities might be perceived by the developing child?

Further reading 📖

If you are interested in the potential of small 'multigrade' schools here are three interesting websites:

- National Association for Small Schools: http://www.smallschools.org.uk
- 'Human Scale Education': http://www.hse.org.uk
- The multigrade research group at the Institute of Education: http://multigrade.ioe. ac.uk/index.html

Karpov, Y.V. (2006) *The Neo-Vygotskian Approach to Child Development* (new edn). Cambridge: Cambridge University Press. In this book Karpov discusses how Vygotsky's ideas form the foundation for the work of the Neo-Vygotskians who depict play as the 'leading activity' of the preschool years.

Vygotsky, L.S. (1978) *Mind in Society: The Development of Higher Psychological Processes*. Cambridge, MA and London: Harvard University Press. The argument in this chapter about the importance of play in children's learning is unavoidably simplistic. In a lecture delivered in 1933 Vygotsky made a powerful case for play in early childhood (see Chapter 7).

Section 4

THE CHILD AND THE COMMUNITY

Schools have an integral and dynamic relationship with the community. This section explores how you can be aware of and engage with the wider community to bring about improved outcomes and well-being of the children you teach. It aims to raise awareness and extend your knowledge of agencies that work with children and their families and how you can build positive relationships with them. Important issues of safeguarding of children and attendance are addressed. We reflect with you on the key contributions that parents, governors and classroom assistants have to make to children's development and to school life. The section shows that as well as preparing pupils for the wider world the school also needs to draw on the community as a rich source of learning.

CHAPTER 16

THE SCHOOL IN THE COMMUNITY AND THE COMMUNITY IN THE SCHOOL

Jo Lang and Eleanor Cockerton

Chapter overview

The school in which you will work is part of a dynamic and often complex relationship with the wider community. Jo Lang and Eleanor Cockerton explore this relationship and how you can make the most of partnership activity with others in your teaching and in your work with children.

Introduction

Children don't exist in splendid isolation. Around them are families, friends, communities, services, expectations and aspirations. Deep in the mix are the members of the school community working with the child – teachers, children, teaching assistants, midday assistants, the school crossing patrol, the cook, the governors, the administrators and the cleaning and caretaking staff.

You may already be aware of some of the debates about schools and communities. We have been developing extended services for years now, ensuring communities have access to school facilities out of hours and that children get their needs for breakfast, before and after school care and holiday activities met. There has been an expectation of schools to work collaboratively with neighbouring schools and increasingly to commission resources and services which meet their collective needs (see also Chapter 2).

It is a complex picture, not simplified by the fact that such a perspective is ideological as well as confusing. Should schools look inwards and focus on learning and teaching and educational outcomes? Should they look outwards and concentrate on exploration, social understanding and thinking skills? Should they be balancing the two, taking a holistic view of the child in his/her social context, working with other agencies to create supportive and appropriate responses to issues, engaging parents, offering opportunities to get new experiences, and, of course, achieving fantastic test results at the same time?

In this chapter we will look at how teachers operate in this world and how you can use the opportunities it creates to:

- improve outcomes for the children you work with
- extend your knowledge of agencies working with and around children and their families
- understand better how to create positive relationships with people and organisations outside the school.

When we started thinking about this chapter, we became aware that the school in the community and the community in the school is an enormous subject and potentially a right muddle. Sometimes you need to look at it from the point of view of an individual child, and sometimes from the point of view of the whole school. So to get it under control a bit, we are going to start with the individual child and look at how meeting the needs of children involves a wide range of people and organisations, with each of whom you will need to build a working relationship and may need to welcome into your classroom.

Building relationships with parents

Think of a child. They will have parents or carers (from now on we will say parents, but will mean parents and carers) whose engagement with you will be critical to the child's educational success, but who may be uncomfortable with, or resistant to, your best endeavours to demonstrate a confident, professional and caring persona. How do you set about building a relationship with them? Well, put yourself in their shoes. What would/do you want from a professional involved in the life of your child? We'd suggest you would want to be treated as an equal partner, someone who is respected and listened to, who has things explained clearly but not patronisingly, whose views are given the same weight as those of others. So perhaps that is how you begin to build up relationships with parents – not as the only expert in the conversation, but as a partner, engaged in a two-way sharing of information in order to facilitate the best outcomes for the child, not for the parent or the teacher. It will be a relationship where you take responsibility for being honest, open and adult, and which enables the parent to be the same. Easy to say, not always easy to do, especially when you are brand new and the parent (and/or perhaps the head) wants a quick fix on their child!

It is sad but true that the parents we come most often into contact with will be those whose children are having difficulties, or those who are themselves having difficulty with the school. Being a parent is tough. Being a perfect parent is impossible. Being a parent who wants the best for their child and who is prepared to learn every step along the journey – arm in arm with you while you are teaching the child – is the best we can aspire to. Don't expect parents to agree with you, do what you suggest or change their world view to fit yours. Do your best to remain pleasant and approachable, even when you feel threatened and unsure on the inside, because presenting a defensive or aggressive stance will always be counterproductive. Recognise that you will need to influence their thinking, widen or deepen their understanding, challenge and support them. The problem is always the problem, not the child or the parent or you.

The partnership approach is summed up in the Early Years Foundation Stage Guidance:

- liaise with any other educational settings the child spends time in
- work closely with parents to identify learning needs and any areas of difficulty
- work with professionals from any other relevant agencies in order to provide the best learning opportunities and environments.

There is more information on the Department for Education website (http://www. education.gov.uk).

Parents as classroom volunteers

Many schools welcome parents into the classroom as volunteers. They may be listening to readers, preparing resources, supporting with the Christmas play. It will be useful for you to read all the school policies that touch on this. There may be a specific policy on parental involvement which gathers all the information together, or one on volunteers, but it may be that your school has the information in curriculum policies. You should familiarise yourself with the safeguarding policy so that you can advise parents whether they will need full criminal records checks before they come into the classroom and whether or not the school will get these done.

Policies and guidelines will help you understand what the school expects from parent volunteers, but it will always be best to talk it through with the headteacher and other staff. Written documents give you the letter of the law, but the practice may be different, so ask your colleagues about how, when and where they like to get parents involved. Some new teachers worry about being watched by parents, and it is true that some parents can be judgemental about teaching. They may be critical of how you handle situations with their child, or the things you say, or how you look. But do remember that they would feel just as awkward if you went into their place of work or observed them parenting at home. Don't be tempted to play to them as an audience or change how you work to please them. You are the professional here, and you should go on teaching as you always do. If their child needs to be challenged, do it! If their child deserves praise, praise them. If there is an incident involving their child, you might want to take some time at the end of the session to talk it through with the parent and explain what you did and your reasons for it, not out of self-defence but because it will be useful for the parent to understand what your expectations are and how you work to get them met. School has changed considerably in the last three decades and this is an easy way of showing how the children are learning. Occasionally a child will behave in an uncharacteristically difficult way when a parent is present, with attention-seeking behaviour or by being very clingy. Talk to the parent about this. Maybe working in another class would be better or just leaving it for a while and trying again later.

Not all parents want or feel able to get involved. Some of these will fall into the 'hard to reach' category. Hard to reach is a phrase we use for those children, parents or community members who may need services but who don't seek them out or who refuse them. Hard to reach parents might be the ones whose children are frequently absent without authorisation – no phone call, no note, no explanation – or those who don't come to parents' evenings. They may not respond to letters home and may change their mobile phone numbers often.

There are many reasons why parents behave like this. They may not know any better or they may be deliberately avoiding involvement. Some parents have low levels of literacy, find schools intimidating or had issues when they went to school and find authority hard to deal with. Perhaps they work long hours and commute long distances and find it hard to get to the school during normal hours. The only way to find out why they have become hard to reach is to have a conversation with them. Don't jump to a conclusion. Try ringing them and telling them some good news about their child. Then you can bring the conversation round to how nice it would be to see them at school and find out whether they have any reasons not to come along. In some cases grandparents might be a viable alternative, especially if they play a large part in the child's life.

When Eleanor, one of the authors, was teaching in a nursery class she had a 'Parent helper rota' and tried to persuade all the parents to sign up at least once a term. One mother was reluctant until Eleanor suggested she just came and watched and she would be free to leave whenever she wanted. By the end of the morning she was sitting at the dough table absorbed in her play with her son beside her. She had grown up in care and playing was something she had had very little positive experience of. She willingly signed up again and happily took her paintings or other work home at the end of the morning.

Parental involvement

Sometimes parents will want to support their own child, perhaps because the child is unhappy or unsettled. This can be useful for the child, the parents and you, but there are occasions when it is unhelpful and makes the situation worse. Don't prejudge this, though, even if your colleagues tell you this is an overanxious mum with a clingy child and they need to be separated. If you can, sit and talk to the parent about the issues and what they want to achieve by coming in. Agree when and for how long they will be in the classroom. You might want to start with an hour first thing, which gradually reduces, and to start with the parent working one to one with their child and gradually separating by working with the child in a small group and then in other groups without the child. Keep reviewing with the parent and the child so that you are all keeping in mind the aim that the child becomes independent and learns how to enjoy school without a parent by their side.

It is easy to become cynical or blasé. Very soon you will have seen many children and parents come to terms with separation and will know that it is almost invariably OK and that a few tears are normal. But each occasion is unique and worrying for the parent and child involved, so be reassuring and professional but never dismissive.

There is plenty of evidence to show that parental involvement in education is one of the key factors in educational success for children. Interested parents can boost motivation, provide support with learning and encourage children to give their best. They are the first educators of their child and their influence is key. The way parents feel about the school, or about school in general, will colour their child's view, so it is worth working hard to get parents on board.

How do parents get involved?

- Fundraising through parents' or friends' associations
- Parents' evenings
- Open days
- Family learning
- Classroom volunteers
- Taking small groups for specific activities like cooking or music
- Parental surveys or focus groups
- Parent governors
- Managing the website
- Seeking sponsorship

Different schools have different expectations of parents and of you as a classroom teacher. But all schools will expect you to treat parents with respect, and to make them feel welcome and valued.

Classroom support

Learning support assistants (LSAs – sometimes known as teaching assistants) bring much more than an extra pair of hands. They may have been in the school a number of years and so have knowledge and experience about the children, families and staff which can help you get a head start. They may be able to advise on the 'how we do things here' which can be so difficult to get your head round in a new workplace. Not that you take everything you are told at face value, of course, and once you understand the school a bit better you will be making your own mind up about where to accept the status quo and where to make suggestions for improvement.

It is important that you work on the relationship you are building with your LSA. Admit your inexperience and openly be willing to take advice. But the bottom line is that you need to be able to give clear, explicit directions to your LSA, making sure that they understand what you expect from them and how you expect them to work in your room, whether they are there to support a single individual or the group as a whole. Being wishy-washy because you are frightened of causing offence will lead to confusion and may undermine the confidence of both you and your LSA, so work on your calm assertiveness so that you can direct activity while listening to suggestions and opinions non-judgementally.

A key part of building the relationship is to get to know your colleagues' strengths. They may have done many training courses or bring to the job a wide range of life skills which can be used to the children's benefit. They may even have trained as a Higher Level Teaching Assistant and be able to take on greater responsibility. Talk to them, too, about whether they like to be an active part of the planning process or whether they prefer to be given written notes.

The more team spirit you can develop with your LSA the more rewarding for both of you, and you can use your shared understanding to raise expectations and standards for the children you are working with.

Working with external agencies

A child may have support from services outside the school – perhaps with social care, a hospital, behaviour support services, a mental health worker, an educational psychologist, attendance services, police, or advisors from a minority ethnic or Traveller achievement team. There may be a CAF (see below) in place with a lead professional coordinating services and regular meetings to discuss services. The family in turn may be accessing support for their own issues, such as housing, probation, drug rehabilitation, therapy, etc. in addition to those faced by the child.

A CAF is an assessment of a child or young person, carried out by a concerned professional using the Common Assessment Framework. It captures all the information needed to make a judgement on what services may be needed to work with the child, and it provides the basis of referrals on to more in-depth services. All parts of the children's workforce (all those working to provide services to children) including schools should be using CAFs to identify the needs of a child in terms of resources and interventions, and there will be a process in the locality for what happens to the information once the form has been completed. CAFs are often completed by special educational needs coordinators (SENCos) or inclusion managers, but they can be filled out by class teachers, too, and are always developed and sent on with the written agreement of the parents or carers. (For more information see http://www.everychildmatters.gov.uk, but bear in mind that government policy is changing.) Each area will have its own procedures for dealing with the CAF and arranging the support identified on it, so ask your SENCo or headteacher what your local procedure is.

The CAF is different to the documentation provided for a child with special educational needs, which will involve an Individual Education Plan outlining what the child needs to enable them to access their education, possibly a Statement of Special Educational Needs which gives a formal assessment of what the local authority must put in place for the child, or a Consistent Behaviour Plan to guide how adults in the school support an individual child.

Support to meet the needs identified in the CAF comes from a range of agencies, some through health providers, some through the local authority, some through charities. Wherever it comes from, it is important that you build good working relationships with the representatives. You shouldn't be seen to be taking the side of the school against the parents, or against an agency you feel has served the child or family badly, because if you are, you won't be taken seriously. You are each there for the child. Did you realise your communications skills would be so thoroughly tested in this job?!

Some professionals will come into the classroom to observe the child's behaviour or learning before making an assessment or writing a report. They might be an educational psychologist, a behaviour support teacher or a specialist teacher. They are there to see how well the child is accessing their education and how your strategies for them are working.

They will give feedback on the child's needs and make suggestions about how you can change the way you teach or interact to improve the situation. Be open to what they say and don't take it as personal criticism. You can't possibly get everything right all the time, and even the most experienced teachers benefit from another pair of eyes. If you have been struggling to deal with a child's behaviour, it doesn't mean you are a bad teacher. It means you haven't yet learnt the technique that will best serve this child and this can happen even after many years' experience. It is very important for your professional development and your emotional survival that you learn not to take feedback personally and that you find a way to accept negative comments as support for your learning.

Once again, you are looking to take an adult, professional, open stance which in effect says to the other agencies: 'This is the situation. How can we all work together to improve it?' Explore the options together, but if you believe the child is being short changed then remember – your first responsibility is to the child, so say so, in as adult, professional and open a way as you can!

Meetings may be formal or informal depending on the setting; so get someone who has been to one before to tell you what happens. Child protection conferences are very formal and can be quite intimidating, especially as you may have to say things in front of the parents that may cause them distress or anger. Some referral meetings have huge numbers of people round the table, and you can find the true situation of the child you have referred gets a little lost as professionals debate and discuss the alternative interventions available. Don't be afraid to bring them back to reality if you need to. Phrases like 'Could you tell me a bit more about how that fits with this situation' or 'That sounds very interesting, and I'd like to know what outcomes we could expect' help other practitioners to reflect on the practicality of suggestions.

Try to avoid using the word 'Why?' Even when it is intended in a supportive way, it can come across as overly challenging and generate a negative or defensive response. Instead of saying 'Why did you suggest that?' call on all your reserves of tact and try 'That sounds interesting, tell me more'. Find a phrase that you can feel comfortable with and use it whenever necessary. And practise your 'interested' face!

In all these situations there will be times when, deliberately or not, something is said which sounds or feels derogatory about your teaching or your school. Try to listen to it without being defensive – easier said than done, we know! – but there is no point in joining in with a blame game. The child is what matters, so keep positive and professional. When you unpick what has been said and reflect, you may find there are things you can learn, and there is no shame in that. The more open you are to learning about your job, yourself, the children and the world the better teacher you will become.

You could ask – and many people do – what all this has to do with schools and, in particular, with teachers. But the truth is that in order for children to learn successfully they have to have many other things in place. They need to have a safe home life and a good diet, be healthy, have any special learning needs met, be free from significant mental and emotional problems, feel secure, respected and valued in school. In every class you teach you will have children who are more vulnerable to poor outcomes because of intrinsic or extrinsic issues. For you to be able to help them achieve their best possible outcomes you will need to engage with people from other professions, get used to them being in your classroom observing, offering advice, and possibly challenging the way you work or what you say. Each of them will help you learn more about the child and about your profession.

Sometimes you will be the first person to identify a difficulty. Being in a new environment can cause a child to demonstrate uncharacteristic behaviour. Watch and make careful, dated notes and if the difficulty persists ask the SENCo for advice.

Chat with parents to understand whether what you see in school is also manifesting itself at home.

A new child in Eleanor's class was pale and often not engaged. She explains:

When I talked to her parents they were disappointed that she was not producing the level of work they knew she was capable of. I kept talking and listening and it became apparent that they were having great difficulty in persuading both this girl and her little sister to go to bed at night. They were often up at 11 or later and consequently getting up for school was a difficult process. After further discussions and advice it was arranged for them to attend a family clinic but I would never have been able to do this if I had not taken the time to find out more.

Safeguarding

This is a term you will come across early on in your training and it is important you understand what it involves and how you deal with any issues that arise. Your school should have a safeguarding policy which you must read and a safeguarding officer who is your first point of contact if you need help or advice.

Safeguarding and promoting the welfare of children is defined as:

- protecting children from maltreatment
- preventing impairment of children's health or development
- ensuring children are growing up in circumstances consistent with the provision of safe and effective care.

Child protection is a part of safeguarding and promoting welfare. It refers to the activity that is undertaken to protect specific children who are suffering, or are likely to suffer, significant harm. (http://www.education.gov.uk/childrenandyoungpeople/safeguarding, accessed 9 December 2010)

Occasionally a child in your care may be the victim of abuse. It could be physical, emotional or sexual abuse or neglect. If you suspect this, record any evidence you have and make sure it is dated. Talk to the designated safeguarding person in your school who will advise you how to proceed. If a child chooses to tell you about being abused (known as 'disclosing'), stay calm, listen and be supportive. Don't promise to keep what they say confidential. Do not ask questions, jump to conclusions or interrupt while they are talking. When they have finished, reassure them and tell them what you will do next, i.e. explain simply the school safeguarding procedure. Contact the designated person immediately and record your conversation with the child as accurately as possible. You will be told how to proceed. Your Local Safeguarding Children Board will have a website with up-to-date information on procedures in your area (DCSF, 2010b).

Helping children to attend

The Education Welfare Service can be a good ally where attendance is an issue. They visit parents when a child's attendance falls below a certain percentage and discuss what barriers the child or family have to regular school attendance. They can arrange various forms of support before resorting to fines and legal action, and often know families well enough to give you advice on dealing with them.

One group of parents who can be very hard to reach are those from Traveller communities. It can take a long time and a lot of effort to build trust with these parents, as many of them are uncomfortable with the formal establishment and that is what you will be representing. But it is equally true that most of them are passionate about their children's happiness and safety. Some schools with high numbers of children from Traveller families make daily calls to parents as a matter of course, giving them good news, reassuring them about the child having settled in and being happy, making suggestions about some homework. That way, when things go wrong or the child is absent without explanation, the relationships with parents are strong enough for the school rules to be restated and expectations explained. Some schools are lucky enough to have community liaison workers making the calls and visiting homes, but in others this will be up to you, and you may want to make it a call a week rather than a call every day.

You may have parents who speak very little English, or who are deaf, and you may need an interpreter or signer to help them in formal meetings. Make an effort to learn something in their language even if it is just how to say hello and welcome. Children with known language or communication difficulties will probably be getting extra support in the classroom, but sometimes a few words or signs to the parents are worth gold.

CRITICAL ISSUES

Sixty-two per cent of parents who responded to a Parentline Plus survey (Stanley and Todd, 2010) had felt patronised, sidelined or ignored when trying to deal with an issue in their child's school. This was an alarming statistic, particularly when viewed alongside the fact that 64 per cent of teachers responding to a Teacher Support Network survey said that they had been subjected to verbal or physical abuse by a pupil's parent. It is clear that steps need to be taken to improve understanding and strengthen relationships between families and schools.

What do you think are the main factors that can make relationships between teachers and parents difficult? What would you do to cross this divide? What specific actions could you take to build relationships with parents and how would you know if they had proved successful?

School governing bodies

Your school's governing body is the most formal representation of the community in the school. Governors are drawn from local people and parents who have the interest, time, commitment and skills to act as a 'board of directors' to the school. The headteacher is the professional (managing director) and retains responsibility for the day-to-day management. Governors should be actively involved in creating the school development plan, monitoring progress, evaluating outcomes and holding the head and his/her staff to account. Governors should become familiar faces around the school, coming in to monitor particular aspects of school life, perhaps talking to pupils or parents, talking to teachers, finding out what is happening and how it happens in the school. It is reasonable to expect governors to visit once or twice a term, though the chair and chairs of committees may be in more often. Governors help the school to understand and reflect the interests, concerns and aspirations of the local community, as well as those of parents and staff, and can bring a fresh, often non-educational, insight into issues and situations.

Governors do not have the right or the role to judge teaching and learning in the classroom. The closest they should get to this is to accompany the head when he/she is monitoring teaching and learning, but even this is for information and understanding, not so that the governor can judge what you do. Most governors are nervous about making school visits. They don't want to get in the way or step out of line. So if you are on the timetable for a visit, make sure you allow five minutes before the start of the lesson to meet the governor and brief them on what you will be doing and what the outcomes should be. Do you want them to sit at the back and keep quiet or sit with some children and join in the lesson? If they see some bad behaviour should they alert you or keep quiet? Are there any children with particular needs that will be disturbed or worried by a stranger in the room? Gently but firmly establish your framework for the visit, bearing in mind the school's policy for governors' visits. Try to find time after the visit to talk to them about what they have seen and to find out if they have any questions. If they cross over the boundary and begin telling you how to teach better, remind them that they should have that conversation with the head, not you!

If you are asked to give a presentation at a governors' meeting or to go to an event such as development planning where governors will be, remember that they may know the school better than you, but they may not have the same understanding of jargon. Try to walk the tightrope between blinding them with your knowledge and patronising them.

Governing bodies:

- are responsible for setting the school's strategic direction, monitoring and evaluating progress and making executive decisions about certain aspects of the school such as appointing heads and deputies and agreeing the budget
- have representatives from different parts of the community, including staff, parents and local people

- bring different perspectives to a school
- act as the school's champions, supporters and challengers.

Working with the wider community

Parents are a good resource for bringing the community in or giving children the chance to go out into the community. If you are looking for some elderly people to sing carols for at Christmas a parent who either works at or has relatives at a nursing home can be very useful. Simple things like carol singing, doing a local litter pick or washing cars for charity help raise the profile of the school and give your pupils a chance to contribute to the local community. Such activities should always be carefully planned with risk assessments and finished off with thank you letters, information about how any money raised was spent or an invitation to the school play.

The idea of taking lessons out of the classroom isn't new and beyond the school grounds there are fantastic resources and opportunities. One example is the Forest School movement. Forest Schools have been around for many years, starting in Europe, and have really taken off in Britain recently. Children can gain huge amounts of self-confidence, independence in their learning, a better understanding of the environment, the ability to work in teams, enhanced social skills and better developed physical coordination. Forest Schools offer a structured programme of learning for pupils of any age, with weekly visits to one woodland spot to build shelters, play games and talk about the changing nature of the countryside. Programme length varies but is usually at least a year so that the children can become comfortable in their new environment.

It is worth searching on the Internet for research and further information if the thought of taking lessons into the woods inspires you!

Most arts and heritage organisations have a remit to provide education and this will often be a requirement of a financial grant that enables them to operate. This gives you access to a huge range of resources, from community artists to museums and historical re-enactments. The Museums, Libraries and Archives Council has developed a strategic commissioning programme which is leading the enhancement of education provision in this area (http://www.mla.gov.uk/what/programmes/commissioning).

Gibbs and Tofi-Tsekbo (2010) argue that:

> A well-planned school visit offers the opportunity to engage with original objects, artworks or documents, tangible and intangible heritage, the past, present and future. Museums and archives are places to develop ideas and explore difficult topics within a safe, neutral environment. They offer creative interaction through art, drama or writing. They provide memorable experiences for young people, who often return with family members or friends. Teachers observe that a visit can encourage engagement and participation from more reluctant learners, as well as stimulate high flyers to make new connections. (p. 48)

Some arts and heritage organisations charge but not all, and if you want to get involved in a large-scale project – a multimedia show, or a town-wide local history project – it might be better to work with other local schools and organise a joint activity.

Most national museums in Britain and around the world offer videoconferencing opportunities for schools. They operate differently, but you can research what they provide on the Internet. You can set up a videoconference where a curator will introduce your class to a range of objects relevant to the topic your children are studying. The children can ask questions and make comments – not as good as actually holding a historic object but better than looking at photos with no interpretation. It is a great way to bring the world into your school and there are far fewer risk assessments to be carried out than on a day out!

Videoconferencing is also great for spreading your community involvement across the country and across the world. There are a number of organisations helping schools to establish links with partner schools in different countries. Most children are fascinated by how their peers in other countries live, so e-mail friends can inspire them to work on their literacy skills. If you have a number of children from a minority ethnic community, they may like it if you establish a link with a school from their country of origin and they may be able to act as interpreters, but make sure you talk to them and their parents first. If they have come to the UK in difficult circumstances, they may have strong views about keeping in touch. While it could be very helpful for the children to know their peers and their teachers are interested in their previous home country, it could spark off bad memories, fears and conflict for them.

Charities are another very useful source of information and engagement. With a bit of imagination and time you can find people from local charities, or local representatives of national charities, to come into your school to give a different perspective on aspects of your curriculum. Many will run education activities that you can get involved in – perhaps sporting challenges to support health charities or fundraising for development organisations. If your class is studying animals in science, for example, you might find a local rescue centre which will bring some animals to the school and talk about them in return for some tins of pet food. The children will be able to ask questions about animal health and welfare, and you will be able to make links between the lessons you have been teaching and the animals in front of you.

If you love gardening, you might be able to involve children, parents and local people in developing allotments. You could 'pay' volunteers in vegetables and fruits, as well as supplementing the school dinner menu, and surpluses can be sold off to raise money to pay for more plants, seeds and equipment. A Harvest Festival with your own produce would be so much more meaningful for children than tins, and you could have a collection to raise money for the school's usual beneficiaries instead of distributing processed food.

If you would like to develop good relationships with your local community, find ways to support events and activities already going on. Enter a float for the local carnival, organise a parent and child litter pick on the main routes to your school (this makes the roads look better and encourages parents and children not to drop the litter in the first place) or set up family and/or adult learning opportunities for local people.

Family learning refers to classes or workshops where parents and their children learn together. You might organise this to fit in with the curriculum, perhaps by inviting parents in to be shown how the school teaches numeracy – particularly good if you can turn the children into teachers for the event. Or it could be something else, like cooking or mending bicycles, where the adults and children learn together. Dads are often reluctant to get involved in schools, so workshops with a practical bent, like building a bird house or self-defence, can be useful to encourage them to come into school with their child. Parents are often well placed to lead workshop sessions, for example on basic Spanish for holidaymakers or the safe use of Internet auction sites. You could ask for volunteers through a letter home or just spread the word when you are talking to parents at the end of the day.

Some primary schools take being at the heart of their communities even further. They open their sports fields to local teams, their hall for groups and choir practices, classrooms for ICT training and kitchens for parent and child cookery lessons. Some rural schools have even considered finding space for a threatened village post office and general stores. This can be a source of rental income, particularly where a school has a falling roll and a reducing budget, as well as a good way to generate positive local feelings about your school (and so more likelihood of being the school of first choice for local parents, not having issues over planning consent or licensing for the school fete and so on).

A school at the heart of its community

The principle that a school should be at the heart of its community and that the facilities should be available for wider use outside of school hours is firmly embedded. The recent push to 'extend' schools – creating opportunities for children to attend breakfast, after-school and holiday clubs offering a varied menu of activities, ensuring that areas have enough childcare available, providing parenting support, enabling access to adult and family learning, ICT and sport, and ensuring families have swift and easy access to targeted services such as speech and language therapy – demands that schools look beyond the classroom and support the holistic development of children in their area. Education policy is changing in this area so check the website at http://www.education.gov.uk for the latest information.

A school cannot on its own meet all the needs of every child, and neither can you as a teacher. Working with and in the community should bring delight, challenge and new opportunities, not an ever increasing sense of panic and overwork. You really don't have to conquer all of this in your first term! But knowing that the world out there is a huge basket of resources just waiting to engage with you may spark your imagination. It won't always be easy. Money, time, other people's expectations can all prove difficult to overcome. But bringing the community into your classroom and taking your pupils out into the community will bring huge rewards to you all. You will be helping to raise the aspirations and outcomes for the children, and even for their parents, and creating a sense of ownership and belonging within the community.

Summary

- The relationship between you as the teaching professional and parents of the children you teach is a crucial one. So it is important that you aim to involve parents in their children's learning and use what they tell you to improve the child's learning experience.
- Read all relevant policies and documentation in school and ask for help from those around you.
- Governors are key members of the school community and you need to consider how you will relate to and work with them.
- Investigate improving links with the community and using it as a two-way process to improve understanding and learning opportunities.

Issues for reflection

- Think of a time when you have had to have a difficult conversation with a person in authority, perhaps a doctor, a manager or a tutor. How did you feel and what could they have done to help you respond better to what they were saying? If you have friends with children at school, talk to them about their relationships with teachers and head teachers. Ask them how things could be improved.
- Put the name of your hometown into a search engine and see what opportunities you can find for schools to get involved in your local community.
- Practise your skills of diplomacy so you can present a positive face when you feel challenged or criticised by parents or other professionals.

Further reading

Alexander, R. (ed.) (2010) *Children, Their World, Their Education.* Abingdon: Routledge. This is the final report of the Cambridge Primary Review which is a comprehensive examination of English Primary Education based on extensive, recent research. Chapter 18 contains some interesting insights into Schools and Communities and Chapter 20 focuses on Schools, Local Authorities and Other Agencies.

Sylva, K., Melhuish, E., Sammons, P., Siraj-Blatchford, I. and Taggart, B. (eds) (2010) *Early Childhood Matters*. Abingdon: Routledge. This contains the findings from the EPPE (Effective Pre-school and Primary Education) project on which the Early Years Foundation Stage Guidance is based. It has chapters on 'Why children, parents and home learning are important' and 'Vulnerable children: Identifying children "at risk"'.

Section 5

DEVELOPING THE TEACHER YOU WANT TO BE

In this final section the focus is on your first teaching post and the career that lies ahead. To equip you on this journey we look at how to develop skills to evaluate your performance as a teacher, as well as specific guidance on job applications, the interview process and the continuing professional development you will undergo as a newly qualified teacher and then as an experienced practitioner. We aim to leave you viewing your career horizon where you are both excited and secure in the decisions you are about to take for your future development and success as a teacher.

CHAPTER 17

HOW AM I DOING?

Ann Oliver

Chapter overview

What does successful teaching look like? How do I develop the skills to evaluate how I am doing as a teacher? In what ways can I make sure I continue to improve? These are fundamental questions that you will be asking yourself not only as you begin your career. They also inform the continuing reflections of all experienced teachers as they seek to hone their practice. In this chapter Ann Oliver provides sensitive insight and a range of practical strategies to help improve your performance, including effective use of observations, mentors and various forms of feedback and evidence.

The purpose of this chapter is to discuss how training teachers can develop professional responsibility to measure, review and improve their performance.

The training period is just the beginning and the question 'How am I doing?' will remain in your thoughts throughout your professional career.

Introduction

Teaching is an observable performance with two main elements: a behavioural component and a cognitive component (Kitson and Merry, 1997). The behavioural component is a set of observable actions. The cognitive component is a combination of perceptions, interpretations and decisions.

Professional Standards for Teachers (TDA, 2008), Ofsted expectations, course competence guidelines and Career Entry and Development Profiles are all part of competence-based training. At the time of writing training teachers and assessors are bound by this documentation and a mentor will almost invariably assess a training teacher's teaching competence against the criteria of standards in *Qualifying to Teach* (TDA, 2006). With all this in place the overriding concern for each and every student teacher will be 'How am I doing?' What needs to be understood from the outset is that teaching is complex. For a training teacher, being in the classroom and not knowing where to start is a common feeling. This is not helped by the fact that an experienced teacher can make the process look dauntingly easy. The beginner may even think 'the teacher didn't do anything and the children all did exactly as she wanted.' What the novice needs to understand is that no teacher becomes an expert easily or ever feels completely satisfied with their teaching.

All good teachers are continually honing their practice to improve the experience and support they give their pupils. Perfecting practice is something which is evident in much of a teacher's behaviour. Informal discussions and letting off steam in the staffroom, for example, are indicative of an ongoing evaluative process of reviewing effectiveness of teaching and learning. Conversations revolve around 'disastrous' lessons or 'difficult children' or specific comments such as 'Ryan just doesn't get it.' Conversely a teacher may enter the staffroom beaming and can't wait to say 'That was brilliant. They really got involved, the conversations were magical and so funny' or 'I think I've cracked it, at last Molly can play the guitar in time with the others.' However brief or ephemeral such comments may be they are based on the teacher's view of how they are doing. The important questions emanating from this behaviour apply to a training teacher, a novice teacher and an experienced teacher. The main difference is that experienced teachers will have skills to measure success and a repertoire of experience to draw on to improve their teaching. This will be new to the beginner and for a training teacher measuring, reviewing and improving teaching is a skill to be learnt and developed. So where to begin?

Building on success

As discussed throughout this book, it is useful for training teachers to recognise their successes and reflect on them to inform future practice. Analysing the reasons for success is an ideal way to begin. In discussion mentors might ask training teachers, 'What have you enjoyed? What do you think went well? Were you pleased with anything that happened?' followed by the important *why* questions which are intended to help training teachers reflect on how their actions, decisions and choices affect children's learning; 'Why did you decide to do that? Why do you think the pupils were so fascinated? Why do you think that went so well?' These are important questions to be used in reviewing your own practice and progress; however, many training teachers initially only focus on their own progress, performance and achievement. This indicates clearly a misunderstanding of the process of teaching. The important questions relating to enthusiasm, engagement, motivation, progress and achievement of pupils are not given due attention. To help balance your perspective, when reviewing success, think carefully about the children's experience. For example, what would it be like to be one of the children in your lessons? What experience would they have had? You may even go as far as considering what it would be like to be the most able child or a compliant child or a child with learning difficulties. Thinking about the impact your teaching has on involving pupils in the process of learning is a crucial skill and often requires a shift of thinking for a new training teacher. In the following anecdotal example, think about the different experiences had by the children and the potential learning outcomes of different stages of the lesson and beyond. In reviewing how you are doing the best marker is to consider how the children are doing.

The children's experience

Louise was teaching a group of Year 2 children science/English. They went on a nature walk and collected things which they brought back to the classroom including leaves, acorns, blackberries and an old sock. The children were interested in the sock because moss and grass were growing on it and they couldn't pull it apart. Two of them got over-excited doing this so Louise took the sock away. The discussion which followed was designed to allow the children to develop language skills, raise questions and put forward ideas, thereby linking the English and science curriculum. Louise asked them about the blackberries (had they eaten them?) and the leaves (had they seen them before?; which plant did they come from?). Almost immediately there were some problems with children not listening to each other or her. They did not appear interested and some started to be silly. Louise then began to draw pictures on a flip chart and encouraged the children to take part by adding to the pictures or doing their own, afterwards explaining to the group what they had drawn. One boy added roots to the grass and a discussion followed about what it was like under the ground. All the children drew a picture of roots under the ground. One in particular was detailed with twists, overlapping each other across tiny worms and insects spaced about. Louise then asked them if roots needed the ground to grow. The lesson finished with the promise that they would plant some seeds, beans and cress and watch them grow. Louise asked the class to think about what they would like to grow their seeds on other than soil, suggesting sand, carpet and toilet paper. The children became animated and the boy who had drawn the complicated root drawing asked if he could grow his in a glass jar. He wanted to see all the roots growing (he had done this at home). Another boy wanted to grow them on his sock. A girl wanted to try mud. When the children left they were still talking about what the roots might look like. The next day the girl brought in some seeds.

In discussion with the mentor Louise cited the second part of the lesson as a success. She felt very pleased with the outcome, but was concerned that she had not followed her plan. She was not happy with the way the children responded to her questions about the blackberries. She said she began to panic as she could see they were not interested and was worried about losing control. The drawing activity was not part of her plan, but she decided to introduce this to involve the children in a different way and hopefully regain their interest. She was surprised it worked so well and felt that from then on the questions, ideas and interest generated were very rewarding for both her and the children. She enjoyed this part of the lesson and was looking forward to the next time she would work with this group. She realised that the initial discussion had not progressed well because she was more concerned with trying to follow her plans rather than responding to the children's interest. In planning she had covered the science and English content but she had not considered how the children might react. By restructuring her questions and involving the children in a way which encouraged them to develop their own lines of enquiry she achieved her objectives: 'to develop language skills, raise questions and put forward ideas'.

It would be naive to think that all situations could be easily redeemable and as productive as the above example but what is important to consider here is the shift of thinking from what the teacher expects regarding a prescribed outcome to involving children in the learning process. 'How am I doing?' depends very much on 'How they are doing?'

A positive response to the following questions will act as a measure of success:

- Were the children thoughtfully engaged?
- Did the children ask relevant questions?
- Was there evidence of children working collaboratively?
- Did children become involved beyond your expectations?
- Was the atmosphere conducive to learning?
- Was there evidence of progress in understanding?
- Did pupils mindfully add to your agenda?

At first you might look at this list and think this will be difficult to accomplish. Of course nobody expects any teacher to achieve this in every single lesson. In reviewing your own success and identifying progress be realistic and pleased with small successes and build on them. The important premise is to recognise success in its many forms. While training, and once you are a teacher, this will be crucial to your progress and achievement. It begs the obvious question: 'How can I improve if I don't know how to identify success?' Observing a range of teaching styles, teachers and learning situations is a good place to start as is reflecting on your own experience as a learner. What you value and believe in will have been influenced by your experience as a learner and this is something to be aware of when observing teaching.

Observing teaching

Observing teachers teach is an invaluable experience if you have the knowledge and skill to identify good practice (see also Chapter 5). This is not a simple process and you will benefit from the support of teachers, mentors and guidelines offered by government agencies. Taking the initiative in developing a professional dialogue is crucial as every training teacher will have different needs. You may have been a teaching assistant or taught abroad before beginning formal training. You may have had only a few days' experience of being in a classroom. You may have been a lawyer, carpenter or househusband. You may have Grade 5 in piano playing or a PhD in Physics. You may have run a Montessori nursery or been a farmer. Need I go on? It is easy to see from this list that starting points regarding expertise and experience are diverse in the extreme. Your desired outcome, however, is common, namely qualifying to teach. But remember every new teacher will develop their teaching at a pace that will reflect their ability and it is not helpful to compare your progress with your perceived progress of other students. Every teaching practice placement will be unique and the challenges presented will vary not only from school to school but also class to class. Professional relationships will differ, geographical location will vary and, most influential of all, each and every child will be different and require particular support.

Identifying good teaching

Time given to reflecting on your own learning experiences of being taught will help you identify good practice. As a training teacher you will be supported in this by mentors, teachers and even peers. At this point it might be worth comparing good and not so good experiences you have had of being taught and even making a list of reasons why you have made the distinction. But please remember that it is natural to make judgements in retrospect based on feelings of success, enjoyment, frustration or even anger. An experienced mentor will be able to guide you in this process. However, a mentor will have their own way of gathering evidence to support assessments of teaching progress, development and ability. This is useful for the trainee to know. Mentors gain evidence of the training teacher's teaching ability by observing them teach, reading their file, observing pupils, looking at the classroom and discussing progress and concerns with the trainee and the teacher. Although evidence is gained in this way, because of the nature of teaching there is no set sequence or order in which judgements are made. The trainee might not be aware of what the mentor's particular focus is or that it changes as a result of observations made.

Mentors are used to the classroom and realise that even the best plans can go awry. They recognise the arbitrary nature of their visits and make allowances for this. No decisions about failing training teachers are made on one observation by one mentor. A mentor's visit is part of an ongoing catalogue of visits. Assessment of a trainee teacher's progress and ability involves the trainee, mentors and teachers. What is important is that training teachers have realistic expectations, recognise success and failure and learn from them. In adult-based training routes like the Graduate Teachers' Programme (GTP), and School Centred Initial Teacher Training (SCITT), this visit is likely to be carried out by an LA advisor or a participating school headteacher.

Understandably some training teachers find the whole process of being observed when teaching a nerve-wracking experience. Hopefully, by being made aware of what a mentor is looking for, insights will be offered which will help allay such fears.

The training teachers' perspective

Teaching practice can be a lonely time if experiences are not shared. It is quite common for training teachers to feel isolated and think other training teachers are having an easier time. A mentor observing several students has a very different perspective. All training teachers at some time experience problems. How these situations are handled and how you respond to them is all part of learning to teach.

Jamie was teaching a maths lesson to a Year 6 class. It was towards the end of his second teaching practice. His mentor sat at the back of the room taking notes as part of a formal assessment of Jamie's teaching. The children, a top maths group, were collecting and collating information about individual shoe sizes. The lesson progressed well with pupils working collaboratively in small groups. Questions posed to develop their understanding of mode, mean and median were at an appropriate level to help develop understanding. In the plenary Jamie asked questions about frequencies of shoe sizes. He wrote these on the board. He then started to explain about the mean, but after only a few words said nothing. The silence only lasted for seconds but was obvious to the mentor. With a big smile Jamie turned to the class. Holding out the chalk and in a bright voice, he said to a girl at the front, 'Rachel would you like to explain to everyone how we find the mean shoe size in this class?' At first Rachel looked shy but was very pleased with herself when she finished and was praised by Jamie. He then carried on with the lesson in a confident way. In discussion with the mentor after the lesson Jamie said that he froze and couldn't remember what he wanted to say, so he asked Rachel, one of the more able pupils, to explain. When she had finished he felt composed enough to carry on. The children did not realise his dilemma and Rachel's involvement was seen as a planned part of the lesson.

Jamie was nervous about being assessed, which is understandable, but his quick thinking worked and even enhanced his teaching. This was recognised by both Jamie and his mentor. To retain a sense of humour and have realistic expectations can sometimes be difficult. But if we learn by consequences then mistakes could be seen as a vital part of the process of learning.

How to be prepared for a formal observation of your teaching

First, it is important to think through the lesson to be observed, making notes if necessary. Think about management and organisational and teaching strategies which address learning objectives and involve children in a meaningful way. Think about how you view a successful outcome. Ask yourself: 'What will I be doing? What will the children be doing? How will the children be doing what they are doing? Why will the children be doing what they are doing? How can I tell if they are progressing and learning?' Secondly, think about contingency plans. What will you do if things do not go to plan, for individuals or the class? What strategies will you use to keep children on task? How will you deal with disruptions? It is impossible to cover all eventualities, but if contingencies are made this can add to your confidence even if you do not follow them through.

The following suggestions offer a checklist for training teachers.

If possible make sure

- the children know there will be a visitor
- the teacher and the mentor are introduced
- the classroom is well presented
- there is somewhere for the mentor to sit.

If relevant, discuss with school staff

- your plans
- their role
- organisational problems
- resources, space, time
- pupils' needs
- how the visit may affect other staff.

Ensure that

- your teaching file is well ordered, up to date and available
- there is a copy of your lesson plan for the mentor
- the mentor is aware of any special circumstances, for example pupils with special needs
- the mentor has a clear understanding of your intentions

- any displays are well presented
- children's work is marked.

Identify for discussion

- aspects of your teaching which are successful
- areas of concern
- questions you want to ask
- difficult situations or problems.

Remember a mentor will not see everything. Make sure you sell yourself and point out aspects of your teaching that you are pleased with or feel enthusiastic about. This might, for example, involve asking children to show their work, talking about a display or relating a particular incident in which you recognised a leap of understanding – yours or the pupils'. Talking about individual progress, learning difficulties or changes in behaviour or attitude will inform the mentor of your understanding of individuals as well as continuity and progression of learning.

Using your mentor's visits effectively

Early visits

On early visits the mentor's agenda will be concerned with how the trainee is beginning to teach. Not surprisingly, being observed can be a daunting experience even for the most capable individual. When training teachers start teaching few are used to the noise, activity and constant involvement needed to make sense of everything that is happening in the classroom. There is a lot to take in. The significance of the teacher's actions, the interplay or intervention needed to encourage learning as well as dealing with disruptive children means it is difficult for the trainee to know where to start. Mentors are aware of this concern about where to begin. The need to identify specific targets crucial to training teachers' development is a major aspect of the mentor's role. To decide which aspects have the biggest knock-on effect to teaching effectively involves the ability to recognise individual needs and progress.

Many training teachers prefer points to be written down by their mentor or to make their own notes as the mentor is talking. Guidelines concerning teaching strengths and areas for development typically form the basis of feedback. The class teacher, trainee support teacher and other teachers in the school have day-to-day contact with the trainee which the mentor may not have. Mentors only gain snapshot evidence of the training teacher's experience on teaching practice but they have the breadth of experience of working with a range of training teachers. Therefore it is important that everyone works as a team and talks about the training teacher's progress together. This should be seen as an essential part of a mentor's visit.

Identifying areas of concern

On a mentor's early visits it can be difficult to identify areas of concern on which to focus. Quite often training teachers lack the skills for recognising significant problems or they feel nervous about telling mentors about their perceived weaknesses. Relationships between the mentor, trainee and teacher are new. The mentor has little experience of working with a particular trainee and is learning how best to support them.

Appreciating that relatively simple adjustments can make a major difference to teaching is often a surprise to the trainee.

Ian had organised his Year 6 children into groups for a history lesson. In each group there were five or six pupils. Handouts about siege weapons were on each table, as were pencils (rollers), bricks (heavy objects) and Newton meters. Instructions were on another handout. The lesson was not successful, several children did very little and some did nothing. Ian became increasingly stressed and ended up shouting at children for not taking part. The lesson was not completed in the planned time. Understandably this was a distressing experience which Ian had no wish to repeat.

The mentor suggested two main changes: a demonstration before the children embarked on the activity and smaller groups to ensure that individual involvement could be monitored. The mentor also asked Ian to think about what he said as he moved about the room and to try to focus his comments on the task rather than behaviour. To the experienced teacher such adjustments will seem obvious but to the novice this is often not the case. A crucial aspect of the mentor's role is to provide an environment conducive to discussion in which successes and difficulties are examined openly. To gain understanding and develop reflective skills, training teachers need to be able to raise concerns and ask questions. The mentor's visit is an ideal time to do this. Until training teachers see the relevance of advice related to their own experience it is difficult for them to learn. A two-way dialogue in which mentors and training teachers communicate openly is ideal. A skilful mentor can do much to enable this to happen. Often, however, a trainee can help the process significantly. Consider the implications of the following hypothetical conversations.

Example 1

Mentor: How did you feel the lesson went?
Trainee: OK, the children all did what I wanted them to do.
Mentor: Were you pleased with how the more able children participated?
Trainee: Yes, I think they found it interesting.
Mentor: What about Craig and Jenny? They finished quite a while before any of the others.
Trainee: Yes they always do. They did it very well. I was pleased with their poem.
Mentor: They sat quietly and waited.
Trainee: (looks at the mentor)

Mentor: I saw you go over to them after a few minutes. What comments did you make?

Trainee: I told them it was good and that they had done well and that I liked the way the poem made me feel.

Mentor: How did they feel about their work?

Trainee: I'm not sure, I think they were pleased.

Mentor: You then asked them to read.

Trainee: Yes, for the last 10 minutes.

Mentor: Next time they finish early what might you do?

In the above conversation the mentor led the dialogue to ascertain the training teacher's awareness of how to offer learning opportunities for early finishers. Although the mentor's questions were answered, very little about the training teacher's intentions was discovered. In this case it would be easy for the mentor to assume that the trainee had not considered the need to respond to early finishers or differentiate expectations of brighter pupils.

Example 2

Mentor: How did you feel the lesson went?

Trainee: OK, the children all did what I wanted them to do.

Mentor: Were you pleased with how the more able children participated?

Trainee: I think they found it interesting. I was concerned that they finished so quickly. I felt that Craig and Jenny had done what I asked very quickly but I was pleased with their poem.

Mentor: They sat quietly and waited.

Trainee: I realised that they had finished but I was talking to another group and it took me a while to get to them.

Mentor: Perhaps you could indicate to them that you knew they had finished and tell them you would be over in a minute. Perhaps think of a short task associated with their work which they could do until you were ready.

Trainee: Yes, but I still feel nervous about talking across the class when you are in the room, so I didn't.

Mentor: We can discuss ways in which you can practise this. For example, talk to a child on the next table then increase the range. Is it a problem for you when I am not here?

Trainee: Not when I am on my own with the class, but when a teacher is in here it is.

Mentor: I saw you go over to them after a few minutes. What comments did you make?

Trainee: I told them it was good and that they had done well and that I liked the way it made me feel.

Mentor: How did they feel about their work?

Trainee: I'm not sure, I think they were pleased. I would have liked more time to discuss it with them. They had used adjectives well but adverbs were not so well used. I could have asked them to pick out the verbs in their poem and try to think of a few adverbs to describe each one.

Mentor: You then asked them to read.

Trainee: Yes, for the last 10 minutes. I don't think I thought it through. It surprised me that they finished so early. Next time I will have an extension task ready or try to give them a task as a result of what they have done. The paired poem idea works well for some children, but there are some pairs which do not work so well. I need to talk to you about this.

In this conversation the trainee responded in a more open way. The mentor was able to ascertain her reasons for lack of action, awareness of missed opportunities and future intentions. The trainee, herself, identified concerns and suggested ways forward. Consequently, the mentor could offer advice which related to the training teacher's identified needs.

Observing training teachers teach

Typically, training teachers will be told the criteria on which they are being assessed: at the present time these are given in Professional Standards for Teachers (TDA, 2007). Training teachers also tend to know that the mentor will be observing and collecting evidence of their planning, teaching, assessments, reflections and aspects of their professional development.

What they probably do not know is how a mentor goes about collecting evidence. It might be helpful if they did. In the following section one mentor's perspective is offered. The mentor's agenda is based on final teaching practice visits, when all aspects of training teachers' teaching are assessed.

During final teaching practice assessment is rigorous, involving the mentor in gaining evidence of how trainee teachers:

- help pupils learn and develop
- deliver the curriculum
- develop their teaching style
- enhance relationships with pupils and staff.

To gain evidence the mentor considers questions such as:

- What do I need to ask the class teacher?
- How do I need to respond to what the class teacher says?

- What would it be best for me to do when I am in the classroom observing a trainee teaching?
- How can I best give advice?
- What will be the most effective way to support the trainee?
- How useful is the advice I give?
- How can I encourage the trainee to become more independent?
- How can I make the trainee feel able to talk openly?
- Is there evidence of development in the training teacher's learning as a result of my actions?
- Has the trainee become more reflective?
- Is there improvement in areas of identified weakness?
- How can I now best support the trainee?

The mentor's agenda

Although there is not always a definite sequence to actions, the mentor has a set agenda. On entering the classroom, if the children are present, the mentor scans the room gauging pupil involvement, eye contact and facial expression. (In the early stages of teaching training teachers are surprised by this and often expect the mentor to concentrate on them.) The mentor is observing the trainee but trying to do this in a way that is not obvious, by looking at the training teacher's notes or reading a child's book. If possible the mentor smiles at the trainee to try to put them at ease and briefly asks, 'How is it going?' or tries to make a quick, positive comment, 'This display looks interesting' or 'I hear you had a very good PE lesson yesterday'. The mentor asks to look at the training teacher's folder and indicates what he or she will be doing. 'I will read your file, watch you teach, talk to the children and look at their work. Afterwards I will talk to you and your teacher about the lesson and your teaching. Please try to ignore me. I'm looking forward to your session.'

In making conscious decisions about what to say on entering the room the mentor's intention is to inform and relax the trainee. The mentor wants the trainee to be able to teach without wondering or worrying about what the mentor is going to do. If training teachers want to introduce the mentor to the class they could say, 'This is Mrs X. She has come to watch us work today. She might talk to you about what you are doing, but don't worry as she used to be a teacher and likes talking to children about their work.'

To be able to observe and analyse training teachers teaching as thoroughly as possible it helps if the mentor can move about and talk to members of the class. This obviously has to be done in a sensitive manner and is not always appropriate. Nevertheless, it offers good insight into children's involvement and learning as well as the training teacher's teaching.

Gaining evidence

At first the list of standards in Professional Standards for Teachers (TDA, 2007) will seem very long, especially to a trainee on first teaching practice. You might find it helpful to use the list to inform your teaching, aid planning, analyse your practice, focus reflections and support discussions with teachers and mentors.

A mentor will gain evidence of the training teacher's ability to address the standards in a variety of ways, including the following methods.

Written evidence

In the training teacher's teaching file, the mentor looks for:

- session plans with clear, purposeful learning objectives, relevant to the National Curriculum and pupils' attainment levels, allowing for progression and continuity, planned assessment opportunities and safety considerations
- tasks and activities, differentiated to involve children in addressing learning objectives in an interesting, creative and appropriate way, offering a degree of independence
- planned use of a range of appropriate resources to enhance learning
- lessons which accommodate all pupils including SEN and EAL (English as an Additional Language)
- planned expectations of learning support assistant (LSA) support
- reflections and evaluations which focus on learning and individual needs and which are used to inform future teaching
- assessments of pupils' progress and achievement.

Teaching evidence

Observing a trainee teach, the mentor looks for an enthusiasm for teaching, a clear ability to put children at ease and engage them in learning and a good understanding of the subject. Evidence will be found of the way a trainee teacher manages, organises and communicates learning. A mentor will look for the following.

Good communication and interpersonal skills which sustain interest and involvement including:

- effective and varied use of voice and non-verbal communication
- clear explanations and demonstrations
- well-focused questions at an appropriate level
- clear communication with other adults

- interventions which enhance learning
- discourse rather than superficial conversation.

Skilful management and organisational strategies to ensure pupils focus on learning, including:

- organisation and preparation to ensure the smooth running of the session
- effective management of individuals, groups and the class
- appropriate differentiation for groups and individuals
- encouragement of peer support and collaborative skills
- organisation of a variety of appropriate resources
- efficient use of adult support
- effective strategies for maintaining discipline and control.

An ability to productively engage children in an enthusiasm for learning by:

- providing an atmosphere conducive to learning
- demonstrating good subject knowledge
- a creative interpretation of the curriculum
- clear and realistic aims
- high expectations
- a sound understanding of individual pupils and their needs
- purposeful monitoring and record-keeping to inform assessment
- opportunities which encourage independence
- a flexible approach in response to children's needs
- skilful handling of misconceptions
- supportive, targeted feedback.

Pupil evidence

Observing pupils, the mentor looks for:

- how children work and respond
- a willingness and enthusiasm to participate
- good study skills, involvement in the task
- cooperation and collaboration
- evidence of productive learning
- the enjoyment factor
- the quality of pupils' contributions
- a positive learning ethos.

Classroom evidence

Observing the classroom the mentor looks for:

- well-presented displays of pupils' work
- interactive areas connected with aspects of study
- well-organised resources
- areas for independent exploration
- quiet corners
- a visually stimulating environment
- an environment which encourages involvement
- a sense of order.

Discussion following a mentor's visit

In discussion following a teaching observation, the mentor and trainee may discuss any of the above observable components of teaching. The cognitive aspect of the training teacher's teaching will also form an important part of any discussion and feedback. By talking to you as a training teacher about your perceptions, interpretations and decisions the mentor will gain valuable insights into your beliefs, your values and ideas, your style and your development. The mentor will base feedback not only on your performance but also on your:

- understanding of pupils and their needs
- reflections on pupils' learning
- awareness of the relationship between aims and practice
- ability to analyse implications of performance
- reasons for choices and decisions
- consideration of alternatives
- ability to assess success and consider ways forward.

Verbal feedback: what to expect

The mentor will make comments and ask questions about particular observations across the range of standards in *Qualifying to Teach* (TDA, 2006). Such conversations are not usually documented but are useful to the trainee.

For example:

It was really good to see the children sprawled across the floor doing their history drawings of the Egyptians on such a big scale. It would have been restrictive just using the desk top. They really had a chance to explore ideas on a grand scale. Don't you think it was impressive how well they cooperated with each other and how they knew exactly which part to work on? We were able to talk about your teaching without being interrupted. Not many training teachers would have had the confidence to let children work like that. I really enjoyed watching them. How did you decide to organise the groups? Who decided who did what? What are your plans for the finished pictures?

In this case feedback refers to the fact that children worked collaboratively and that the training teacher's control of the class was good. The mentor was able to find out about the training teacher's choices in group design and task allocation. From a brief discussion a great deal of information was gleaned about the training teacher's teaching ability. This type of evidence is crucial in building a picture of progress but is not always so apparent in detail in formal written feedback. Interactive dialogue, involving the trainee and the mentor, is to be encouraged and is a good time for both parties to raise any points or concerns they wish to discuss.

Written feedback: what to expect

Most training teachers, understandably, place a great deal of importance on written feedback. Often after a session they find it difficult to take everything in, especially in the early stages of teaching. They find productive comments relating to building confidence, improving practice and considering alternatives useful to analyse their teaching and guide their learning. The mentor should be aware of the need to make suggestions, channel thinking and give a clear framework in which training teachers can develop ideas and experiment. Reflection on practice can be developed in this way. Helpful comments will:

- praise performance, building on the positive, recognising strengths and commenting on them
- focus on one or two areas which are weak or need developing, suggesting alternatives and discussing possibilities to improve practice
- encourage conversation so that training teachers have the opportunity to analyse their teaching, ask questions and consider their development
- explain what is required and clearly state what the trainee is expected to do in a problematic or failing situation
- empathise with a particular set of circumstances, including class size, previous experience and inherent difficulties
- focus on individual pupils and their development
- provide targets for the trainee to work towards.

Giving reasons for comments made and offering alternative suggestions increases the value of the mentor's feedback because it offers the trainee a way forward. Inviting comment from the trainee in a way that would aid reflection on practice might include asking them about:

- particular choices made interpreting the curriculum
- where they got their ideas from and ascertaining if more than one source was used. What degree of autonomy did they have?
- talking to the trainee about pupils to gauge understanding of individual needs, relationships, expectations and development. Asking about changes they would like to make and why.

CRITICAL ISSUES

... Learning begins with the need for some motivation, an intention to learn. The learner must then concentrate attention on the important aspects of what is to be learned and differentiate them from noise in the environment ... (Svinicki et al., 1996, p. 265)

Classrooms are noisy busy places, nothing is simple. To concentrate attention on the important aspects of what is to be learnt is a crucial skill in developing teaching confidence and competence. Consider the quote given above and reflect on your experience of the way training teachers are supported and assessed in achieving success. What implications does this have for the way you make sense of and evaluate your teaching? What new understanding have you gained from this training about your performance in the classroom?

Conclusion

I can hear you say, 'What a complex and complicated process ... I'll never do all that ... Do teachers really do all these things? ... It's so demanding, challenging, difficult!' This is all true. It takes time to teach well. There is always more to learn. There are no easy answers. What works with one group might not work so well with another. Learning to teach can be viewed as an ongoing process which is both rewarding and frustrating. It is not a smooth passage and often there are no easy answers. Remember: a mentor's visit is not only about assessing progress but is also about supporting development.

Career entry and development profile

Towards the end of your final teaching practice you will be expected to fill in a document called a Career Entry and Development Profile (CEDP). This will involve identifying your particular teaching strengths and areas for professional development. Choices made as to which criteria to select will be as a result of discussions with mentors in school and university mentors but will be your responsibility. Once you decide which targets identify your professional development needs you will enter them into your Career Entry Development Profile at transition point 1. Your CEDP will act as a focus for your professional development at the beginning of your teaching career and should be taken with you on your first teaching post.

Summary

- In making observational visits the role of the mentor is to support the training teacher's progress and assess their competence against the standards in *Qualifying to Teach* (TDA, 2006).
- To gain evidence on which to base judgements the mentor observes the trainee teach and talks to them about their teaching.
- Ideally an open dialogue in collaboration with teachers and the trainee offers the mentor insight into the training teacher's development.
- Trainee competence is assessed using stated criteria although mentors will have their own methods of gaining evidence.
- Typically assessment of trainee progress involves identifying areas of strength and areas for development. Identifying specific targets and offering advice is crucial for individual development.
- To alleviate the stress factor training teachers are advised to prepare thoroughly for a mentor's visit.

Issues for reflection

- To what extent might your contribution to any dialogue be helpful in recognising your concerns? Can you think of questions you might ask to help identify problems?
- A positive approach to feedback is generally advised but does this enable mentors to give a frank account of a training teacher's progress?
- In what ways might mentors help training teachers to become aware of alternatives without 'telling them what to do'?
- To what extent might a training teacher's own understanding or reflection influence a mentor's judgement of their development in a positive/negative way?

Further reading 📖

Clegg, D. and Billington, S. (1994) *The Effective Primary Classroom*. London: David Fulton. The section on pages 26–35 'What we know about effective classrooms' provides some insight into reflective practice.

Ghaye, T. (2010) *Teaching and Learning through Reflective Practice*. Abingdon: Routledge. The author takes the stance that focusing on success is powerful in supporting reflective practice to improve the quality of teaching.

Hayes, D. (2004) *Foundations in Primary Teaching*. London: David Fulton. The child, learning and teaching are explored in a personal way, providing a comprehensive introduction to all aspects of teaching.

Hayes, L., Nikolic, V. and Cabaj, H. (2000) *Am I Teaching Well?* Exeter: Learning Matters. Self-assessment strategies to encourage reflective practice feature highly in this book. Its emphasis on self-reflection and self-evaluation will be particularly valuable to trainee teachers.

Hobson, A. J., Malderez, A. and Tracey, L. (2009) *Navigating Initial Teacher Training: Becoming a Teacher*. Abingdon: Routledge. This book is written by experts in teaching and is based on a major study of 5,000 beginning teachers. The text is useful in offering reassurance to the novice through sharing the experience and perceptions of other new teachers.

Kitson, N. and Merry, R. (1997) *Teaching in the Primary School*. London: Routledge. This book is a coherent introduction to teaching written by experts in primary education. There are several relevant chapters extremely useful to training teachers with a clear focus on learning relationships.

Proctor, A., Entwistle, M., Judge, B. and McKenzie-Murdoch, S. (1995) *Learning to Teach in the Primary Classroom*. London: Routledge. This is a very comprehensive book which includes several highly relevant chapters by experienced teachers to support trainee teachers in the school-based element of their course.

CHAPTER 18

YOUR FIRST TEACHING POST

Anne Cockburn and Graham Handscomb

Chapter overview

You have successfully trained and are now set for the delights of securing your first teaching post! In this chapter Anne Cockburn and Graham Handscomb discuss some of the best ways to look for your first teaching post, how to prepare your application to show yourself in the best possible light, the interview process and the next steps. Throughout they stress the importance of thorough preparation and recognise the need to make career decisions about which you feel comfortable.

Introduction

In this chapter we describe the main considerations you should take into account when applying for jobs and briefly discuss the induction period. People are often surprised by how demanding and time-consuming the whole process can be. Do not be caught short: read on so that you do not have a last-minute major panic on your hands.

When it seems as if you have only just begun your pre-service training people will start asking you about jobs:

- Where are you planning to work?
- Which pools have you applied to?
- What have you written in your personal statement?

Some local authorities (LAs) start looking for newly qualified teachers very early on. Indeed, it is not uncommon for some applications for 'the pool' to be in before the end of January. Other LAs are much more laissez-faire and many of their jobs do not come up until May, June or even July. Both extremes can be hard for the people concerned. It is not easy, for example, to complete an application form demonstrating your confidence and experience when you feel that there is so much to learn and you still break into a sweat when you have to plan, and teach, several class sessions in a day. Nor is it easy to stand back and watch all your colleagues land jobs when you are desperately waiting for a post in your area and coping with the demands of your final assessments. Knowing that applying for jobs is invariably stressful generally helps but rarely makes it any easier. Fortunately, however, there is a strategy which can lighten the burden, namely preparation.

Where and when to start looking

If you are at a college or university it is likely that they can advise you on where and when to start looking for your first post. Many universities now also run specific recruitment fairs where representatives from all over the country can give you information about schools in their local authority. Here are some additional pointers which might prove helpful.

It is important to recognise that job hunting may well take considerable time and attention. During your training you are unlikely to have much time and attention to spare. It is vital, therefore, if at all possible, to plan times when you can devote yourself to the task. It may be, for example, that you will have time over the Christmas holidays to update your curriculum vitae and outline your personal statement. Or you might have some time available between assignments. We would suggest that you begin the drafting process sooner rather than later as it will give you time to reflect on what you have written and improve your application as a result.

Pre-service teachers tend to find out about jobs in one of six ways:

- the *Times Educational Supplement*
- weekly education supplements in newspapers such as the *Guardian* and the *Independent*
- lists issued by local education authorities (obtained by telephoning specific authorities)
- logging on to local authority websites and searching for 'jobs in schools'

- your university or college
- word of mouth (for example, it might be your teaching practice school).

Think carefully about when you are going to start applying for jobs. Factors to consider are the urgency to obtain a post, your personality, the popularity of the area where you wish to apply, your relevant experience and your other commitments. For example, if you are an anxious person who requires a job as soon as possible, then you may wish to start applying sooner rather than later. If that is the case remember that, if you are undertaking a one-year programme, it is unlikely that you will be able to write much about your course or your teaching experience on your application form. In contrast, you may wish to wait until you are fairly confident that you are going to complete your training successfully and then turn your attention to looking for jobs. There you run the risk of having fewer jobs to apply for but having more relevant information to include on your application form. Whatever you decide your prospective employer should appreciate how much teaching experience you are likely to have.

Choosing your area

Rather than applying for every job advertised, in the first instance it is a good idea to sit down and consider where you really want to teach. Discuss possibilities with family and friends. If you are relaxed about where you might work it is often easier as you are likely to have greater scope if you are prepared to move to a new area. Nevertheless it is important to remember that going to another part of the country would not only involve starting a new job, but also entail moving house, finding your way around, making new friends and so on. In other words you would have a lot on your plate. However, if you relocate early on in the summer, just after your training has finished, you will have a chance to get settled, coupled with the excitement of meeting new people and beginning a new career.

Planning where to apply can also include decisions as to whether you want to consider applying to a local authority 'pool' and/or opt for individually advertised jobs. In essence – although there are regional variations – if you decide on going for a 'pool', you complete a general application form. In most areas, if it meets with success, you will then be invited for an interview.

Again there are likely to be regional variations but, basically, two or three people will interview you (usually including a headteacher and a representative from the local education authority). Depending on your performance they will grade you – A to D, for example. This information will then be made available to schools in the area. The higher your grade the more likely you are to be offered 'a look round' a school and, with luck, a job. Typically, a formal interview at the school is unlikely in these cases.

In other areas where there are such general applications your form will simply be made available to any headteachers who wish to consult it in their search for new staff.

If your application appeals to them you will then be asked to an interview for their specific school.

You may decide to apply to both a 'pool' and individual jobs or focus on one or the other. Individual posts tend to start being advertised from late February (when there are very few) onwards. If you have not seen anything suitable by April/early May do not worry as there tends to be a flurry of jobs in early June. These arise as half-term – typically the last week in May – tends to be around the last date teachers can hand in their notice if they intend leaving at the end of the academic year. Not only are there a reasonable number of posts therefore but most of the applicants will be people in your position or people returning to teaching after a break.

Two cautionary comments before focusing on applications: it is important to have a fairly clear idea about where you wish to teach at this stage. If you are too vague you will waste a lot of time, energy and money. If you are too specific you will dramatically reduce your chances of finding a job: while it might be very convenient to teach just around the corner, the job – if there is one – may not be advertised for ages. You may not get it and there may then be very few other jobs available. Added to which, many would argue that you should only stay in your first job for two to three years and then move on (see below). It is also important to remember that not only moving house but also moving to a new area can be highly stressful. Making new friends, finding your way around and so on takes time and energy: both may be in short supply when you take on a new job.

Applications

It is well worth putting considerable time and thought into your applications: if your efforts are not of a sufficient standard you will fail to get over the first hurdle. Again there are variations but you will almost certainly have to provide one, some or all of the following:

- an application form
- a personal statement
- a curriculum vitae (CV)
- an accompanying, covering letter.

The early sections in application forms are generally straightforward requests for biographical information. You will be asked for details of examinations taken. Try to be as detailed and accurate as possible: the fact that ten years ago you took a GCSE in music or art may make all the difference to whether or not you are asked for an interview. If you have to complete a standard form consider the information required and the space you have been given. For instance, think about the grades you obtained in schools and higher education: have you been given too much or too little space for them? How can you best fit them in?

Having written your application, make sure to check it thoroughly for spelling mistakes, grammatical errors and style.

Personal statement

Later sections of the application tend to be more tricky. You may be asked specific questions about your views on various issues and/or you may be asked for 'a personal statement' with little or no guidance provided. These are often seen as the most challenging part of the application procedure. They do, however, provide you with an opportunity to demonstrate what you have to offer in terms of personal qualities, philosophies and outlook. Here – with the help of some of Anne's past PGCE students – we provide you with some helpful suggestions.

When drafting responses to such requests it is important to keep the following in mind:

- As people who do the shortlisting of applicants, it is a fairly boring task sifting through application forms: make yours stand out by presenting it in a lively and interesting style.
- You are not only unique but – however, tired and lacking in confidence you are – you have a range of strengths you can offer a school. Think back to all your achievements and interests, remembering, apart from anything else, that you would not have been offered a place to train as a teacher if you did not have the potential to be successful. Yate's (2001) 4th rule when preparing a job application is, 'Remember that people get great joy from pleasant surprises. Show a little gold now, but let the interviewer discover the mother lode at the interview' (p. 11). Eve, who recently landed a post teaching Year 5 and a former student of Anne's, advises 'Make sure you are thoughtful about the process of educating. Give good examples of innovative and creative lessons.'
- Show an awareness of the specific post you are applying for and, as nursery teacher Paola advises, 'Study the person specification in detail.' Also demonstrate a familiarity with the wider educational context ensuring, for example, that you follow Zak's advice by being '… aware of what is on the government's agenda'.
- In applying for a specific school post briefly try to relate the qualities and outlook that you have to the particular school. It helps to give readers of your statement a 'mental picture' of what it would be like for you to be fulfilling this job in their school. Balance this with avoiding 'second guessing' too much detail about the school or making big assumptions based on the limited evidence.
- Be honest. While it might be tempting to imply that you are an expert at this, that and the next thing, don't do it as you might find yourself (with your Grade 1 piano certificate) playing in front of an entire school at assembly. More appropriately, you might say that you have an interest in 'x' or 'y' which you would be keen to develop if the opportunity arose. In addition, avoid volunteering for numerous extra-curricular activities even if you would like to take some on. You might be

landed with more than you bargained for and, without beating about the bush, your first job is likely to require all your time and energy without extra demands being put upon you.

- You may find it helpful to make use of, and reference to, the *Professional Standards for Teachers* (TDA, 2008), drawing on some of the language used in them to show how you meet the specific requirements of the job description.

- You may be applying for several jobs in different counties but remember to include some specific statements about the particular school or region to which each application is destined. It is important for both you and those involved in the selection process, after all, to be sure that you are appropriate for the post or area in question. You might, for example, comment on the support provided for newly qualified teachers or the opportunities in information communications technology.

- Be concise but not list-like. It would be inappropriate to provide your life history and, indeed, even if selectors were interested they would not have time to read it. On the other hand, a list of achievements, attitudes and aspirations would be very dry and lack substance. Rather than 'I think play is very important', for example, try something along the lines of: 'Having worked in three contrasting reception classes, read some of the relevant literature and attended lectures on the subject, I am developing a view that play can have a very effective role in children's learning. For example, one day, I observed ...' (then give a brief account of a child, or children, learning through play).

- Think very carefully about how you present your personal and professional philosophies. Again there is a need to be as honest as possible without shooting yourself in the foot in the process. If you have strong views about how particular subjects should be taught (for example, through a play-based approach) and you would be reluctant to teach in any other way then you may feel it is only right to say so. You should, however, recognise that, by doing so, you may well be significantly narrowing your choice of jobs. It is not necessarily that the interviewing panel would disagree with your philosophy but more that they might be hesitant in employing someone who appeared to have rigidly held views.

- Sometimes personal statements are included as part of the application form and sometimes they are not. If they are not it is usually a good idea to include them in your covering letter.

- As part of your application you will almost certainly be invited to say something about your personal interests and hobbies. Selection panels want to be reassured that you are a lively and interesting person who has a range of interests and friends but that you are also someone who enjoys their own company and who is not always dependent on other people for their rest and relaxation. It is worth noting that Yate (2001), citing a survey that reported that those who played sport tended to earn more than their less energetic friends, concluded: 'The interviewer is looking for your involvement in groups, as a signal that you know how to get along with others and pull together as a team' (p. 177).

Curriculum vitae and letter of application

An opportunity to present details of your examination results and other notable achievements is very likely to be included in the application form, but if it is not or if you deem it insufficient, you may wish to provide a copy of your curriculum vitae. The style of such documents can vary but, to be successful, they need to be word-processed and presented in a professional manner.

Crafted with care, the curriculum vitae can be a very effective way in which to present the main details of your background and experience, and some of the key messages you wish to convey. A concise and well-organised CV can help shortlisting panels to take in quickly who you are and what you might bring to the post. However, for some applications you may be instructed not to supply a curriculum vitae. This is because some schools prefer the applicant's details to be presented in a common format structured by the application form. They consider that this makes it easier to compare applicants. In these cases it is advisable not to be tempted to enclose your curriculum vitae 'just in case'. This may duplicate information you put in the application form frustrating the selection panel and giving the impression that you do not pay attention to detail.

Within the body of the application form it is likely that you will be asked to write a letter of application. Sometimes this incorporates the personal statement. There is often a blank page towards the end of the form for this letter of application, and you may also be instructed to provide a separate page if needed. It is important that you write enough but not too much. If you are given full details about the post, school or local authority it is useful to gear what you have to say about yourself and your outlook to this information. Having read many applications it is often frustrating to deal with letters which just list a person's personal and professional history – a sort of potted biography – with little attempt to relate this to the job being applied for!

Remember that the selection panel is likely to be dealing with a number of applications. So your job is to make its task as easy as possible by presenting the main details about yourself and your approach to the post in a clear accessible way. Don't worry about leaving some fine details out. Keep in mind that there will be opportunity to discover more about you through the interview process. The goal of the application is to say enough to interest the selection panel and to secure an interview. Finally, make sure you address the basics of neatness and accuracy. Do not use lined paper, and do not make spelling or grammatical errors. If you are unsure, find a book on the subject such as those listed at the end of the chapter.

As part of your application form or your curriculum vitae, typically, you will be asked to include the names and addresses of two referees. Specific details as to whom you should approach (for example, your personal tutor) may be included but it is usual to use someone involved in your pre-service training (for example, the head of one of your SCITT or GTP schools or a PGCE tutor), and a lecturer who worked with you on your first degree. Sometimes it may be appropriate to include one of the headteachers from a teaching practice school. Whoever you select, be sure to ask them before you send in your application and thank them after the event. Apart from the obvious courtesy, it is important to remember that you may need to call upon such people again in the future. It is also important to ask referees to supply a reference for each job you apply for, rather than for them to provide an obviously generic reference to everyone, headed 'to whom it may concern'.

When sending the application off it is useful to attach a covering letter. This can be very brief and almost a courteous formality along the lines of 'I enclose my application for the post of ... Thank you for your consideration'. Nevertheless, be sure that it is neat and professionally laid out.

Some vital last points to remember are, before you post your application, be sure to:

- Ask two or three constructively critical friends to read it to check for spelling mistakes, misleading statements and grammatical errors. They will also be able to tell you if you are under- or over-selling yourself.
- Take a copy so that you can refresh your memory if you are asked for an interview.

Interviews

Preparation

As with the applications, it is important to prepare as thoroughly as you can for interviews. Hawkins (1999) invites us to

> JUST THINK ... you could spend at least 40 years of 40 weeks and 40 hours a week in employment. That's a long time to be stuck in a job or a career you can't stand! Yet, incredibly, most people devote more time in planning their annual holiday than thinking about a whole lifetime in work. (p. 2)

If you do not know the school you have applied to, it is a good idea to visit it beforehand to ensure that you know where it is: you do not want to be wandering round the streets on the day of the interview trying to find it.

Prior visit to the school
Sometimes it is possible, and indeed encouraged, to look round a school prior to the interview day. Seize the opportunity if you can but, on the one hand, try to avoid missing any important sessions or teaching opportunities and, on the other hand, try to visit when the school is in action! Phone the headteacher beforehand and check whether a visit is feasible and arrange a mutually convenient time to meet. Generally schools will be very pleased to be approached and welcome the fact that applicants are showing such an engaged interest. If your request is denied, do not be dismayed as it may be that so many people wish to visit that it is not possible to accommodate them.

You can learn a tremendous amount about a place by the way staff and pupils greet you. Is the school somewhere you would like to work or do the people in it make you feel uncomfortable and unwelcome? If you are in the midst of teaching practice when you are invited for interview it is often possible to visit a school when the children have gone home. When visiting be relaxed and yourself, but also be aware that, while this is not a formal part of the interview process, you will nevertheless be 'on show' and so be conscious of the impression you are making. Make the most of the opportunity to find out more about the school and think through any questions that you might want to ask beforehand. Don't overdo the questioning so that you appear 'pushy', but show interest in the school and the post on offer. Make eye contact, smile, be attentive and show genuine interest when people talk about their work. Avoid giving the impression that you are only interested in gathering information for your own fact-finding purposes.

Prepare and practise

Prior to your interview it is important that you prepare as well as you can. Remind yourself what you have written in your application, but also think about the questions you might be asked. As Hodgson (2005) points out, 'Interviewers are seeking the answers to three fundamental questions: "Can you do the job?" "Will you do the job?" and "Will you fit in?"' (p. 2). Remember that the interviewers will have your application to hand and may want to explore aspects of the information that you supplied. Ask colleagues what questions they have been asked and think how you might have answered them. Some fairly standard questions include:

- Why do you want to teach?
- What do you think makes a good teacher?
- What makes you want to work with children?
- Can you describe the range of experience you have had in the classroom?
- What are your views on the role of play in the curriculum?

Practise your replies out loud to encourage your fluency. You will not be able to prepare for all the questions you will be asked (see below) but if you have thought through some of your answers you will present a more relaxed and confident view of yourself on the day. 'The key is drawing the positive out of the normal – the convincing out of the average and the extraordinary out of the ordinary' (Hodgson, 2005, p. xiv). Although it is useful to prepare for the sort of questions you may be asked, it is important to realise in advance that there may be questions you do not anticipate. Try not to be phased by this! It is always useful to pause for a moment to collect your thoughts before launching into an answer.

Having practised answering questions you would also be wise to consider whether you have any questions. Remember, interviews are a two-way process: you need to be sure that you want the job on offer (see below) just as much as the interview panel need to ensure that you are the best person for the job. Typical questions you might prepare

are: 'If I were to be offered the post, what provision will there be for me as a newly qualified teacher?' or 'I have grade 8 piano; might there be any possibility to join in, or start, an after-school music club if I were successful today?'

Some schools ask candidates to do a short presentation on the day of the interview. Others ask interviewees to take a class for a story or some similar activity. Again, thorough preparation is of the essence. As far as possible practise what has been asked of you beforehand. Make your life as easy as possible by, for example, preparing index cards with key words or phrases on them in case you 'dry up' on the day. If asked to teach a class prepare this as thoroughly as you would during your initial teaching training and see if you can ask a tutor or a colleague to look at what you have prepared beforehand. Tamsin, who teaches a mixed Year 3/4 class advises, 'Don't over-complicate your lesson plan.'

In recent years prospective teachers have increasingly found themselves being interviewed by a school's council. It is important to take this seriously. Young people's questions can often be very incisive and can explore aspects of teaching, the classroom experience and the teacher/pupil relationship that may not be fully examined in other parts of the interview process. For example:

- Why did you want to be a teacher?
- Why do you want to come to our school?
- How would you make our lessons fun?
- What do you do when pupils are naughty?

Sometimes questions may be phrased clumsily and come over as inappropriate, but it is important to see beyond this to the issue that lies behind the question. We have been told that candidates are often asked if they know any good jokes so it is as well to have a couple of simple and appropriate ones at the ready!

Finally, several days before the interview, think about what you are going to wear for the great day. This may sound trivial but first impressions are crucial. Corfield (2009) goes so far as to say:

> Your appearance is the most important aspect of the first impression you create. This cannot be stressed too much, and if it is the only thing you learn from reading this book, it will be valuable ... Your choice of clothes indicates your attitude to yourself and other people. (p. 49)

When surveying your wardrobe for the appropriate outfit select something that is smart but not overpowering. For females we suggest a skirt or a dress rather than a top designer suit. Men, we think, should opt for a jacket and tie. A suit is a possibility but we certainly do not think it is worth buying one just for the occasion. Corfield (2009) explains:

> The right clothes do not draw attention to themselves; rather they show off the person inside them, and in the right colours you will receive compliments on how well you are looking rather than on your clothes ... Keep your clothes that get attention for your social life and let your abilities and ideas do the talking in the interview. (pp. 50–1)

Whatever you decide upon, ensure that it is comfortable, crease-resistant and unlikely to show any stains. (There is a certain law which states you will spill something on your outfit a few minutes prior to your interview!) In summary, it is important that you appear smart, as this conveys the message that you value the interview opportunity and are treating it seriously and with the appropriate respect. Given this, we suggest that you choose clothes which feel natural and help you feel comfortable and at ease with yourself, while also portraying yourself as a professional.

The day of the interview

Allow plenty of time for your journey and arrive at the school in plenty of time. We would suggest 10–15 minutes early. Any earlier and you have too long to panic. Any later and you may begin panicking about whether you will make it there on time. If you find that you are running late owing to unforeseen circumstances, telephone the school to explain and give an approximate arrival time.

Arrival

On arrival at the school, unless you have been told otherwise, make your way to the school office. Several possibilities might happen at this point – a tour of the school, a coffee, the interview – but, be warned, as soon as you come into contact with anyone at the school you are likely to come under scrutiny! It is not uncommon, for example, for interviewees to be shown round the school by a member of staff, or a pupil and your guide's opinion canvassed afterwards.

When it is your turn to be interviewed, again remember that first impressions are crucial. Over 50 years ago Springbelt (1958) suggested that interviewers often make up their mind about a person's suitability within the first few minutes of the interview. We understand this point of view but, even if this is the case, professional interviewers will make sure that they spend the rest of the interview thoroughly testing such an initial judgement rather than assuming that it was correct in the first instance. We have found that despite such initial impressions we quite frequently change our minds, so do not worry if you do not appear quite as you might like – a good interviewer should be able to see well beyond appearances.

The interview

Enter the room with a smile on your face and try to give the impression that you are delighted to be there. Sit back, but do not lounge, and try to relax: if you are physically relaxed you are more likely to be mentally relaxed. If you are too laid back you are likely to come over as arrogant, unaware and complacent. The key is to be positive and professional.

The number of interviewers is difficult to predict but, usually, there will be between two and four. One of these is likely to be a headteacher and, depending on whether it is a pool or specific job interview, the others might be a school governor, a teacher or a member of the local authority. Typically they will start with simple factual questions or questions they imagine you will have prepared, such as:

- What made you apply for a job at our school?

Answer as honestly and fluently as you can, having listened carefully to what you have been asked. People will expect you to be nervous so take your time and do not worry if you stumble over the odd word or two. It is important to include everyone in your answer. In other words, rather than stare fixedly at the person who asked the question, look at the other interviewers too as you answer the question. If you do not understand a question say so! This is not always easy but, we can assure you, it is better than providing a totally inappropriate and incoherent response.

A common failing of interviewees is that they are either too verbose in their responses or monosyllabic. Remember that your interviewers are trying to find out about you so, rather than one-word answers, they need some clues as to who you are. They do not, however, require your life history. Talking too much or too little is often a sign of nerves but it can also indicate a lack of awareness of your audience: not a good characteristic in a potential teacher. So, in your answers try to give a clear response to the main issue in the question and, if possible, a brief example to illustrate your point. In other words, address the heart of the question, and say enough to interest and intrigue, leaving the panel to ask any supplementary questions if they want more from you on this issue.

During the course of the interview you may well be asked questions you had not anticipated. Try not to panic! It is quite in order for you to take a couple of minutes' thinking time. Interviewers will often pose questions that they know you could not have prepared to see how quickly you can think when on the spot. They will not expect a perfect answer but evidence that you are intelligent, practical and thoughtful, and not someone who will blurt out the first thing that comes into your head when put under pressure. If you are asked a question that has more than one part do not be afraid to ask the second part to be repeated. If you really do feel caught unawares Sam, a Year 1 teacher, advises: 'Be yourself – a school is looking for a friendly, down-to-earth team member, *not* a machine.'

CRITICAL ISSUES

Anke Tigchelaar and her colleagues (2008) use the term 'revolving door effect' (p. 1530) to describe career changers who opt for teaching, remain in the profession for a short time and then move on to another type of job. Is this necessarily a bad thing? What are the arguments for and against such behaviour? Would the same reasoning apply to those who changed schools at regular intervals? Why? Why not?

Some interviewers are highly experienced and will use techniques designed to show you at your best. If, for example, you have given rather a short answer they will provide you with a prompt which will encourage you to say more. Other interviewers are not so adept and you may find yourself being asked what you consider to be rather facile questions. Keep cool and try to respond in a mature and intelligent manner. Even if you later decide that the job is not the one for you, remember that word can get around and it is as well to keep your negative thoughts to yourself.

Your questions

Towards the end of the interview you will almost certainly be asked if you have any questions. It gives the impression that you are thoughtful and well prepared if you have one or two queries. Any more and the interviewers will be watching the clock. If it has not already been discussed, you would be wise to ask about induction arrangements (see below). Eggert (1992) warns, however, that you would be unwise to: 'break out of the role of interviewee and interview the interviewer by asking for ... opinions or suggestions' (p. 73). You may, of course, be interested in how much you might be paid; Corfield (2009), however, cautions: 'If money is not mentioned, avoid discussing the subject at the interview' (p. 119). Instead she advises, 'If you are offered the job, you can say: "I'm certainly interested in the position, but haven't yet had full details about the conditions of employment. Perhaps you could tell me the salary for the job?"' (p. 119).

If you have no questions you would be wise to say something along the lines of: 'I found your brochure/introduction so informative that I don't have anything to ask, thank you.'

Arnold et al. (1998) warn that some interviewers are overly influenced by the 'recency effect'. In other words, they have a tendency to give too much weight to the last thing a candidate said or did. Accordingly, be sure to smile and thank the interviewers before leaving the room.

After the interview

It is likely you will hear whether you have been successful on the day or within a day or two of the interview. Before you receive the letter or the telephone call decide whether you want the job, regardless of whether you are offered it. It is important that you think you would be happy in the post but try not to be too discriminating. In many schools it is common practice to ask applicants to wait and then to give them the outcome of the interview on the day. Opinions vary on this, but many people feel it is bad form to go through the whole interview process and then turn down the post, particularly if the school has given a lot of opportunity to visit, tour and get to know the school. Indeed, in some interviews one of the questions might be, 'Having had an opportunity to view the school are you still interested in the post?' So, if possible, it is better to do your thinking about whether you would accept the post beforehand. You can reject one, or possibly two, jobs after interview but you are tempting fate – and creating a bad image – if you decline any more.

If you do want the job and are offered it – congratulations!

If you are unsuccessful try to view the experience constructively. Don't be too down-hearted. Remember that not being appointed is not necessarily a reflection on you. The interview process involves a number of ingredients – the nature of the school and the job; what the other candidates bring which is not in your control; the appropriateness of the fit between the job and the applicant and the varying judgement of the individuals on the panel. All that you can do is prepare well and present all that you have to bring to the post as positively as possible.

It is common practice for interview panels to offer feedback and, however challenging, we strongly advise that you heed the advice given. If an offer is not forthcoming, it is perfectly in order for you to ask for a debriefing. Sandy recommends that you '... try to stay positive and learn from feedback.' This is not always easy, especially if it is delivered in a clumsy manner which, unfortunately, can be the case with inexperienced and embarrassed interviewers.

Should you find that you have been rejected after two or three interviews, have a chat to your tutor or headteacher, or visit your local careers centre. It may be that, unluckily, there is someone better qualified than you for the jobs you have applied for or it may be that you are making some simple mistakes which can be easily rectified. Remember, you were successful in gaining a place to train as a teacher, so you must be pretty good! Moreover, the fact that you were offered an interview suggests that you are well on the way to securing a post and that it is probably just a matter of time.

If you have not succeeded in finding a job by the end of your initial teacher education put your name down on the supply list and/or volunteer at your local school. If you make yourself known, respected and liked it should not be long before you land your first job.

Induction

At the time of writing all students undertaking teacher training successfully in England have to complete literacy, numeracy and ICT tests prepared by the Training and Development Agency for Schools (TDA) by the end of their first year of teaching. In addition, in order to continue in the profession, newly qualified teachers must pass a period of induction. This was introduced as part of the Teaching and Higher Education Act 1998 and 'should combine support, monitoring and assessment of your performance as a new teacher' (DfES, 2001b, p. 1).

The induction period is usually one academic year but may be completed pro rata if you decide to work part-time. For example, if you take on a 50 per cent post, your induction will take two years. Should you opt for supply work, you may only count periods of one term or more in a school and only if the headteacher agrees at the start of your employment. There is currently no time limit for starting your induction (unless you have completed the equivalent of four terms' supply) but you would be wise to complete it as soon as possible after your training to make the most of the expertise you have acquired.

Most of the schools you are likely to apply to should be able to offer you an appropriate induction programme. If you are planning to work in the independent sector, however, you should check whether this is the case. You should also be cautious if you are considering a school under special measures as particular conditions apply. In some cases such schools will not be able to appoint NQTs.

In all schools your headteacher will be formally responsible for your induction programme and will either act as your induction tutor or delegate this to a senior member of staff. Provision should be tailored to meet your needs. It should be based on the strengths and weaknesses identified in your Career Entry and Development Profile (see Chapter 17) which, very early on in your post, you and your mentor will convert into an action plan designed to help you consolidate and develop your teaching skills.

As a newly qualified teacher you will be given a lighter timetable than more experienced colleagues. All teachers now have 10 per cent time for preparation. On top of this as an NQT you should have an additional 10 per cent and 'the remaining hours must be protected and used for professional development' (Clarke, 2000, p. 30). During your induction period you should be observed and have a number of formal review meetings. You should also be given the opportunity to see more experienced colleagues teach. Towards the end of your programme your headteacher should tell you whether or not you will be recommended for successful completion – in essence this means whether you can meet the standards laid out in Professional Standards for Teachers (TDA, 2008; see also Chapter 17). Good practice in support for newly qualified teachers entails colleagues being given ongoing mentoring and coaching, clear arrangements for monitoring and evaluation, and regular feedback on performance and encouragement. The LA has a responsibility to monitor and ensure that schools are providing the appropriate quality of support, development and management of its NQTs. Although rare, if you feel that you are not being treated appropriately then you should contact the named LA officer about your concerns. In the unlikely event that you should be unlucky enough to fail you may appeal to the Secretary of State but, in our extensive experience, the vast majority of newly qualified teachers complete their induction period successfuly.

Good luck!

CRITICAL ISSUES

Many years ago Schaffer (1953) observed that people who experience the most job satisfaction tend to be those who select careers which most satisfy their needs.

Starting with Maslow's (1943) 'Hierarchy of Needs', search the literature to explore the range of people's personal and professional needs. Consider how they relate to you and your choice of teaching as a career.

Summary

- Applying for jobs is demanding and stressful: take it one step at a time.
- Think carefully about where you wish to apply.
- It is worth spending time and effort on your applications.
- Make the most of any opportunity to visit and tour the school.
- Prepare thoroughly for interviews and remember to reread your application.
- During interview aim to keep calm and focused, and show interest.
- Remember it is in the interviewers' interest that you show yourself at your best and they will want to help you do this.
- Where possible do your thinking about whether you want the job beforehand.
- Try to be constructive and learn from your experiences, even when unsuccessful.
- Remember that you do not have to accept a job if it is offered to you.

Issues for reflection

- Think about your strengths and weaknesses and be prepared to discuss both!
- What sort of school would you really like to work in? Large? Small? Rural?
- Decide what you would want to gain from the opportunity to visit the school before interview.
- Can you articulate your professional philosophy? What, for example, do you think are the most important aims of primary education? What should be the role of parents in their child's education?

Further reading

There are numerous books on job applications and interviewing but here are two you might like to look at:

Corfield, R. (2009) *Successful Interview Skills*. 5th edition. London: Kogan Page. We think that this book lives up to its claim that it is an '... extremely useful guide which shows you how to exude professionalism and confidence and take control of the interview process' (back cover).

Hodgson, S. (2005) *Brilliant Answers to Tough Interview Questions*. 2nd edition. London: Pearson. This is a very clear and practical book which is intended to show you off at your best. On the back it explains that it is designed, for example, to help you 'avoid panicky gibberish' and explains 'the art of turning every question to your advantage'.

Finally, we suggest you read the regular guidance column and articles for teacher trainees and newly qualified teachers in the *Times Educational Supplement* and commend the following as very practical guides to your first year in teaching:

Cowley, S. (2009) *How to Survive Your First Year in Teaching*. 2nd edition. London: Continuum.

Lush, V. (2009) *Get Ready to Teach*. London: Pearson.

McNally, J. and Blake, A. (eds) (2010) *Improving Learning in a Professional Context*. Abingdon: Routledge.

Rogers, B. (2003) *Effective Supply Teaching*. London: Sage.

REFERENCES

Ainscow, M., Booth, T. and Dyson, A. (2006) *Improving Schools, Developing Inclusion*. London: Routledge.

Alexander, R. (1992) *Policy and Practice in Primary Education*. London and New York: Routledge.

Alexander, R. (2001) *Culture and Pedagogy: International Comparisons in Primary Education*. Oxford: Blackwell.

Alexander, R. (2004) Still no pedagogy? Principle, pragmatism and compliance in primary education, *Cambridge Journal of Education,* 34(1), pp. 7–33.

Alexander, R. (2006) *Towards Dialogic Teaching: Rethinking Classroom Talk*. 3rd edition. York: Dialogos.

Alexander, R. (2008) *Towards Dialogic Teaching: Rethinking Classroom Talk*. 4th edition. York: Dialogos.

Alexander, R. (ed.) (2010) *Children, Their World, Their Education: Final Report and Recommendations of the Cambridge Primary Review*. London and New York: Routledge.

Alexander, R., Rose, J. and Woodhead, C. (1992) *Curriculum Organisation and Classroom Practice in Primary Schools: A Discussion Paper*. London: DES.

Anning, A. and Ring, K. (2004) *Making Sense of Children's Drawings*. Maidenhead: Open University Press.

Armstrong, M. (1980) *Closely Observed Children: The Diary of a Primary Classroom*. London: Writers and Readers in association with Chameleon.

Armstrong, M. (2006) *Children Writing Stories*. Maidenhead: Open University Press.

Arnold, J., Cooper, C.L. and Robertson, I.T. (1998) *Work Psychology*. 3rd edition. London: Pitman.

Assessment Reform Group (1999) *Assessment for Learning: Beyond the Black Box*. Cambridge: University of Cambridge School of Education.

Assessment Reform Group (2002) *Ten Principles of Assessment for Learning*. Online at: http://www.assessment-reform-group.org/CIE3.PDF (accessed 2010).

Baker, M. (2010) *Are Exams Really Getting Easier?* BBC News, 30 April. Online at: http://www.bbc.co.uk/news/10094248 (accessed 1 May 2010).

Barnes, D. (1976) *From Communication to Curriculum*. Harmondsworth: Penguin.

Barnes, R. (2006) Behavioural management and positive ethos. In A.D. Cockburn and G. Handscomb (eds), *Teaching Children 3–11*. 2nd edition. London: Sage, pp. 116–37.

Bennett, N. and Dunne, E. (1992) *Managing Classroom Groups*. London: Simon & Schuster.

Black, P. and Wiliam, D. (1998a) *Inside the Black Box: Raising Standards Through Classroom Assessment*. London: School of Education, King's College.

Black, P. and Wiliam, D. (1998b) Assessment and classroom learning, *Assessment in Education*, 5 (1), pp. 7–74.

Black, P., Harrison, C., Lee, C., Marshall, B. and Wiliam, D. (2003a) *Working Inside the Black Box: Assessment for Learning in the Classroom*. London: Department of Education and Professional Studies, King's College.

Black, P., Harrison, C., Lee, C., Marshall, B. and Wiliam, D. (2003b) *Assessment for Learning: Putting It into Practice*. Maidenhead: Open University Press.

Blyth, W.A.L., Cooper, K., Derricott, R., Elliott, G.G., Sumner, H. M. and Waplington, A. (1976) *Place, Time and Society 8–13: Curriculum Planning in History, Geography and Social Science*. Bristol: Collins/ESL.

Board of Education (1931) *Report of the Consultative Committee on the Primary School* (The Hadow Report). London: HSMO.

Bolton, G. (2010) *Reflective Practice: Writing and Professional Development*. 3rd edition. London: Sage.

Bolton, G. and Heathcote, D. (1995) *Drama for Learning: Dorothy Heathcote's Mantle of the Expert Approach to Education* (Dimensions of Drama). Portsmouth, NH: Heinemann.

Britton, J. (1992) *Language and Learning: The Importance of Speech in Children's Development*. Harmondsworth: Penguin.

Brophy, J. (2010) *Motivating Students to Learn*. 3rd edition. New York: Routledge.

Bruner, J. (1960) *The Process of Education*. New York: Random House.

Bruner, J. (1962). *The Process of Education*. Revised edition. Cambridge, MA: Harvard University Press.

Bruner, J. (1996) *The Culture of Education*. Cambridge, MA: Harvard University Press.

Bubb, S. and Earley, P. (2010) How to ensure staff development makes a difference, *Professional Development Today*, 13, pp. 22–6.

Buzan, T. (1993) *The Mindmap Book*. London: BBC Books.

Byron, T. (2008) *Safer Children in a Digital World: The Report of the Byron Review*. London: Department for Children, Schools and Families.

Carini, P.F. (2001) *Starting Strong: A Different Look at Children, Schools and Standards*. New York: Teachers College Press.

Carrington, V. and Hodgetts, K. (2010) Literacy-lite in BarbieGirls™, *British Journal of the Sociology of Education*, 31(6), pp. 671–82.

Central Advisory Council for Education (CACE) (1967) *Children and Their Primary Schools* (The Plowden Report). London: HMSO.

Chapman, C. and Gallannaugh, F. (2008) How to … mentor and coach, *Professional Development Today*, 11, pp. 29–42.

Clark, L. (2007) Half of state secondary schools fail to provide children with a good education, says Ofsted. *Daily Mail*, 18 October. Online at: http://www.dailymail.co.uk/news/article-488054/Half-state-secondary-schools-fail-provide-children-good-education-says-Ofsted.html (accessed 7 January 2011).

Clarke, S. (2000) No way back, *Times Educational Supplement,* 16 June.

Clarke, S. (2001) *Unlocking Formative Assessment*. Abingdon: Hodder Murray.

Clarke, S. (2003) *Enriching Feedback in the Primary Classroom*. Abingdon: Hodder & Stoughton.

Clarke, S. (2008) *Active Learning Through Formative Assessment*. London: Hodder Education.

Cockburn, A.D. (2006) Motivation and learning within the classroom. In A.D. Cockburn and G. Handscomb (eds), *Teaching Children 3–11*. 2nd edition. London: Sage, pp. 70–81.

Cook-Sather, A. (2007) Registering the impositional potential of 'student voice' in educational research and reform, *Curriculum Enquiry*, 36, pp. 359–90.

Corder, C. (1990) *Teaching Hard, Teaching Soft*. Aldershot: Gower.

Cordingley, P., Bell, M. and Temperley, J. (2005) Mentoring and coaching for learning, *Professional Development Today*, 8(2), pp. 15–19.

Corfield, R. (2009) *Successful Interview Skills*. 5th edition. London: Kogan Page.

Corsaro, W. (2009) Peer culture. In J. Qvortrup, W. Corsaro and M. Honig (eds), *The Palgrave Handbook of Childhood Studies*. Basingstoke: Palgrave Macmillan.

Creative Learning Journey Ltd (2011) 'The Creative Leaning Journey'. Online at: http://www. creativelearningjourney.org.uk (accessed 23 January 2011).

CUREE (2010) online at: http://www.curee.org.uk (accessed February 2011).

Dawes, L., Mercer, N. and Wegerif, R. (2000) *Thinking Together: A Programme of Activities for Developing Speaking, Listening and Thinking Skills for Children 8–11*. Birmingham: Imaginative Minds.

Department for Children, Schools and Families (DCSF) (2007) *The Children's Plan: Building Brighter Futures*. London: DCSF.

Department for Children, Schools and Families (DCSF) (2008) *The Early Years Foundation Stage: Setting the Standards for Learning, Development and Care for Children from Birth to Five*. London: DCSF.

Department for Children, Schools and Families (DCSF) (2009a) *Independent Review of the Primary Curriculum: Final Report* (The Rose Review). Nottingham: DCSF Publications.

Department for Children, Schools and Families (DCSF) (2009b) *National Curriculum Assessments at Key Stage 2 in England 2009*. Online at: http://www.dcsf.gov.uk/rsgateway/DB/SFR/s000865/index.shtml (accessed 20 October 2010).

Department for Children, Schools and Families (DCSF) (2010a) *Assessing Pupils' Progress*. Online at: http://nationalstrategies.standards.dcsf.gov.uk/primary/assessment/assessingpupilsprogressap (accessed 9 October 2010).

Department for Children, Schools and Families (DCSF) (2010b) *Working Together to Safeguard Children*. Online at: http://www.publications.ed.gov.uk (accessed 9 December 2010).

Department for Education (DfE) (2010) Discussion about teaching of evolution in the primary curriculum with representative from British Humanist Association. Personal communication [letter], 1 September. Online at: http://www.humanism.org.uk/_uploads/documents/ReplyfromDfE01.09.10.pdf.

Department for Education and Employment (DfEE) (1999) *The National Curriculum: Handbook for Primary Teachers in England Key Stages 1 and 2*. London: DfEE/QCA.

Department for Education and Skills (DfES) (2001a) *Special Education Needs Code of Practice*. Annesley, Nottinghamshire: DfES.

Department for Education and Skills (DfES) (2001b) *Learning to Teach: A Strategy for Professional Development*. London: HMSO.

Department for Education and Skills (DfES) (2003) *Excellence and Enjoyment – A Strategy for Primary Schools*. Nottingham: DfES.

Department for Education and Skills (DfES) (2004a) *Excellence and Enjoyment: Learning and Teaching in the Primary Years*. London: DfES.

Department for Education and Skills (DfES) (2004b) *Every Child Matters: Change for Children*. Nottingham: DfES.

Department for Education and Skills (DfES) (2004c) *Five Year Strategy for Children and Learners*. London: DfES.

Department for Education and Skills (DfES) (2005) *Excellence and Enjoyment: Social and Emotional Aspects of Learning: Guidance*. London: DfES.

Department for Education and Skills (DfES) (2007) *The Early Years Foundation Stage*. London: DfES.

Department for Education and Science and Welsh Office (1987) *Report of the Task Group on Assessment and Training*. London: DES.

Doddington, C., Flutter, J. with Berne, E. and Demetriou, H. (2001) *Sustaining Pupils' Progress in Year 3*. Cambridge: Faculty of Education, University of Cambridge.

Doyle, W. (1977) Paradigms for research on teacher effectiveness. In L. Shulman (ed.), *Review of Research in Education*, Vol. 5. Itasca, TX: F.E. Peacock.

Drake, J. (2009) *Planning for Children's Play and Learning*. 3rd Edition. Abingdon: Routledge.

Drummond, M.J. (1996) Teachers asking questions approaches to evaluation, *Education 3–13*, October.

Dweck, C. (2000) *Self-Theories: Their Role in Motivation, Personality, and Development*. Philadephia: Psychology Press.

Dyson, A. (2001) *Building Research Capacity*. London: National Educational Research Forum.

Earley, P. and Porritt, V. (2010a) Effective practices in CPD – what works, *Professional Development Today*, 13, pp. 5–9.

Earley, P. and Porritt, V. (eds) (2010b) *Effective Practices in CPD: Lessons for Schools*. London: Institute of Education, University of London.

Edwards, D. and Mercer, N. (1993) *Common Knowledge: The Development of Understanding in the Classroom*. London: Methuen/Routledge.

Edwards, T. (2003) Purposes and characteristics of whole-class dialogue. In *New Perspectives on Spoken English in the Classroom*, NC Discussion Papers. London: QCA.

Eggert, M. (1992) *The Perfect Interview*. London: Century.

Ekins, A. and Grimes, P. (2008) Inclusion in action: joined-up thinking and development, *Professional Development Today*, 11(3).

Ekins, A. and Grimes, P. (2009) *Developing an Effective Whole School Approach*. Milton Keynes: Open University Press.

Essex County Council (2002) *Educational Enquiry and Research in Essex*. Chelmsford: Forum for Learning and Research Enquiry (FLARE), Essex County Council.

Essex County Council (2003) *Early Career Professional Development*. Chelmsford: Forum for Learning and Research Enquiry (FLARE), Essex County Council.

Fielding, M. (2004) 'New Wave' student voice and the renewal of civic society, *London Review of Education*, 2, pp. 197–217.

Fish, D. (1995a) *Quality Mentoring for Student Teachers: A Principled Approach to Practice*. London: David Fulton.

Fish, D. (1995b) *Quality Learning for Student Teachers: University Tutors' Educational Practices*. London: David Fulton.

Freedman, S., Lipson, B. and Hargreaves, D. (2008) *More Good Teachers*. Policy Exchange. Online at: http://www.policyexchange.org.uk (accessed 14 June 2010).

Frost, R., Handscomb, G. and Prince, R. (2009) *Active Enquiring Minds: Supporting Young Researchers*. Chelmsford: Forum for Learning and Research Enquiry (FLARE), Essex County Council.

Fulwiler, T. (1987) *The Journal Book*. Portsmouth, NH: Boynton/Cook.

Galton, M. (1995) Do you really want to cope with thirty lively children and become an effective primary school teacher? In J. Moyles (ed.), *Beginning Teaching; Beginning Learning*. Buckingham: Open University Press.

Galton, M. (2007) *Learning and Teaching in the Primary Classroom*. London: Sage.

Galton, M. and Williamson, J. (1992) *Group Work in the Primary Classroom*. London: Routledge.

Galton, M., Simon, B. and Croll, P. (1980) *Inside the Primary Classroom*. London: Routledge & Kegan Paul.

Galvin, P., Miller, A. and Nash, J. (1999) *Behaviour and Discipline in Schools*. London: David Fulton.

Gardner, H. (1993) *Multiple Intelligences: The Theory in Practice*. New York: Basic Books.

Gaskins, S., Haight, W. and Lancy, D. F. (2007) The cultural construction of play. In A. Goncu and S. Gaskins (eds), *Play and Development: Evolutionary, Sociocultural, and Functional Perspectives*. Mahwah, NJ: LEA.

Gibb, N. (2010) Nick Gibb Speech to the Reform Conference, 1 July. Online at: http://www.education.gov.uk/news/speeches/ng-reform-conference (accessed 1 July 2010).

Gibbs, K. and Tofi-Teskbo, J. (2010) Creative professional development! Museums and archives supporting teaching and learning, *Professional Development Today*, 13(3).

Gillard, D. (2007) Presaging Plowden: an introduction to the Hadow Reports, *FORUM*, 49(1 & 2), pp. 7–20.

Gillespie, H., Boulton, H., Hramiak, A. and Williamson, R. (2007) *Learning and Teaching with Virtual Learning Environments*. Exeter: Learning Matters.

Gleeson, D. and Husbands, C. (eds) (2001) *The Performing School: Managing, Teaching and Learning in a Performance Culture*. London and New York: Routledge/Falmer.

Gove, M. (2010) Speech to Westminster Academy, 6 September, Department for Education. Online at: http://www.education.gov.uk/news/speeches/mg-westminsteracademy (accessed 24 September 2010).

Grugeon, E., Hubbard, L., Smith, C. and Dawes, L. (2005) *Teaching Speaking and Listening in the Primary School*. London: David Fulton.

Hall, N. and Martello, J. (eds) (1996) *Listening to Children Think: Exploring Talk in the Early Years*. London: Hodder & Stoughton.

Handscomb, G. (1995) Sense of Purpose, *Education 21*, April, p. 12.

Handscomb, G. (2002) The rise of collaboration, *Professional Development Today*, 5(2), pp. 3–6.

Handscomb, G. (2002/3) Learning and developing together, *Professional Development Today*, 6, pp. 17–22.

Handscomb, G. (2004) Collaboration and enquiry: sharing practice. In P. Earley and S. Bubb (eds), *Leading and Managing Continuing Professional Development*. London: Sage.

Handscomb, G. (2009) Developing the Enquiring Profession, *Professional Development Today*, 12, pp. 3–5.

Handscomb, G. and MacBeath, J. (2003) *The Research Engaged School*. Chelmsford: Forum for Learning and Research Enquiry (FLARE), Essex County Council.

Handscomb, G. and MacBeath, J. (2009) Professional development through teacher enquiry. In A. Lawson (ed.), *Action Research: Making a Difference in Education*. London: NFER.

Hargreaves, A. (1986) *Two Cultures of Schooling: The Case of Middle Schools*. London: Falmer Press.

Hargreaves, D. (1998) *Creative Professionalism: The Role of Teachers in the Knowledge Society*. London: DEMOS.

Hargreaves, D. (2003) *Working Laterally: How to Make Innovation an Education Epidemic*. London: Publication in partnership with DEMOS, the NCSL and DfES.

Harris, A. (2002) *School Improvement: What's in It for Schools?* London: RoutledgeFalmer.

Hart, S., Dixon, A., Drummond, M.J. and McIntyre, D. (2004) *Learning Without Limits*. Maidenhead: Open University Press.

Hastings, N. and Wood, K. (2002) *Reorganising Primary Classroom Learning*. Buckingham: Open University Press.

Hawkins, D. (1974) I, thou and it. In D. Hawkins (ed.), *The Informed Vision Essays on Learning and Human Nature*. New York: Agathon Press.

Hawkins, P. (1999) *The Art of Building Windmills*. Liverpool: Graduate into Employment Unit.

Haydn, T. (2007) *Managing Pupil Behaviour: Key Issues in Teaching and Learning*. Abingdon: Routledge.

HM Inspectors of Schools (1978) *Primary Education in England*. London: HMSO.

Hodgson, S. (2005) *Brilliant Answers to Tough Interview Questions*. 2nd edition. London: Pearson.

Holly, M.L. (1984) *Keeping a Personal-Professional Journal*. Victoria: Deakin University Press.

Hord, S.M. (2009) Professional learning communities: educators work together towards a shared purpose – improved student outcomes, *JSD*, 30(1) (National Staff Development Council). Online at: http://www.nsdc.org.

International Primary Curriculum (2011) 'International Primary Curriculum'. Online at: http://www.internationalprimarycurriculum.com (accessed 23 January 2011).

Katz, L. (1993) *Dispositions as Educational Goals*. ERIC Digest (EDP-PS-93-10).

Kitson, N. and Merry, R. (1997) *Teaching in the Primary School*. London: Routledge.

Krathwohl, D.R. (2002) A revision of Bloom's taxonomy: an overview, *Theory Into Practice*, 41, pp. 212–18.

Lawson, A. (ed.) (2008) *Research Tool-kit: The How-to Guide from Practical Research for Education*. Slough: NFER.

Lawson, A. (ed.) (2009) *Action Research: Making a Difference in Education*. Slough: NFER.

Lawton, D. (1994) *The Tory Mind on Education 1979–1994*. London and Washington, DC: Falmer Press.

McAteer, M. with Hallett, F., Murtagh, L. and Turnball, G. (2010) *Achieving Your Masters in Teaching and Learning*. Exeter: Learning Matters.

MacBeath, J. and Stoll, L. (2001) *A Profile of Change*. In J. MacBeath and P. Mortimer (eds), *Improving School Effectiveness*. Buckingham: Open University Press.

McIntyre, D. (2001) *The Expert Teacher*. MEd presentation, Essex LA/University of Cambridge.

Maclure, M. (1992) The first five years: the development of talk in the pre-school period. In K. Norman (ed.), *Thinking Voices: The Work of the National Oracy Project*. London: Hodder & Stoughton.

Mantle of the Expert (2011) Mantle of the Expert.com – a dramatic-inquiry approach to teaching and learning. Online at: http://www.mantleoftheexpert.com (accessed 23 January 2011).

Marshall, H.H. (1988) Work or learning: implications of classroom metaphors, *Educational Researcher*, 17, pp. 9–16.

Maslow, A.H. (1943) A theory of motivation, *Psychological Review*, 50, pp. 370–96.

Mason, J. (2002) *Researching Your Own Practice: The Discipline of Noticing*. London and New York: Routledge Falmer.

Mercer, N. (1995) *The Guided Construction of Knowledge: Talk Amongst Teachers and Learners.* Clevedon: Multilingual Matters.

Mercer, N. (2000) *Words and Minds: How We Use Language to Think Together*. London: Routledge.

Mercer, N. and Dawes, L. (2008) The value of exploratory talk. In N. Mercer and S. Hodgkinson (eds), *Exploring Talk in School.* London: Sage, pp. 55–72.

Mercer, N. and Hodgkinson, S. (eds) (2008) *Exploring Talk in School.* London: Sage.

Mercer, N. and Littleton, K. (2007) *Dialogue and the Development of Children's Thinking: A Socio-cultural Approach*. Abingdon: Routledge.

Moon, J. (2006) *Learning Journals: a Handbook for Reflective Practice and Professional Development*. 2nd edition. Abingdon: Routledge.

Mortimore, P., Sammonds, P., Stoll, L., Lewis, D. and Ecob, R. (1988) *School Matters.* Wells: Open Books.

Myhill, D. (2006) Talk, talk, talk: teaching and learning in whole class discourse, *Research Papers in Education*, 21, pp. 19–41.

National Curriculum Council and National Oracy Project (1991) *Assessing Talk in Key Stages One and Two*, Occasional Papers in Oracy No 5. York: National Curriculum Council/National Oracy Project.

National Gallery (2011) 'Take One Picture'. Online at: http://www.takeonepicture.org/index.html (accessed 23 January 2011).

Nicolopoulou, A., Barbosa de Sá, A., Ilgaz, H. and Brockmeyer, C. (2010) Using the transformative power of play to educate hearts and minds: from Vygotsky to Vivian Paley and beyond, *Mind, Culture, and Activity*, 17, pp. 42–58.

O'Brien, T. (2010) *On the Road: The Action Learning Set (ALS) Journey Towards Becoming a Research-Engaged School*. Nottingham: National College for Leadership of Schools and Children's Services.

Office for Standards in Education, Children's Services and Skills (Ofsted) (2002) *The Curriculum in Successful Primary Schools.* London: Ofsted.

Office for Standards in Education, Children's Services and Skills (Ofsted) (2008) *Curriculum Innovation in Schools*. London: Ofsted.

Office for Standards in Education, Children's Services and Skills (Ofsted) (2009a) *The Importance of ICT: Information and Communication Technology in Primary and Secondary Schools, 2005/08*. London: Ofsted.

Office for Standards in Education, Children's Services and Skills (Ofsted) (2009b) *Virtual Learning Environments: An Evaluation of Their Development in a Sample of Educational Settings*. London: Ofsted.

Paley, V. G. (2001) *In Mrs Tully's Room: A Childcare Portrait*. Cambridge, MA: Harvard University Press.

Palmer, S. (2006) *Toxic Childhood: How the Modern World Is Damaging Our Children and What We Can Do About It*. London: Orion.

Pedder, D. (2005) *Consulting Pupils.* Presentation at FLARE Conference, Chelmsford, 27 May.

Pedder, D. and McIntyre, D. (2004) The impact of pupil consultation in classroom practice. In A. Arnot, D. McIntyre, and D. Ray (eds), *Consulting in the Classroom: Developing Dialogue About Teaching and Learning.* Cambridge: Pearson.

Perkins D.N. (2009) *Making Learning Whole: How Seven Principles of Teaching Can Transform Education.* San Francisco: Jossey Bass.

Pollard, A. (1999) *Reflective Teaching in the Primary School: A Handbook for the Classroom.* 3rd edition. London: Cassell Education.

Pollard, A. (2008) *Reflective Teaching.* 3rd edition. London: Continuum.

QCA (1999) *Teaching Speaking and Listening in Key Stages 1 and 2.* London: QCA.

QCDA (2000) *A Language in Common: Assessing English as an Additional Language.* Online at: http://www.qcda.gov.uk/resources/assets/A_language_in_common_-_Assessing_EAL.pdf (accessed 12 November 2010).

Richards, C. (1999) *Primary Education – At a Hinge of History?* London: Falmer Press.

Rickinson, M. (2009) How to … plan your research project, *Professional Development Today*, 12(2).

Robinson, K. (2005) What is education for? *Times Educational Supplement,* January.

Rogers, B. (1990) *You Know the Fair Rule.* Harlow: Longman.

Rogers, B. (1998) *You Know the Fair Rule.* 2nd edition. London: Financial Times/Prentice Hall.

Rogers, B. (2011) *Classroom Behaviour: A Practical Guide to Effective Behaviour Management and Colleague Support.* 3rd edition. London: Sage.

Rose, J. (2009) *Independent Review of the Primary Curriculum: Final Report* (The Rose Review). Nottingham: DCSF.

Rosenthal, R. and Jacobson, L. (1968) *Pygmalion in the Classroom: Teacher Expectations and Pupils' Intellectual Development.* New York: Holt, Rinehart & Winston.

Roth, W.-M. and Lee Y.-J. (2006) Contradictions in theorizing and implementing communities in education, *Educational Research Review*, 1, pp. 27–40.

Rudduck, J. and Flutter, J. (2004) *How to Improve Your School: Giving Pupils a Voice.* London: Continuum.

Sadler, D.R. (1989) Formative assessment and the design of instructional systems, *Instructional Science,* 18, pp. 119–44.

Schaffer, R.H. (1953) Job satisfaction as related to need satisfaction in work, *Psychological Monographs: General and Applied,* 67, pp. 1–29.

Schön, D.A. (1983) *The Reflective Practitioner: How Professionals Think in Action.* New York: Basic Books.

Sharp, C. (2009) How to … ask the right questions, *Professional Development Today,* 12, pp. 1–26.

Sinclair, J. (1993) 'Don't mourn for us', *Our Voice* (Newsletter of Autism Network International), 1(3).

Smith, A. (1996) *Accelerated Learning in the Classroom.* Stafford: Network Educational Press.

Smith, A. and Call, N. (1999) *The Alps Approach: Accelerated Learning in Primary Schools*. Stafford: Network Educational Press.

Smith, P. (2010) *Children and Play*. Chichester: Wiley-Blackwell.

Springbelt, B.M. (1958) Factors affecting the final decision in the employment interview, *Canadian Journal of Psychology, 12*, pp. 13–22.

Stables, A. (2003) Learning, identity and classroom dialogue, *Journal of Educational Enquiry, 4,* pp. 1–18.

Stanley, J. and Todd, J. (2010) *Beyond the School Gate: How Schools and Families Can Work Better Together*. London: Parentline Plus and Teacher Support Network.

Stenhouse, L. (1975) *An Introduction to Curriculum Research and Development*. London: Heinemann.

Stenhouse, L. (1981) Action Research and teacher's responsibility for the educational process. In J. Rudduck and D. Hopkins (eds), *Research as a Basis for Teaching: Readings from the Work of Lawrence Stenhouse*. London: Falmer Press.

Stephens, P. and Crawley, T. (1994) *Becoming an Effective Teacher*. London: Stanley Thornes.

Stevenson, A. (1989) *Bitter Flame: A Life of Sylvia Plath*. Boston, MA: Houghton Mifflin.

Stoll, L. and Seashore Louis, K. (2007) Professional Learning Communities: elaborating new approaches. In L. Stoll and K. Seashore Louis (eds), *Professional Learning Communities: Divergence, Depth and Dilemmas*. Milton Keynes: Open University Press, pp. 63–76.

Stoll, L., Bolam, R., McMahon, A., Thomas, S. and Wallace, M. (2006) *What Is a Professional Learning Community? A Summary*. London: DfES.

Svinicki, M., Hagen, A. and Meyer, D. (1996) How research on learning strengthens instruction. In R. Menges and M. Weimer (eds), *Teaching on Solid Ground*. San Francisco: Jossey Bass.

Swaffield, S. and MacBeath, J. (2006) Embedding learning how to learn in school policy: the challenge for leadership, *Research Papers in Education, 21,* pp. 201–15.

'Sweet like chocolate' (2008) *Junior Education Plus*, March, pp. 33–6.

Teacher Training Agency (TTA) (2003) *Qualifying to Teach: Handbook of Guidance*. London: TTA.

Tigchelaar, A., Brouwer, N. and Korthagen, F. (2008) Crossing horizons: continuity and challenge during second-career teachers' entry into teaching, *Teaching and Teacher Education, 24*, pp. 1530–50.

Tizard, B. and Hughes, M. (1984) *Young Children Learning*. Cambridge, MA: Harvard University Press.

Training and Development Agency for Schools (TDA) (2006) *Qualifying to Teach*. London: TDA.

Training and Development Agency for Schools (TDA) (2007) *Professional Standards for Qualified Teacher Status*. Online at: http://www.tda.gov.uk/upload/resources/pdf/s/standards_qts.p (accessed February 2010).

Training and Development Agency for Schools (TDA) (2008) *Professional Standards for Qualified Teacher Status and Requirements for Initial Teacher Training* (revised). London: TDA.

UNESCO Institute of Statistics (2000) *Education for All 2000 Assessment: Executive Summary.* Montreal: International Consultative Forum on Education for All.

Vygotsky, L.S. (1978) *Mind in Society: The Development of Higher Psychological Processes.* Cambridge, MA and London: Harvard University Press.

Ward, G. and Rowe, J. (1985) Teachers' praise: some unwanted side effects or 'praise and be damned', *Society for the Extension of Education Knowledge*, 1, pp. 2–4.

Watkins C. (2010) Learning, performance and improvement, *Research Matters,* 34, Summer.

Wells, G. (1987) *The Meaning Makers: Children Learning Language and Using Language to Learn.* London: Hodder & Stoughton.

Wells, G. (1999) *Dialogic Enquiry: Toward a Socio-cultural Practice and Theory of Education.* Cambridge: Cambridge University Press.

Wells, G. and Ball, T. (2008) Exploratory talk and dialogic inquiry. In N. Mercer and S. Hodgkinson (eds), *Exploring Talk in School.* London: Sage, pp. 167–84.

Whitehead, M. (2004) *Language and Literacy in the Early Years.* 3rd edition. London: Sage.

Willes, M. (1983) *Children into Pupils.* London: Routledge and Kegan Paul.

Williamson, B. (2009) *Computer Games, Schools and Young People.* Bristol: Futurelab.

Woods, D. (2000) *The Promotion and Dissemination of Good Practice.* London: Education Network.

Woolfolk, A., Hughes, M. and Walkup, V. (2008) *Psychology in Education.* Harlow: Pearson Education.

Wragg, E.C. (1997) *An Introduction to Classroom Observation.* London: Routledge.

Yate, M.J. (2001) *Great Answers to Tough Interview Questions.* 5th edition. London: Kogan Page.

Zipes, J. (1995) *Creative Storytelling.* London: Routledge.

INDEX

Added to a page number 'f' denotes a figure and 't' denotes a table.